D G Colley
1996

K.C.

D0939664

DOUGLAS HOW &
RALPH COSTELLO

K.C.

THE BIOGRAPHY
OF K.C. IRVING

KEY PORTER·BOOKS

Copyright © 1993 by Douglas How and Ralph Costello

All rights reserved. No part of this work covered by the copyrights
hereon may be reproduced or used in any form or by any means —
graphic, electronic or mechanical, including photocopying, recording,
taping or information storage and retrieval systems — without the prior
written permission of the publisher, or, in case of photocopying or other
reprographic copying, without a licence from the Canadian Reprography
Collective.

The publisher gratefully acknowledges the assistance of the Canada
Council, the Ontario Publishing Centre and the Ontario Arts Council.

Passages from Ralph Allen's articles on K.C. Irving, which appeared
in *Maclean's* on April 18, May 2, and May 16, 1964, are reprinted by
permission of *Maclean's*.

Canadian Cataloguing in Publication Data

How, Douglas, 1919–
    K.C. : the biography of K.C. Irving

Includes index.
ISBN 1-55013-493-0 (bound) ISBN 1-55013-620-8 (pbk.)

1. Irving, K.C. (Kenneth Colin), 1899–1992.
2. Industrialists – New Brunswick – Biography.
3. Capitalists and financiers – New Brunswick –
Biography. I. Costello, Ralph. II. Title.

HC112.5.I7H6 1993   338.092   C93-094229-9

Key Porter Books Limited
70 The Esplanade
Toronto, Ontario
Canada M5E 1R2

Photographs not otherwise credited are from the Irving archives
or family.

Design: Annabelle Stanley

Typeset by Indelible Ink in Monotype Times New Roman.

Printed and bound in Canada

95 96 97 98 99 6 5 4 3 2 1

In Bouctouche you learned which end of
a wheelbarrow to take hold of.
— *K.C. Irving*

Contents

Preface

Douglas How is a journalist and author who grew up in the small New Brunswick community of Dorchester. It is not far from the village of Bouctouche, and when he was eight years old he overheard Elva McNairn, a roomer in his mother's home, talk about the marriage there of her sister Harriet to a rising young businessman named K.C. Irving. How would not think of this again for more than fifty years, by which time he'd started out as a reporter with the Moncton *Daily Times*, been a soldier and war correspondent in the Second World War, a member of Ottawa's parliamentary press gallery, an assistant to a cabinet minister, and a member of the editorial staffs of both *Time* magazine and the *Reader's Digest*. By 1980, he had also written several books, had returned to the Maritimes to study Canadian history in a belated college education, and was deemed a natural choice to write a biography of the man who had married Elva McNairn's sister.

K.C. Irving was in his eighties then, and his family felt it was time for someone to produce an objective account of his life and legendary accomplishments. How, it was agreed, would write the book as he saw it, through the eyes of an experienced journalist,

ix

giving it fairness and balance. It turned out to be a difficult task. The secretive Irvings gave him limited access to their multitudinous operations, but he was free to do his own research, seek out his own sources, and form his own conclusions. Before the book was finished, How had spent about 90 hours with Irving himself.

The research and writing took two years, and by the time these were completed the Irvings had had second thoughts. Eventually they decided they should not be involved in the project. The bulky manuscript went into a filing cabinet.

It was Ralph Costello, publisher of the Saint John *Telegraph-Journal* and *Evening Times-Globe*, who had recommended How to the Irving sons, and as the time approached for retirement he thought of tackling his own book on Irving. But first he inquired about the How manuscript, and after several discussions, and with some reluctance, the Irving family agreed to turn the manuscript over to him to do with it as he saw fit. His reaction: "I realized immediately that there was only one thing I should do with Doug How's manuscript. I should have it published. It was, in my opinion, the most exhaustive, definitive portrait ever compiled on the man who had changed forever the economic face of New Brunswick."

But this didn't turn out to be an easy task, either. Costello inevitably had proposals of his own, ideas he felt would strengthen an already massive documentation of Irving's life and accomplishments. How, on the other hand, wanted to preserve his manuscript in its original form. He was concerned about changes that might alter the objectivity of his work. At the same time, he realized that Costello, as the key man for many years in the Irving newspapers, as one who had risen from reporter to publisher within that Irving world, knew things that could enhance and help shape the book. Two more years, numerous meetings and a candid and extensive dialogue between the two would go by before agreement was reached and the work was ready for publication.

Costello updated some sections, recalled Irving anecdotes, included intimate glimpses of Irving and his family, of people such as Canada's noted trial lawyer John J. Robinette and John D. Park, a brilliant engineer who had an unlikely and finally unpleasant business relationship with Irving in the 1950s and '60s. He added to stories from Leigh Stevenson, Irving's beloved cousin, and provided personal insight into what was said about the Irving newspapers, how they were operated, and their ordeals under the scrutiny of Parliament and the courts. He gave the views of the men who worked in the newsrooms, and of those critics who believed the newspapers protected Irving and everything he did. Finally, he told of a human legend moving reluctantly, and yet at times with surprising grace and humour, into old age.

Nevertheless, this remains very largely How's work, one which he feels does strike a reasonable balance in saluting Irving's accomplishments without glossing over his faults and failures, and one which reflects many hours of exposure to the incredible range of Irving enterprise. In hours of talk with the man himself, How found that it was always Irving who, in his eighties, was most ready to carry on, always took his coat and always called him Mr. How. He found, on their tour of Saint John, that perhaps the most astonishing thing of all was the modesty with which Irving talked about what he'd done to change the city's face and future.

It was during a pleasant reunion with Elva McNairn that How was told a story that goes to the heart of what may turn out to be Irving's most meaningful achievement: the dedication of his heirs to his wide-ranging life's work. One day, she said, the Irving family descended on an Irving project in the forests of New Brunswick; K.C. was there with his wife, sons, assorted grandchildren and great-grandchildren, and workers stopped what they were doing to gather around to welcome them. At this moment a very young great-grandson looked up at his own father and, in a tone of admonition, said: "Look, Dad, men not working."

A dynasty was continuing into the next generation.

Acknowledgements

To identify all those who had a hand in making this book possible would be a daunting task. Yet there are many we wish to thank for their co-operation and especially for those personal recollections and anecdotes that will greatly expand the public understanding of the man who was known as K.C.

The logical person to start with is Leigh Stevenson. For most of his life he watched with bemused amazement and pride as Irving galvanized New Brunswick to new heights in business and industrial development in a career spanning much of the twentieth century.

Stevenson was Irving's cousin, boyhood chum, short-term employee (when Irving was six and he was ten), flying instructor (in the First World War) and lifelong friend. His stories — delightful, amusing, and informative — give colour and substance to a man few people really knew and fewer understood. This book, and history, are the beneficiaries. We are grateful to him.

Others who added a new dimension to Irving's complex reputation included friends from his youth and some of his early business associates. Their stories have created a fresh picture of a man who was a paradox all his life — especially to writers, who for years attempted to determine what made him tick, analyzing his life, his motives, and virtually everything short of his soul. Few came even close. Of all those who tried, Ralph Allen was the exception. One of Canada's great journalists of this century, he was a contributing editor to *Maclean's* magazine in 1964 when he wrote the most penetrating series of articles ever done on Irving. In a rare break with tradition, Irving granted him several interviews, invited him to his home, escorted him on tours of his industries, and provided him with information that more than justified *Maclean's* claim that the series was "the first full account of Irving's extraordinary character and his even more extraordinary activities." That series remains a classic. It provided valuable background for this book, as it has for countless other articles over the years. We are indebted to Ralph Allen.

Other writers have added bits and pieces to Irving lore. They included David Pickard, writing in *Canadian Business*, Cyril Robinson in *The Standard* of Montreal, Byron Fisher in *Liberty Magazine*, David MacDonald in *Maclean's*, Dal Warrington for *The Canadian Press*, William French in *The Globe Magazine*, and Jack Carrington in *The Northern Miner*. Also helpful were reports that appeared through the years in *The Globe and Mail*, *The Toronto Star*, *The Monetary Times*, *The Sackville Tribune*, *The Atlantic Advocate*, Saint John's *Telegraph-Journal* and *Evening Times-Globe*, *The Times* and *Transcript* of Moncton, and *The Daily Gleaner* of Fredericton. All served as references and check points, as did the following books: Dalton Camp's *Gentlemen, Players and Politicians* (McClelland & Stewart, 1970), *The Art of the Industrialist* by Russell Hunt and Robert Campbell (McClelland & Stewart, 1973), Alden Nowlan's report on the New Brunswick newspapers in *Canadian Newspapers — The Inside Story* (edited by Walter Stewart, Hurtig Publishers, 1980), John Edward Belliveau's *Little Louis and the Giant K.C.* (Lancelot Press, 1980) and *Citizens Irving* by John DeMont (Doubleday Canada Limited, 1991). Any reference to or use of material originating from these publications, however limited or indirect, is gratefully acknowledged. Valuable material was also found in reports of the Davey Senate Committee on The Mass Media, the Kent Royal Commission on Newspapers, court records of the combines case against the New Brunswick newspapers, reports of the Royal Commission on Corporate Concentration, records of the New Brunswick Legislature, and other sources.

We would hope, however, that the tone of this book has not been set by legislative reports, court documents, and recycled material of another time in history. Rather, we believe it is in the words of those who knew Irving personally — those who worked with him and for him — that the personality of the man comes to life, that something essential in his character is revealed. One such person was Eddie Sheehan, an engineer and project manager from the United States. He explains in riveting detail how and why he came to hate the sight of K.C., yet ended up admiring and respecting him. It is a compelling, warts-and-all examination of Irving and his tough, unbending nature — a story that contributes immeasurably to the scope of this work.

Lawyers and business associates, politicians and clergymen, giants of industry and commerce, labour leaders and construction workers, critics and fans alike march through the pages of this book. Some, interviewed in their nineties, knew Irving as a boy. Others were with him in the early days and remained for a lifetime. Their stories, many interlaced with Irving's own yarns — and some bitter memories — have fleshed out a montage of a man who emerges as much more than a driving industrial tycoon. This still evolving portrait of Irving comes from the memories and candour of men like Stevenson and Sheehan, longtime Irving architect Sam Roy, Irving Oil's super salesman Arnold Payson, Sydney businessman Eddie MacDonald, lawyers Louis McC. Ritchie, Adrian Gilbert, Yves Pratte, lawyer and former UNB president Colin Mackay, Lord Beaverbrook, Harrison McCain of the vast McCain food processing conglomerate, forestry expert Barney Flieger, construction foreman Earl Emeneau and countless others.

We are grateful as well for the encouragement of Anna Porter, who was determined to be the publisher of the first book to be written by two New Brunswickers who actually knew Irving and had extensive access to him. Jack McClelland, for many years president of McClelland & Stewart, was one of the first to read the manuscript of *K.C.* His enthusiasm and advice helped keep the wheels turning. Maritimer Fraser Sutherland did the first editing and trimming, followed by the editing and guidance of Renée Dykeman, who had the advantage of having grown up in New Brunswick, aware of the Irving presence and influence. To all of them — and to all those unnamed who also helped along the way — we say thank you.

Prologue:
A Few Coins

A SLOW TRIP IN HEAVY TRAFFIC HAD UPSET THE DRIVER.
Now the customer was standing at the entrance to New
York's LaGuardia Airport with his hand out. Waiting for
his change.

The taxi driver made no attempt to mask his feelings. He
hadn't wanted the late afternoon trip to the airport in the first
place, but the passengers had piled into the cab before telling him
their destination. He resented that, too. When he cursed it wasn't
to himself or under his breath.

The Old Man — he was in his seventies and vigorous — stood
and waited. Patiently. Unperturbed. His hand out. The driver had
his money and he wanted his change. All of it. He, not the cabbie,
would decide whether there would be a tip, and how much. The
cabbie's face was flushed. New York cabbies are experts at intimidating their customers, but the Old Man didn't scare easily. When
he received his change he said, "Thank you." He said it politely.
He meant it. By nature and training he was a polite man. There
was not the slightest hint of sarcasm in his voice.

The Old Man counted the money before reaching into his pocket. He was looking for some spare coins. Finally, he selected a dollar bill and several coins and held them out to the cab driver. For the driver it wasn't enough. His eyes registered disdain as he spread the money out on his left hand and went through a ritual of appearing to count it. A dollar bill and three quarters.

But the cabbie wasn't through. Not yet. If he couldn't break the Old Man at least he would shame him. He pocketed the dollar and dropped the three quarters. He didn't throw the coins. He simply let them slide off his fingers and they fell to the ground. "Stick it," he said. "You need that more than I do."

"No." The Old Man had a way of speaking slowly, calmly, and deliberately when he wished to make a point. "No," he said, "I don't think so, but if you don't want it I can certainly use it." He bent over and picked up the coins.

He was Kenneth Colin Irving and he didn't need those three quarters, but it would have been out of character for him to leave them there. As importantly, he was not going to be faced down by a bully of a New York taxi driver. Or anyone else, come to think of it. As his whole life testified.

CHAPTER ONE

❧

Mr. Irving Buys a Pulp Mill

"Where did you find that Huckleberry?"
– WASHINGTON BUREAUCRAT'S COMMENT ON MEETING
IRVING FOR THE FIRST TIME.

THE YEAR WAS 1942. KENNETH COLIN IRVING WAS FORTY-three years old and about to try to purchase the Dexter Sulphite Pulp and Paper Company in upper New York State. In Washington to discuss the deal, he was accompanied by lawyer A.R. Cornwall of Watertown, New York, who represented the Dexter Company as well as the U.S. Federal Refinance Corporation, which now controlled Dexter. Cornwall was looking for someone to save the troubled company, someone to perform a miracle. In Irving, he believed he had the man.

The Dexter Company had defaulted on a mortgage held by the Refinance Corporation. It also owed Irving money for pulp it had bought from his D'Auteuil Lumber Company of Quebec. It was about to collapse, but Irving believed he could save it — and recoup his own losses at the same time.

He and Cornwall were meeting with a Mr. Plow of the Recon-struction Finance Corporation. After some discussion, Irving said: "Well, Mr. Plow, do we have a deal?"

"Mr. Irving," said Plow, "I don't know. I just don't know. I'm going to have to think about it." Then, a bit awkwardly, he added:

3

"There's another matter I have to discuss with Mr. Cornwall. I wonder if I could get in touch with you later at the hotel?" That seemed like a strange way to end the meeting but Irving agreed and left.

Years later he'd still be chuckling over what Cornwall said when he came back to the hotel, grinning from ear to ear. He loved to repeat it.

"Do you know," Cornwall had asked as he entered the room, "why Mr. Plow wanted to see me privately?" Irving confessed he had no idea why he'd been asked to leave. He just thought it a bit strange. "Well, after you left," Cornwall had related, "Mr. Plow said: 'Where did you find that Huckleberry?'"

Now it was Irving's turn to be surprised. "A huckleberry? Why did he call me a huckleberry?"

The reason, as it turned out, was pretty basic. Of those interested in purchasing the Dexter Company, none had offered to pay more than 10 cents on the dollar for the mortgage. "And now you bring me this huckleberry who says he'll pay 100 cents on the dollar with interest if we agree to a four-year extension!" But could he come up with the money? Yes, Cornwall had said, he could get the money.

And he did. He purchased the Dexter Company and it took him into the pulp and paper business because Plow decided to give him that chance. In fact, he had little choice. Irving's proposal was by far the best he had received.

In later years Irving would recall that it was at the Dexter Company that he really learned the pulp business. Dexter had two mills, 640 employees, and big problems. So Irving did what was to become one of the hallmarks of his career. He looked at Dexter not as a company that was going to cost him a lot of money, but as an opportunity. He examined it with a piercing eye for detail and with a knowledge of how things worked. All he had to do was make it work. That, in many ways, was the ultimate attraction — turning a company around, putting it back on its feet, experiencing the exhilaration of making a business solvent and prosperous where others had failed.

So the deal was made. On May 1, 1942, Kenneth Colin Irving took over the company that had been started by two brothers, who had since died and left it to their widows. For years people would wonder how he did it. How did he get the money? It wasn't easy, but Irving had been handling money all his life and had a bank account from selling vegetables at five years of age. In this case the major obstacle was the Canadian government's wartime rules on foreign exchange. When a Canadian bank agreed to back him, the Foreign Exchange Control Board refused to let the funds leave Canada. Still, he found a way. He went to firms that bought from Dexter and got them to advance money on future sales. He used the money to improve and replace machinery, to put in new power facilities, and applied the profits to reduce the mortgage.

He had found a born pulp man in Austrian-born American engineer Frank Lang: "He knew what I didn't and vice versa." He hired Lang away from another company and put him in charge. He spent days, weeks, half his time in New York selling pulp and doing other business. He saved, built Dexter as a market for D'Auteuil, dovetailed them, fitted them into that pattern of mutually reinforcing businesses that became characteristic of his career. And he paid off that mortgage, with interest, in less than four years.

Frank Lang would tell a story of his own that helped explain how he did it. He said he called Irving to say a problem had arisen and he was afraid they were going to have to close down. He didn't want to close down. Irving wondered about a mechanical detail, a valve. Had it been checked? "Oh yes," said Lang. "I'm sure it must have been," but just before they hung up Irving came back to it. "Mr. Lang," he said, "I wonder if you would check that valve." When he did Lang found to his consternation that it had not been checked and that when it was, the problem was solved. There was no shutdown. But what amazed Lang was that Irving even knew the valve existed.

K.C. Irving did know these things — minute details in a sweep of complexity — and he would amaze many people besides Frank Lang with his knowledge of them. For he combined great skill at high finance, the instincts of an entrepreneur born and schooled, the merchandising talents of a man who had sold cars for years, and an iron will — all this plus a fascination about how things worked. As a boy he had never been much of a student but he had liked to take cars apart and put them together again. An eminently practical man who watched him work all one night to get a ship's faulty engine going called him "the best mechanic I ever saw." A professional in the field said he'd rank him as the equivalent of a trained mechanical engineer. The owner of a construction firm said he knew more about construction than anyone else he'd ever met.

One man who believed he knew the secret of Irving's success was Leigh Stevenson, a cousin, boyhood chum, and lifelong friend. He was convinced he knew what made K.C. Irving different — or one of the things that made him different. "He had a computer mind," said Stevenson. "I never met anyone else quite like him. It was amazing the things he could work out in his head while financial people were adding and subtracting figures and punching information into their pocket calculators or working their slide rules."

Stevenson was talking about Irving's ability to remember the smallest detail of information he had picked up years before, and his uncanny knack of getting to the core of complicated calculations as quickly as he was given basic information. He remembered Irving talking once to some of his executives about estimating the cost of a project under consideration.

"Ken said, 'It will cost about $750,000, perhaps a little more.' Then he asked his people to confirm his figures. They said they'd need time. About a week later they came back with fact sheets, graphs, financial calculations, and the cost, they said, would be around $790,000; no more, perhaps a little less.

"The figures were basically the same. But the difference was that Ken did it in his head, as he talked, in a split second."

Leigh Stevenson remembered something else about Irving. "He always had several projects in the works; he was always doing one thing, thinking of something that had to be done and planning still something else. You know, I think he had the ability somehow to think of several things at the same time. Either that, or he shifted gears so fast that he covered a dozen subjects in the time it would have taken someone else to deal with one."

Many others found his memory astounding. Together, these traits would make him fabulously successful, the creator of an interlocking network of companies that numbered in the scores, then the hundreds, largely headquartered in a New Brunswick where many people found it hard to survive let alone succeed and prosper.

The worth of his "empire" — a term he disliked intensely —
came to be estimated in the millions and then billions of dollars.
He ignored all such estimates and refused to speculate on what its
dollar value was. In truth, it was not something he considered
important. He was a builder and that was his great challenge and
accomplishment. What he loved to do was take a troubled company
like Dexter and give it new vitality. "I like," he'd explain, "to see
wheels turning."

He became a controversial figure, the focus of many battles, a
social phenomenon compared to a revolution or a war. His methods and his ways produced two conflicting images. His manner
was usually so gentle, so unassuming that a taxi driver said, "He
ain't stuck up one bit," and a banker called him "the most courteous man I ever knew." Yet anger could make him tremble, and
many found it hard to square his personal attributes with his
hard-nosed corporate reputation. He worked day and night, generally seven days a week. When he made a rare surrender and went
on a fishing trip off Mexico with H.R. MacMillan, the British
Columbia lumber baron, cousin Leigh Stevenson urged him to
relax and have fun. Irving looked at his cousin with baleful eyes.
"I guess," he said, "you'll never understand me. My fun is work."

He was imbued with a granite-like self-confidence, an abiding,
paramount conviction that what he did was right, a conviction
one subordinate likened to that sense of divinity in ancient kings.
"I am right and you know I'm right," he stormed at a provincial
premier. When his obsessive, lone-wolf secrecy yielded to an
explosive outburst before a legislative committee, he left the members stunned. When he faced a Senate committee probing his ownership of all New Brunswick's five English-language newspapers,
one reporter wrote that it was a manifestation of raw power. Even
in the backwoods of his province, neighbours argued over whether
he was a saviour or a monster.

He was called the King of the Maritimes, the Last of a Breed
of Kings, the last and greatest of the feudal barons who'd dominated New Brunswick, a Quiet Croesus, a mystery millionaire, the
last of the rugged individualists, a fossil, a dinosaur, an anachro-
nism whose deeds could never be repeated. He was called a pirate,
a man people loved to hate. Others saw him as a saint. He himself
professed to find nothing unusual in anything he did.

His critics were numerous. His admirers were legion. On one point many of both camps agreed: he was a genius, a builder who did amazing things. This huckleberry.

He rather liked the term huckleberry — his eyes would sparkle when he told the Dexter story — perhaps because he had come out of the village of Bouctouche on New Brunswick's east coast, where Mark Twain's Huckleberry Finn would have felt entirely at home. It had a river — not a Mississippi perhaps, the Bouctouche, but a good, wide, virile river where you could fish and sail and skate and swim and upon whose waters the logs came down each spring to feed his father's sawmill. Bouctouche had one long main street without a name — it later became the Boulevard Irving — and sailing ships came in with sailors who liked to drink and fight, and it was so small that everyone knew everyone else. Its 800 or so people were of French-Acadian, Scottish, English, and Irish stock. They got along well. One of the rooted elements of a complex personality was that, quite simply, Irving loved the place. Of all the things he would reminisce about in his seventies and eighties, Bouctouche came increasingly to dominate. The last thing he'd want, he would say, was to have anything printed about him that would say anything bad about Bouctouche.

By the time he was born there on March 14, 1899, his family was four generations deep in the lumbering-farming-fishing county of Kent. In Scotland they went back much further, to 300 AD when Nuath, the son of a Cambrian prince, owned lands in lowlands Annandale. From his grandson Kinder Irin or Irwin stems the modern name Irving.

In 1549 Richard Irving, commonly known as Duke Richie, was granted the Hoddom Charter at Lower Annandale. From these Irvings of Hoddom descended the Irvings of Kent. In 1822, at age fifty-one, George Irving left Dumfries and sailed to New Brunswick aboard the square-rigged vessel *Ellen Douglas*, which made many voyages to Britain and brought many Scots back. Irving and his wife, the former Jane Stitt, went up the Richibucto River to take a government grant of 200 acres at Mill Branch, in an area now known as Beersville. There George cleared the land, built a house and barn, and later a new house of more hand-hewn timbers, moving his farm buildings farther back from the river. He fathered ten children, one of them Herbert, born the year they arrived.

At eighteen, Herbert himself took up land at Galloway, on the post road midway between the Richibucto and Bouctouche rivers, and set about pioneering too. This tall, well-built man once said that when he started he walked miles and came back with his week's wages on his back: a bushel of potatoes. Married to Catherine Durgavel, he built himself a fine farm in the forest, did well enough to send some of his seven children to college, and eventually became a justice of the peace.

His fifth child, and second son, James Durgavel, born in 1860, spent only a few years at school and around twenty-one years of age left home to buy a sawmill and settle in Bouctouche. He married Minnie Hutchinson and she bore him three children, Herbert, Jane (Jen), and a son who died in infancy. Minnie Irving died at twenty-five in 1889 and James D. later married Mary Elizabeth Gifford. Their three children were Lou Dorothy, Kenneth Colin, and Marion.

Kenneth Colin Irving, widely known as K.C., would become a legend in his time, a man who transformed his native province, injecting new life, industry, dignity, hope — and controversy — into an economically backward section of Canada. What follows, then, is the story of K.C. Irving, a.k.a. "that huckleberry."

CHAPTER TWO

&

The Boy From Bouctouche

*"She told me never to touch liquor and I'd never want
to; and I never did."*
– K. C. IRVING REMEMBERING HIS MOTHER'S EARLY TEACHINGS.

KENNETH COLIN IRVING WAS BORN WHEN THE BOER WAR
was being fought, when Queen Victoria was on the
throne, when the British Empire knew no setting sun,
when modern Canada was not quite thirty-two years old and
nobody foresaw the overwhelming changes that would affect his
life and career — the wars, the prosperity, the Depression, the
recessions, the inflation, the soaring growth of government. It was
a time when villages like Bouctouche lived much within themselves, when people grew much of their own food, when there were
two worlds: your own community, and everything else.

There was no television or movies or radio: people entertained
themselves. Men gathered in kitchens and told stories, and when
they got too ribald the young were told to leave. The older men
loved to talk about local events, and young Kenneth Irving loved to
listen. They told the story of the man who would go to the Irving
woodpile each day and help himself to a stick or two of stove wood.
It was only a stick or two. Not something that would ever be missed.
J.D. Irving himself knew about it but looked the other way. It wasn't
going to break him. But finally two of Kenneth Irving's uncles

decided to do something about it. They selected a healthy-looking stick of wood, bored a hole in it and put enough gunpowder in it to teach the man a lesson. The only trouble was that the family maid unwittingly put it in the kitchen stove, and ended up on the floor in profane dismay. That was the day the Irvings learned she could cuss better than any man. And it was a story that Kenneth Irving would remember and tell for the rest of his life.

Or the story oldtimers told of his Uncle Arch, the town lawyer, who was invited to a stag dinner and enjoyed every minute of it until he discovered that his hosts had stolen the chickens from his own flock. They told of the time the boy's mother entertained the Women's Missionary Society, served them dandelion wine and was later told, to her rigidly teetotalling horror, that her guests were seen stumbling away, holding onto the picket fence. Whether the story was true or not, she descended into her cellar and did away with every last vestige of the suspect brew.

The boy's father was the acknowledged patriarch of the immediate Irving clan, the one to whom brothers and sisters turned for guidance and advice, a man who built his own local empire embracing the sawmill, a general store, a gristmill, a carding mill, a lumber business, and three farms. He also marketed fish and other produce. The Irvings were *the* family in town and J.D. Irving was its leading citizen. He was small — about five-feet-seven — thin, wise, affable, generous. "He had a big heart," recalled Dossitha (Dos) Savoie, "awful big." Savoie had reason to know. Irving took him in as a fatherless, unschooled boy, gave him a home and work, "raised me as good as his own." Many years later Dos Savoie's eyes twinkled when he remembered the winter's day J.D. told him to take one of the family horses "and give it a few miles. Take your girl." With a comely lass under a buffalo robe in the sleigh beside him, Dos "felt rich that day." At ninety-six, it still made him feel rich.

J.D. Irving, he said, "couldn't see nobody stuck. If a man had no job, he'd find him one. If a man had no clothes, he'd tell him to go into the store and get some." A priest told of J.D. Irving asking if he knew of any families in need, and sending things to them. It was something that happened often in those times long before anyone ever dreamed of social assistance or UIC benefits. At the time of the historic Halifax ship-collision explosion in the winter of 1917 Irving rounded up hundreds of windowpanes wherever he could find them, in town and out, put them on a railway car, took several men with him, and headed for the shattered city. That generosity he paid for. He slept in the cold railcar and came down with the bronchitis that would dog him for the rest of his life.

K.C. Irving loved and admired his father, respected his good judgment, his abundant common sense. From him he got a mechanical aptitude, knowledge of how to run a many-pronged business, a grasp of politics, and a loyalty to the Crown. Flags and bunting decorated the home and store on coronation days and on other occasions when royalty was honoured. When elections came, said J.D. Irving's daughter, Jen (Irving) Rettie, "the house just boomed. Father was a great Liberal, heavens above!" He was, in fact, recognized as the Liberal party in town.

J.D. was, as well, the pillar of the local Presbyterian church, the man who would write a cheque if it needed money. "We weren't particularly churchy," said Jen Rettie, but the family went regularly. The church had no permanent minister, just summer student theologians, one of whom annoyed J.D. and others with his urgent pleas for union with the Methodists in a new United Church. The Presbyterians of Bouctouche, thirty to forty of them, were known as strict, hard-line believers and when union came to a national vote Presbyterian they remained; Methodists they didn't especially like. K.C. Irving said he never considered himself religious: "I went to Sunday School because I was sent there." He generally abided by the stern strictures about a no-nonsense Sabbath. "You could shine your shoes but you couldn't go skating."

Cars fascinated him, though they were so rare in his early days that "you might see one in a year." But in 1905 his father bought a Pierce-Arrow. It went fifteen to twenty miles an hour and "you stopped at every culvert and for every frightened horse." At eight, Kenneth Irving could drive it, and half a dozen times he took it apart and put it back together again.

The family home was surrounded by fields, gardens, his mother's roses, and dozens of thoroughbred cattle and horses. There were fourteen seats at the dining-room table and they were often filled. Priests came to lunch, relatives were forever coming. Years later Mary (Archibald) Taylor would recall going there with her mother and her father, a Presbyterian minister and staying for several days. It was an accepted thing. Leigh Stevenson was there often over the years. A harness-maker would come and stay for days. Indeed, the house was so busy that in 1911 J.D. rebuilt and expanded it, put in electricity, and had a large upstairs room where great parties were held.

Kenneth Irving absorbed all this. He remembered a rambunctious pony from the coal mines of Cape Breton that kicked his straw hat off and missed him a few other times. His father "wouldn't let me on him, but you couldn't keep a young fella off a horse's back." He got up daily at 6:30 a.m. to get cream from the separator so he could have it with his oatmeal porridge. He saw the last years of his grandfather who sat on the verandah communing with the Bible. He sat at the knee of his mother's aunt who read him Scripture. He joined in the grace that was said three times a day.

But there was another world outside the Irving home to which he gravitated at a young age. He admired blacksmith Johnny Walker, a devout Presbyterian who taught Sunday School and let him work at his forge. He admired Dr. King who had brought him into the world, who drove his horse all over the country and "never called a quarter of his bills; if people couldn't pay, that was all right." He formed a high respect for the Roman Catholic priests and what they did to keep the village on a straight and narrow path. He liked the Acadians, learned the French of the wharf and the bush: "I was able to get by in it, but it wasn't good French." He was devoted to Dave Evans, the brawny foreman of his father's farms, and to Dos Savoie: "In many ways they brought me up." He was devoted, too, to George Weeks who ran the gristmill. These men became his mentors and his friends. But it was his mother who became a crucial element in shaping his life.

Mary Elizabeth Gifford had had, it was said, a hard life as a child. Her parents died when she was very young and she lived for a time with relatives, then left and walked nine Kent County miles to live with an uncle and aunt who owned a sawmill. She didn't go to school; they taught her. She learned bookkeeping. She eventually went to Bouctouche and kept house for the widower J.D. Irving, and then married him.

Eighty and more years later Leigh Stevenson could still vividly remember the Mary Elizabeth Gifford Irving he knew when he was a young boy. He remembered her as small, neat, meticulous, and prim. He remembered her home where he spent so much of his youth. It was a home where everything was in its place.

She was a serious woman and from her young Kenneth got his seriousness, his tenacity, his determination and perseverance. Of that, Leigh Stevenson was certain. Almost a century later, Stevenson could remember that trim, brisk little woman declaring: "If you are going to do something, do it right." She didn't say: "You might as well do it right." There was a difference in those two attitudes. She said, if you are going to do something, *do it right*.

It was more a directive than a comment. It was something K.C. Irving would say hundreds, probably thousands of times, during his life. It was practically a family creed. The grandchildren and the great-grandchildren of Mary Elizabeth Gifford Irving would say it, too — but it was not simply a saying. It was a challenge and a hallmark of excellence. It was something that had been hammered into the Irvings from their earliest days as children. It was something they said — but they also believed it with a passion. And it all started, in Leigh Stevenson's opinion, in the kitchen of Mrs. Irving.

"Ken learned a great deal from his father, he respected him and always spoke highly of him. Ken was an Irving, there was no doubt about that, but he had Gifford in him, too. He had the looks of an Irving but I'd say he was mostly a Gifford. The strong influence that made him what he was came from his mother."

Her one son became the idol of her life. "No child," said Jen Rettie, "could be adored as he was and not love his mother." She was small, quiet-spoken, reserved, "terrifyingly neat; her house was spotless." To Kenneth Irving she was all a mother should be. His eyes could water in remembering her. "I liked her very much," he'd say in his understated way. "She was reasonably strict. She demanded and gave respect and she didn't mind what others thought. She was a tremendous help to me."

She taught him many things. "She told me never to touch liquor and I'd never want to, and I never did. She was death on liquor." She told him never to smoke. He tried it once, got sick and never smoked again. She said to waste anything was a sin. She kept a garden and when her son started to sell the vegetables at five, she made it larger so he could sell more. She taught him to keep his money in a large dining-room clock and when it rose to

$10 or so to put it in the bank: "She'd never let me carry it around."

From her, from his genes, from his environment, from the Calvinist creed that has produced many millionaires, there stemmed that passion for work, the enjoyment of it, and a restless obsession to acquire, build, expand, and improve that would dominate his life. "He went fishing a bit," said Leigh Stevenson, "but he never played much. He was more serious than the rest of us, though he could laugh his head off at a joke."

At an early age he took violin lessons. As Leigh Stevenson remembered it, a couple arrived in Bouctouche to teach music. There wasn't much to do in a small town, so soon many of the children were taking music lessons, including young Ken Irving. "Uncle Jim (Irving) bought violins for Ken, for Marion and Lou, and he bought one for me, too. They cost about $25 each and they came from the Williamson Company in Toronto. Mind you, $25 was a lot of money in those days and those were pretty good violins."

Did Irving learn to play the violin? "Sure, he learned to play it all right. Now, maybe he wasn't all that good, but he played well enough for a beginner." Later, after the war, Stevenson played at parties and dances. His favourite tune, and maybe Ken's, too, was "The Dark Town Strutters' Ball."

In later years, long after his fiddling days were over, Stevenson said that whenever he was with Irving and a piano was available he'd rip out a few choruses of "The Dark Town Strutters' Ball." "That would break the ice and we'd start talking about our favourite subject — Bouctouche and how much fun we had there as kids." But Irving recalled that he had given the violin lessons up "because I wasn't a natural." One did well what one did best. He would say of certain people that "they couldn't play the violin." He meant they were trying something beyond their talents. He admired practical men and he was, as engineers, lawyers, businessmen, and politicians would learn, a practical man himself.

"In Bouctouche," he would say, "you learned which end of a wheelbarrow to take hold of."

Leigh Stevenson recalled, "when Ken was six years old he got one of those little four-wheel carts. You know, the kind with a pull handle. Another youngster might have spent his time riding down a hill or just pulling it around the back yard, but Ken decided to go into business.

"He came up with the idea of cleaning out basements and cellars. He'd clean the cellars and in return he would keep whatever there was that could be salvaged. Usually, it was just bottles, but bottles were worth something and once they were cleaned up there was always someone who was ready to buy them.

"Soon he had me and Addie McNairn cleaning those cellars, carting away the trash and washing the bottles. We were older, about ten, but he was the boss. He owned the pull cart and he ran the show. We might get four cents between us out of every 10 cents he made. He got more than both of us put together, but we didn't mind it a bit. It just seemed like the thing to do at the time. We were great pals, you know. It was natural, I guess. My mother was his father's sister. We weren't much alike. Ken could laugh and have a good time, but we didn't have the same sense of humour. He was always proper, circumspect. Always diplomatic. He took me as I was, and I accepted him as he was. We didn't try to change each other — and I know this for sure, I'd never have been able to change him."

The unchangeable Kenneth Irving helped thresh grain. He worked on the farm. He helped drive the family cattle to distant fields when the grass was right, helped round them up. He built ice shanties and other things as soon as he could handle a saw and hammer. He sold cucumbers at two to three cents, bundles of carrots at four to five cents. He spent hours taking nails out of boxes, straightening them, selling them. He saved lead foil from tea packages and found a market in the local junk dealer at four cents a pound. He sold newspapers. He raised ducks, dozens of them, and when his father complained about the noise he sold them for $150. He packed smelt at one cent for a 10-pound box. He bottled cod liver oil: Nobody else would do it.

He got farmhands to save binder twine from stooks of grain, and he got co-operation in the precise way it was to be done: it made a lot of difference how it was cut. It was worth twice as much when it was cut at the knot as it was when it was cut in the middle, for it was a nice, clean cord then, about 15 inches long and just right for tying up grainbags at the gristmill. He'd been selling it for eight cents a pound but when George Weeks took over the mill he said he'd only pay three cents. Weeks told him: "Your father would fire me if I paid more than it's worth." The boy held out for two or three years, then succumbed. It was a lesson. He would later agree that you don't pay more for something than it is worth, or more than you can afford, but at the time "it took the edge off collecting twine."

It was this small, wiry George Weeks who was told by the boy's father "to bring him up right" and who won the boy's affection in doing it. Many years later Irving would say: "I thought of him as one of us." Weeks was involved in one of the boy's early financial coups. He had bought a Ford and decided to sell it in a lottery. Anthony McNairn won it, this open, windowless vehicle, only to find that he was so big he couldn't get behind the wheel. The boy offered to buy it for $8. McNairn said he'd have to have $12, "but a week later he said I could have it for $8. I went to George Weeks and said I wanted to hide it: I didn't want my father to know I had it. He said the best place was the woodshed at the gristmill, so I dug a hole in a pile of slabs and hid it there. A week or so later father asked if I owned a car, and I said yes. 'Well,' he said, 'let me tell you two things: don't you run it, and get rid of it.' Father was a serious man. There was no question he was the boss. I had to get rid of that car."

George Weeks suggested they call Joe LeBlanc, who ran a hotel in Rexton. LeBlanc, he said, had been interested in buying it. So they called, and he asked what the boy wanted. Eleven dollars, he said, and Joe LeBlanc dickered a bit and then took it. It was the first of many cars Kenneth Irving would sell. He was eleven or twelve years of age. Where did he get the $8 he'd paid for it in the first place? "I had it in the clock."

He'd worked on the car while Weeks owned it. Weeks let him use his carpenter's tools to build things, "but God help me if I damaged one and didn't tell him or if I didn't put them back where they belonged." Weeks was on the school board. He ran skating races. When the boy built a boat to fish smelt and go on the river, he enlarged the design and found he couldn't get it out of the gristmill basement. It was Weeks who found a way. But when Weeks raised a beam and got it out, the boy hesitated when called over to see. Something had happened to put a strain on their relationship.

Weeks taught boys to box, and one day he told Kenneth Irving he couldn't hurt a fly: "I saw an opening and hit him in the eye," Irving recalled years later. "He never said a word. He went off holding his eye. I threw off the gloves and out the door I went."

For days Kenneth avoided the man. Then came the day when Weeks called out that he had a birthday present. The boy had doubts. "You're sure?" he said from a distance. "You're not mad?" When he saw the boat in the outdoors sunlight he knew their rift was healed.

Young Kenneth Irving fought quite a lot in those early days in Bouctouche, mostly bare knuckles. It was almost a way of life there, a form of entertainment, "no more than shaking hands today. If you didn't look after yourself it was a bit of a reflection on you." Sailors drank at the half-dozen hotels and then battled in the streets or on the wharf. It became a mark of distinction to be good at it. On Labour Day weekends men came in from Moncton and elsewhere, and many fought. Jim Wry, owner of one of the seven schooners in town, was often tried and never bested: "All the Wrys were good with their fists."

What men did, boys emulated. The Irving farm foreman, Dave Evans, would halt his horse and watch Kenneth Irving in battle, urge him on, then tell him to get up on the wagon where he would preach to him the wisdom of more holy ways. The fact was that the boy liked to fight: "You had a certain amount of energy. You had to get rid of it somehow." His eyes would light up years later in recalling it. He won, he estimated with a grin, about half the time.

It was fighting that led to a one-year exile. Two boys had given him a beating. Next morning he caught up with one of them and sought revenge, one on one. A teacher came out and ordered him into the school. The boy replied that they were outside both school grounds and school hours. The teacher told him what he'd get, and the boy began heaving stones at him. He never, he said, spent a more worrisome day in school than he did that day, and he soon had orders from his father: he was going to Millerton, a village to the north in the Miramichi Valley, to live with his half-sister Jen and her husband, the Rev. Alex Rettie.

He was fourteen then, and he had never really liked school. "He found studying hard," said Jen Rettie. Fellow Bouctouche students remembered him as serious, popular, though he did like to pull the ribbons from girls' hair. He was, he said, "always up to something, making a nuisance of myself."

In Millerton, things changed. On his first day in class Principal Percy Robinson said, "Kenneth, stand up. You've come to learn.

I'm going to teach you. I'm the boss. If you fight for one minute it's going to be too bad for you. Now we'll find out where you are in class. You say Grade 9. I'll just check you." His finding was that the boy had until Christmas to catch up, and he gave him extra lessons to do it. At nights, beside a kerosene lamp, Alex Rettie helped him too. It took effect. "By gosh," he'd say, "I got so I liked school." And he never forgot what those two men — Alex Rettie and Percy Robinson — did for him. "They taught me responsibility and discipline."

Jen Rettie had never liked seeing him so devoted to the pursuit of money, and in unspoken ways she and her husband set about diverting him. She thinks it worked: "I doubt that he earned a penny that year." He became a bosom pal of two Simpson brothers. They fished, roamed the fields and the village together, found and looted Jen's cakes no matter where she hid them. When he was well into his eighties Irving remembered it all as "probably the best thing that ever happened to me." Jen Rettie remembered it as "a lovely year."

ta

Enlisting for Himself

"I've decided to enlist."
  – KENNETH IRVING IN 1915.
"You get yourself to school."
  – J.D. IRVING'S REPLY TO HIS SIXTEEN-YEAR-OLD SON.

A T FIFTEEN, THE YEAR THE FIRST WORLD WAR BROKE OUT, Kenneth Irving was back at school in Bouctouche. He worked in the family store and the mills. But now he was swept up in a new fervour. He wanted to join up and go to war. At sixteen, he could wait no longer. He got a drive to Moncton and went to see a Dr. White for a medical checkup prior to joining the infantry.

At first, the doctor was co-operative. "This," he said, "will make a man of you." But when he got around to filling out forms and checking family details his attitude changed. "So you're Jim's boy," the doctor exclaimed, and from his tone of voice Kenneth Irving knew he had a problem.

"You get the hell out of here and back to Bouctouche," the doctor said, but after further talk he relented and agreed to sign the medical section of the form. "Now," he said, "if Jim signs this, you're in." Next morning the boy told his father he had something he wanted him to sign.

"What is it?" asked J.D. Irving.

"I've decided to enlist."

20

"You've what?" his father said. Without waiting for an answer he pulled out his watch, glanced at it, and rasped: "You get yourself to school."

"His boot," said his son years later, "just missed me."

At seventeen, tall, gangling, and still restless to join the army, young Irving was packed off to Dalhousie University in Halifax to enrol in a special arts course. Its records show that his high-school matriculation marks were less than distinguished: English 58, History 61, Geometry 40. His roommate was a wounded veteran back from the war. Irving enrolled in the officers' training corps. He tried again to enlist, this time in an artillery battery, but his father thwarted that, too. He wrote no exams, and his father, deciding that there were too many military distractions in Halifax, shifted him the next fall to Acadia University in small, quiet Wolfville, N.S.

The fervour remained. Boys were enlisting. Veterans were common. One morning his Latin instructor told him to translate a passage. "Not today, sir," he said quietly, but with firmness and finality. He picked up his book and left. "Young fellas get rebellious." As he walked down the hall his roommate asked where he was going. "I'm going to enlist in the Royal Flying Corps," he said. "By God," said the roommate, "I'm going with you."

He enlisted in the spring of 1918. His parents yielded. His mother "felt bad but everybody was going. She let me go." He would remember his military experience fondly. He liked the discipline, the guard drill, the camaraderie. He found machine-guns no problem: "They were up my line." He exulted in studying engines. He got a perfect mark in navigation. He became a second lieutenant. In England for advanced training, he caught up with Leigh Stevenson, now a pilot after long months in the trenches as an infantryman. Together, in a two-seater Sopwith Camel, they took off. A long, rich, and distinguished life lay ahead of Stevenson, but he would always remember the day when he put that plane through every intimidating trick he knew. It was, he'd say, a flimsy, temperamental machine with a short flight time — but long enough to "scare the daylights out of a fledgling pilot." A modified Camel, it had dual controls and a gas tank removed to make it a two-seater training plane. In it, he did rolls and loops and dives, "everything I could think of. Let's face it, I was showing off. I wanted to let him know how good I was — and I wanted to give him a little scare."

Did it work? Leigh Stevenson, seventy years later, still didn't know. "If he was frightened, he didn't say so. But, then, he would have been too stubborn to let me know."

Various people agree that Kenneth Irving would probably have made an excellent fighter pilot in action, but he never got the chance. On November 11 he and friends were in a London hotel when they heard a commotion outside. As they went out into the shouting streets, someone said the war was over. His reactions were mixed: "We were disappointed not to see action, but we knew we were lucky to be alive."

He came home in 1919. Years later he said, "All I thought was that I was going back to a great deal of very hard work and I might as well get used to it." But the summer of 1919 turned out to be something else. Irving's sister Lou had half a dozen young ladies visiting with her at the family home and Stevenson remembered playing the violin or the piano at dances "anywhere we could find them." He also remembered that twenty-year-old Ken Irving did a lot of dancing that summer. "That was one of the best summers of my life," Stevenson recalled, "and it was the last summer, perhaps the only summer, that Ken really loafed.

"It was a summer of fishing and loafing and going to every dance we could find. We had a wonderful time and it was the only time in all the years I've known Ken that he took it easy. I think it was one of those crossroads of his life. He was thinking about leaving Bouctouche, but his heart was there and he wanted to stay and get more involved in the family business."

At the end of the summer Leigh Stevenson headed west to pursue a career in flying and the Royal Canadian Air Force; he would end up an air vice-marshall.

Irving himself would remember that summer of 1919 as one of the most unusual in his life. He remembered the loafing, the fishing, the parties, and the dances. Especially the dances. "Why," he recalled, "by the end of the summer I'd danced myself right down to skin and bones, and I had to stop and go to work before the loafing killed me."

But there were other forces at work too. Even before Irving got home, the thrust of labour restlessness had penetrated the isolation of tiny Bouctouche. J.D. Irving's sawmill workers were threatening to walk out for higher wages. Leigh Stevenson was there visiting, and he had never seen a strike. He remembered putting a revolver under his coat, "in case things got rough," and going with his uncle and watching him stand on a lumber pile and look out into dark, brooding faces. It was a head-to-head collision between two schools of thought: one that the Irvings could and should pay more, the other that but for the Irvings there would be little work at all.

It didn't last long, that confrontation. J.D. Irving said he couldn't pay more, that he would if he could but he was operating on a pretty narrow margin. He was blunt and forceful. When the whistle blew he told the men to go back to work, and they went. It was over, but for Irving's son it cast both light and shadow on things to come. In the frail, patched, and chronically aching economy of New Brunswick, it was the forerunner of many such confrontations.

During that first year of peace he saw melancholy reasons for what his father had done. They left in him impressions time would never erase, and they largely influenced what he did with his life. For one thing, a budworm infestation had swept through the forests of Kent County and other parts of the province, decimating the trees that were its economic lifeline. Numerous sawmills had closed or were closing. People were selling out and leaving. His ailing father kept his sawmill going but by the 1930s that would have to close too. There wasn't enough wood to sustain it.

Nor was that the only blow. A powerful rival had emerged to threaten the family store. It was new, it was exciting, and it captured the interest and imagination of longtime customers who were being wooed away from their traditional shopping habits. Eaton's catalogue had arrived in Bouctouche.

In Moncton and elsewhere Eaton's were in the mail-order business. Their catalogues were becoming a national institution. The competition was devastating in many small towns, for they offered a great sweep of merchandise and, worse, they drained off cash and left many of their local rivals to fret over reduced business done on credit. It wasn't long before the Irving store found its profits drastically slashed.

Kenneth Irving joined the fight to rescue it, but he soon had cause to wonder at his skills. "I placed an order for what at that time would be considered a substantial number of neckties, some of the most colourful ties ever seen — all colours of the rainbow.

They were considered by Mr. Bourgeois, the manager of the store, as not for this world. He said they would be suitable for a bunch of circus clowns, but they would not sell in Bouctouche. He said I was going to ruin my father."

Then in came hotel-keeper Andrew Hebert, a man who once said he'd bought so many vegetables from a younger Kenneth Irving that he'd set him up in business. "He looked at the display of ties, grabbed the brightest and declared, 'Now that's what I call a tie.' He purchased it immediately and he talked so much about that tie — and they were talked about so much in the store — that they were soon all sold."

There was a lot more at stake in the second experience. His father was away at the time potatoes came to harvest. The Irvings bought and sold them, and Kenneth kept buying as fast as they came in from an excellent crop. It wasn't long before every available inch of space was filled. By the time his father returned there was no room for more — and the market was sick. They had regular customers in Montreal, Boston, and other cities but they either wanted no potatoes or, if they did, offered less than they'd cost.

"You've even got potatoes stuck between the joists," his father said. "They're going to sprout. Take them out on the ice, get rid of them." Instead, a disconsolate Kenneth Irving sent off a flock of telegrams. To his surprise and pleasure, back came two orders for two carloads each and the message: "If you have more we'd be glad to have them." He wired back and raised the price. "Bang, they accepted. Six cars. I asked what they'd offer for more. One buyer suggested we sell on commission. He said he thought he could get $10 to $12 a barrel, a lot more than I'd paid. I shipped more to New York and got $18 net." It was years before he learned why the market had changed so radically. Then he discovered that frost had killed the crop in rival American areas.

In 1920, as the store floundered, he took a prophetic step. He did it on his own to help restore the business. At six o'clock one morning he started to dig a hole in front of the store. By the time his father came in he had a 250-gallon gasoline tank nearly covered. With cars becoming more and more common, they had, in his father's name, become a "barrel agent" for Imperial Oil.

J.D. Irving asked what he was up to. "I'm darned sure," said his son, "we're not going out of business." But within a year he decided the business was not big enough for his half-brother Herbert, his father, and himself. To what degree did Kenneth Irving's later penchant for controlling his own interests develop out of his relations with this half-brother? They didn't see eye to eye in numerous ways: "We had different ways of doing things." Herbert was fourteen years older, likeable, popular. Average, said his loving sister Jen. He didn't have Kenneth's dynamism, drive, or brains. He didn't approve of the gasoline experiment. He doubted that the store could survive Eaton's competition and suggested, said Kenneth Irving, that they close it. Because he was older, he had seniority, and Kenneth Irving didn't like it. In Leigh Stevenson's words, "He didn't like being under anyone."

CHAPTER FOUR

🔊

A Ford in His Future

*"You had to have happy customers ... you didn't leave
people in a lot of trouble."*
— K.C. IRVING'S EARLY SALES' PHILOSOPHY.

THEN THERE WERE THE ESCAPADES OF THAT LOVABLE
rascal Addie McNairn. That's how he was remembered by
K.C. Irving and Leigh Stevenson. He loved to drink, play
poker, and mostly he loved to live by his wits. He wasn't a bad
man. In fact he was good company, but he was always on the edge
of getting himself into trouble.

Stevenson remembered McNairn winning a lot of money playing cards on a troopship coming back from the First World War,
but it was gone as quickly as he made it. He also remembered an
incident in wartime France when a Scottish regimental paymaster
rode into a small French town and hitched his horse in the street
while he went into the temporary army headquarters to do his
business. When he returned a short time later the horse was gone,
never to be seen again. At least, never to be seen alive or in one
piece. Addie had not only stolen it, he had sold it to a local butcher, saddle and all. "It was a quick sale, for a low price, and Addie
had a wonderful party that night." The next day, there were some
choice cuts of meat in the butcher's window. The townspeople
were happy to get any meat and cleaned out the store in no time.

The saddle? "We never saw it again," said Leigh Stevenson. For a time Addie McNairn was K.C. Irving's best friend. They were as different as day and night. They crossed Canada together and almost went to Australia.

In 1921, with a postwar depression sapping the country, Irving concluded that he should join Kent County's exodus. McNairn had come home from the west and said he was going to Australia. "Overnight," Irving said, "I decided to go with him."

En route, they stopped in Saskatchewan to earn money harvesting grain, slept in sheds, and never ate better in their lives. It was an experience Irving would talk about for years. "Western Canada was an eye-opener," he once told a writer. "We shocked 160 acres of oats and another 160 acres of wheat for a Mr. Simpson of Milestone, and we did so well that Mr. Simpson sent us on to a Mr. Thompson near Weyburn. We started spike-pitching, real hard work, for, I think it was, $4 a day.

"What struck Addie and me was how different farming in western Canada was from farming back home. Mr. Simpson was originally from Virginia and he told us he spent one winter out of two in Virginia and the other in California. He spent not more than half a day in the fields. Farming to us — even if you owned the farm — meant getting up at 4 a.m. to feed the stock and milk the cows, and then looking after the crops or working all day in the woodlot when the weather was right. This new look at life in the wide-open spaces made us all the more determined to go to Australia. We went to Vancouver and started looking for a boat."

They never took one. While he was visiting a relative a wire came from his father, urging him to come home. The family tie proved too strong. Irving went back to Bouctouche and soon after so did McNairn. He lived in Bouctouche until his death in the early 1960s.

Now twenty-two-year-old Kenneth Irving was given charge of the store. By day he sought improvements, greater volume, got in new lines of merchandise. He put in electricity from the gristmill's generator, made a switchboard out of a tombstone. He saw things improve, profits rise. By night he sold cars. He had earlier sold Chevrolets briefly for a dealer who needed help and capital. Now Arthur Maillet of Richibucto got him selling Fords. Maillet found it tough selling for the Henry Ford who had revolutionized American industry with his assembly line, who would market his celebrated Model T until 1927. Ford, said Irving, made his dealers finance his operations, gave them quotas, got cash. The cars came in around the year but in Canada no one bought them in winter; the roads were blocked by snow and ice. They came in, moreover, with the wheels off, the body and chassis separate, and had to be put together. With Ford riding him, Maillet turned over southern Kent County to Irving within a couple of years.

His father said he would be the ruination of the countryside, that farmers couldn't afford cars. Kenneth found a way: "If you thought a farmer was serious, the first thing was to get him to say he wanted a car. Then he'd say he didn't have any money. You'd ask him when he was going to get some or how much he did have. Then you had to work it out. You made a lot of suggestions. You took in on trade all sorts of things — horses, carriages, harnesses, cattle. Then you had to sell them too. Moving around that way, you got a good idea of how you could dispose of things. I even took in a load of groceries."

He was neat, his shoes polished — by himself, a lifetime habit — his books kept in his pocket. He kept a list of prospects. He was surprised to find that "people would tell you everybody's business but their own. They had more time then." He learned, too, that "you had to have happy customers. You didn't leave people in a lot of trouble." He sold his Model Ts for $385 and made $80 on each car he sold. He showed buyers how to crank them, with your thumb down to keep out of trouble from the kickback. When starters came in, they cost another $85. He extolled them. He talked about every asset he could think of: "You had to have things to say." He learned that one happy customer led to another.

"William Graham of Main River was one. He farmed and ran a small store, and he wanted a light delivery truck. He bought it and in a few days he called to ask me to come up and get it started. I did, and he said, 'You were good enough to come up here; I think if you went to so-and-so in Bass River you could sell a car.' Sure enough, I sold a touring car. I'd make maybe $105 on that. Mr. Graham kept calling me with tips. He helped me sell perhaps five cars. Sometimes he'd even go with me when the crops were in."

Irving never, he said, had a bad debt. He did well. He made far more this way than he did in the store. In 1924 he made $20,000; in 1925, $22,000. What made it even better was that "I never enjoyed anything more than talking to those farmers."

Tom Nowlan once recalled a conversation in this period of Kenneth Irving's life. J.D. Irving asked him if he didn't think his son was tackling too much, spreading himself too thin, and Nowlan said, "No, leave him alone. Let him go." He was impressed by Kenneth Irving: "He'd bargain with you but he'd never come out on the short end. I knew when he started you couldn't hold him." Indeed, he would later lend Irving money and get it back with good interest.

Nowlan was a good-hearted, popular local small businessman. In an era of widespread coastal rum-running, he imported and sold. In later years he owned a farm across the river from Moncton. In Bouctouche he was a kindly benefactor of local events and causes, a good customer of the Irving store, and the subject of one of Irving's chuckling tales. A minister came one time and said in privacy that he would appreciate it if Irving would go to Mr. Nowlan and inform him that he'd had a call from a Customs officer in Saint John to the effect that he would be paying him a call at a certain time the next day. When Kenneth Irving informed him, Mr. Nowlan thanked him and said the Customs officer had been good enough to call him as well. Though they never discussed his business then or later, all was in order for the visit.

Probably it was in 1924 that Jim Irving expressed his reservations to Nowlan. The family story is that he was disappointed that his son was not going to stay in the family business, that his career was clearly taking a pattern of its own. That year the son built a garage and service station to sell Imperial products, repair cars, and assemble the Fords he continued to sell. He said he invited his father and Herbert to join him but they declined. "All right," he said, "I'll do it alone." The family store by then was on its feet, doing four times the business it had done at its lowest ebb, and in their own niches they remained, though Herbert would soon depart for Montreal.

The garage arose across from the store, on the family land. The only complaint from Irving's mother was that it blocked her view of the street. But that was part of the strategy. There is a picture of it, and it is clearly and importantly visible from a distance, under an early version of those canopies that would become a hallmark of his life's work.

He hired carpenter Ephrem Cormier to build it but he hammered many of the nails himself. He would say that he borrowed

$2,000 from a bank and had a month's credit and had to run fast to make the business go. It did well. He came to do 95 per cent of the gas and oil business in town, then got a truck and drove it out into the country seeking more. He had an efficient secretary in one Harriet McNairn who had come to Bouctouche in 1919 to work in the store. She kept his books. He liked and admired her. There is a story that he once went to a basket social and outbid a rival for the basket she'd brought. In time, she would marry him and become the most important person in his life.

Neil Ross came in one day and asked if Irving knew that Imperial Oil had bought a lot in town and was naming Joe Bourque its full-time agent. Irving didn't know, and he called Imperial's supervisor in Moncton to ask what was going on. He was told there had been complaints from town merchants about buying oil and gas from a family they competed with in other businesses. Imperial decided to have a full-time instead of a part-time agent. Irving spoke hot and angry words. He blamed the Moncton supervisor for what happened: "From Imperial's standpoint the move made sense but he might have told me what he was going to do."

In Irving's reaction lay his future. He met the new competition with competition of his own. In his own small, local sphere, he took on a national giant backed by an international giant. He wired Charles Noble, a supplier in Tulsa, Oklahoma, and got regular shipments of gas and oil in tank-car lots confirmed. In Bouctouche they said he would get skinned alive. He didn't care. He ordered an $800, 10,000-gallon tank from Toronto. The story in Bouctouche to this day is that two tanks arrived on railway flat-cars on the same day — one for Imperial, the other for Irving — exciting curiosity for miles around. What Irving remembered was that his heart hit bottom when he had trouble getting his own in place. Then a fire marshal arrived and said it was too close to buildings, and he had to do it all over again, moving it with ropes and skids.

From Noble he ordered gasoline to his own specifications. Mixing it with natural gas to give it the right boiling point. At a time when many cars still had to be cranked, he preached that his gasoline gave a faster start. He charged five cents, then three cents more than his rivals. Imperial had a brand called Premier, Canadian Oil a brand called White Rose. He combined the two and called his Primrose. He had "Primrose" painted on three trucks, and peddled it around the country. He did a lot of business. When asked later whether Imperial might have been the real sire of Irving Oil he replied, "No, I think it would only have been a matter of time before I went into business for myself anyway." He did not profess the sort of long-range vision that people supposed. He was simply reacting to the situation that faced him. Cars were coming in. They needed gas and oil. He sold cars, and he sold gas and oil. It was, he said, just common sense.

In 1925 Irving built a second service station, in nearby Shediac in Westmorland County. The first of many expansions had begun, but in that same year something else happened: Ford reacted to complaints about his aggressive selling of cars. Its senior regional official came to Bouctouche and said Irving would have to stop selling in Moncton and in Westmorland; the local dealer was complaining about competition. Irving agreed in later years that if he'd been in that dealer's place he'd have complained, too, but that wasn't what he said to the Ford representatives back in 1925.

"It's open territory."

"You've got to stop," the Ford man insisted, "but don't get mad. Wait. I'll be back next week."

He was back within a day or two to ask Irving if he'd like to take over the franchise in Saint John. It sounded big — big enough to raise doubts: "I didn't think I could handle it. I said I'd have to take a look." He looked. He decided to go. He was twenty-six.

CHAPTER 5

Saint John: Irving Among the Loyalists

"Our policy is better and more satisfactory service."
– FORD DEALER IRVING'S FIRST FULL-PAGE NEWSPAPER
ADVERTISEMENT IN SAINT JOHN.

THE K.C. IRVING WHO LEFT BOUCTOUCHE WAS READY FOR larger things. He was combative, determined, accustomed to working far harder than most men. He knew a great deal about a variety of businesses, already knew the virtues of diversification, and had seen how a troubled business could be restored to health. The family store had been an excellent training ground.

From the intricate guts of automobiles and learning how to sell them, from the cutting, processing, and sale of lumber, from twenty-one years of making his own money, he had come to the conclusion that if you had responsibility you also had to have authority. You had to have control. He had come into close contact with three corporate giants, Imperial Oil, Ford, and Eaton's, and in the process of dealing with them he had learned how vulnerable a small operator could be and how dependent the Maritime provinces were upon an economy whose power centre lay far away, controlled by men swayed far more by larger designs than local interests.

As a young boy he had once gone to Saint John with his father to an animal show. He saw a man enter a lion's cage and suddenly

32

hours of Sunday School, of Biblical instruction at a great-aunt's knee, came flooding back. "There," he blurted out to the amusement of the audience, "is Daniel in the lion's den." It was a fitting, if premature, introduction to the city he would make his headquarters for forty-six years, where he would polarize opinion between those who felt he could do no right and those who felt he could do no wrong — a Daniel in the cage of public opinion.

Saint John in 1925 was, as it is now, the largest city in New Brunswick, a seaport fringed by forests. Its red-brick and rectangular wooden buildings, its faded, harassed face occupied the place where the St. John River yielded some 400 miles of waters to the Bay of Fundy, where the Kennebecasis contributed its own waters to the St. John. Champlain had been there in 1604. There Lady LaTour had lost her husband's fort to his fur-trading rival, Charnisay, in the days of French rule in Acadia. There New Englanders later founded the tiny community to which Loyalists flocked in their thousands in 1783 with the defeat of the British cause in the American Revolution. One year later, New Brunswick was hewn out of Nova Scotia. One year later still, Saint John became the first city incorporated in what is now Canada. For the next two centuries it prided itself in being the Loyalist City.

Neither the city nor the province ever came close to achieving the ambition stated by one Loyalist leader: to create in this wilderness "the most gentlemanlike society on earth." Nor to making the society a permanently prosperous one. For a few decades in the middle of the nineteenth century the city did boom in an era Maritimers still think of as the age of wooden ships and iron men. Saint John produced the legendary *Marco Polo*, the "fastest ship in the world," and hundreds of others. It became the home of the world's fourth-largest accumulation of vessels. Then sailing ships lost their pre-eminence in the very period when a new Canada emerged with the Confederation of 1867, a coincidence many Maritimers would for years believe was more the penalty of political folly than of economic change.

By 1925 Saint John had tried for half a century to restore its vanished glories. Irving arrived in Saint John the year the Admiral Beatty Hotel opened on King Square, within easy sight of the Loyalist Cemetery whose caretaker would say whimsically years later that "there's none of the Irving family buried here, and I wish there was. Not that I wish them any harm but it would give the place some prestige."

Prestige Irving did not have in 1925. When he made the trip from Bouctouche to Saint John in a Model T, he was an obscure outsider who needed Saint John more than it needed him.

Scrubbing-board Surprise Soap, destined to be one of many New Brunswick products eliminated by the incursions of remotely controlled capital, was selling for 10 cents a bar. The automotive age spoke out in advertisements urging people to "Fill 'er up with FUNDY, better gas." Human needs were reflected in ads for winter underwear and medicinal potions certain to cure virtually any bodily complaints known to man. Tory Arthur Meighen and Liberal Mackenzie King were locked in mutual hatred in a federal election campaign. The Pittsburgh Pirates were beating the Washington Senators in the World Series. The St. George's Society went on record as protesting the suggestion that there should be a Canadian flag. "The Union Jack," it resolved, "is the proper and the only flag." Tourism, said an article, had grown 50 per cent in the past year with the arrival of 25,000 cars. Editorially, the *Telegraph-Journal* said Maritime Union "could become an intensely practical issue" but for the moment "we should concentrate on Maritime co-operation for Maritime advancement." Advancement was precisely what was being sought in a widespread movement to assert Maritime rights, claiming a larger, fairer share of the growing Canadian prosperity of the 1920s.

A full-page newspaper ad announced Irving's arrival in Saint John on October 14, including his picture — short, dark, cropped hair over a thin, resolute face and a stiff collar: "His reputation as a successful Ford dealer and for business integrity had preceded him." In capital letters it proclaimed that "OUR POLICY IS BETTER AND MORE SATISFACTORY SERVICE, TO BE HONEST IN OUR RELATIONS WITH OUR CUSTOMERS." To this end, he had not "spared expense in equipping our Service Department so that service can be rendered promptly and efficiently." He had chosen his staff "from among those who have attained success in their respective departments." The "improved Ford models" were now on display in a renovated showroom, the parts department had been enlarged "to handle a complete assortment of parts and accessories," and ladies were "especially welcomed."

The *Telegraph-Journal* ran a five-paragraph story on page nine. It quoted Mr. Irving as "highly enthusiastic over his organization," said he was "well known in the New Brunswick automotive world as secretary-treasurer of J.D. Irving Ltd. and a Ford agent," and that his new premises had been "in the hands of carpenters and painters for the last few weeks or so," resulting in "some pleasing renovations, especially in the showroom."

Irving's showroom-garage stood at 300 Union Street. His Ford franchise cost him nothing. Ford officials were happy to have a young, aggressive salesman in charge of sales in Saint John, and his mandate was to sell more Model Ts. Irving sold himself. He stayed at the Royal Hotel, and he worked day and night. Still, he was so young, so unknown, that there were reservations about him in financial circles. As far back as 1921 he had saved $5,000, but now he needed a lot more. He went almost at once to a bank to establish a line of credit, got a jolt, and met a man whose name would course through the careers of numerous Canadian businessmen. His name was Enman. Horace L. Enman.

As Irving told the story: "The bank was prepared to give me the line of credit I asked for but wanted my father's guarantee. I had then been in business one way or another for five years or more, and I had fulfilled all my obligations to the bank. I was now the new Ford dealer in Saint John and felt I should not ask my father to sign a guarantee for me. But the bank demanded that extra protection.

"At that very time, who walked into my new place of business but Mr. A.J. MacQuarrie, the manager of the Charlotte Street branch of the Bank of Nova Scotia. I shook his hand. His first words: 'How could you do it, Kenneth?' He went on to say he had been a family friend for years. He had visited with us in Bouctouche, and he had gone fishing with my father. 'How could you come to Saint John and not do business with me?'

"Little did he know how much I wanted a friendly banker who wanted my business. So I apologized and said I was prepared to give him my business providing he was prepared to arrange a certain line of credit. With that he wheeled on his heel and said, 'I'll call you in the morning.'

"He called back within the hour and said we had an appointment with the regional supervisor of the Bank of Nova Scotia,

Mr. Horace Enman. The next morning, after spending some time in Mr. Enman's office, I said, 'Mr. Enman, we came here for a purpose and I am wondering if you have come to any decision?' He jumped up from his desk, a smile all over his face, and said, looking over at Mr. MacQuarrie, 'Didn't he tell you?'"

Irving got his lines of credit and, even more significantly, he became acquainted with Horace Enman, a man who would become president of his bank. But Enman would live in Saint John for a long time and delight in bringing together economic prospects and the men who might best take advantage of them. He would become a friend and confidant of K.C. Irving — at least to the degree that anyone ever did.

In this first period in Saint John Irving would acknowledge he pursued a curious mixture of business ventures. He thought small. He also thought big, but he tried never to pass up a business opportunity. He took advantage of little ones: "A big company wouldn't be bothered with them but that's all there was for someone in my position." Tom Enright, for instance, was running a bus line out to Rothesay and had no place to shelter the bus. Irving gave him a key and said he could use the garage at night. "It didn't disturb anything," said Irving. "He'd park it there at night and we'd move it out first thing in the morning." Enright was happy. He had a secure place for his bus at night, and Irving had another longtime customer and supporter.

And so it continued — big deals, small deals, and growing sales. Ford was impressed and rewarded his efforts by giving him a franchise in Halifax and the Maritime franchise for its tractors. Then, in 1927, Ford got him into "an awful mess." It announced, with a great flourish, the Model A as successor to the Model T it had been marketing for seventeen years. The cars were due in the spring, but they didn't arrive until fall and for months Irving and his salesmen were left only with pictures, propaganda, and the powers of persuasion — and wondering, waiting customers. He even filled some of the gap with surplus Chryslers he got from a rival dealer.

Amid these day-to-day tribulations, he was thinking ahead. Significantly, he formed K.C. Irving Gas and Oil Ltd. A car dealership subjected him to corporate decisions he could not control. In the gas and oil business he saw the opportunity to build *and* control what he did himself. He was soon absorbed in the business in Saint John and elsewhere, selling what he got from Noble and, when that became uneconomic because of freight rates, utilizing other sources. When his first Saint John gasoline customer ran into trouble, it was Irving who rushed out to Three Mile House to attend to it. He found a row of stalled and irate customers stretching away from the fruit stand of an Italian immigrant who sold Irving gasoline under a name of his own concoction: Blue Spark. Water, Irving discovered, had found its way into the gasoline. The matter was straightened out and Irving admonished the dealer to make certain that watering was confined to the fruit and vegetables.

He established outlets in various communities and bought service stations in the city. He found a good man in Ray Tanton, a Prince Edward Islander who had tried homesteading in Saskatchewan, and leased him an outlet. Recognizing the impact of a famous name, he made a partnership agreement with Charlie Gorman, "the man with the million-dollar legs." He was too busy to watch Gorman, a war veteran wounded in the leg, win a world ice-skating championship in a 1926 blizzard on Saint John's Lily Lake before 25,000 fans, but he found the time to set the speed skating champion up in the service station business.

There are those who claim Howard P. Robinson, the city's dominant businessman, once threatened to "chase that fellow Irving back to Bouctouche." To the contrary, Irving said their relations were always friendly. It was, indeed, Robinson who was also reported to have said that Irving was the best thing that ever happened to him: "Before he came along, everyone was trying to pull me down. Now they're trying to pull Irving down." It was Robinson who called to ask Irving if he could do anything for Gorman. Gorman in turn predicted that "Irving will be the greatest man this country has ever seen."

CHAPTER SIX

~

The Ford Dealer in
a Cadillac

"He got more advertising out of that car! It got people talking about him."
  – GENERAL MOTORS DEALER MIKE LAWSON SPECULATING ON
  WHY FORD DEALER K.C. IRVING DROVE A GENERAL MOTORS
  CADILLAC IN THE DEPRESSION YEARS.

IN 1927 K.C. IRVING WENT BACK TO BOUCTOUCHE AND married Harriet McNairn. In 1928, the year his first son was born, he came into contact with two men who would be his allies for many years. One was Louis McCoskery Ritchie, a patrician lawyer who had forsaken the trenches of the First World War for the Royal Flying Corps. The other was K.B. Reed, a small, sharp businessman who had opened his own service station in 1924 after trying other ventures. The three men were brought together when one of Lou Ritchie's clients got an option on Reed's service station but ran into problems and couldn't handle the deal. Ritchie called Irving to ask him if he'd be interested in taking over the station. Irving said he'd be right down.

He, Ritchie, and Reed formed a company called Haymarket Square Service Stations Ltd. At the end of its first year there were no dividends. "K.C. Irving," Ritchie discovered, "doesn't like to pay dividends." Instead, he bought out his two partners and gave Reed a job that lasted almost sixty years.

Why did Reed join him? "Irving," he said, "seemed to be the rising star. He had a lot of people guessing. He was doing so well that a lot of jealous people thought it wouldn't last." Irving hired Reed for the new Irving Oil Co. Ltd. In establishing it in 1929, he used Lou Ritchie as a lawyer for the first time, raised $300,000 in a financing handled by Frank Brennan of Eastern Securities. He made the preferred shares callable, and he called most of them as soon as he could.

He hired Reed as an auditor, and to find dealers. He was already selling gas and oil not only in Saint John but in Bouctouche, Shediac, Moncton, Sussex, Campbellton, and St. Stephen in New Brunswick, and he was invading Nova Scotia. He bought Moncton's Bore Motor Fuel Co., and with it a service station in Truro. There he found more famous athletes in hockey stars Doggie and Skeets Kuhn and set them up with a lease, their station known as The Bearcat in honour of the celebrated local team. When a large gasoline tank rolled into town to service it, it was Irving who did much of the work of getting it into place near the railway tracks. When Russell Fraser of Halifax told Irving he had just finished paying for the installation of several new gas tanks for other companies and didn't have money to install more, it was Irving who came back in overalls and with a pipefitter, and put in his own tank. When he made a deal with Joseph Wright of Westville to sell his gas, Wright didn't like the contract. Irving told him to draw up his own, and they did business for years.

As part of another deal he acquired one of his most loyal employees. He wanted to put a tank in front of George Hankinson's store in Weymouth, N.S., and Hankinson said he could do it if Irving would give a job to his teen-aged nephew. That nephew, Arnold Payson, started driving a 1924 truck in the Yarmouth area in 1929 and he soon had a story that flustered and then amused his boss: The brakes gave way on a hill and he demolished three Imperial Oil tanks in front of a country store. The proprietor came roaring out and told him to replace them fast. When Payson got them in, the store owner snorted, "But those are Irving tanks." Payson said he was sorry but that was all he had, and within a week the man was happy because he'd never sold so much gas.

In Amherst, Irving got a service station as part of a company purchase and hired Ted O'Neill to handle the district. He put a

10,000-gallon tank on the marshy outskirts of town. From it, O'Neill peddled gas around the area, using a second-hand truck, then a new one. He fixed pumps. He ran the business from his own home and did his reports at night after a long day. He started at $28 a week. Irving would drop in occasionally. He had a stock question he asked O'Neill and many others thousands of times: "How's business?" Business, O'Neill found, came tough at first: "It was hard to get in anywhere." He sold only 100,000 gallons of gas a year, a fraction of what a single station later sold.

In Halifax, Irving offered a job to accountant Hilus Webb. Webb wanted $40 a week. "No, no," said Irving, "I can't afford that." He offered $27.50. Webb told him if he could get an accountant for $27.50 he'd better do it. He started out the door three times before Irving gave him what he wanted. Then Irving said if he was such a good accountant he'd better set up a bookkeeping system to handle his scattered business. Webb wasn't too sure he could do it. He wrote to the American school that had trained him and got help. The system proved so good that it was adopted for the Saint John headquarters. Webb soon found that Irving gave loyalty for loyalty received. But when he went to work for him he figured the man was going to do one of two things: "He was going to be big or he was going to go bust."

Thus selling cars, building his network of service stations and other outlets, K.C. Irving was growing when the stock market collapsed in late 1929 as the prelude to the most devastating economic depression the modern world had seen. But one thing was soon apparent: Irving had no intentions of going bust.

His response to the Depression was typical. He simply did what he did best. He worked harder. He also did things that demonstrated both optimism and defiance of hard times. One out-of-character act occurred in 1931 at a motor show in Montreal when he saw a lavish, black, 16-cylinder Cadillac. Irving bought it, taking care to see that the sale was made in the name of Roy (Mike) Lawson, a friendly rival who sold GM cars in Saint John. The splendours with which the Cadillac was endowed were just too much for him. The Cadillac had luxurious upholstery and seven seats. It cost $11,000 and consumed so much gas that one service station operator said, laughing, "It burns it up faster than I can put it in."

Irving's Ford allies were not too pleased that he hadn't bought a Lincoln. "I didn't want a Lincoln. I wanted that Cadillac." He drove it about the Maritimes, and wherever he stopped, people gathered to feast their eyes on it. His colleagues would talk about it for years. Several autumns in a row he gathered friends into its lush interior and headed for New York to watch baseball's World Series. On a Nova Scotia dirt highway Lou Ritchie somehow managed to ram into a wagon. "Holy Moses," said Irving, "the horses' collars went flying and they took off like wild moose." Then Dr. George Watts, his brother-in-law, ploughed it into a ditch and a tree and it got nicknamed "the timber cruiser."

Irving kept the Cadillac for several years, then yielded to the sterner faith in which his mother had raised him. He decided it was costing too much and relegated it to a prim and solemn fate: it became a hearse. In later years he'd regret selling it, but while he had it that Cadillac provided him with much more than luxury transportation. Said Mike Lawson: "He got more advertising out of that car! It got people talking about him."

The Dirty Thirties didn't faze him. That was when he grew. Nothing discouraged him. Nothing scared him. Other oil companies, said K.B. Reed, pulled in their horns; Irving kept expanding. According to Bob Sutherland, who joined Irving Oil in 1930 to take charge in western Nova Scotia, "He never mentioned the Depression." Mike Lawson said, "He only knew one road, the road ahead. He had no horizons." Hilus Webb remembered that "he came through those years on the upswing all the way." Irving himself was quoted as saying it was easier to do business then because there was less competition. He contended in later years that the Depression was a stimulant to work harder: "You had to use your head and your ingenuity. You couldn't sit around sucking your thumbs. You could be twice as busy as you had been because you had to be out looking for business."

He was on the road half the time. Lunch often consisted of a chocolate bar. He seemed tireless, partly because he could nap anywhere. He did business until people went to bed and there was no more business to be done, then got into his car and headed for a place of rest. "I don't suppose," he'd say, "there is a community in New Brunswick or Nova Scotia I don't have memories of from those days, and very few of them are bad ones. I've never been happier." He cherished those memories of the boarding houses and hotels where he slept and the places where he ate, of the big table at Yarmouth's Grand Hotel where commercial travellers gave him business tips; of a lady who was a terror for neatness; of his agent Captain Norman Smith of Barrington Passage, N.S., who commanded ships in both world wars, who once saw a German submarine surface and said, "Give me a rifle." The sub submerged. Smith who once caught an Imperial Oil man using Irving cans, jumped off the wharf and started swinging before he reached the boat below.

Despite his optimism, he was operating, Irving said, "on a pretty narrow margin from 1929 on." He kept going. He bought two small petroleum-marketing companies in Prince Edward Island and went into business there. He got into Quebec's Magdalen Islands. He got into Newfoundland only to face rebuff. When its economy collapsed in 1933, Britain took over. The government borrowed money from Imperial Oil and gave it the exclusive right to sell oil and gas.

He didn't have too many service stations in those early days, said Bob Sutherland, "but he put in a lot of tanks." His customers, storekeepers, and garagemen steered him to other opportunities. He dug holes and put in tanks himself. At one small place in Nova Scotia he saw fishermen coming ashore from an island to buy gas and oil. He bought a boat and took it to them. If a garageman was busy, he put gas into cars. He took chances on people. Daniel Mullen of Mount Stewart, P.E.I., told of the time in 1933 when he built a small service station with thrity-five cents in his pocket and the offer of a $200 loan. Other oil companies wouldn't look at him but Irving said he'd put in tanks if Mullen guaranteed to sell 5,000 gallons of gas a year. Mullen said he couldn't make the guarantee. Irving put the tanks in anyway — and they exceeded the 5,000 gallons from then on.

As the Depression deepened, he cut salaries 10 per cent, then, Ted O'Neill and others found, made it up with a Christmas bonus. He promised that his Primrose gas would mean "more miles, more smiles," and preached service to his employees. "Mostly we were selling service," said Hilus Webb, "and we had to make sure we gave it." Irving bought a lot of land, insisted on seeing it before he did: "I enjoyed that sort of thing. If you get land at the right price," he'd say, "you can't go wrong." A colleague remembered

Irving turning down one lot in Petitcodiac, N.B., because it would cost $100. He could get lots on the Miramichi, Irving said, for $50.

He laid out lines for service stations, once causing comment in Amherst when he did it on a Sunday. He gave architect Sam Roy, an older man from Bouctouche, the tender to build his first station in Halifax in 1930. Roy said he made $4,300 on the $12,800 deal and was foolish enough to tell Irving. From then on he was on commission, 10 per cent above cost. In his biggest year, 1938, Roy supervised so many construction jobs for Irving that he made $100,000. The stations no longer were made of brick, as the Halifax one had been. They were wooden and they cost considerably less. Roy soon learned that he had his own ideas about how he wanted those service stations built. "No one was ever really an architect for K.C. Irving," he said.

In 1930, when an outlet did well to sell 200 gallons of gas a day, Irving sold 8 million gallons a year. Within six years he was selling not much less than that in New Brunswick alone. He employed 212 people in Saint John and 482 elsewhere. He was selling at 100 garages, and folklore was thickening around him in a blend of antagonism, awe, and speculation. Arnold Payson, posted to Saint John to run an outlet in 1933, remembered a man telling him he had no use for Irving, didn't like his methods, never bought his products. Payson told him Irving was an honest man to work for, and provided many jobs when jobs were rare indeed. He asked the man how many people he employed. There was no answer, said Payson, but the man bought Irving gas from then on.

It puzzled people, said K.B. Reed, that Irving was able to do things others couldn't. He was said to be that rarity, a millionaire, but his doom was frequently forecast. When Sutherland left Swifts, the meat-packing firm, he was told Irving would soon be gobbled up. An executive with the then McColl-Frontenac oil company recalled Irving being cited at a staff meeting as a threat, and the top man present saying: "He'll be gone in two years." Reed said people thought Irving was crazy when he erected his five-storey Golden Ball building in 1931. It got its name from Saint John history; a golden ball had apparently been used to mark the corner of Sydney and Union Streets as a site for auction sales. It cost him about $250,000, land and all. He planned it as a combination of car showroom and service station garage, and as a place to park and store cars. In one sense the doomsayers were right: the parking plan was not successful. His response was typical. He came up with new ideas and snap decisions.

The regional managers of national companies had to consult headquarters, and it could take days or even weeks to get a decision — and, often as not, by then Irving had already grabbed the opportunity. Moreover, Imperial's regional managers had to justify each new station on its merits and give evidence that it would be profitable. Irving wanted representation, and if a station didn't pay, so be it! The profits from the other stations would carry it. Still, rivals like Imperial decided it was better to have him around than to let other multinationals into the Maritime market. But eventually all the multinationals got in and gobbled up smaller firms, including McColl-Frontenac. About the only one they didn't gobble up was Irving Oil. By the time the competition began to notice Irving, it was too late.

It was in the 1930s that a new chapter opened in his relations with Imperial. He had made a deal with Cities Service, a U.S. company, for supplies to be shipped in from Massachusetts. They helped him finance bulk-tank farms at Saint John and Halifax. The tanks were in and the products were flowing north when in 1930 the new federal government of Conservative R.B. Bennett took protective measures to shore up the sagging Canadian economy. One regulation made it uneconomic for Cities Service to continue the deal. It was cancelled, but Irving had his tanks.

He went back to Imperial and they agreed to supply him from their refinery near Halifax. Eventually they backed Irving in a bank loan and talked with him about buying him out, but he decided against it. Irving himself would make both public and private criticisms of Imperial in the years ahead, and he would bump into their resistance as he sought wider horizons, but in his eighties a more mellow Irving said: "If I'd had any sense, I'd have kept my mouth shut." Over the years, he added, "they were good to me."

Paradoxically, it wasn't long after he renewed his ties with Imperial that he cut his ties with Ford. A company official came to the Golden Ball building and didn't like where Irving had his car showroom. He thought it should be more prominent, said the time had come for Irving to decide whether he would confine himself to

44

selling Fords. Irving said that if he had to give up something it would be selling cars, and that was the end of that.

Mike Lawson, a man who got his own General Motors dealership in 1938 and in time became a millionaire, then lost it all, thought Irving was the best car salesman he ever knew. Now, though Irving would buy Ford products for years and sell cars through staffs in dealerships elsewhere, his main franchise was gone. But the selling skills he'd learned remained.

It was not, in fact, a one-way street to success. In those days of massive unemployment, lengthy breadlines and countless hoboes on countless trains, he had triumphs and troubles. Though colleagues soon noted that he hated to get out of something once he was in, he'd do it when it was necessary. He once said, "I always had more ideas than a dog has fleas." In the 1930s he gave ample indication that it was true.

When the parking plan didn't pay off, he used some of the Golden Ball space to build buses and some of it for a new company, Commercial Equipment, to sell automotive supplies. He started another company called Maritime Tire. He ran buses of his own and, through them, got into memorable battles. He got into shipping because of another battle. After his father died in 1933, he bought out other members of the family and revived budworm-ravaged timber operations on their 7,000 Kent County acres of forest. He produced lumber, pulpwood, and mine pit-props, and he used these ventures as a school for far larger things to come. He got into politics because of a political rebuff. He, Lou Ritchie, and Frank Brennan teamed up to try for a licence to fly a New Brunswick–Boston route; they were turned down. He became involved in veneer woods. In the back country of Nova Scotia, he got into gold mining, and out again. He got into the newspaper business, and out again. He got into finance, and out again, ending his direct link with Irving-Brennan in the 1930s, because, he decided, that was a violin he didn't play well; he didn't feel at home in stock and bond issues, left them to Brennan, and used his services when he needed them. On the other hand, he got into shipping because he felt he was forced to, and it would become a major factor in his success.

CHAPTER SEVEN

&

The Coasting Trade

*"The Government of New Brunswick can't buy a roll
of toilet paper without Irving's approval."*
– *NOVA SCOTIA HIGHWAY MINISTER (LATER PREMIER)*
A.S. MACMILLAN IN THE LATE 1930S.

IRVING'S INVOLVEMENT IN SHIPPING COULD BE TRACED BACK
to a bleak and threatening day during the Depression, in
1932, when the Canadian National Railways raised his freight
rates and all but dared him to go into the coastal trade. In effect,
the CNR thought it was calling his bluff, but he was not bluffing;
he was angry. In later years Irving acknowledged that it was a
conflict with the government-owned CNR that forced him into
shipping. To sustain his growing network of gas and oil outlets
Irving had been using the railway for bulk deliveries. Then, as the
Depression hit rock bottom in 1932, the CNR raised the rates it
charged him.

At first he was upset. There wasn't any extra money for higher
rates, he argued; anyone who was staying afloat was doing it by
the skin of his teeth. But his words fell on deaf ears. That was bad
enough but then he learned that the CNR wasn't raising the rates
for Imperial Oil. It said Imperial Oil was different: it had a refinery. That made Irving furious, and all the more determined. Off
and on, for some two years, they wrangled, Irving on one side, the
CNR's regional headquarters in Moncton on the other. They

called it company policy. Irving looked on it as blatant discrimination. He got nowhere. To stay alive in a game he believed was rigged against him, he said he would have to do what no other company was doing. Unless the rates were cut, he would get into coastal tankers. The CNR refused to budge. After all, he didn't have a single tanker to start up his coastal service. It had to be a bluff.

As Irving recalled it, it was 1934 when the CNR told him where he could go and what he could do. There would be no lowering of the freight rates he was being charged. If he didn't like it he could go into water transportation. In those rough and tumble days of the Depression it was a take-it-or-leave-it proposition. Irving decided to leave the proposition — and the CNR.

Now, for Irving, there was no turning back. That summer he set off for Britain with a colleague. It had just broken daylight on the dirt road between Edmundston, N.B., and Rivière-du-Loup, Que., when they suddenly saw a bridge was out, swerved their car and nearly went into a stream. They made it to Quebec City in time to catch a liner on July 12. He remembered the date for years because it was his wife's birthday.

In Scotland he saw what he had come to see, a tanker for sale. The *Elkhound* was a year old. She had had a fire and was being converted from diesel power to steam. She could carry 95,000 gallons, and he bought her. He bought more trucks too, and he began a three-year program of building more bulk terminals at strategic places — large white, round bellies for what he had to sell. It was to one of these, at Moncton, that the *Elkhound* made her first delivery. That historic trip brought her through the Bay of Fundy, into Shepody Bay, into the muddy Petitcodiac River to that sharp and narrow bend that had given the city its original name — Bend of Petitcodiac. It was an occasion Irving never forgot.

Loaded with gasoline from Imperial's refinery, *Elkhound* came up that brown river on the tide that followed its celebrated bore, and wheeled at the bend. On Irving's new wharf, a mile from the CNR's regional headquarters, an audience waited, a distinguished one, for in the thirties any sign of economic thrust was cause for celebration. *Elkhound* nosed into the wharf, and an order went out. It should have commanded her engines to silence. Instead, to the horror of Irving and all who watched in disbelief, the engines

47

were switched to full speed back. In the confusion that followed —
as new orders were shouted to the engine room and crew members
scurried about to disengage the stern and bow ropes, the *Elkhound*
plunged into the muddy bank of the Petitcodiac where she halted.
Dead in the water. The dignity of the great occasion was shattered. The *Elkhound* was beached.

The guests departed and for hours, as the tide receded, men
worked to free her. Irving worked with them, with a shovel, slipping, slopping, "all of us mud from head to foot." Slowly the
Elkhound's bow was cleared, and when the tide came back at 2:30
a.m. he and his men held their breaths and hoped. They saw her
respond to the rising waters and to her engines. They saw her budge,
move, and then slowly slide out — and keep going down the river.
On the next tide she came back and did it right. The new service
was operating but the fight with the CNR was far from over.

In 1937 the CNR confronted Irving again. "Fine gentlemen
and some of them even personal friends," he recalled, but their
message was cold and their purpose melancholy. "They told me I
should withdraw the tanker from service. This was no veiled
threat; it was simply an outright statement. If I did not remove the
tanker, the CNR said it would cut its rates so drastically that my
competitors would have an advantage over me in every community
where I was shipping by coastal tanker. When I refused to take off
the service they had forced me into in the first place, the CNR cut
freight rates to all competitive points by amounts ranging from 28
per cent to 45."

Irving saw it as "a tough, even vicious policy." He met it in his
own way. He bought a second ship, the barge *Molly G.*, and kept
on going. He was in the shipping business to stay.

In the mid-1930s, Irving got into a second form of transportation that made him, among other things, a rival of the CNR. He
established SMT (Eastern) Ltd., a bus line. The name — one he
first saw in Scotland — meant Shore Motor Transport in New
Brunswick and Scotia Motor Transport in Nova Scotia. The company came to have sister organizations, Island Motor Transport in
Prince Edward Island, and city services in Saint John, Fredericton, Moncton, and Sydney.

Irving built his own bus bodies, hired expert James Fitzsimmons
from Ontario to take charge of assembling them atop imported

British Leyland chassis. The work began as an offshoot of his Golden Ball garage and soon employed thirty-five. He called it the manufacturing division of Universal Sales, the firm he had formed to sell Fords. It kept expanding, moved into new quarters, got into building trucks, and made buses for other companies.

As paved roads came in and travel increased, there was hectic competition for passenger traffic. Irving bought up small companies and their franchises, some of them one-man, one-bus operations, some in debt for his oil and gas, some that found it uneconomic to meet tougher new government standards. He smiled at CNR cries of unfair competition from its highway rivals, and quietly went about planning further expansion of his bus business. But it was when he went after the franchise to operate a city system in Saint John as a subsidiary of SMT that he ran into problems that would exhaust far more time and effort, leading to twelve years of intermittent legal and political counter-punching.

Here, as elsewhere, he came up against Fred C. Manning of Halifax, a man whose career and enterprises were strikingly similar to his own. Like Irving, Manning was a Presbyterian from a small town, Falmouth, N.S., a man who started small and made things grow. Like Irving, and in competition with Irving's franchise in Halifax, he sold Fords. Like Irving, he got into the gas and oil business. They knew each other well. When Irving went to Halifax, he would say, "We must go see Fred." If, in fact, there was an equivalent of Irving in Nova Scotia, it was Manning.

With partners, notably millionaire industrialist Roy Joudrey, Manning had established Super-Service Stations Ltd. In 1935 he published a brochure–highway map of Nova Scotia and used it to extol the services he had to offer, mentioning that Super-Service had stations in twenty-seven communities, twenty-four in Nova Scotia and three in New Brunswick, including one in Saint John.

One year later Manning made a Saint John move with larger implications. The New Brunswick Power Company, a subsidiary of the Federal Light and Traction Co. of New York, had announced that it wanted to sell a package of Saint John properties that included a street railway, a power plant, and a gas manufacturing and distributing network. Both Manning and Irving wanted to replace the street railway system with a bus route. Both fought for it, and at least twice it appeared that Manning had won final civic approval.

Irving fought him every inch of the way, in the city's common council, in crowded and acrimonious hearings of Legislature committees in Fredericton, and in the courts. He argued that citizens of Saint John were entitled to preferential treatment. Meanwhile, amid confusion, bitterness, and litigation, the city's aged transportation system sagged and came close to winter collapse.

For two years the battle continued and then there was a hiatus. By 1939 Irving had a tentative but unsigned agreement from the power company to sell him its street railway system if it sold to anyone. Then Manning beat him to the punch. He bought a controlling interest in the power company itself. With it he got the street railway system and the city transportation rights. Still Irving fought on. He said he had been advised that he could get what he wanted if he paid a certain bribe, but refused to have anything to do with what he called "that monkey business."

It would not be until 1947 that the issue was resolved. The Liberal New Brunswick government expropriated the power generating and distributing systems Manning had taken over. A month later fire destroyed his car barn and nine of the buses he was using. When Saint John common council voted to seek legislative authority to end his city transportation rights, amid complaints that the service was inadequate, a disheartened Manning testified that "the main reason the system had not been improved is that every time we go to make a major move we are blocked by SMT," and he saw no end to it. The Legislature approved the common council's action and on July 1, 1948, Irving's City Transit Ltd. buses — seventeen new ones and twenty older ones — began operating under a renewable thirteen-year franchise. The fight was over.

By then, however, there had been another, shorter confrontation with Manning. It, too, involved a collision over bus routes. Irving's SMT had for some years been operating Nova Scotia routes from Amherst to Halifax and Truro to Sydney. It had no franchise because until 1938 there were no franchises to be had. Then the Liberal government of Premier Angus L. Macdonald directed the Public Utilities Board to decide who should have one for provincial routes. Both Irving and Manning sought it.

K.B. Reed took a room next to the board chairman at the Carleton Hotel in Halifax so he could, if opportunity offered, salt the arguments more personally. But Manning lived next door to

Highways Minister A.S. MacMillan, and he made the most of the counter-argument that he should get preference as a Nova Scotian.

A decision was close when Irving was invited to call on Premier Macdonald — and came up against a truculent MacMillan. Macdonald, Irving said, seemed to favour SMT but he called MacMillan in, and the minister arrived "with a chip on his shoulder." He accused Irving of "rascality" in his gas and oil business, of cutting prices, of offering improper, under-the-table incentives to dealers. Irving, denying it, said, "You are getting pretty rough under your Gasoline Act; you're being pretty rough with us." MacMillan said he found it strange that every construction company in the province was using Irving Oil products, and he wondered why it was so. Irving said he liked to think it was because he provided better service than his rivals. "Hah," snorted MacMillan, and the funny thing, laughed Irving years later, was that the minister had a construction firm of his own — and didn't mention that it, too, was an Irving customer. That alone, he would say, should have convinced him. Nor did MacMillan's company stop buying from Irving Oil when the episode was over.

But the minister, the man who would become premier when Macdonald became Canada's navy minister in 1940, said something else that day. He said the government of New Brunswick "can't buy a roll of toilet paper without K.C. Irving's approval," and he wanted Macdonald to know this was a situation he thought should not be encouraged by the government of Nova Scotia.

Within twenty-four hours it was announced that the Public Utilities Board had awarded the provincial bus franchise to Manning. SMT was out, and it embittered Irving. "He wasn't used to being treated that way." Even so, the rebuff didn't stop Irving from making a new deal — even with Manning. The problem faced by Manning was that he had a franchise but no buses. Irving now had buses but no franchise. He rented buses to Manning until Manning got his own.

"You don't," he would say, "let a setback affect your business judgment. You don't close doors on opportunities."

CHAPTER EIGHT

❧

A Toehold in Politics

"There'll be no business for Mr. Irving.... No business whatsoever."

– NEW BRUNSWICK CONSERVATIVE PREMIER
J.B.M. BAXTER IN 1931.

WHAT A.S. MACMILLAN HAD SAID ABOUT IRVING'S political leverage in New Brunswick was increasingly being said in New Brunswick itself. The gossip was that two men had great influence on the Liberal government of Premier Allison Dysart: one was K.C. Irving; the other was C.C. Avard, publisher of the twice-weekly Sackville *Tribune*.

There was a certain basis for the gossip in both cases. Avard had a lucrative sway on the government's decisions about printing and advertising contracts. Irving had become personally involved in the Liberals' electoral fortunes. In his recollection, it stemmed from a rebuke by J.B.M. Baxter, the Saint John lawyer who was Conservative premier in 1931.

"I sent one of my senior men to see him to say we would appreciate some government business," Irving recalled. That is the way things were done in New Brunswick in the 1930s. If you wanted to do business with the government you went to see a politician, and if you could manage it, right to the top man, the premier.

Irving had gasoline to sell and the government was a potential customer, so he dispatched an emissary to see the premier. It was a mission Irving's representative would not soon forget.

John Babington Macaulay Baxter was an impressive figure, one of the great politicians of his day and something of a legend in New Brunswick. Forced by economic circumstances to leave school at fourteen, he worked first as a dry goods clerk and later as a butcher's accountant. He was a cub reporter for the Saint John newspapers while serving at the same time as a clerk in a law office. It took him nine years to get his law degree but from that day on he never looked back. He had a brilliant career as a lawyer, politician, and finally as chief justice of New Brunswick.

Baxter was a politician's politician, a tall, handsome, articulate man who was at the peak of his political career that day back in 1931 when Irving's agent called on him in Fredericton. Quick-witted and noted for his humour, he knew how to put a visitor at ease and for the first few minutes Irving's representative was sure he was going to walk out of the premier's office with the kind of response his boss was waiting for. But then the premier started to ask more pointed questions.

Almost playfully, in a cat-and-mouse exchange, he rolled the Irving name over his tongue a few times. "Irving . . . Irving . . . K.C. Irving?"

"Yes, sir," said his visitor, "Mr. K.C. Irving of Saint John."

"K.C. Irving . . . Mr. K.C. Irving . . . Why, isn't he the son of J.D. Irving of Bouctouche?"

"Yes, I believe so."

"Why," said Baxter, "J.D. Irving's the Liberal who fought us for years. No, there'll be no business for Mr. Irving. No, no business whatsoever!"

But if that was the end of the conversation and the meeting, it was also the beginning of a new chapter in Irving's life. Baxter had made it clear that business would go to friends of the government, and Irving had no difficulty understanding that message, or remembering it. Though four years would intervene before the next election, and though two more Tory premiers would succeed Baxter after he went to the bench, Irving did not forget. "Baxter pitchforked me into politics," he'd say. "Or put it another way: what he said that day did nothing to convince me I should stay out."

That memory was with him on a summer day in 1934 when he sat on the verandah of Moncton's Brunswick Hotel with Allison Dysart and Fred Magee, the able Port Elgin businessman who had been the Liberal party's treasurer through arid years in opposition. Irving knew Dysart well because Dysart had come to Bouctouche to set up a law practice after Arch Irving died. He came from Cocagne, down the coast, and it was J.D. Irving who convinced him he should make the move. He was an amiable, bluff man, gregarious, outgoing, popular, given to grandiose phrases. He came from a farm family. One son, as he went out into the world, undertook to educate the next to follow. One would become a Supreme Court Judge in Manitoba, two others prominent accountants in Boston. Allison Dysart got into law and politics and became leader of the provincial opposition in 1930.

Irving found Magee an excellent man, and he soon got to know him better. Magee packed and canned fish, and Irving would get him to make cans for his oil. But that day in Moncton Magee was in a gruff, rebellious mood, and Dysart had a purpose in inviting Irving to join them. There was going to be an election soon, and he said he could win it.

"The hell you can," Magee said.

"I've got a young fellow named McNair who can even win York County."

"That will be the day."

With that, Magee embarked upon a mixture of lecture and lament. "I've been cursed with you politicians all my life," he said.

Whereupon Dysart beamed upon Irving. "Kenneth," he said, "will help me. You owe me something, Kenneth. Your father got me to go to Bouctouche. He got me into politics. Now you've got to help me." And Irving agreed to do it, in his words, "to do footwork to raise money for the Party." He pitched into it with his habitual fervour, canvassing from New Brunswick to Ontario. He went to Toronto and met Liberal premier Mitchell Hepburn, and Hepburn sent him to his own bagman, Laura Secord Chocolates head Frank O'Connor, at the King Edward Hotel. He saw O'Connor more than a few times, and from him got names of others who might help. He raised a lot of money, some of it his own, and it helped produce a victory.

In June 1935, Dysart's Liberals whipped the Tories of Premier L.P.D. Tilley. When the Legislature was dissolved Tilley had held twenty-seven seats, the Liberals fifteen and there were six vacancies. In the election the Liberals took forty-seven seats, the Conservatives five. The Liberals even won York for lawyer and one-time Rhodes Scholar J.B. McNair — the same McNair that Dysart had touted as a winner a year earlier. That night at the wharf in Bouctouche, Irving's *Elkhound* blew her whistle so long and so loudly that someone had to tell her captain to stop. It was widely said that K.C. Irving had financed the Liberal win.

Four years later, in the fall of 1939, only weeks after the beginning of the Second World War, charges of Irving's influence on the Dysart government became a public issue in another election campaign. The charge was heard throughout the campaign. Perhaps it crystallized one afternoon in a classic oldtime Conservative rally in a large, bare hall in the village of Albert: bronzed country people perched on hard wooden chairs, their faces stoic in the silence of shared allegiance and belief. On the wall were pictures of King George VI and Queen Elizabeth, who had only recently toured and enraptured Canada. The speaker stopped occasionally to replenish his indignation from a jug of water and to mop his perspiring face, his thick, plump body heaving with his message. It was New Brunswicker R.B. Hanson, a former cabinet minister in the Conservative federal government of R.B. Bennett, a later Opposition leader in parliament. And the core of what he had to say was that K.C. Irving had a stranglehold on the Dysart government and on the New Brunswick gasoline market, and that the situation must be investigated.

"But what can you expect?" cried Hanson. "Irving financed Dysart's 1935 campaign and you taxpayers are now paying the bill." It was a theme the Conservatives expounded at length. They called Irving "the phantom premier." They called the administration the "Dysart–Irving government," the "Primrose government." Sackville's Avard became "the infantile publicist," Dysart's "Goebbels," the equivalent of Adolf Hitler's Nazi propaganda minister.

All this took place against a background of war, as Russia's Foreign Minister Molotov championed Stalin's peace pact with Hitler's Germany, blamed the conflict on Britain and France, approved Hitler's conquest of Poland, and accepted a share of the spoils. There was fighting at sea and in the air, and the advance party of Canada's First Division arrived in Britain. Meanwhile, in Moncton, Trans-Canada Air Lines, the precursor of Air Canada, inaugurated its cross-country service, and Irving's SMT bus drivers won acceptance of their union and got a raise. Throughout the province there was the commotion of political mayhem, of charges and counter-charges, jabs, punches, haymakers.

Years later, K.C. Irving said that his political influence was grossly exaggerated but he would neither confirm nor deny that he got from Allison Dysart what he was denied by J.B.M. Baxter. He did say that, under the Tories, Imperial Oil got all the government business. The popular perception was that once they were out he got plenty himself, but anyone trying to pin down the facts faced some baffling realities, including a reminder of the vaulting growth of government. In 1939 the annual provincial budget ran to some $9 million. A little more than 50 years later it had increased to almost $4 billion.

In their 1939 campaign oratory the Conservatives tended to be long on generalities and short on figures. A popular notion then was that Irving was getting practically all the gasoline business from Dysart's Liberal Government. The Conservatives didn't need any encouragement to fan that fire. But records for the years between 1935 and 1939 provide fascinating reading. If Irving controlled the provincial gasoline market, it wasn't borne out by figures revealed in the Legislature. In 1937 and part of 1938 his oil company sold about 6.2 million gallons of gasoline in New Brunswick. Imperial Oil sold more — 6.8 million — and ten other companies, if combined, outsold each of them. In 1936 Dysart was asked whether the Department of Public Works had purchased any gasoline tanks. Yes, he replied — all of them from Imperial Oil. What companies supplied gas and oil to those tanks? Answer: five companies, including Irving's.

The public accounts, in turn, spell out in teeming detail where the government's money went, even down to a 25-cent payment to SMT. Indeed, the biggest contracts of all for oil companies appear to have come from selling asphalt for the paving contracts that began in 1936. They went to Imperial and BA (later Gulf Canada), and they ran well into thousands of dollars.

From the figures available, then, it would have been difficult to prove either that Irving received inordinate benefits directly from government, or that rival companies were excluded. But Tory leader F.C. Squires had another point to make: "The franchises for bus, truck, and freight business on the highways of this province are almost completely in the hands of one company, which also does a most profitable gas and oil business with the government."

Certainly Irving remembered 1936 as the year surfaced roads began a major change in New Brunswick transportation. He did well in supplying contractors who built them, but said, "Dysart had nothing to do with that." There are no public records that disclose whether he did better than others. He continued to be outrun slightly by Imperial Oil in overall gas sales in the province. In fiscal year 1943–44, for example, with the Liberals still in power, the figures were very close to those for 1937–38: 6.1 million gallons for Irving, 6.8 million for Imperial.

As things turned out, the 1939 campaign ended with a Liberal counterattack that may well have backfired. In its final days the party got information that led to charges that Squires, seeking campaign funds, promised Canadian and U.S. firms that, if supported and elected, he would do certain things. It arose from a lawsuit launched in Montreal by one H.B. West, who said he had acted as personal agent for Squires and hadn't been paid. He maintained that he had seen Squires solicit a $100,000 contribution from a major executive of a prominent oil company on a promise that, if elected, he would reduce the gasoline tax from ten cents to eight cents a gallon and undertake to cancel the licences or bring about the cancellation of the licences of the Irving Oil Co. in New Brunswick.

In Sackville, Avard printed the information and sent thousands of copies hustling through the province. In Woodstock, on the Thursday before the Monday, November 20, vote, Attorney General McNair turned it into platform accusations. A woman who was there remembered the audience stiffening in indignation, for Woodstock was Squires's home town and he was a respected man. It was unfair, many felt, to drag out such a major issue when the Conservatives had so little time to reply.

Still, in haste and massive condemnation, the Liberals did. Avard's *Tribune* called it "the sordid story" of how Squires tried to sell the province down the river: "You'll need to hold your nose as you read the awful record." Squires made two speeches: he denied everything, threatened legal action, and called it a slanderous plot by the Liberals to cover up the "ghastly" provincial finances.

Moncton's *Times* had for weeks devoted daily columns to Conservative rhetoric, blandly reporting that Liberal meetings were poorly attended and that many people left before they dragged to an indifferent end. Now it cried that the charges against Squires constituted vicious, false blackmail. It didn't deign to print the charges themselves, but predicted they would boomerang.

Some Liberals shared this conclusion. To them the use of the information, made so late, was a mistake, bringing into the scales a hostility between Protestants and Roman Catholics — many people felt Dysart, the first Catholic ever elected premier, was defaming the Protestant Squires.

No one will ever know how much the charges did sway voters, but the results hint that they may have swayed many. The Liberals survived with twenty-seven seats but the Conservatives gained sixteen, ending up with twenty-one. McNair and two other cabinet ministers were defeated.

Irving had again helped raise Liberal funds, though not as actively as in 1935. Allison Dysart resigned within a year of the election to become a judge, and when he did, Irving said he himself withdrew from direct political activity. He continued to contribute to the Liberals but collected no more party funds. A prominent Conservative may have had at least part of the explanation. He said Irving began to donate money to both parties.

CHAPTER NINE

&

The Bull of the Woods

*"I'll put you so far into the lumber business you'll
never get out."*
— AIMÉ GAUDREAU'S 1941 PROMISE TO K.C. IRVING.

I RVING TURNED FORTY THE YEAR THE SECOND WORLD WAR
begin. His office was in a triangular building overlooking the
landing place of the Loyalists, and there he had radio equipment to keep him in touch with his accumulating interests — his
oil company, his bus lines, his ships, his timber and other businesses. No detail was too small for his attention. When asked if he had
to oversee every detail himself, Irving replied: "You do if you want
to stay in business."

He never had a headache, perhaps in part because, as one colleague put it, "he never cluttered his mind with unimportant
things." He rarely said anything bad about anyone: "You don't,"
he'd say, "want to cast reflections on people. What's the use of
that?" For some time he played weekly poker at the Cliff Club —
"I usually made a dollar or two" — but he gave it up because he had
so little time to spend with his wife. He drove cars fast, passing
others on the road. He delegated very little authority; when someone asked him why he didn't delegate more, he said, "because I
can't stand to see people make mistakes." His knowledge of their
work drove employees to greater efforts. Said troubleshooter

Duncan Wathen, "When your boss knows more about your job than you do, it keeps you on your toes." When he sent Arnold Payson to take charge in Truro, he told him, "At times you will make a promise that's not justified. If you make it, keep it, but don't do it again." He would tell someone else, "If something is the law, abide by it. If it's a bad law, try to get it changed."

By 1939 he had two badges of progress. One was his first plane, a five-seater Stinson with both floats and wheels. The other was an ulcer, a penalty for the life he led, "just grabbing food, eating too fast." The ulcer announced itself on a day he had a hot dog and a bottle of pop in Fredericton and was still going at ll p.m. in St. Stephen. His weight was up to 215 pounds on his six-foot frame. He acknowledged he was too heavy and decided to do something about his health. He drank milk for a long time, pampered and eventually beat the ulcer.

Irving was still troubled by the ulcer when he went tramping with Ray Estey of Grand Falls to inspect some woodlands. Estey took with him plenty of grub, including steaks. When he first brought it out to cook over a campfire, Irving asked if he was expecting guests. No, Estey said, but he liked to eat well and figured Irving did too. Irving was still eating cautiously and little, and he passed up the feast. "Someone," he said, "recently wrote that I was a millionaire. I don't know which I'd like more: the money or a stomach like yours." The Lahey Clinic in Boston cured the ulcer in 1941, and he never had the problem again, though he watched what and how he ate from that time on.

In the early days of the war Irving went to Ottawa to discuss New Brunswick industries that could be developed or adapted to participate in the war effort. He came away unhappy. From the cabinet he got the message: existing industries, primarily in Ontario and Quebec, would be the centre of activities and wartime defence work. That answer didn't satisfy him. He went back to Ottawa and this time he made his point. Soon he had a contract to manufacture landing barges for attacks on Nazi-dominated Europe. He built them in Bouctouche, set up facilities near the old gristmill, built bunkhouses on the family farm, and brought in scores of workers.

But his main link with the war, and perhaps New Brunswick's greatest contribution to the war effort on the home front, came through the production of skin-thin veneer woods for the swift, all-wood Mosquito fighter-bomber that could fly all the way from Britain to Berlin and back. The veneer sheets were produced in Saint John in a converted cotton mill by Canada Veneers Ltd., a company that was almost bankrupt when Irving entered the picture in 1938. No one then could have speculated on the vital war role the company would soon play. Irving was simply responding to a company that was about to go belly up.

Canada Veneers had been launched in Saint John in 1933, primarily to turn out material for orange crates for the local Wilson Box and Lumber Co. The plant was housed in a converted race-track grandstand, and in 1936 it burned down. It was re-established, but by 1938 R.H. (Red Hugh) McLean, vice-president, and largest shareholder, withdrew his guarantee of a mere $17,000 bank loan. The position of the company was so precarious that the calling of the loan meant bankruptcy.

Irving said that Robert McMillan, president, and Frank Brennan, a director, came to him several times to seek financial aid. He would later say he felt Brennan had been misguided in getting into the business in the first place. Nor did he consider it good business to accede to the company's requests for help. However, he and Brennan had been partners in Irving-Brennan Co. Ltd., which in 1936 had underwritten an issue of $100,000 of Canada Veneers preferred shares. Though he withdrew from that investment firm early in 1936, Irving obtained shares in the company and on January 6, 1938, agreed to guarantee a bank loan of $10,000. In return, he got control of the company. Brennan was soon on his way to England to end dealings with the firm buying veneers for aircraft construction and make a new arrangement with Sarbo Laminated Wood Products Ltd., a subsidiary of the giant Sanders-Roe, which produced a much better contract.

Still, the company had trouble getting high-grade yellow birch logs and consequent difficulties in meeting its obligations. So in 1940 Irving became involved in another way. He undertook to supply better logs at $20 a thousand board feet. He formed Eastern Timbers Ltd., and set out to find them.

Irving found the logs he wanted in New Brunswick, Maine, Quebec, and elsewhere, and the company surged into production. Working day and night, seven days a week, it employed 500 people and became the largest supplier of its kind. In C.A. Kessler, an elderly American, the company found the expert it needed to slice wood accurately to a minute fraction of an inch. What equipment Kessler wanted, Irving got, said Art McNair, then understudying Kessler and later a postwar head of the firm. Irving himself was in the plant for hours, night after night, seeking efficiencies, improvements, ironing the bugs out, learning. He was in his element mastering the details of one more business: "I could do that sort of thing all night and never get sleepy."

Nevertheless, there was friction. Robert McMillan continued as president, but he and Irving came increasingly into conflict. The stand-off lasted until 1941, when Irving gained control of a majority of common shares. An Irving man, Wendell W. Rogers, another alumnus from the Royal Flying Corps in the First World War, was put in charge. McMillan was bitter but Irving wanted changes. At the end of a long and bristling meeting Irving had his way. From then on, with Rogers in charge, his control was unchallenged, and he eventually bought McMillan's shares.

Was Irving right in getting rid of McMillan? Was he an opportunist, or was this just another case where he had to have his own hand on the tiller? To Art McNair, a relative of Robert McMillan, who had hired him at Canada Veneers and who supervised plant production when the aged Kessler retired during the war, the answer was that the company could not have produced so much and so well for the war effort if Irving had not become involved.

ﾟ&

Irving had help in all his forestry-related activities. Aimé Gaudreau was Irving's kind of man — hard as nails, honest, loyal, down-to-earth, self-taught, driving, intelligent, ambitious, and successful. He was one of Irving's best friends and perhaps his best-ever partner. As for Gaudreau, he believed they broke the mould when K.C. Irving was created.

Irving never favoured partnerships, but Aimé Gaudreau was the exception. Together they made a formidable team. Together they also made a lot of money. Their involvement began in 1941 when Quebec's D'Auteuil Lumber Co. came up for sale on the death of its owner. E.F. Malkin, a shareholder who had been Irving's associate in the 1930s, recommended Irving and Gaudreau, the latter already in charge of buying pulpwood and the operations of D'Auteuil. The company itself bought and sold pulp, and the proposal, said Malkin, was that Gaudreau would run things, and Irving would act as an adviser. When a deal was made Irving got 55 per cent of the company, Malkin 15 per cent, and Gaudreau 10 per cent with others involved.

Irving and Gaudreau took to each other immediately. To Gaudreau, nine years his senior, Irving became a god. To Irving, Gaudreau became the best partner a man ever had. Gaudreau was, in fact, the epitome of the archetypical Irving man, not long on formal education but schooled by the knocks and knuckles of learning on the run, supremely practical, hard-working, ardently loyal. He was a big man, about five-feet-eleven and solid, a real woodsman. He could procrastinate because he always wanted the last detail, he always wanted to be extra sure. Irving spoke and understood French no more than adequately. Gaudreau had about 300 words of English, but there was never any doubt about what he meant.

Gaudreau grew up in a large family on a Charlevoix County farm. His father died when he was young. He quit school early and went to New England to work in textile mills, then came home and became a lumberjack. When they became partners, Gaudreau told Irving, "I'll put you so far into the lumber business you'll never get out." It happened, and it made Gaudreau rich and Irving richer.

They made a team in which Irving became far more than an adviser. They snowshoed together through forest vastnesses, their eyes making arithmetic from the march of trees, they escaped serious injury, even death, in a plane crash — and they embarked upon expansion. Gaudreau called Irving the best mechanic he ever saw. Irving honoured him in other ways: he named a ship and a sawmill complex after him. When Gaudreau was old and spent he sold his D'Auteuil interests to Irving. Irving said he would only buy them if Gaudreau remained the partner he had been. Before he died in 1976, aged eighty-six, Gaudreau would sit trembling with anticipation when told Irving was coming to see him.

From Wilfred Grenier of Quebec City came another story of the Irving of those days. Grenier was an engineering graduate of Laval University, a surveyor. Irving and Gaudreau got him to come to New Brunswick to see the railway lands Irving would buy later. They had already flown over them and gone into them on foot, but they wanted more precise information. In particular, Irving was looking for yellow birch for Canada Veneers. Grenier found plenty of good stands mixed with evergreens or high and alone on rolling hills. And thousands of potential feet of softwood. The three of them spent several days in the woods snowshoeing about, tenting at night. Irving wanted to see and know everything for himself. How could Grenier take an inventory of such a large area?

The answer was that one sample was enough to tell you what was available in a much larger tract. The key was to know where to take it. You ran baselines with a compass, blazed trees, used rivers as a cross-reference point. If there were no rivers, you made lines at right angles to the first ones. Now you had lines going in two intersecting directions, numbered. You cruised along those lines and every so often you took a sample, built up an inventory, studied what kinds of timber were there, their age, their quality. Then, finally, by multiplying, you knew.

Irving was fascinated. Grenier suggested he get an inspector to check out what veneer logs there were. Irving got one but still wanted to see for himself. By the hour he and Gaudreau tramped down the lines and then at night Irving would match his own findings against those provided by the inspector, Grenier, and information from an earlier survey made by another woods company. Finally, all the facts meshed and came together, largely to the same conclusion. Only then was Irving satisfied. And with Gaudreau he would talk business, always business. Gaudreau was the man at Irving's right hand when he bought Dexter Sulphite in 1942. Only weeks earlier, on March 30, they bought for D'Auteuil a tract of forest in New Brunswick as part of the dismemberment of an empire dating back to the nineteenth-century railway era.

For Irving, this was only the start of his involvement in vast forest holdings, woods operations, pulp and paper mills, and reforestation. The New Brunswick and Canada Railway and Land Company had acquired its empire in the 1870s in the same way the Canadian Pacific Railway got millions of acres of western Canada for building a railroad to the west coast. It proposed to build a railroad of its own from Fredericton to Rivière du Loup, and the New Brunswick government agreed to cede it 4,047 hectares for every 1.6 kilometres it built. The company ended up with 647,520 hectares. It built the line but eventually went broke and leased it to the CPR for 999 years. Nor did the company harvest its own timber. Instead, it leased the land for stumpage to various firms. It did this for years in the valleys of the Restigouche, the Miramichi, the Tobique, and other rivers, maintaining small staffs to check the lumber cut and oversee operations. Its headquarters were in Saint John.

In the war years the people who owned the company's shares decided they wanted out. Costs had begun to eat too deeply into the profits from the leases. School taxes kept growing, sometimes from districts that overlapped: they couldn't raise enough stumpage fees to cover overheads. Only the choicest hardwoods were being cut and there was a lot of overmature wood. If all this were not enough, key shareholders lived in Britain, and Britain was repatriating every cent it could find to finance a costly war.

So W.E. Golding, the general manager in Saint John, was told to sell and he set about shopping. The firms that held leases got the first options but passed them up. Some spurned the opportunity because they thought they could get all the lumber they needed from crown lands. O.B. Davis of Grand Falls believed he could only make a profit if he had a pulp mill. Davis passed. The New Brunswick government passed. Others passed.

In a 1949 court case in which Irving protested against tax assessments, the story of who bought what and for how much finally unfolded. On January 10, 1942, Fraser Companies of Edmundston bought 85,652 acres on the Green River for $300,000, or $3.50 an acre. In March, D'Auteuil got 40,000 acres in the St. Francis area, in that thumb of land protruding from northwestern New Brunswick. It paid $3.42 an acre. A year later Frasers purchased 627,840 acres on the Tobique for $2,000,000, or $3.18 an acre. Within a month Irving paid the highest price yet for close to 176,000 acres on the Restigouche: $710,000, or $4.03 an acre. A month later again, in the counties of Victoria and Carleton, the firm of Flemming and Gibson, which had been cutting there on lease, picked up 30,248 acres at the lowest price to date, $2.14 an acre. Golding, in brief, got prices that reflected the market of the time and disparities in the quality of the forests he had to offer. For nearly two years he sold no more.

In March 1945, Hugh John Flemming of Flemming and Gibson, the son of a former Conservative premier and destined to become one himself, made his maiden speech as a member of the Legislature. His remarks illuminated a time — the war in Europe would end in exactly two months — when the country stood unknowingly on the verge of unprecedented prosperity yet had an economy still haunted by memories of the Depression. A New Brunswick Development Board had just been created, signalling the gathering momentum of the state's movement into the economy. In 1944, however, it spent just $12,438. Wildland taxes were $2 an acre. The province, lamented Flemming, had too many ghost towns or towns heading that way because lumber operations no longer sustained them. Furthermore, too many lumber companies that did exist — and he named seven that controlled 2.4 million acres — were exporting wood out of the province, including D'Auteuil, an exporter of pulp.

Finally, he came to the New Brunswick Railway Company. Since the company had sold land to Fraser and Irving, he said, its principals had applied to Ottawa for reduction in capitalization from $3,000,000 to $30,000 "and, I presume, have distributed tax-free the $2,970,000. They still owned some 700,000 acres, said Flemming, and there was a rumour that they are negotiating for the sale of the company to pulp mill interests, outside New Brunswick — and Canada too." If, he said, this sale went through, his own community would become a ghost town. If the lands are to be sold, they should be under the control of the people. He suggested that the government add to crown lands the 700,000 acres and that all transfers of large tracts of land should be subject to review and approval by the Department of Lands and Mines before being made final.

The Liberal government of John B. McNair — he had been re-elected in a by-election and became premier in 1940 — replied through Lands Minister F.W. Pirie. He twitted Flemming as a champion of free enterprise who now proposed state intervention. Then he revealed that one of the first things he did on joining the cabinet in 1935 was to discuss with New Brunswick Railway the possibility of the province's buying their lands. He had told Golding that he would recommend paying $2 an acre.

Golding referred him to the company president in Montreal, and the president referred him back to Golding. This time Golding told him — and Pirie agreed — that the time was hardly proper for negotiations because the company was engaged in a lawsuit with its bondholders. The ensuing suit went all the way to the Privy Council in London and was not settled until 1939. By then the war had come and Pirie said he had no time to negotiate further. Then he had seen a deed showing that Fraser Companies Ltd. had bought the first tract. Again he went to Golding, who confirmed that the sale had been made.

Pirie said, "I could not see any reason why we should complain as long as those lands were being bought by people carrying on industry, and therefore it did not disturb me very much." Pirie went on to say that "he understood that recently the controlling stock of the [New Brunswick Railway] company had been purchased. But as long as the purchasers were carrying on industry they had a perfect right to own these lands." His words confirmed the rumour Flemming had heard.

Irving's own story was that he had discussed the purchase of further land with Golding, and that Golding had told him to wait. "Then later he told me the company itself was for sale, and asked me if I was interested." He was. He bought the company shares and, with them, 698,000 acres of land at a cost of $1.2 million. But since the company had net assets of $112,000, that 1949 court case was informed, the actual price was $1.50 an acre. The purchase raised Irving's total holdings to close to 914,000 acres.

His first interest arose from his need for wood for Canada Veneers and for his barge program. He got some of his yellow birch from the N.B. Railway lands, and when the federal government got into the act, forming a crown company to buy wood for veneers, he predicted that it would jump the price sharply. It did. The price, however, wouldn't affect him if he got his timber from his own lands. That was a primary reason for his purchases, but there was another: he was looking ahead.

In any case, one bit of Irving folklore was that Fred Pirie had helped him get the railway lands. Other companies may have bought railway lands and still others rejected them; that didn't matter. The focus, as it would long be, was on Irving. Pirie was a wealthy, self-made man, a driving, combative one. He was in Grand Falls what J.D. Irving had been in Bouctouche.

Pirie had said in the Legislature that the government had nothing to do with any of the railway land purchases. But for a long time, friends said, the rumours of Pirie's supposed role in Irving's case would dog him. Those rumours were remembered in Grand Falls even in the 1980s. Irving was driving about the former railway lands when the subject was raised. He professed surprise. He asked his son Jim if he had ever heard the rumours. Jim said he hadn't. Irving asked a senior member of his staff if he had heard them. The man said he had. Pirie, Irving said, had nothing to do with any of his purchases. The first Pirie had heard of the purchase of the company was when Irving told him.

On that drive through his forests, Irving was told that now, in a day when government intervention in the economy was prevalent and growing, some people might feel that Pirie had made a mistake in not buying them for the Crown. He looked out over woodlands stretching as far as the eye could see, but especially at some of the tens of millions of trees he had planted in a huge, continuing program of reforestation. Then he spoke with quiet certainty. "Well," he said, "I'll tell you one thing: if the government had bought these lands, those trees wouldn't be here."

CHAPTER TEN

ता

The Dawn of a Dynasty

*"Never do business with someone who has the ignition
on and his foot on the accelerator."*
— EARLY LESSON LEARNED BY THE PROPRIETORS OF THE JIM,
ART AND JACK FARM.

W HEN IT WAS VERY LATE, K.C. IRVING'S WIFE WOULD
sometimes call down to him from the second floor of
their huge white-pillared home that sat well back from
the street on the crest of a hill on Mount Pleasant Avenue overlooking Saint John. This was especially the case in later years
when she thought he was working too hard and staying up too
late. "Kenneth, it's after eleven . . ." Or, "Kenneth, it's midnight."
And he would answer: "All right, Honey, I'll be up shortly."

It didn't matter who was there. He called her "Honey," or
sometimes "Hon." The warmth in their voices could make a visitor
feel like an intruder. But for them it was natural. They came from
two small Kent County towns, he from Bouctouche, she from nearby Galloway. They said what they meant and what they felt. They
did not flaunt their feelings for each other, but neither did they try
to hide them. Their marriage was, by many accounts, one of the
smartest things Irving ever did, because from the first she was a
formidable buttress in his life, a partner admirably suited to his
character and his needs and to raising a family amid his frequent
absences. Irving would say they never had a quarrel, but he was

embarrassed when it came to talking about their courtship. He found it unseemly. No one, however, agreed more enthusiastically than he with a statement that she became a great factor in his success.

She accepted what he was, his constant travels, his absorption in work, his outrageous indifference to time. He once took one young son to Moncton and left him in a hotel room while he made a brief call. Hours later he remembered with a jolt and rushed back to get him. He once called his wife and said he would be home very soon for a rare quiet evening together. He arrived hours late. "Don't you ever blow up at him?" a friend asked Mrs. Irving. "I nearly did that time," she laughed.

Wealth, it was widely agreed, did not change her one bit. She once showed some distinguished visitors around Saint John and pointed out the humble apartment where she had first lived. This greatly impressed the visitors. Friends remembered that she packed countless boxes for the poor. Lowly Irving workers who did jobs around the family home tell of being invited in for coffee, of Mrs. Irving making sure she chatted with them. Arnold Payson told of her teaching him and others to cook when he was working in Saint John on his own.

Certainly the Irvings led what one acquaintance called a close, family life. Mrs. Irving took her sons to St. John's and St. Stephen's Presbyterian Church. She joined in its affairs, in church suppers, in the ladies' organizations. She worked in the Kindness Club for young people initiated by Hugh John Flemming's wife Aida. Annually for some years she threw a skating party for its Saint John members. It was she, Ray Tanton recalled, who called him at his service station one day and said her young sons wanted some telephone wire to string to a neighbour's house during a Bouctouche summer. She wondered if he could help. He called her back and quoted the price for new wire. Mrs. Irving said she was afraid the boys would find it too high. Tanton shopped around and found he could get it more cheaply second-hand. She said the boys would be delighted and thanked him very much.

There were three sons, James Kenneth, born in 1928, Arthur Leigh in 1930, and John Ernest in 1932. Jim, Art, and Jack. They would learn the hard lessons of commerce at their father's knee, but they would learn much from their mother too. If the world of New Brunswick came to live at times in awe of K.C. Irving's accomplishments, and if the sons shared a sense of pride in what he did, they were no less impressed or influenced by their mother. They idolized her.

In later years they acknowledged that she put up with a lot as they passed through their rambunctious teen-age years. Those were busy times for Harriet Irving as they started their own business ventures even before they were in their teens, and just about everyone who knew the family agreed on her patience and tolerance.

The sons would race from school to the Golden Ball building to get salesmen's samples from Kathleen Scribner's stationery supplies — then sell them. All three sons sold magazines door-to-door to earn pocket money: *The Saturday Evening Post*, *Liberty*, the old *Montreal Standard*, *Maclean's*, and *Chatelaine*. But their most profound early lessons in business were in a more uncertain and capricious field. It all started when the brothers decided they had enough experience to diversify. The Jim, Art, and Jack Farm run by brothers, aged twelve to eight, went into the egg business. They bought twelve hens and sold eggs to neighbours. When the hens stopped laying it was time to get rid of them, so they put an ad in the newspaper, and learned another lesson: "It pays to advertise." Someone called to say he wanted to buy the hens. The deal was made and hens were delivered as agreed.

Then they learned another lesson. Jim Irving recalled: "The buyer put the hens in his van, got behind the wheel and passed the money through the window. He was just about to take off when we realized he'd short-changed us, but he hadn't locked the door so I pulled it open and jumped in. We told him we weren't leaving until he paid us what he owed us. He finally paid — but we didn't do any business with him after that."

Later, when the brothers were in business on a grander scale in Bouctouche, they would go to Moncton each week to sell eggs and chickens. On one occasion they tried to make a deal with a Moncton grocer who wanted the chickens but didn't want to pay the price. "He wanted to pay us forty-two cents a pound and we needed forty-five or forty-seven cents. We couldn't make a deal so we went to a hotel and talked to the chef. He agreed to take the chickens off our hands — at our price.

"However, he didn't have enough cold-storage space so we drove over to the back entrance of a store where the chef said he had made storage arrangements. It was the same store owner we had tried to make a deal with earlier in the day. We transferred the chickens and then the store owner started to pay us — at forty-two cents a pound. It turned out that he owned the hotel, too. There was another long argument and finally we got our price, but in one day two outlets had dried up for future business — the store and the hotel."

The young Irvings had learned three valuable lessons: "Never do business with someone who is in such a hurry that he has the ignition on and his foot on the accelerator. Always know who is going to come up with the money when you are making a deal and, finally, don't cut off too many customers. You may need them in the future."

But the real lessons, the lasting lessons, were learned at home — business principles from their father and lessons in tolerance and compassion and charity from their mother. While still very young, they learned that service to the customer is the first rule of business. Jim Irving recalled the night his father came home and found two dozen eggs on the kitchen table. It was New Year's Eve. "Dad woke me up and I thought he was going to wish me a Happy New Year. Instead, he asked me what the eggs were doing on the kitchen table. I told him I was supposed to have delivered them but I had forgotten. I'd do it tomorrow. At 12:30 a.m. on New Year's Day, I was pounding on the kitchen door of a neighbour's home. They were having a party and I had to wait a long time before someone came to the door, but I got the eggs delivered. When I got home my father wished me a Happy New Year — and I never again forgot that work came first, no matter what."

There were other things the brothers would never forget about those early days in business. For one thing, their neighbours were tolerant, if tolerant is a strong enough word, because at one time they had as many as 125 hens and 1,500 baby chicks in a brooder converted from a garage behind the family's home. And if their neighbours were tolerant, their mother's forbearance, they all agree, went far beyond any normal measure of maternal affection. There was, for instance, the night the brooder stove went out. Half a century later the Irving brothers would recall that they got all the little chickens — all 1,500 of them — into the kitchen where they were trying to keep them alive with heat from the kitchen stove. That's when their mother arrived, and pitched in to help.

The next day, though, the chickens had to go to Bouctouche, and that pretty well ended the Jim, Art, and Jack Farm business in Saint John.

In middle age the brothers could smile at the memory of their early escapades and marvel, in retrospect, at the patience of a mother who could be so understanding and unflappable. In their early teens the three sons tagged along like so many pups behind their father. They would come away from a visit to an Irving company, with the father questioning the sons on what they had seen and learned. He took them everywhere and patiently explained the mechanics, the techniques of the things they saw. As soon as they were old enough, he put them in summer jobs to learn for themselves.

He didn't push them into projects, though they might ask his opinion about something they had built. Earning their own money was their own idea, but whatever they did had to stand on its own. Their father didn't yarn about the projects of his own youth; it wasn't until they were grown and running businesses themselves that they heard of most of them. But he did take them to places where men worked for him, and they watched and they came to want to emulate him. Irving himself would say that if anyone wanted to discuss this, they should "talk to the boys." The boys recalled that from their early years they were absorbed in what he did. "We never," said Arthur, "knew anything else."

In their early teens the boys left the schools of Saint John to attend Rothesay Collegiate, a nearby residential school. Tom Legassick was on duty in the office the day Irving arrived to enroll one of them. "I was nervous," he said, "about dealing with such a man. Then I realized he was as nervous as I was." At R.C.S., the devotion to projects continued. Legassick, on the staff for a quarter-century, remembered an evening when he chanced into a heated discussion. Jim Irving was deeply involved. A group of boys had gone into the business of fishing through the spring ice on the Kennebecasis River and selling what they caught. "From what I could gather," Legassick says, "some of the boys wanted to be paid a dividend and others wanted to plow the profits back into expansion." The latter argument was vintage K.C. Irving.

At R.C.S., too, nicknames were rampant. The Irving boys became "Oily," "Greasy," and "Gassy" — names cited in articles for years. In a private school populated in large part by sons of the well-to-do, it was an unwritten schoolboy law that no student boasted of distinctions or possessions. Those guilty of transgressions suffered social condemnation. The Irving boys, said then headmaster Dr. Humphrey Bonnycastle, were well-liked. He found all three different. None, he remembered, was academically inclined. Jim was "a reasonable student, a good, steady leader." Arthur had a good mind was "a bit harum-scarum. He was into whatever was going on, high jinks, the author of minor mischief." Jack was quieter, had more of the gentle side of his father's character. But Legassick recalled the time he made Jack manager of the basketball team. "Suddenly everything was run as it should be, everything was where it was supposed to be," kept neatly and with great attention to detail. They played basketball, football, and got into track and field, and their parents came at times to cheer them on. On weekends the boys went home and often took friends with them.

Bonnycastle found the father a generous donor, and once at least his sense of humour came out. Years after his sons had left R.C.S. he laid the cornerstone for a new building, saying there was a time when he'd had a call from Bonnycastle to the effect that "I had one son in residence whom I could take back any time. I won't tell which one it was. Don't worry, Arthur, I won't give you away."

From R.C.S. the sons went on to Acadia University. There they were remembered as modest, full of life, athletic, and interested in girls. None of the three was a distinguished student, or graduated. They simply weren't interested in a university education. They wanted to get back to New Brunswick and start what they considered the real learning process — on the job. Jim quit at nineteen, and when he did, he says, his father accepted it with one comment: "Get to work."

Each summer during college days they went home to work as ordinary hands at ordinary jobs in various company businesses. Jack worked at construction jobs. Jim loved the woods. As they got older, Irving would take them to business meetings. Arthur sat quietly, listening. Arthur, however, proved the most volatile of the three sons and at later meetings would be told by his father to sit down and close his mouth: "Don't burn your bridges."

All the boys went into the family businesses and they would all, in time, bring up their own children much as they were brought up themselves. Thus the homilies K.C. Irving had learned from his mother, the lessons he had learned from his father and others were imparted to a third and fourth generation. Lessons that stuck.

&

CHAPTER ELEVEN

The Postwar Push

"You did that well, Payson."
– K.C. IRVING'S CASUAL COMMENT AFTER HIS DRIVER SKIDDED
IN AND OUT OF A DITCH ON A SNOW-COVERED NOVA SCOTIA
HIGHWAY.

FOR IRVING OIL THE SECOND WORLD WAR WAS LARGELY A matter of marking time, of abiding by government restrictions, of waiting to grow again. K.B. Reed remembered it as a time of official supply quotas, of monthly meetings to work them out, of sales remaining just about where they had been. Hilus Webb remembered it as a scrambling time, of salesmen going out all day long to find what markets they could. He remembered the decree that ended the days when one outlet could sell gasoline for various companies. Government ruled that it was wasteful to have so many trucks going to single destinations, and that each must now rely on one supplier.

Once, an Irving ship put into Shelburne, N.S., without notifying authorities. The only reason it wasn't fired on, said an official memo, was that the man in charge of the guns was out to lunch. Arnold Payson remembered particularly the day Irving came to Truro — Payson had taken charge there in 1938 — and said he had to get to Moncton, some 110 miles away. There was a snowstorm raging, which Payson noted aloud, but Irving said he had to go. Payson knew that if Irving went he would have to drive him, but still he hadn't heard the worst of it.

In those days before snow tires, Payson had chains on. Irving told him to take them off; they would wear the tires, and tires were going to be hard to get. Payson never forgot that trip, slewing and sliding in the driving snow, passing through small towns hooded white, nor Irving's reaction when the car plunged off the road, bucked, careened, and got back on again. Irving had been reading documents. As Payson fought back to the highway, he looked up and said, "You did that well, Payson," and went on reading.

Danger didn't bother Irving. What bothered him was having Irving Oil mark time. By 1945 his construction of buses was uneconomic, and he got out of it. The conflict with Manning for the Saint John bus franchise dragged on. But his forward movements far surpassed all this. He built barges. He got control of Canada Veneers. He bought the railway lands. He bought control of D'Auteuil. He bought Dexter Sulphite. He bought his first hardware store. He acquired Saint John's daily newspapers. He even got into the shipping business in the Caribbean by finding winter work for the *Elkhound* carrying syrup from Cuba to the United States.

But, as much as anything, that period in his life convinced Irving that he should take a major step that would end his reliance on others for the production of his oil and gasoline. It convinced him that he must have his own refinery. He'd been thinking about it for at least fifteen years. In 1945 his ambitions were still relatively small: he was thinking of a refinery with a capacity of 7,500 barrels a day. He knew he didn't have the expertise to build and run one himself, so he went to Imperial Oil and they put people to work on a design. The project was aborted, but it was a herald of things to come.

As peace returned, he did something that indicated he was faring well and hoped to fare better. He asked Leigh Stevenson, that cousin four years his senior, to go into business with him. "Just look at all the things to be done down here," he argued. "Just look at them." Stevenson looked but was not convinced that a business association would be right for either of them. Man and boy, he had been Irving's closest friend. They had been friends from their earliest memories and they'd be friends until the day Stevenson died at ninety-four in 1989, but there was more to Irving's offer than friendship. Stevenson had great talents of his own, so it was not simply nostalgia that caused Irving to court his boyhood chum.

In fact, one of Stevenson's great strengths was demonstrated in his ability to realize that a business relationship with Irving was not in the cards for him.

"We were too far apart in our way of thinking, in our general philosophy of life," Stevenson would say many years later. Stevenson believed in working hard, but he also wanted something else from life. He was warm, outgoing, gregarious. A man's man, he looked forward to the cocktail hour. In his nineties, he'd say: "I drink all the time." He didn't mean he was a drinker in the classic sense of the word or that he was a problem drinker. Simply put, he took a drink. He enjoyed a drink. Irving didn't drink. Period. Stevenson, a witty happy man, enjoyed telling a story, reminiscing, the funny side of life. He worked hard during his life and was successful. But for him there was time for play, too. A time for relaxing. That was the one thing Irving never learned to do.

By 1945 both Irving and Stevenson were successful, Irving in business and Stevenson in the RCAF, where peacetime service had prepared him for high responsibilities in the Second World War. In 1940 he was promoted to air commodore and posted to England as commanding officer of the RCAF overseas. He would return to Canada in 1942 as an air vice-marshall to take charge of Western Air Command in the wake of the Japanese raid of December 7, 1941, on Pearl Harbor. In 1944 he was appointed senior Canadian officer on the staff of Lord Mountbatten, Allied Commander in South East Asia, when plans were being formulated to use Commonwealth air crews to bomb the islands of Japan. This was abandoned when the atomic bomb brought the war in the Pacific to an end.

This, then, was the man that Irving wanted to join him in 1945. He had also sought him as a business associate when he moved to Saint John in 1925, and when Stevenson declined, Irving wondered if it indicated a lack of confidence in his future. Twenty years later, Irving's success was apparent, and when he made a second proposal he spiced it with something which stressed this. He wrote out a cheque and offered it as an inducement to link their careers. The cheque, said Stevenson, was for $1 million. He turned it down. Once, later, when he and Irving were dining with two other men, one of them asked Irving if it was true. "Ask Leigh," Irving said. "It was his decision." He turned it down, Stevenson said, for the same reason he did in 1925: "He'd have killed me."

"With work," Irving said, and Stevenson confirmed it. He wasn't geared for the relentless pace Irving would expect. He wasn't interested in dedicating the rest of his working life to the things that interested, drove, impelled this cousin. He settled down, instead, in British Columbia, got into business and politics and served as a member of the provincial legislature.

If Stevenson declined to join Irving's work force, there was no shortage of others almost as talented.

&

Shortly after the war twenty-five-year-old Ken Hankinson was a car salesman in Digby, N.S., and thinking of bigger things. He was the son of that George Hankinson who had let K.C. Irving put a gas tank in front of his Weymouth store provided he gave Arnold Payson a job. He knew he could get a General Motors dealership in Weymouth but needed someone to put up a place for him to do business. He figured he might get an oil company to build one and lease it to him if he sold its products. But he was broke and none of the oil companies he approached would have anything to do with him.

Irving had bought land across from George Hankinson's store, and Irving paid heed to the son's appeal. Ken Hankinson told Irving he didn't have a licence to sell gas and oil. If backed, he would get one. Irving soon started building him a garage. By the time it was up Hankinson was still having trouble with the provincial Public Utilities Board. They kept rejecting his bids for a licence, and he kept making more. Two years went by before he got one, and what impressed him was that Irving did not complain once in that time. A generation later they were still doing business.

About the time George Hankinson made his deal with Irving, Alex Ross made another. He had been living in Pictou, N.S., in 1934 when Irving was looking for customers for a new-fangled idea, oil-fueled home furnaces, and he bought the first Irving oil burner in town. Soon after the war he, too, wanted to go into the car-and-gas dealership business. He had just about given up hope of finding a site on Moncton's Main Street when Irving heard about his problem, cleared out a bus depot and let Ross have it. "I can truthfully say," Ross commented years later, "that I would not be in business if it had not been for his help."

Soon after the war Steve O'Regan of Parrsboro, N.S., also decided he wanted a garage. He had come off a farm up the road, and he was already selling Irving Oil products, cars, and lumber, and wheeler-dealering his way to becoming a millionaire. He was a born salesman. "The way of it is," he would say, raising his peaked cap, and the pitch would flow. There is a story that a rival once tried to convince two rural ladies, O'Regan customers, that he could offer a better car deal, that O'Regan would feed them Irish blarney, flatter them, cajole them. "Yes," one of the ladies said, "all this may well be true but, you see, we like it."

When O'Regan wanted his garage, Irving came to dicker over terms — so much rent, so much of a split on oil and gas sales. O'Regan then retreated to consult his sister Kate who had, he said, the sharpest business brain in the family. Kate said never to go into a deal without getting more than the other fellow. O'Regan decided to hold out. That, he figured, was the way Irving himself would do it. Irving got into his car and left, but when he got to Moncton he called and said it was a deal. They got, O'Regan said, as good a garage as you could want to see, without a contract, without anything more than that call from Moncton.

About the time it was being built, Irving and Bob Sutherland drove across a new causeway at Barrington Passage, N.S., to the island to which they had once arranged to take fishermen oil products by boat. Irving Oil already owned sites on both sides of the mainland end, but as they came back Irving saw a better one, dead ahead, occupied by a house. He got Sutherland to buy the house, eventually to be moved to make way for a service station.

With moves like these, as even Sutherland's Irish setter Rusty could see, Irving was again expanding his oil and gas business now that the wartime lull was over. Rusty kept a sort of Irving Oil inventory: if Sutherland drove past one of its service stations the dog was apt to knock his hat off.

The number of service stations and dealers was growing. So were other things. In 1946 Irving established Kent Lines Ltd., a shipping firm, and started buying up war-surplus corvettes, those tough little heroes of the Royal Canadian Navy in the Battle of the Atlantic. He bought Steel and Engine Ltd., a rundown company in Liverpool, N.S., and used it to convert eight of them to cargo ships.

To D'Auteuil Lumber he added other acquisitions in Quebec, began to buy up small oil-marketing companies as an early step towards a larger invasion, and bought Chinic Hardware Inc., a Quebec City hardware firm that traced its history back to 1805. He'd bought Thorne's Hardware, a long-established Saint John company, in 1942. He had bought plenty of hardware from their big King Street store and he figured that it could supply things his and other companies needed. When he took it over, he told its executives never to refuse shipment of an order, never to reproach a customer, and never to have a bad debt. Typically, he soon knew more about the business than anyone in it — what it should buy, how it should sell. When the time came for big decisions it was always Irving who made them, and he soon had profits at a point that more than reimbursed him for what he'd paid for the company in the first place.

Chinic, too, he bought partly to supply his other companies, and he soon added Lewis Brothers' two hardware stores in Montreal and, with them, a branch in Toronto. He had little use for a hardware store in Toronto, but it came with the deal. Before long, he had what amounted to the second-largest chain of hardware stores, primarily wholesalers, in eastern Canada.

He took D'Auteuil into production of its own pulpwood for Dexter Sulphite and other markets. This, too, was part of a larger design. As he'd said when he bought the New Brunswick Railway lands: "I thought we'd have a use for them. We were in the lumber business to stay." Yet even that vast tract didn't seem enough. He wanted more forests still, and he found them in Quebec and Maine. In Quebec, especially, he had his troubles — from politics. His moves there coincided with the heyday of the long rule of Premier Maurice Duplessis and his Union Nationale party. Amid its rumoured and later certified corruptions, colleagues say, Irving would have nothing to do with payoffs to get what he wanted. He never gave much to Quebec political campaign funds, either. As a result, one former executive said, his companies didn't get much political support.

It may have been Duplessis who disrupted D'Auteuil's plans to produce its own logs. During the war the company had bought and sold them as a broker, shipped them to Dexter, to the veneer plant in Saint John, to West Virginia, and to firms in Canada and

Newfoundland. Then Irving and Aimé Gaudreau sought and found land they could cut on for themselves. Known as the Nicolas Rioux Seigniory, it was a large tract twenty miles inland from the south shore of the lower St. Lawrence River, between Trois Pistoles and Rivière-du-Loup. It was held in fee simple with the wood free of any stumpage charge. But the uninterrupted tenure was brief. The forests had been leased to others for stumpage in earlier years, and there were soon protests from the people who had cut, but cut no more. They were Duplessis supporters, and they petitioned him. He listened, and in 1951 he acted. He told Gaudreau he must issue stumpage permits. Gaudreau refused. "We need that wood," he said.

This provoked a more serious threat. Duplessis said he would expropriate. As Irving recalled it, Gaudreau protested, "You can't do that, Mr. Premier." The eyes of Duplessis roamed the law books that lined his office. "I know of nothing in those," he said, "which says I can't."

"But," said Gaudreau, "there is a larger law. The Bible bids us to be fair to our neighbour."

Duplessis took the land, anyway, then in recompense five years later provided D'Auteuil with other forests on the north shore of the St. Lawrence. They would remain government property, he said, but D'Auteuil could cut for thirty years as much as it would have cut on its previously held tract. After that it would pay stumpage. Irving and Gaudreau already had acquired other woodlands nearby and around Baie Comeau. Now they had access to more. But in time they would face yet another expropriation.

In Maine, Irving came across another formidable French Canadian, a bull of a man named Edouard Lacroix. Like Gaudreau, he was raised in a large impoverished Quebec family, had little early schooling, and started working in American textile mills at age fourteen. He later learned English at Nova Scotia's St. Francis Xavier University. He became a lumberjack and grew into a baron of the forests in Maine and Quebec's Gaspé Peninsula, employing 6,000 men. When he was elected to Canada's Parliament in 1924, his men gathered in a Maine camp cookhouse and gave him a gold cane. "In Quebec," they said, "you are a member of the House of Commons. In Maine, you are a King." From then on he was King Lacroix.

But by the end of the war he was ill, and he and his brothers in business with him were willing to sell things. Irving was willing to buy. He took to Lacroix and would bestow upon him that laurel he employed for those he liked: "He was a good chap."

In Irving's amphibious plane, he, Gaudreau, Lacroix, and Wilfred Grenier flew over the Lacroix holdings in Maine and northern New Hampshire. A deal was made, then another. The Great Northern paper company was after an exchange of lands with Lacroix's Van Buren and Madawaska Corporation. Lacroix, said Grenier, was happy to sell to Irving but he personally didn't want to make the swap with Great Northern. Irving bought the land and made the swap. He ended up with thousands of acres in the Allagash River watershed not far south of D'Auteuil holdings in northern New Brunswick. With them he got a large sawmill at Keegan, Maine, across the St. John River from St. Leonard, N.B. He also bought, at the mouth of the St. John, beside Saint John's Reversing Falls, the faltering pulp mill the Lacroix family owned and to which they had for some years driven logs by water over hundreds of miles.

It wasn't the first time Irving had looked at it. Horace Enman had suggested in the 1930s that he buy it. Others had, too, but he would say, "No one ever told me how I could run it profitably." Expert advice suggested he might make $2 on a ton of pulp — and he might lose $2. It wasn't good enough. Instead, Lacroix bought the mill.

By 1946 things had changed. Irving now had his forest lands in New Brunswick and Maine. He had learned a lot about the pulp business through Dexter, and had Frank Lang's expertise. He figured that if others could run pulp mills in New Brunswick, why couldn't he? He decided he could drive the required logs down the St. John and he could make it pay if he had not one but two mills to consume them at its mouth, one the pulp mill, the other a large new sawmill.

He made arrangements with a national investment house to handle the financing with a bond issue, but there was a setback. The investment house sounded out authorities in Fredericton and was advised not to touch the deal. It withdrew. Irving turned to Frank Brennan and Brennan put out a $2-million bond issue. With the money, Irving got half the ownership of the mill, and eventually all of it.

The mill perched on historic ground. For a century there had been mills on Union Point, a knob of land protruding into the river in the heart of the Saint John–Lancaster urban area. In 1899 a sawmill on the site gave way to one of Canada's first pulp mills. It went through a succession of owners until, in 1932, it was purchased by Lacroix's Port Royal Pulp and Paper Company. It still had that name when Lacroix sold it to Irving in March 1946.

The mill was worn and antiquated. Shutdowns had dogged it repeatedly. Employees got at most six months' work a year. Wages were low, raises scarce and puny, and the men were denied a union. Most of the work was done by hand. Water supply was a problem; in summer months the city cut it off for weeks. The quality of the pulp was poor. The location was by no means ideal. There were transportation problems.

For such reasons it had scared off the investment house, and spurred the doom-sayers to forecast that this time Irving *had* made a mistake. As for the workers, they didn't know what to think, but some of them were scared too. They soon felt more optimistic. One employee went up to the new manager with a complaint shortly after the takeover. The manager said he didn't want to entertain individual complaints: "Where is your committee?"

"What committee?"

"Your union committee."

"We have no union. Lacroix didn't like unions."

"Then get one," the manager said.

In fact, Irving and Frank Lang, satisfied with their union experience at Dexter, had already accepted the reality of unions. It wasn't so much a matter of whether there would be a union as when. Local 30 of the Canadian Pulp and Paperworkers Union was in business within weeks, and out of the first negotiations came a nineteen-cent-an-hour raise. The members greeted it with "total disbelief," said Charles Lynch, local president for ten years. Moreover, there was work day and night, seven days a week. Irving, they found, didn't even want to close down for maintenance. For Lynch, "it was the best thing that ever happened when Irving got the mill."

Somehow the water problems ended too. Irving suspected the pipes from Spruce Lake were leaking, and he got the city to check. The pipes *were* leaking. There was at least one big hole. The city assigned men to fix it on a holiday, and Irving went out early that morning to watch. He found no workers there. He liked and admired J.D. McKenna, the mayor of the day. He called him. McKenna was still in bed but, said Irving, "I could almost hear his feet hit the floor when I told him what was going on." The workers were soon there. The water began to flow adequately. The mill soon began to function better.

Irving became part of the mill's existence, frequently there, shaking hands, conferring with Lynch and other officials, grabbing a tool and going to work, mastering the idiosyncrasies, the machinery, the methods. Of none of the major plants he would own did he get to know more than he did of this one. Anecdotes bloomed around him. A novice labourer, unaware of who he was, once told him to get out of the way. Irving, smiling, obliged, then looked up the man on later visits to make friendly talk with him. He was once advised to shut the mill down, markets were so low. He refused to stop production even for a day and soon the pulp was piled in sheds, railway cars, abandoned buildings, anywhere he could find until things looked up again.

Men got used to seeing him around long after most people were in bed. "Night visits," he would say, "are the best way to find out what is going on. If you know both ends and the middle of a business you should be able to make the right decisions. You can learn an awful lot at nights." Jimmer McMullin once saw a car parked in the mill yard well after midnight. Mrs. Irving was in it, alone, knitting. She asked McMullin if he'd seen her husband. "Yes," he said, "he's in the mill." She asked him to relay the information that she felt it was time to go home.

Over the years, Irving would keep expanding that mill despite its restricting site. He would boost its production higher and higher and build, at nearby South Bay, a sawmill capable of turning out 30 million board feet a year. He would make Saint John the largest consuming point for forest products in eastern Canada.

Why did he do these things? Why was he constantly on the move, always looking for opportunities to change, improve, and expand what the public called the empire but he called the company? His own explanations include the oft-quoted "I like to see wheels turning" and to "create activity." He had another with a lyrical touch: "I've always enjoyed what I did. If you are busy, you get interested.

It's like the fiddler at the dance. You'd almost play for nothing." Or, "When you get things going right, it's really music."

He expounded what he saw as a sort of iron law of business: "You've got to keep going. Expansion is the thing. The trouble with many businessmen is that when they have made some progress they sit back and take a rest. We can't progress while standing still." He created many companies in such a way that each could be judged on its own, so he could see whether it could stand on its own feet.

Why New Brunswick? A place of thin and scattered population, up to three-quarters of a million or so in his lifetime, dominated by 85, perhaps even 90 per cent forest, split and sluiced by rivers — the St. John, the "Goodly River" of the Indians, a north–south vertebral column; the Miramichi, that mesh and mass of tributary arteries and veins through high, quiet hills; the Tobique, the Nashwaak, the Restigouche? The Petitcodiac running with the innocence of crystal into Moncton and the brown, engulfing Fundy tides. The Kennebecasis, a lovely name for lovely waters fringed by tall elms and fertile fields. The many others with liquid names from vanished wigwams. And in their valleys and on the coast small villages, small towns, small cities, united by road and water and divided by the armies of trees. A province haunted by the memories of the Acadians, those who fled expulsion and those who returned from it; the Loyalists who fled revolutionary persecution in an expulsion of their own; the Scots who had to leave their lands when their landlords decided that sheep were more profitable; the Irish who fled the famine that brought death to millions; the English who had fled the poverty of their homeland; the Indians with their legends and their ache of knowing all this was once theirs and was no more.

New Brunswick, a place where men voted as grandfathers had, where for years the French were overwhelmingly Liberal and the British largely Conservative, and no other creed of politics amounted to much. A place without the mystique of Quebec or the wealth of Ontario or prairie space, a rugged, beautiful, trying place. In the euphemistic vernacular of economics, a have-not province that fostered in its young a love that was beyond it to fulfil and sent them forth in chronic exodus to larger hopes. A province where the things Kenneth Colin Irving did were judged the more remarkable because they happened here, and until he did them no one thought they could be done.

Why the Maritimes when his closest parallels in monumental success were a group of men who went away to achieve it, and who, in doing so, became testaments to what had happened to their homeland? There were seven of them born between 1870 and 1885, and they could be seen as the most prodigious progeny of the golden age of sail. They just missed it, but they grew up among its immediate memories and its slow, sad dying. Their careers became an epitaph, for they all saw that it had gone, and they all departed too. But they reflected, in their energy and their reach, what it had been.

Nearly all of them came, like Irving, from small coastal towns. Max Aitken, who made a fortune through corporate mergers in Montreal, went to Britain and became a press lord, a political power, Lord Beaverbrook. R.B. Bennett became rich as a Calgary lawyer, and later rose to become prime minister of Canada and a British lord. Alfred Fuller, America's "Fuller Brush Man," was once called the greatest huckster of his time. Cyrus Eaton became the financier-industrialist of Cleveland, Ohio. Sir James Dunn of Algoma Steel was once called by a powerful American financier "the greatest financier of us all." Louis B. Mayer ran his father's Saint John junkyard at fourteen, and later dominated Hollywood. Izaak Walton Killam had a spectacular if secretive career in finance.

But Irving stayed home, and many people would speculate about what would have happened if he, too, had chosen a more prosperous area for his enterprise and expansions. Many think he would have soared even higher than he did. K.B. Reed remembered asking him whether New Brunswick and the Maritimes were the logical location to be in: "Is this the place?" He never got a clear answer. But Irving himself, as a threat or tactic, or on occasions simply out of frustration, grumbled that he would leave. He grumbled, but he would not go. And when he spoke from the heart he would say: "No matter where you go you'll find problems. New Brunswick is a good place."

In 1947 he was offered a chance to get in on Alberta's early oil play, turned it down and was told by his son Arthur that he had missed a golden opportunity. "I didn't want to live in Alberta," he'd say. "I wanted to stay here. This is where I wanted to live. It's nice to stay home. You couldn't get a better place than the Maritimes." Besides, he'd note, "it took years for Alberta to boom on oil," and in time the boom slackened.

Quite simply, he was happy where he was. Some charged that he came to confuse what was good for him with what was good for New Brunswick, but that didn't bother him too much. He went on doing what he felt was right, convinced and happy that it benefited the area as well.

Irving became a voice for the region's soured hopes, an architect of its aspirations, as close to a New Brunswick nationalist as the province has known. He saw vacuums everywhere around him, and he kept expanding into them, raising another question: Where did he get the money to do it so often? He got it in various ways. He could raise it through issues of stocks and bonds. He could tap the profits of his existing companies, though he preferred to leave them where they were to finance their own expansion. He could, as with Dexter Sulphite, pay off the costs of acquisition with the profits acquisition eventually brought.

Primarily, he stood well with the banks and abided by that business maxim that says a wise man uses someone else's money. "I always," he'd say, "borrowed a lot of money; I don't really know of a bad bank." He once bought an old bank building, borrowed the money from the bank itself when it moved the branch to new premises, fixed up the old one, and paid off the loan with rental profits — some from another bank. He got one company by backing a bank loan with the resources of another, quickly built the second's profits, then used its assets to back a bank loan for a third.

He borrowed millions and only once, he'd say, was he threatened, to the great embarrassment of Horace Enman. Enman was ordered by his Toronto head office to call a large Irving loan, and Irving saw it as an attempt by rival interests to take him over. Enman apologized, gave him as much time as he could, and died regretting what he'd had to do.

Irving survived it. He found other money and paid off the loan, and he later heard that the bank official responsible said he'd never have called it if he'd known Irving could do it. He and Enman remained friends, did other business, and as Irving grew, so did the number of banks interested in lending him money. The time soon came, said one bank manager, "when he didn't go to the banks; you went to him."

As added protection, added leverage, what Irving built became increasingly his own. In early years he issued shares, and Sam Roy says he and others did well by them: "He cut us in on things." But Irving called shares as soon as he could. He preferred the security and the satisfaction and simplicity of being in control. He found that "the minute you make money, people spend all their waking hours trying to get it out of you." Certainly he remembered his mother's warning that to waste it was a sin.

In a Nova Scotian town one day he was with men building an oil tank farm, making sure the grade of its earth foundation met his always exact requirements. A penny was struck under a level, and when the job was done the coin had vanished in grass. The others started away. Irving remained, looking for it, and when someone noted it was only a cent he looked up and said, "Look after the pennies and the dollars will look after themselves." He kept looking until he found it.

The money he used, the control he achieved, gave him the advantage of calling his own shots: "When you go public, you have certain rules you have to go by. Those rules may not be the most convenient way to accomplish what you set out to do. You can take a calculated risk if you only have to account to yourself."

He took numerous risks, but never on a hunch, always after careful calculation. In 1946 his Saint John pulp mill was seen as a risk indeed. But he took it, and plunged into a new phase of operations — his log drives down the St. John River to supply it.

CHAPTER TWELVE

❧

Driving the Logs

*"He did it all and never asked anyone to do anything
he wouldn't do himself."*
— ARTHUR IRVING DESCRIBING HIS FATHER'S LIFE ON THE
ST. JOHN RIVER.

HORACE PETTIGROVE WAS WITH IRVING THE NIGHT ONE
drive went through Fredericton. As a senior government
labour official, he had been in Geneva attending a meeting of the International Labor Organization, and the two men
chanced upon each other while waiting for a plane in Montreal. It
was a boiling hot day and Irving suggested they go to a movie. In
his early years in business, Irving had been a great man for movies.
He'd drop hectic things and go to one to calm down. This time,
however, Pettigrove didn't think much of the idea; cramped theatre
seats didn't much suit his long legs. But Irving said it was one
place they could find air conditioning, so they went.

On the plane, Irving did something he often did to refresh
himself. He put on slippers, excused himself and slept for twenty
minutes, then took up the conversation exactly where it had ended.
When they got to Fredericton after midnight, he insisted on driving Pettigrove home in the car he'd left at the airport. Pettigrove
protested that he lived in the suburbs. "Why, I know where you
live, Mr. Pettigrove," said Irving, a bit hurt at the suggestion he
didn't, for they had known each other for years.

As they crossed the river, Irving stopped on the bridge, got out and shone a flashlight down into the waters. He was wondering where the log drive was, and Pettigrove suddenly heard him shouting, as excited as a boy. "This," he exclaimed, "is a wonderful drive. It will be over in nine days." Cars now were waiting behind them, and Pettigrove said, "Mr. Irving, I think we're holding up traffic."

"Well now," said Irving, "I believe that's so," and climbed back in. When they got to Pettigrove's home, Irving carried one of his bags. He was invited in for coffee but said he had to get on up the river to see more of the drive. When he was gone, Mrs. Pettigrove asked who he was.

"That, my dear," said her husband, "was K.C. Irving."

Irving, meanwhile, was already driving north to see more of one of those drives that were to be part of his life for some twenty years.

"My father," Arthur Irving would say, "was the Main John Glasier of his day. He's walked the St. John River from end to end. He's been up to his back in water. He did it all and never asked anyone to do anything he wouldn't do himself." It was true. The stories of K.C. Irving's involvement in the river drives are legion and the comparison to the Main John Glasier apt. Both men were giants and legends of their times, and of log drives down the St. John River.

Glasier lived, flourished, and made his reputation during the nineteenth century. He was a river boss and the first man to take a drive over the torrential drop at the New Brunswick town of Grand Falls. Because there were other bosses named John, an Irish cook dubbed him the Main John Glasier. The name stuck and by the time he died in 1894 he was immortalized: the term Main John Glasier was applied to the manager of any big lumber operation as far away as the western United States.

Irving had been familiar with river drives as a boy and young man in Bouctouche and he would throw himself into the operations after acquiring the Saint John mill and the distant New Brunswick and Maine lands that fed it. He acknowledged that he "had a lot to do with them." That was an understatement. Irving said he knew enough to do most of the jobs and "was familiar with most of the activities." Which is to say he was often there, dressed in a mackinaw and high boots, often flew low over them, took food to the men, supervised, questioned, watched, worked. So was his family, down eventually to his grandchildren. At times men heard his wife giving instructions on the radio that controlled the operation.

Lacroix ran the first drive for Irving, then Irving's own men took over. He had exclusive rights to the river. The drives made the river a highway that began in Maine and bore hundreds of thousands of logs south in a rite of the seasons, a marvel of organization and timing, a pageant of sweat and muscle. They are virtually gone now everywhere, but while they lasted they were a spectacle.

When he quit college Jim Irving worked on one, then took over. "A born straw boss," someone called him, a tall, sturdy man who would tell his workers, "I knew nothing when I started; I learned from you." He was hot tempered, given to arguing with men who felt they knew more than he did, but, said one of them, "of good heart." He made his home for some years in St. Leonard, not far from Grand Falls. He learned the French of the forests, working out changes that speeded the drives.

In the beginning, veterans say, "they started in snow and came home to snow." They began as soon as thawing spring ice would let them, became one long cavalcade of logs, men out front, men in the rear to clean up. They slept in large tents, worked in sun and rain maintaining momentum, pushing errant logs back into the water with long, pointed picaroons. At night they slicked up and went into small towns to find what fun there was.

For greater efficiency, the drives came to be divided into sections, each with ten miles of river, its own foreman, its own wagon or supply boat. There would be fourteen or fifteen sections, each with its own combination cookhouse and bunkhouse. The meals, it was generally agreed, were wonderful: "Irving was fussy about food." If a cook wasn't good enough he was soon gone. Each made his own bread.

The men wore short boots; tall ones were too warm and they were dangerous if you fell in the water, as men did, from boats. They used boats with powerful motors to make things move faster. The wooden boats that had to be towed through Grand Falls gave way to steel-hulled ones that were taken apart and moved by truck. Men who worked the river drives said the Irvings picked up any equipment that would help.

The men were mostly French-speaking from northern New Brunswick — tough and hardy. They had their stars, and Felix Therrien was one of them. He, like the others, worked seven days a week. He started at forty cents an hour and got up to $1 with no extra pay for overtime. The worst part of it all, he said, was missing home and family on Sundays. He was glad when the drives were speeded up in a precise carefully calculated system that read the river like a book. On one tributary after another — the Quisibis, the Salmon, the Little, and others — men awaited Jim Irving's radioed word to dump into the water thousands of cords of pulpwood to join the drive exactly when required. Timing was vital. If the river was too high, logs drifted ashore. If it was too low, logs were hard to move. At times they had to build small dams to get enough depth.

In places the river ran fast, in places it ran slow. There were islands to avoid, feed-in brooks where logs could go wrong. At Grand Falls it posed its greatest obstacle, a drop of seventy-five feet with its own legend — of the Maliseet maiden Malabeam who promised to lead her Iroquois captors to attack her settlement and took them instead to their deaths over the falls. In spring when the ice broke the whole town roared with the sound of it, and the falls were a tumult that hurled logs like so many toothpicks to rocky banks. There was a boom there, a holding place, and annual conferences with the men who operated the concrete dam. The whole process of timing came to a head there, for if the drive came too early the logs would wash ashore; if it took too long, power was lost.

When the drive went through people came to watch over several days, saw the river solid with them, saw a drama of leaping, churning wood descending into a long gorge with cliffs 200 feet high. From there the logs moved into an area known as "the coffee mill," where rounded, rocky banks reduced momentum to sluggish, circling lethargy, and logs could pile up in great, tangled jams that sometimes could be freed only by opening the dam wider, or all the way, to blast them out with sheer force.

There, in the coffee mill, one day K.C. Irving and his son Jim were seen working alone, in the water for hours, pulling out snarled logs with ropes. In a place, one worker said, where others wouldn't go for money, they were seen to be in danger, but when someone told Irving he only laughed and said there was none. He enjoyed it. Stories spread that his mind was turning to other things — to a plywood factory in St. Leonard that was actually started and then abandoned because someone else had built one first; to a pipeline that would take chips from a groundwood mill to Saint John with chemicals that would turn them into pulp by the time they got there.

Other stories spread and brought more controversy to his life. Vandals preyed upon his property, slashed tires and smashed bridges. Guards were needed to protect booms. It was said that he had too much and paid too little. Protests grew as machines came in more and more, as bulldozers trampled the shoreline, as people resented the bark that fell in the river and the periods it was solid with logs. To all this would be added long, involved arguments with government as power demands led to the Beechwood dam in the 1950s and to the Mactaquac dam in the 1960s.

The drives eventually ended — Mactaquac killed them. Therrien sat thinking only briefly when he was asked if he missed them. He remembered the laughter. He liked to remember the days when the drives reached Maugerville and yielded to tugs to take them through slow waters to Saint John, when K.C. Irving would be there to shake hands and thank them all. But the drives themselves he did not miss, though he wouldn't mind just one more so young people could see how hard men worked in more demanding times.

Félice Poitras told of the Irving woods that nourished the drives from the great, green watershed of the Restigouche, with its many tributaries. He was a jolly, earthy priest, like a character out of Chaucer, one of twenty-seven children born to a farmer who talked to his horse in English so his sons would not acquire the profanity he used, which, the Reverend Félice recalled with a grin, they did anyway. He went into the lumber camps for years, by horse and sleigh, then by car over icy roads. He said Mass in cookhouses, he heard confessions, he got men laughing. He spiced his sermons with tales, with worldly jokes cleansed with scriptural passages. He told of the cold nights in early days, of standing in front of a stove for hours to keep warm while weary lumberjacks slept like the logs they cut, of the hearty, bountiful meals.

The first time he met K.C. Irving was in a camp cookhouse. Irving invited him to stay as long as he wished, as often as he wished, then just before strapping on snowshoes to go he slipped

Poitras two $10 bills. When Félice told that story to a camp fore-man, the foreman said he was amazed that Irving carried any money at all.

Poitras and Jim Irving became great friends. Poitras loved to hunt and fish. For some time, when he was paying for a farm, he largely fed himself in this way from the Irving lands. Once he and his brother saw a moose. It was out of season, but the temptation was too great. He shot it and took the meat, and Jim Irving found what was left. Not knowing who was guilty he reported it and Father Poitras ended up before a magistrate, saying "I have come to confession." He was fined $100, which was, he said, not a bad price for 800 pounds of meat. When he retired, he built himself a house on Lake Quisibis, and behind it a garage and over the garage a chapel. People would fill it every Sunday and in one of his sermons he said they would be pleased to know that he had shot his first deer of the season. He paused, then he added, "legally."

Irving was often in the woods too. He got lumber camps going, would come in on a bulldozer or truck sent through the snows to get supplies. He took pride in the statement of the local health inspector that his camps were the first to make life better for the men, by providing sheets, electricity from a diesel motor, central heat, washrooms, showers, furniture. He built good camps of lum-ber instead of logs. He insisted that new roads be cut straight, that hill grades be gradual to reduce accidents on ice. He banned liquor and guns. "He didn't like smoking but he let us do it."

He also kept growing, building, expanding. He built his sawmill in Saint John and when Mactaquac ended its life he estab-lished another at Estcourt, Que., in that area where Quebec, New Brunswick, and Maine come together. He built another on the Restigouche lands, at Veneer Siding. He gave work to hundreds of men. They worked long days, walked out Saturday night, and came back Monday morning. At first those who cut down trees did it with saws they worked by hand. A good man might cut two and a half cords a day for which he received $5.50, then $6.50, a cord. Changes kept coming. Teams of horses yielded to trucks and tractors and skidders, handsaws to power saws that could cut wood far faster.

Jim Irving was in charge for some years. Once he woke up with his hair frozen to a bunkhouse wall. Félice Poitras remembered him taking the bus from St. Leonard and walking from the highway into camp to save money. He was learning firsthand one more phase of the business in the woods — learning by doing, as his father had before him.

CHAPTER THIRTEEN

❧

"It Never Pays to Talk with Your Coat On"

"I'll chase Irving out of town with the arse out of his pants."

– *UNION LEADER ANGUS MACLEOD.*

BY 1948 K.C. IRVING WAS ATTRACTING THE ATTENTION OF national publications, and from the first they tried to estimate what he was worth. They started with a guess of up to $100 million and the estimate would keep increasing. That early guess came from David Pickard in a cover article in the February 1948 issue of *Canadian Business* magazine. The cover featured a sketch of Irving, bald, with fringes of white hair. The estimate received no confirmation or even comment from Irving. A year later Cyril Robinson tried his hand for the *Standard*, a Montreal weekly. Like Pickard, he got nowhere delving into personal matters. He found Irving willing to talk at length about industrial opportunities in New Brunswick or a Chignecto Canal, "but what he told me about himself I could have put on the back of a postage stamp."

In their articles, both Pickard and Robinson brought up a subject that was causing increasing speculation about Irving. "Many," wrote Pickard, "have associated him with ownership or control of the *Telegraph-Journal* and the *Evening Times-Globe*, the Saint John morning and afternoon newspapers." Irving, he found, would neither confirm nor deny the rumour, "dismissing it with

'I'd rather not discuss the matter.'" Robinson, too, said there were rumours that Irving owned the papers. By the time Robinson's article appeared in 1949 Irving had owned the papers for five years. He said years later that he had once approached Howard Robinson and asked him if he would sell. Robinson turned him down but said he would sell to Irving if and when he decided to get out. In 1944, a bit earlier than Irving expected, the call came that put him back in the publishing business. With the deal came the radio station CHSJ and the house Robinson owned.

The house became Irving's home, and the media became part of his mystery. No announcement was ever made. The men who had been directors continued to be directors. The legal arrangements that had closed the deal remained locked in silence. Even when his ownership was taken for granted, mystery remained. He rarely talked to writers. One veteran New Brunswick newsman who did not work for the Saint John newspapers, said that in thirty-three years he had never written about him, and couldn't say what he thought of him because "I haven't enough to go on."

In 1948 Irving doubled his newspaper ownership in New Brunswick by purchasing the two English-language dailies in Moncton. Some years earlier, someone had suggested Irving buy the *Transcript*. He had known the paper since his youth; John T. Hawke, the colourful and ardent Liberal who edited it, whose mock rooster crowed over every Liberal election victory, had sent Irving's father daily news bulletins to post in his store window at Bouctouche. An approach was made but got nowhere; the owner, Senator C.W. Robinson, wanted too much money.

By 1948, however, the afternoon *Transcript* and morning *Daily Times*, long and bitter political rivals, were jointly owned and politically neutral. Their owner, Jack Grainger, needed money to bring them up-to-date, and someone suggested he try Irving. Irving was interested and the deal was made. As far as the public was concerned, Grainger remained the boss. Clair Ganong, then managing editor, once said he was never informed that anything had changed. But on a Sunday in November of that year the night editor got a call from a man who said something had happened in Saint John on Saturday and he would bet the Monday *Times* would have no mention of it. K.C. Irving, he said, had driven a truck through the picket lines of striking workers.

"And why," asked the editor, "wouldn't we print it?"

"Because," the caller said, "Irving owns your paper."

The editor contacted the Canadian Press correspondent on duty in Saint John and said he wanted a report. He did it, he later said, partly because he figured that if anything would stir reaction from Irving and thus confirm his ownership this might. The CP story came in. He printed it. There was no reaction from Irving.

On that picket line in Saint John there had been a reaction from Irving. Physical. Dramatic. No single episode would ever surpass it in the scarred inventory of union memories of him. For the bareknuckle lad of Bouctouche re-emerged in a forty-nine-year-old man and left an imprint that would last for years.

His opponents were some forty men, labourers, who worked for Irving Oil at his bulk storage plant on Courtenay Bay, a small, compact place with big, white, round tanks, an office, a wharf, a railway line for the cars that brought in what he sold, trucks to take it out. When he got word that union organizers were busy among them, Irving suggested what amounted to a company union. There was a secret vote and the men, instead, formed Local 15 of the National Union of Oil Workers, a member of the Canadian Congress of Labour. In February 1948 it was certified by the New Brunswick Labour Relations Board, and negotiations began with the company. They went on for months, through conciliation proceedings, and got nowhere.

The union wanted a fifty-four-hour, six-day week cut to a forty-eight-hour, six-day week, $27.50 to $35 wage rates raised to $31.20 to $38, time-and-a-half for overtime instead of straight time, and they wanted two weeks' holidays instead of one after five years on the job.

On October 29, Angus MacLeod, a general organizer for the CCL, wrote the company asking that a conciliation board's recommendations be adopted and that the union's demands be met. Union men said he got no firm answer, and an angry meeting instructed him to inform Irving that unless a settlement was reached within twenty-four hours they would strike. When the day arrived, Irving called them together and said he expected all of them to be on the job the next morning, and anyone who wasn't would be fired.

Instead, at 7 a.m. the union members set up a picket line. A driver went out on delivery service, unaware that he bore a sign saying "This is a scab truck." Nothing untoward happened until late afternoon. Then Irving showed up, peeled off his coat and invited any picketer to take him on. There are varying versions of what he shouted. One was, "You may be tough but I am tougher." He later said he wasn't looking for trouble but only obeying a principle that "It never pays to talk with your coat on." One man present towered over him — the six-feet-four local president. "He could have made mincemeat of me," Irving recalled. Instead, the giant grinned, and Irving got in his car and left.

The next morning, a Saturday, an Irving executive tried to get through the picket line into the plant. Blocked, he retreated. That afternoon Irving returned with a group of officials and policemen. The picket lines opened and they drove through. Three loaded trucks were readied to go. The first driver got to the pickets and decided not to go on. Irving told him to get out, climbed in himself and drove through. The police did nothing. Behind Irving drove one of his executives. That car, unionists said, struck a worker but kept on going. The unionists also claimed that a driver following hit two workers, one of whom was taken to hospital.

The pickets re-formed and stayed there until late Monday afternoon. Then a sheriff arrived with legal papers announcing that an injunction has been granted Irving by a judge of the provincial Supreme Court forbidding picketing for thirty days.

The next issue of the *Maritime Commonwealth*, a unionist publication, had an article headlined: "Court Injunction Used To Break Saint John Strike." It was written by union organizer Henry Harm, who had seen it all. "K.C. Irving," he wrote, "has done it again. As usual he is out to smash organized labour and all it stands for, only this time he has gone one better, he has torn off his coat and asked forty of his employees to fight him." Harm called upon unionists in general to fight for men "receiving nothing better than starvation wages." Unionists in general did not press the legal action against Irving on a charge of reckless driving. The charge was dropped.

To their angry accusations, there were publicly unspoken rebuttals. An official of another oil company watched the confrontations from nearby and remembered exulting in Irving's defiance. A high official of another oil company, one that had no comparable union, remembered hearing what happened and rejoicing too. Irving himself kept public silence. He had argued in seeking the injunction that the pickets were illegal because they stalled the flow of trucks from his yard. He left no doubt, in discussing the affair years later, that he thought the strikers were violating premises he owned.

Perhaps the best explanation came from Gordon Ebbett, another man who saw it happen. He had come to Saint John in 1928 and got a job with Irving when jobs were scarce indeed. He was a jack of all trades and, at the time of the strike, was foreman of the plant, left with one other to man it. "I don't think," he said, "K.C. Irving likes anyone to tell him what to do."

But if the oil workers' strike lent itself to union charges, it also fitted into a more complex context. No part of Irving's career yields less to categorical statement than his relations with unions. Certainly he was dogged by accusations that he was anti-labour. No one ever questioned that he could be tough. But there also were unionists who said good things about him, found him reasonable and conciliatory, *pragmatic*, willing to make a deal if a deal was in the cards. But he could play it both ways, depending on circumstances, trends, personalities: he rolled with the punches. In any negotiations, business or labour, he judged his adversaries, met militance with militance, reason with reason. "Irving," said a man who rose from office boy to executive under him, "wasn't anti-union. He was pro-Irving."

Cyril Robinson's *Standard* article, published shortly after the 1948 strike, noted that Irving had faced three strikes at his veneer plant, others among his bus drivers, and now the one at the oil plant. Angus MacLeod, he said, called Irving "a reactionary." MacLeod called him worse than that. A tough Scot, he once threatened "to chase Irving out of town with the arse out of his pants." He said Irving exploited the people and resources of New Brunswick "with equal impartiality." He dubbed him a "little tin god," said he was "the arch-enemy of the labour movement, a tough union breaker." Once, when Irving was nursing ribs broken in a fall, he negotiated with MacLeod and others for five hours at his bedside. When it was over MacLeod was asked how the patient had behaved. "As well as could be expected," he replied dryly.

The two came into conflict over both the oil strike and the veneer strikes. Other labour leaders who knew him well suspect MacLeod actually had a grudging respect for Irving, "though he would never admit it. Irving, in turn, considered MacLeod a radical, and reacted accordingly. Certainly, MacLeod was a militant, well to the left in the labour spectrum. So was J.K. Bell, a senior unionist in the marine and other trades. In his view, Irving long was "notorious for paying as low as the traffic would bear," a "buccaneer." They had "strained and bitter relations" that led "to a lot of unpleasantness" unrelieved by Irving's "Bible-thumping way of swearing, his Presbyterian profanity." Bell once slept in his car on a rural roadside rather than fill its gas tank at a nearby Irving station.

James Whitebone of Saint John, another top unionist, was much more charitable. He faced Irving often, and said he found him a very fine man who provided a lot of employment. "We don't always get what we want but when we get a contract he sticks to it to the letter. You have to respect any man who provides thousands of jobs."

Apart from Irving's pulpworkers, there were others surprised and pleased when he took over. Stewart Smith was president of the city bus union at the time the long fight over a franchise came to an end. It was shortly after the oil workers' strike when he and his executive were called to Irving's office. They were apprehensive, wondering, scared. But Irving not only accepted their union, he gave them the best raise they had ever had. They came, says Smith, to look upon him as a definite improvement as a boss.

A *Telegraph-Journal* reporter-editor remembered once getting a call from Irving. It was something so rare it astonished him. Irving said he had just concluded an agreement with two union leaders, that they were at a local hotel and had a statement to make. The reporter asked what he wished to say on his own behalf. Irving said the union men would make the only statement. When the reporter went to the hotel, he got an amicable one, then said, "Now let's go off the record. What do you really think of Irving?" One of them, he said, "tore the hide off me for intimating he would talk two ways. They both thought Irving was okay, a joy to deal with."

On an SMT bus running between Edmundston and Fredericton one night, a passenger loudly berated driver Fred Bishop for working for Irving: the pay was poor, the hours long, the company anti-union, and there was no pension at the end of the line. Bishop heard him out, then lashed back. The passenger, he said, didn't know what he was talking about; Irving was an excellent man to work for. Bishop's widow says he never changed his mind.

To such anecdotes were added others that helped explain the loyalty many workers felt for him. Said Earl Emeneau, a big Lunenburg County man who ran many construction jobs: "He made you feel you were part of one big family." Bill Connolly, who left a job driving a hearse to join Irving Oil in 1943 and became its head in Prince Edward Island, told of Irving's reaction when he heard a worker had cancer. Irving wanted to fly him to the Lahey Clinic in Boston. A doctor said it was no use. Four Irvings flew over for the funeral. There are numerous stories like that — stories of finding less onerous work for men who were ailing, of not only tolerating but helping alcoholics by sending them for medical help, or sending men out to find them on a bender and get them out of jail.

Yet the same Irving, said a colleague, could let a good man go rather than raise his pay. He could be irritated when a man who worked all sorts of hours for him said he wanted Sunday off to attend his son's christening. He could expect his plane pilots to sit around for days on end, even through weekends, with nothing to do until he finished his business. "It never seemed to occur to him," one said, "that everybody didn't like to work as much as he did."

There was nothing static about the overall picture of his relations with organized labour. If unions were just starting to creep in in 1948, they grew increasingly strong and resistant to Irving's argument that a Maritimes employer faced limitations, difficulties, and costs because he could not be expected to match national levels. National levels would come in time, in some industries, but it would take years, and the results could be varied.

Irving did not believe he was anti-union, but he did believe there were good unions and bad ones, good union leaders and poor ones. He had no use for a weak union leader or one he couldn't trust. And there were businesses where, in his view, unions had no place. "Some operations shouldn't have a union," he said. "Some businesses are just too hard to run." He also thought there were "certain jobs that require individual initiative." He didn't believe unions encouraged individual initiative. On the other hand, he acknowledged that if a union did its job, it could be very good for the company and for the employees. He also was aware that unions could be made the scapegoat for a company's poor performance. He said a poor boss could blame things on a union, and that was something top management or owners had to have the experience and ability to spot.

People who negotiated with him and for him, remembered him in different ways. Men like MacLeod and Bell abrasively; men like Whitebone, Stewart Smith, and the pulp mill's Charles Lynch approvingly. Government officials saw him as one of a breed, not unlike other employers who knew their case and fought it to the hilt. Douglas Cochrane, for years deputy labour minister in New Brunswick and then Manitoba, said, "Irving was no pushover. He was a tough bargainer but, I think, very fair. When he met a good, able, strong union he accepted it. When he met a weak one he didn't. He was no better and no worse than other employers. Some unions are inflexible, but Irving probably had no more trouble with them than others would have. Capable, thoughtful union leaders respected him, and that's what he deserved because he was able to achieve almost miracles. He paid what he had to. In some low-paying industries, he paid low. In the situations he faced, you couldn't afford to be a pantywaist."

Both Cochrane and Horace Pettigrove, a former labour official with both the New Brunswick and federal governments, harked back to days in non-union plants when they saw women packing clams for seven cents an hour in a ten-hour day. There was none of that oppression with K.C. Irving, Pettigrove said. "Irving was a hard-headed businessman, and there are millions like him. People were loyal to him because he deserved it. And he was an angel compared to some employers I've known. There were a lot of bastards around when he started. You talk about exploitation; it was terrible."

Dr. Colin Mackay who, as a Saint John lawyer, participated in labour negotiations on Irving's behalf, found him "a superb negotiator" and felt union leaders had "a great respect for him." Lawyer Yves Pratte of Montreal saw him as "a great negotiator because of his charm and knowledge. He'd never say 'no' in a way that said 'I have the key.' He convinced people that he couldn't be as bad as he was reputed to be."

As a veteran of labour negotiations for both management and unions, Pratte agreed with Cochrane and Pettigrove on one point:

"I have seen employers a lot worse than K.C. Irving." Pratte represented him on numerous occasions and found that, though clearly Irving would have preferred to have no unions, he wasn't unrealistic. When a union was in, Pratte saw no evidence that he wanted to destroy it. Overall, Pratte saw him within the context of his times: "It's a matter of generations. It's not fair to isolate him. In his early days there were no unions. An employer could do what he liked. I could see that it was difficult for him to adjust later, to abdicate authority to unions. But he was typical of his generation."

Pratte remarked on something noted by others too: that Irving never went into labour or other negotiations without first reading slowly through a proposed contract. It could be painful to wait while he did it, but when he was through he had mastered the document thoroughly. To that precise preparation he added something else when negotiations began. His remarkable memory let him recall, word for word, clause for clause, usually in a quiet, unraised voice, what opponents or a contract said, even years before. And, more than one participant remembered, he was always right.

Union troubles were occurring at the time in 1948 when Irving decided to relocate his Saint John veneer plant in Pembroke, Ontario. He said Angus MacLeod wanted more money than he could afford to pay. Some unionists say Irving himself created the issue, that he had already decided to move the plant, making the union look like a villain for chasing an industry out of New Brunswick. But Lloyd Yeo, then a union vice-president, said MacLeod used poor judgment in starting an illegal strike.

Whatever the facts, it was the culmination of years of labour problems at the veneer plant, during the war and after — years of bitterness, struggles within union ranks, illegal walkouts, hard bargaining, and the intervention of government conciliators bent on keeping vital wartime production going. When contract negotiations reached an impasse in 1940 Ottawa stepped in and brought about a settlement. Three years later union members struck for more money and kept on striking even though their own president branded it "illegal and wildcat." James Whitebone, then head of the Canadian Congress of Labour in New Brunswick, urged the strikers to abide by a pledge that there would be no wartime strikes in essential industries. Horace Pettigrove, as a federal official, said only a return to work would lead to further contract discussions. The men succumbed but demanded a new election of their own officers.

The strife kept right on into peace, with walkouts, union charges of company discrimination, a provincial Labour Relations Board finding that there was none, and a month-long strike in 1946 that the company called illegal. Now, too, the company was being harassed by the die-back disease and by a lack of orders. There were layoffs, shutdowns. One shutdown, for a month, was attributed to a shortage of logs and rail cars.

It had become obvious to Irving that New Brunswick could no longer supply the yellow birch needed by the plant. It had also become obvious that the disease that killed them had not affected stands west of the St. Lawrence. He began looking for a new source of supply. The search took him first to northwestern Ontario, to the Sault Ste. Marie area. He and Aimé Gaudreau snowshoed through bitter winter weather to see for themselves. The land was not what they wanted.

Then word came that the answer might lie in Ontario's Algonquin Park west of Pembroke. Robert McMillan, then living in Ontario, said he drew it to Irving's attention because he was still interested in the company. Irving and Gaudreau put their snowshoes back on and went into another wilderness.

This time they were satisfied. The lumbering rights were owned by the Odenback firm of Rochester, New York. Irving bought them and formed Hogan Lake Timber Ltd. to supply a new plant. He got land in Pembroke, but his problems were not over. His plans progressed, halted, progressed again as Britain cut down on orders and sought veneers where it could get them most cheaply. In Pembroke itself there was controversy. There were those who wanted the employment the plant would provide, but some looked on it with distaste. A civic plebiscite finally decided the issue in Irving's favour.

Still, it was November 1951 before Canada Veneers was back in operation, with a $7-million British order to make it possible. It would go on from there and it would do well. Irving was often there. He would fly to Pembroke, then on to Dexter to keep in touch with these most distant of his operations. But in time he sold Dexter Sulphite because troubles arose over getting pulpwood there from Quebec. There were objections to dumping it into Lake Ontario and to driving it up the Black River. Because the alternatives were too costly, he said, he decided to sell. Did he make money when he did? "Yes," he smiled, "we did quite well."

CHAPTER FOURTEEN

🐾

Chances in the Air

"He'd fly when it wasn't fit for a dog. If he was going, he was going."

— PILOT JIMMY WADE.

K C. IRVING FLEW A LOT. HE LIKED TO SIT BESIDE THE PILOT. Sometimes, in the air, he took over himself. He bought a lot of planes: the Stinson, which he gave to the government during the war, then other amphibians, a Grumann Goose, which he bought from the government after the war; a larger Mallard capable of taking ten passengers; a Beaver, a tough little bush plane he got from Fred Pirie. He bought a big DC-3, one of the workhorse Dakotas, brought it from Mesopotamia and reassembled it. Eventually he had a fleet of them headquartered at Saint John's airport under a company of their own, Irving Oil Transport Ltd. Still other planes were purchased to spray forests and fight forest fires.

Planes intrigued him. Dr. Colin Mackay, a Saint John lawyer and one-time president of the University of New Brunswick, told of flying back from London to New York with him and seeing Henry Ford III's private jet parked at LaGuardia Airport. Irving went over, introduced himself to the crew and had a happy time inspecting it. He soon had one of his own.

Irving took his chances in the air. Pioneer pilot Jimmy Wade recalled: "He'd fly when it wasn't fit for a dog. If he was going, he was going." Wade was Irving's personal pilot for years, but he was more than that. He also looked after maintenance and mechanical details. Other owners of private planes had their own engineers for things like that, and they flew with two pilots, just in case. But Wade was in every sense an oldtime bush pilot and Irving relied on him completely.

Raised in Sussex Corner, N.B., Jimmy Wade didn't use instruments for navigation in his earliest days as a pilot. As a result, he learned to rely on sight, and he survived numerous perils, sometimes with Irving, sometimes alone or with others. On one flight, he and a lone passenger were forced down in woods outside Halifax. An air force search finally spotted and rescued them. Flying out of Charlottetown in December of wartime 1942, he and an American flight engineer crashed in a blizzard in an attempt to rescue an American air force crew that had gone down in Greenland. It took them five days on scanty rations to get ashore in a dinghy. They were rescued by Inuit and spent three months in northern isolation before they got home.

In 1946 Wade was back with Irving, and he put down in Montreal on a routine December flight just when intensive efforts were being made to rescue survivors from a plane forced down in the St. Lawrence. Irving was called and gave approval for Wade to join in. On Christmas Eve Wade found a tiny, clear spot amid dangerous river ice, put down his Grumman Goose and saved three men from a floe.

He was eminently cool under stress. So was Irving. One executive remembers the night their plane flew into a blizzard en route to Dexter. One passenger was praying as they bucked on, looking for something that would guide them into a landing. Others took consolation from hearing Wade and Irving calmly discussing what to do. They made it.

Irving said he didn't remember that one — "There were a lot of them" — but he did remember flying just above the Gulf of St. Lawrence waves on a storm-hassled flight from Newfoundland. He also remembered another close call: "We left Montreal for Toronto after dark and ran into a terrible storm this side of Kingston. It threw all the guidance gear out. We couldn't get signals. After three-quarters of an hour we spotted water and wondered if it was Lake Ontario. We sent out a signal that we were lost. We came down low and suddenly saw a lot of dead trees in a flooded area. We climbed and just got over the trees. Then we saw a clear part of a lake. We got down there, and we were just throwing out the anchor when we heard a *putt-putt-putt*. It was a guide, in a motorboat, a camp care-taker in the woods of the Adirondack mountain country. He took us in. He fed us and slept six of us in one room."

And another time when the ice had gone but there was snow in the woods, when he and Wade were about to take off from Quebec City and Aimé Gaudreau caught up with them. Gaudreau wanted to go see a lumber operation, so they went. They came in over a small lake, a saucer of water rimmed by hills, a rough place for a landing. Said Irving: "We had a lot of baggage. We came down steep. We levelled out but, by gosh, the plane wouldn't land. The wind was undercutting us, and there was just one place to get down, at the outlet of the lake. I told Wade, 'You'd better get her down' because he couldn't get up over the hills again. We hit about seventy-five feet from the shore, just missed a dam and plowed into trees. White birches. The wings hit one and I flew out the door. I landed in the branches of a tree, about ten to twelve feet above the ground, and fell into the snow. It didn't hurt me a bit. It was just like falling in a feather bed. We had to take the wings off but the plane wasn't damaged much. We were about two miles from the lumber camp, so we walked in."

By many accounts, Irving was imperturbable in tight situa-tions, and he could be nettled if flying conditions were borderline and a pilot didn't want to fly. He contended that he never asked a pilot to do things the pilot felt he shouldn't do, but once Wade left Irving he found it harder to get his own way. In the early fifties, he picked Freeman Fleming from dozens of applicants. Wade was a good man to get you out of trouble. Fleming felt that he was a good man to keep you out of trouble.

An aviation veteran, Fleming believed Irving had been "lucky as hell" for years. He wouldn't take risks Irving was used to, risks that had made more than one man refuse to fly with him. He flew by instruments, and found Irving keenly interested. Once his boss took the controls himself, got into cloud, and put the plane into a spiral dive. "Take the damn thing," he said, and never tried instru-ment flying again. But his interest continued. "Gee," he said, "how do you do it?"

Once he got used to it, he felt they could fly anytime. Fleming told him every plane had its own limitations, and he abided by them though at times it wasn't easy. "On the ground," he'd say, "you're the boss, but once that door is closed I am." Sometimes Irving would get angry. He'd say, "I don't mean to pressure you, but there's pressure on me, and I know I do it unconsciously." He was, said Fleming, "a hard man to say no to. You had to dig in your heels. I told him I had to make the right decision every time, that in the air you don't get a second chance. Irving said, 'I never thought of that.'" Irving also said, "That damn Fleming — when he says no, he means it."

Fleming once flew the entire Irving family to Jamaica, and he told Irving they could all have been wiped out if anything had happened to him: "He laughed. It didn't bother him a bit." He urged Irving to fly with a second, reserve pilot, to get a maintenance engineer, radar, and de-icing equipment. It took time, but eventually he got the works.

It was a trying job, Fleming said. He could be called at any hour, was expected to be available seven days a week, and did a lot of waiting: "If I had a dollar for every hour I've waited, I'd be rich." He once flew Irving into Quebec City's airport on a winter's day. They planned only a brief stop to refuel because Irving was in a rush to get to Rimouski. But he said on landing that he had one thing to do and would be back shortly. It was bitterly cold, and the hangars were full. After an hour Fleming started the plane's engine so it wouldn't freeze. He did it again an hour later. He did it every hour from 9:30 a.m. until 10 p.m. Then Irving showed up with an executive for the flight to Rimouski. A one-hour stop had stretched beyond twelve hours.

Irving was contrite. He said he'd leave the next move up to Fleming. Fleming, tired and frustrated, opted to go into Quebec City and take a room for the night. It was the sensible decision, but Irving was boiling mad: "I couldn't help but respect the man in the years I was with him, but there were times when I hated his guts," said Fleming. This was one of them. They drove in strained silence. Then the executive turned to Fleming and asked, "And how was your day?" Before Fleming could answer, Irving exploded: "And why don't you keep your mouth shut?" It broke the ice. They all burst into laughter. But eventually Fleming left.

Irving continued to fly in small planes, in helicopters, on commercial airlines, and in the most modern of corporate jets with a succession of pilots, but his fondest memories were of those early days dating back to his training during the First World War and the years with Jimmy Wade.

CHAPTER FIFTEEN

❧

The Power of Dollars

*"Governments those days would do almost anything
to get industry. A dollar bill looked as big as a horse
blanket."*
– R.A. TWEEDIE, LONGTIME ASSISTANT TO NEW BRUNSWICK
PREMIERS, EXPLAINING THE POLITICAL PHILOSOPHY
OF HIS TIME.

IN 1951, THE YEAR IRVING OPENED HIS NEW VENEER PLANT
in Pembroke, he gave his Saint John Sulphite Ltd. mill a new
name, Irving Pulp and Paper Ltd., and launched a $20-million
expansion of the mill overlooking Saint John's famous Reversing
Falls. This had numerous ramifications. He needed steel for the
construction, and steel was hard to get. He spoke to Fred Pirie,
then a senator, and Pirie arranged an interview with C.D. Howe.
Irving told the powerful federal minister that he needed steel.
Howe said there was none available in Canada but there was some
in West Germany. Irving went there and made another deal. This
time he swapped pulp for steel.

Then construction troubles developed with the steel, and he
went back to the company that had provided it. It sent out a
young, university-trained engineer named Hans Klohn, who six
years before had been one of those thousands of mere youths and
old men Hitler rushed into uniform to defend the Third Reich in
the last days of its grotesque life. He was tough and demanding,
workers say, until one of them, a war veteran, told him he was

behaving like a tyrant and he cooled his ways. But he got things done. The steel problems were licked, and the construction itself became folklore. Irving wanted the additions made without disturbing the twenty-four-hours-a-day production of the mill already there, and it was done. Office workers got used to doing their jobs while steel arose around them, to seeing the space converted to new uses. Irving's sons were there, watching, working. Irving himself was frequently there, arguing with engineers, propounding his ideas, saying this could better be done that way. Once he went to use a mobile outhouse and was beaten to it by an employee who didn't know, or care, who he was. Irving grinned and told a witness he was happy to accommodate a man in such a hurry to get back to work.

Even before construction began there were problems. In county and provincial political ranks, there were contentious debates over the concessions Irving sought. In the preliminary rounds, he made proposals, retreated politely before rebuffs and came back again and again: he simply wore them down. The agreements he finally sought included special rates for the 25 million gallons of water the mill would swallow daily, a fixed annual tax of $35,000 for five years, $45,000 for the next ten years, $55,000 for the ten after that, powers of expropriation, freedom from action founded on nuisance, the right to change watercourses, and the right to discharge refuse into the St. John River at its dramatic site beside the Reversing Falls.

Irving said he needed the rights to ensure that the expanded sulphite mill would survive and prosper — rights and powers given similar projects in the past. It was hardly an exaggeration. The explanation lay in an alliance between politicians desperate for industry and businessmen striking hard bargains in making it available. But Irving did seek a legal shield that none of the other industrial giants had received — exemption in law, except by special government permission, from injunctions and suits for such "nuisances" as noise, air, and water pollution. Irving argued that such powers were needed, and he said he had considered other sites in St. Stephen and Grand Falls but had decided on Saint John because its economic needs were foremost in his mind. A lot of trouble in the province and city was due to lack of industry. Somehow industry must be found, he said, and this was a start.

There were hot protests and rejoinders in the county council, in the Legislature, in crowded meetings of its corporations committee. There were amendments. A school tax of $10,000 a year for twenty years was added. The right to expropriate lands "generally for and in connection with all the powers and purposes of the company" was removed; the company was, however, given the power to expropriate what "it shall deem necessary or useful," a power that Premier J.B. McNair noted was subject to cabinet approval.

Opposition leader Hugh Mackay and others raised questions about both the expropriation powers and the right to discharge wastes. In committee, the right to dump wastes was eliminated with Irving's approval, though his lawyer had earlier said "it would be well to have the authority," even though the dumping would continue anyway. To complaints about a stench, the company lawyer said the mill would employ "modern methods and keep odours down to a minimum." From the company's managing director, Frank Lang, came a less consoling answer: the mill would smell because there was no way to have it otherwise. In other communities with pulp mills, he added, there were no complaints about the odour because mills meant jobs and prosperity. Lang's comments were as true as they were candid and for decades odours from the mill created controversy in Saint John. The company spent millions upon millions to reduce the problem, though never satisfying those who believed that somehow it should be possible to have the jobs and the benefits without the pulp mill or rotten egg stench that accompanied them.

The bill became law. Years later Don Garey, then clerk of the municipality of Lancaster, site of the mill, contended that in the conditions of the time it was a good deal. Dr. Stephen D. Clark, then a Liberal MLA and a member of the corporations committee, recalled a full and independent study, not simply a surrender to Irving's will.

The enlarged mill gradually took shape, bringing with it more jobs and a marked increase in production. And with this, a repercussion no one foresaw when it all began. In the erection of the high, grey-white walls, square construction panels were used, made in Saint John by an outside firm that had a patent on them. As the work progressed, flaws were detected, flaws that Irving contended made them unsuitable and below contract demands. He sued. The case went to court, and had a sequel that took him into another line of business.

On a Saint John street corner after a day in court, a deal was made. The defendant said he wanted to settle out of court. Irving said he would settle if the price was reduced on the panels already received and if he got the right to produce them in the Maritimes. The defendant accepted his terms.

Irving went into the business of making the panels, and into something much larger. He wanted to get into steel fabrication, the conversion of steel into construction materials. He had found in the energetic Hans Klohn the man he felt could do it for him. Klohn had become a key figure in the expansion of the pulp mill. He was, it turned out, interested in staying in Canada. He could have gone to the United States; he decided to stay with Irving.

From these developments in the 1950s came a new company, Ocean Steel Construction Ltd. (OSCO), which took Irving into the construction business, not only for his own companies but for many others, into work on hospitals, libraries, office buildings, bridges, and numerous other projects. Becoming the largest company of its kind in Atlantic Canada, in turn, it spawned yet another, Strescon Ltd., which took over the making of the panels but concentrated mainly on making and selling pre-stressed concrete.

OSCO started from scratch, Klohn said, with fewer than twenty men. The capital was borrowed, and repaid out of profits. The first headquarters were in a shack in Saint John, and Klohn was the key. "If it weren't for you," Irving told him, "I wouldn't be in this business." He made Klohn, at twenty-eight, a partner with a minority share, and he saw him develop into one of his key executives, the driving boss of both OSCO and Strescon. Klohn went on from there. A man with a contagious smile, he became an Irving family favourite, welcome in their midst, charmed by the hospitality of Mrs. Irving, and Irving's kindnesses. He brought out his wife and children from Germany and settled down. As OSCO and Strescon flourished, he became well-to-do.

As Irving grew in these ways, he became more and more mysterious in his usual public silence. As a child on a trip to Sydney, N.S., he had heard the ticket collector on a public conveyance ask his father if he was four and thus entitled to ride free. The boy intervened to say he was five. The father paid and smiled that this would teach him to keep his mouth shut. Years later an Irving son observed that a trout wouldn't get caught if it did the same. Secrecy was a family trait that became a corporate guideline. It also contributed to the mystique that grew around him, to the problems of Irving watchers in their attempts to unearth what he was up to, and to the rumours that reflected all this.

In his *Gentlemen, Players and Politicians*, Dalton Camp records a conversation on party strategy between Ewart Atkinson, provincial president of the Progressive Conservative party, and speechwriter Ken Carson:

"Look here, Ken, all you have to do is just ask one question: 'What is the secret deal between Liberal premier John McNair and K.C. Irving?' Just ask that question and you'll have those fellows in an uproar."

"What deal are you talking about, Ewart?"

"Never mind what deal. I know what I'm talking about. Just ask that question."

"Ewart, you can't ask a question like that."

"Goddamnit, Ken, why can't you?"

"They aren't going to answer it."

"Of course they aren't, but everybody in New Brunswick is going to be asking themselves, 'What is the secret deal between John McNair and K.C. Irving?' See what I mean?"

In the seventeen years of Liberal rule that began with the Dysart victory of 1935 and continued through the Depression, the war, and into postwar prosperity, it remained a popular conception that Irving was close to Dysart and his successor McNair, that what he wanted he got, that with his high-priced lawyers and economic clout he overwhelmed the flimsy structure of government, the thin and inadequate civil service, and the politicians hungry for the jobs he could create, that he played off one community or county administration against another to get his way.

Allison Dysart once said Irving never asked for favours. McNair was accused of giving the province away to Irving, and later called it nonsense: "Nobody ran my government. Just because he was known to be a Liberal, the Tories used Irving as a target." Robert Tweedie, top assistant to both these premiers, told the same story. He was not a constant shadow over Fredericton. "The premiers never checked things with him. There was no backroom tie. McNair was a tough and opinionated man. He liked Irving very much. He had a desire in general to meet all reasonable requests, but if they were unreasonable he would be tactful, he might seek compromises but he wouldn't yield on the essentials. Dysart was more easy going, a hellishly decent, fine, compassionate man; Lord Beaverbrook called him 'a dear fellow, full of fun.' But there was a point beyond which he wouldn't be pushed.

"At the same time, it was true that Irving was a man with great influence. If he did call, great attention would be paid to what he said. I don't mean that something would be done automatically, but every effort would be made by the premiers to meet his wishes without compromising themselves. The fact is, he made damned few demands. You could go for months and never see or hear from him. He did have something to say on some things but in general not nearly as much as might be thought. Anything done for him would have been done anyway. Governments in those days would do almost anything to get industry. A dollar bill looked as big as a horse blanket. Irving himself told me it was harder to make one in New Brunswick than any place he knew. As far as I was concerned personally, he was one of the great gentlemen."

A rejoinder to this came from Senator F.A. McGrand, a member of the Legislature for seventeen years, health and social services minister under McNair for eight. In his eighties he said, "You heard that Irving snapped his fingers and the government jumped, and I think it was true. He was a taskmaster." Yet McGrand also said that "all I'm going on is gossip," and that "McNair would never be pushed around." He personally had never had any contact with Irving.

Irving denied stories that there was a pattern to his attitude towards the provincial premiers he knew up to 1960 — that he was friendly at first but always came to have a distaste for them when they wouldn't do what he wanted. He once summed up his attitude to them: "Dysart was all right. He never liked trouble, though not to the point of shunning it. He'd clap you on the shoulder and say 'Better do something else.' He was basically a kind man. He liked to be happy. McNair was a good lawyer but he wasn't in the same class with Dysart as a premier."

The long Liberal rule ended with the 1952 election victory of the Progressive Conservatives' Hugh John Flemming, who crossed swords with Irving legally. The legal case arose over a sequel to Irving's purchase of the New Brunswick Railway Company. Flemming's lumber firm bought stumpage rights from him and, after a contractual dispute, settled out of court, getting pretty much what they wanted.

"I have always been a Liberal and usually have voted that way," Irving said, "but good government is the main thing." Without confirming that he fell out with McNair, he found it "a welcome change to have Flemming in power." Flemming was more reserved: "I never congratulated myself that I had his warm sympathy." He added, "You can say this or that about Mr. Irving but he has been a great asset to New Brunswick. You have to admire anyone who devotes his life to building up industry in our province."

During Flemming's time in office, several major developments affecting Irving's forestry operations surfaced. One involved the problems raised for his St. John River log drives by construction of the Beechwood dam between Perth-Andover and Woodstock. It provoked one of those long, tough, relentless fights that marked his career. The second was a start on a reforestation program that would, more than any other thing, bring him warm and widespread praise. The third was the intrusion of foreign interests who proposed to build a newsprint mill at the very time he was planning one himself. It led to another long battle and it became a factor in taking him into yet another line of business — the building of ships.

Beechwood's dam was heralded as a major step to provide power for a province that needed it if it were to attract industry. As such, it was a political plus for Flemming. It was also the first ever built by the provincial government, and Irving said he favoured that sort of thing. The problem, from his standpoint, was what it would do to up to 300,000 cords of wood, pulp, and longer logs for lumber, that came teeming down the St. John every year. By the late 1950s his Saint John sawmill was in operation and his pulp mill was undergoing another expansion. Those logs were vital to both.

The complex issue involved both the provincial and federal governments. The right to drive was covered by the federal Navigable Waters Protection Act, and Ottawa's permission for Beechwood to be built also specified that it must not interfere with logging. To build holding booms for the drive, Irving needed approval from two sources, the federal Department of Public Works and the provincial Department of Lands and Mines. But his main problem arose in conflicts with the New Brunswick Electric Power Commission which built the dam and was armed with broad powers to erect storages and to expropriate.

The Commission did not object to the drive, but in 1954 it asked Irving to do it earlier because it wanted to move the logs through Beechwood sluices and excess water rather than sap power generation with stored water. Irving agreed, and set about planning a holding boom just above Beechwood that would make it possible. A study by Dr. R.A. Young, a New Brunswicker who taught political science at the University of Western Ontario, showed that it was this boom that "became the source of tremendous contention between [Irving and] the Power Commission, which wanted protection of the dam, safety from flooding, minimal expense along with a boom large enough to reconstitute the early upstream drive and hold it until water was low enough at Maugerville for its safe and efficient release." By 1956 Irving decided that he needed a large boom supported by piers driven into the river bottom. He claimed the right to the undiminished flow of the river and he made demands to back it up: sluices that could pass the drive in thirty-six hours; payment of the costs of the boom by the Power Commission and use of its property in building it; the promise to do everything possible to aid passage; a flow of water equal to pre-dam days until the logs reached Maugerville, and the release of more water if that was not enough to do it; no liability for damages except those caused by gross or wilful negligence; liability by the Commission for any expense to Irving due to the dam.

The Commission refused his terms, pondering the threat of 19.2-kilometre log jams smashing through the boom and over the dam, of flooding, and of damage to the dam itself. Its chief engineer fought against any boom at all, but by 1957 Irving was seeking permission to build one. The Commission, in rebuttal, demanded that it be satisfactory to them, that if it held more than 6.4 kilometres of logs it could be released, that in an emergency they could open it, and that they could apply to have the piers removed if the boom caused jams or threatened property.

On this basis, agreement seemed close. The Commission, headed by a member of cabinet, consented to Irving's application to build the boom if it was found acceptable and met their requirements. But the chief engineer worked to ensure that those requirements should be decided by the Commission staff, and his demands helped to bring a decision by Public Works to hold the Irving application in abeyance. The chances of agreement faded, negotiations resumed, and another year passed, with the drive moving through Beechwood in June without much difficulty. For a time it appeared that Irving had let the matter drop, but by that December his men were surveying boom sites again. This time, however, he asked to be allowed to build a smaller boom with cables rather than piers. To this, the Commission's chief engineer agreed, subject to indemnity terms, and it was built.

Still, Irving had his eye on what he had first wanted. He continued to conduct the drive without accounting to anyone or providing any information, inconveniencing the Power Commission. The frustrations mounted. The Commission was sued by Irving, who sought undiminished river flow. Under these circumstances, the Commission began to wonder whether a pier boom might not be preferable to the trouble of dealing with the Irvings. The drives were getting larger and costing the Commission money. Moreover, by 1960 Irving and Commission interests were both expanding and becoming linked by the burning of Irving oil at the latter's Saint John thermal plant.

In this atmosphere Irving came up with his own interpretation of what co-operation might mean: the Commission should pay half the cost of the piers for a new boom. In 1962 Irving and the Commission's manager finally agreed to relieve the government agency of any liability for Irving's equipment and, after further wrangling, to terms over potential damages. The commission accepted. The piers were sunk. The boom was built.

In the six-year struggle Irving had gained the ability to consolidate the drive on land owned by the Commission, free from public complaint. Now he could truck wood to Beechwood from his Maine forests and add it to the main drive. The Commission got no guarantee that water would not be wasted or that the Commission would receive payment for damage to its property. The Commission's managers had come to sympathize with, in their words,

Irving and "the importance of this operation to the New Brunswick economy."

The whole complex issue was chronicled in academic detail by Dr. R.A. Young. His study revealed the level of bitter contention the boom created — and how demanding and persistent Irving could be.

CHAPTER SIXTEEN

❧

Softwood Will *Grow on a Hardwood Ridge*

"Mr. Irving, those trees are just not going to grow."
– *FORESTRY EXPERT BARNEY FLIEGER'S WARNING AT THE START OF IRVING'S MASSIVELY SUCCESSFUL REFORESTATION PROGRAM.*

BARNEY FLIEGER DIDN'T WANT TO ARGUE WITH K.C. IRVING, but a principle was involved. A professional principle.

Flieger was a professional forester, a former dean of forestry at the University of New Brunswick, an expert in the field. He knew when and where trees would grow, and he was convinced Irving would fail to grow softwood trees on hardwood ridges. "Mr. Irving," he said, "those trees are not going to grow."

"Well now, Mr. Flieger," said Irving, "I think they will. In fact, I'm sure they will, but we're just going to have to wait and see." He liked Flieger. "He was a good chap," Irving would say many years later, "but he was wrong."

The discussion took place in the early days of K.C. Irving's pioneering reforestation program, and Flieger wasn't alone in questioning it. In fact, the trick in those days was finding someone who didn't, even outside New Brunswick.

Flieger was so sure the program was doomed he said he would eat his textbooks if it succeeded. Armand Côté had no college degree and no textbooks to eat, but he agreed with Flieger. Côté had spent much of his life in the woods and he wondered why

Irving wouldn't listen to reason. He remembered standing on a northern ridge where hardwoods had grown, where Irving was transplanting baby softwoods. Like many others, he thought Irving was living in a dream world.

In 1957 Irving owned millions of trees in New Brunswick alone, and it was in that year that he made a historic decision. It was time, he decided, to start planting more. The beginning of his reforestation program coincided with the Beechwood battle, steady expansion of his oil business, arrangements to form corporate alliances with two international giants, and plans to build the oil refinery he had wanted for years. It came at a time when he was planning to broaden the base of his forest operations and get into newsprint.

Reaction to his reforestation plan was not long in coming. It ranged from scepticism to ridicule. The experts said he was wrong and suggested he should stick to things he knew. At the start of what would later be hailed as one of the greatest pioneering steps in forest management in Canada, Irving stood virtually alone. The experts said reforestation was too costly, that it was best to leave the forests to Mother Nature. They said it was wrong to put a single species where variety had grown. They said governments and forest companies should combat fires, control cutting, do something about insect depredations, and leave the rest to nature. It was in this strained atmosphere of disagreement, opposition, and ridicule that Barney Flieger made his long-remembered boast that he would eat his textbooks if Irving proved to be right.

The scepticism didn't bother Irving. To him, at the beginning and later, it was simple: "It had to be done if we wanted any forest at all." He had seen what the budworm did to Kent County. By 1957 a new infestation in New Brunswick had been fought for five years with aerial spraying by chemicals and showed no signs of relenting. His own pulp mill was absorbing millions of trees a year, and he saw the budworm as a deadly threat to continuation of that supply alone. He went ahead with reforestation and he would say his one regret was that he hadn't started twenty years earlier.

Time would bring Irving recognition and honours. But it would take years for other New Brunswick companies to follow him, twenty years for the provincial government to start a major reforestation program of its own. Armand Côté would admit he was wrong. Barney Flieger would admit handsomely that he was, too.

Irving's program started small, in a harsh northern climate, on that hardwood ridge at Black Brook in the watershed of the Restigouche. It was an experiment that was recalled years later by the then chief Irving forester, Frank Barkhouse. He, Irving, and Irving's son Jim saw 3,000 infant softwoods go into the ground. Within a year Irving made it clear that he would go far beyond that modest beginning. He sounded out expert opinion on the soil he wanted. He bought more land and opened a nursery near Juniper. On a tributary of the Miramichi he started with a small, cleared plot that would grow into hundreds of acres.

The whole process — from seed to baby trees, replanted at Juniper when they were big enough, replanted again to the north in four years — became a passion with him. He gave up fishing entirely. Guests might get out a canoe and angle in the Restigouche. He vanished into the woods, to the neat, growing ranks of transplanted softwoods, driving or tramping about, pruning limbs, talking to his workers, making suggestions, changes. He'd stay until dark, and once got angry when people came looking for him long after nightfall. People told him he was covered with mosquito and fly bites. He was oblivious to them. Armand Côté said they were working together one hot day and the flies were so thick he said, "Mr. Irving, they're going to eat us." Irving didn't answer. He kept on going.

He was happy in his element. His forests were so vast that you could look for miles from a hill and everything you saw was his. He got to know them like the back of his hand, got to know the white spruce and black spruce and red spruce, the balsam fir, the white and yellow birch, the maple and tamarack and hemlock, their strengths and frailties. He knew the fir was what the budworm liked best and should get less of. He knew the white spruce would grow fast but was also vulnerable, the red spruce could be caught by frost, the tall, skinny black spruce was the least susceptible to the budworm but tended to grow with agonizing slowness in low, wet areas. He put black spruce in hollows and planted white spruce higher up. He cut down standing trees, tens of thousands a year, for pulp and lumber, cleared the ground with great, crushing machines that created a landscape like something from the barren reaches of the moon.

Félice Poitras recalled seeing the result and being appalled. Five years later he saw the same land, and wondered at the change, at the green, healthy Juniper-raised trees growing there. It got to the point, in time, when J.D. Irving Ltd.'s transplanting followed hard on the heels of the cutting, and before long the transplants of various species numbered not in the thousands but the millions every year.

And every year Irving built more roads. Straight. Like arrows through the wilderness. Every summer he brought in hundreds of people by bus from as far away as Edmundston, and they moved in line, so far apart, each stopping at a given distance to stuff more baby trees into the earth, the distances varying in an experiment to find the best. He brought others into the Juniper nursery to plant and transplant there. He built a large sawmill at Veneer Siding. In time, his company opened another nursery, at Sussex in the southern part of the province.

Through the years he preached one key message about refor-estation. The cooks at his lodge had to get used to serving meals at all hours, never knowing when Irving and his latest visitors would show up, such was his obsession in showing them about, in propounding his views on conservation. He entertained premiers, cabinet ministers, foresters, big businessmen, even a vice-president of the United States. Hubert Humphrey came in the 1960s, and was involved in a comic incident. He was accompanied by a large group of secret servicemen, and early one morning they all came out of the lodge with its big stone fireplace, rows of guest rooms, and view of the junction of the Restigouche and a tributary brook. They were going fishing, and just as they came smiling forth a plane came roaring down the river, low, spewing mist. Pilot Freeman Fleming remembered their consternation, the bodyguards grabbing their revolvers, ducking for cover, pulling Humphrey down to secure the well-being of the second-highest figure in the greatest nation on earth. In fact, the pilot had designs only on the insects that might spoil the vice-president's day, but no one had remembered to tell either Humphrey or his bodyguards.

There were, over the years, many guests at the Irving lodge. One was the chairman of the board of a huge American paper company. He went about with Irving and started to do some figuring. Finally he said he had concluded that reforestation could never pay for itself in Irving's lifetime. Irving replied that he was right, and added that reforestation was an investment in the future.

He took pride in showing guests around his forests, in having groups of children come. He gave them young trees to plant around their schools. He put up signs that said what species were planted, bearing the name of the foreman who oversaw it. On tours Irving would say which plot was coming up next and who had supervised its planting, never making a mistake.

He enjoyed the company of his workers. One evening a group of guests were sitting down to dinner when a foreman passed the windows of his lodge on the Restigouche. Irving called him in and pulled out a chair for him to join the group. The foreman was in his shirtsleeves. Irving took off his coat too, out of courtesy, then got the man to tell what he'd done that day, what kind of trees he'd planted, and why each species had its own place.

He joined in the campaign of Forest Protection Ltd., financed jointly by government and business, which fought the budworm with spray, and he got planes of his own to supplement Forest Protection's work. His foresters came to say his woodlands did much better than others because he sprayed more of them.

New critics emerged — environmentalists and others concerned about potential health hazards from the spraying, people who said the budworm remained as vigorous as ever despite years of it, that spraying interfered with nature's better way of taking care of the budworm. Irving remained a hard-core believer. He stood with those who argued that New Brunswick forests would become a mere shadow without the spraying programs.

In 1970 he joined with the province's resources minister W.R. Duffie in planting the 26-millionth tree on Black Brook hill where it all began. By then reforestation covered 30,000 acres, the Juniper nursery was producing up to 5 million trees a year, and Irving said the figure would be further increased in the future. He had already spent $3 million on the work, was planting 1,000 trees an acre, and his foresters said he could expect to reap four times as much wood as nature would provide — and he would do it in half the time.

By 1974 the Irvings were planting 12 million trees a year and took part in another ceremony marking the planting of the 60-millionth tree. He was planning to boost the program to 20 million trees a year, since the budworm was devastating trees in millions every year. As he put it, "saying we should learn to live with it makes about as much sense as saying we should learn to live with the plague." Two years later Irving planted his 100-millionth tree. By then Irving's reforestation covered 20,235 hectares, and the firm that still bore his father's name was planting 15 million trees a year. In another fifteen to twenty years, Irving said, the trees planted in 1957 should be ready for harvesting.

Above: James Durgavel Irving:
K.C.'s father was the Liberal in
Bouctouche in the early 1900s.

❧

Top left: Mary Gifford Irving: She
was a strong influence on her son.

❧

Left: Young Kenneth, circa 1902: He
would be earning his own money
within three years of this portrait.

The first car K.C. bought and sold —
even before he was in his teens.

&

K.C. at Acadia University in 1917.
He would soon leave to join the
Royal Flying Corps.

K.C., 19, poses for a rare studio portrait — probably for his mother.

Above: K.C. (far left) with Royal Flying Corps buddies at Tadcarter, Yorkshire, England, in 1918.

❧

Left: K.C. in the cockpit of the First World War's famous Sopwith Camel.

❧

Below: A bowler-hatted K.C. (standing, far left) at a 1926 Ford sales meeting.

K.C. with his eldest son Jim in 1929.

Jack (4), Jim (8), and Arthur (6): soon all three would be selling magazines, eggs, and chickens.

One of the original Irving tower design service stations, built in Moncton in the 1930s.

K.C.'s vast transportation system had a modest start in the 1920s.

Pilot Jimmy Wade (far left) and K.C. (centre) walked away when this plane crashed and burned in an airport takeoff in 1952.

ON THIS SITE WILL BE
ERECTED A NEW ARTS BUILDING
TO PROVIDE LECTURE ROOMS,
LABORATORIES AND OFFICES
FOR THE HUMANITIES AND SOCIAL
SCIENCES. FUNDS FOR THIS
BUILDING WILL BE PROVIDED BY
CORPORATIONS AND FRIENDS
THROUGHOUT CANADA AND THE
GOVERNMENT OF THE PROVINCE
OF NEW BRUNSWICK.

THE SOD-TURNING CEREMON
ON MAY 14TH, 1959, MARKS
FIRST STEP IN THE REALIZ
OF THIS MUCH NEEDED
TO THE UNIVERSITY'S FA

TELEGRAPH-JOURNAL

K.C. was sixty when he turned the sod for an arts building at the University of New Brunswick.

ža

That Doomed Canal

"It was one of the greatest mistakes Canadians ever made."

– K.C. IRVING ON CANADA'S REJECTION OF FREE TRADE WITH
THE UNITED STATES IN THE FEDERAL ELECTION OF 1911.

ON A SUMMER'S DAY IN 1957 CANADA'S "MINISTER OF everything," C.D. Howe, visited Saint John to campaign for a return to power of the Liberal regime that had governed in Ottawa for twenty-two years. He asked Irving to drive him to the airport, and on the way he asked a question: "Do you really think a Chignecto Canal would do much for the Maritimes?"

"I most certainly do," Irving replied, and cited reasons why.

"Then," said Howe, "I'm going to do something about it. I'm going to get at it."

In that corner of Irving's mind where the reforestation program was born, none of his hopes surpassed in intensity that for a Chignecto Canal. He argued for years, indeed still argued in his eighties, that it would do big things, that without it the Maritimes could never return to the prosperity of their Golden Age. It was one of those dreams that led sceptics to see Maritimers as a sort of permanent lobby against the will of God. God made Cape Breton an island; but Maritimers linked it to mainland Nova Scotia with a causeway opened in 1955. God made Prince Edward Island what it was; they sought a link to New Brunswick. God created the

18-mile-wide Chignecto isthmus and they sought to cut through it and convert Nova Scotia into an island just at its border with New Brunswick.

No one sought it more ardently than Irving. It became a passion, one of two major things that he was certain would bring boon and benefit to the Maritimes, if only Ottawa could be convinced. If only Ottawa would do something. One dream was a Chignecto Canal. The other was free trade with the United States.

He remembered a night in 1911 when, as a boy of twelve, he saw a bonfire light up the Bouctouche night in celebration of a political victory. The nation as a whole, in one of the decisive elections of its history, had chosen a Conservative government. With it died the fifteen-year rule of Prime Minister Sir Wilfrid Laurier and something else Irving would mourn for many years: the immediate prospect of free trade with the United States, the central issue of the campaign in English-speaking Canada.

"It was," he said many years later, "one of the greatest mistakes Canadians ever made." He looked out a window as at some lost and distant thing, then elaborated: "It was terrible that we lost it. We've never gotten over it down here. We cast aside, for the Maritimes, our natural market in New England, tens of millions of people on our doorstep." He sat for a moment thinking what that might have meant to him alone, and his mind went all the way back to those Model T Fords he'd sold in the twenties. With free trade, he said, he could have sold them for $80 to $90 less than the $385 he charged.

Irving never had those opportunities but he did live long enough to see Free Trade become a reality, and long enough to see his sons and his grandsons moving swiftly and dramatically to penetrate those very markets that he had eyed so enviously and so covetously more than half a century earlier. But it was the canal that captivated him most of all and that illuminated two salient aspects of his career. In the first place, Irving might well have attracted broader support if he had been able to convince more people that he sought the canal for reasons wider than his own personal interests. Secondly, he faced what for him had been virtually a lifetime of frustration in dealing with what he considered a cold, indifferent, and heartless national capital.

New Brunswick's layers of government he could contend with, at times to his considerable success. Ottawa remained difficult, aloof, largely indifferent, grown too big as the years went by to pay much heed to the Maritimes. Soon after John Diefenbaker's Progressive Conservatives turfed out the Liberals in that election of 1957, effervescent trade minister George Hees came to Saint John, and a reception was held for him. Irving and his sons showed up, got him aside and gave him their Chignecto Canal pitch. Toronto's Hees grinned his spacious grin, patted Irving on the knee and said, "You're all right, K.C."

It was, for Irving, the voice of Ottawa, a capital where he was never really at home. Some who know its rituals and ways say he was uncomfortable in lobbying Ottawa — he did not use his Liberal connections and his Liberal background in the many years that the Liberals were in power. Ned Bosse, executive assistant to New Brunswick's spokesmen in the Liberal cabinets from 1935 to 1957, said Irving came to him only to discuss business problems, and then not often, and he "came as a businessman, not as a Liberal." Wes Stuart, long a Liberal MP from New Brunswick, remembered Irving telling him he'd sat in the Commons gallery, wanting to see him but unwilling to send a message during a debate in which Stuart seemed interested. Although Irving spoke only of C.D. Howe with warmth and approval among the many ministers of his time, he saw Ottawa as an instrument for the projection of the will of central Canada, and as a source of difficulties for the Atlantic provinces. It was Ottawa that frustrated his shipping plans, that owned the intractable CNR, that hounded him over his media ownership, his oil business, and other ventures. "Why," he asked, white-faced, "would they do these things to me?"

As a supreme practitioner of private enterprise, he was typical of a breed that tended to see all governments as necessary expressions of the public will that nonetheless took in tax money that private enterprise might well put to better use. He spoke for lower tariffs, for a long-range shipbuilding policy, against tight money and high interest rates, against shipping and energy policies. He called for lower freight rates, for incentives that would enable manufacturers to operate within New Brunswick and reach the markets of central Canada at a competitive price. As inflation gathered strength, he argued that it was not a problem created in the Maritimes and that a national policy to combat it might only add to their chronic unemployment. Above all, he said, Ottawa must not kill incentive with high taxation.

He accumulated in time a litany of grievances against Ottawa. "After 1911," he said, "they didn't have much use for us down here. Most of our troubles are man-made by government. They have done some rough things to us. You might well wonder what their real aim has been for the Maritimes. You can say what you want, but if they didn't discourage industry they were damned indifferent to it."

Irving worried about whether Canada's welfare system, government aid, subsidies, and grants to industries were killing personal initiative. The Irvings accepted government assistance when it was available, but they said they would never launch or expand an industry simply to get a grant. They took government aid, as Irving's son Arthur said, because it was there and competitors were taking it. Still, Arthur said, government intervention in the economy fouls things up. It interfered with competition in which only the fit should survive. He could rattle off name after name of industries that had been stimulated or expanded with government encouragement, only to flounder and die. In 1963 his father said: "I don't believe in government subsidies except as a short-term stopgap or in very special cases."

He appeared more than a few times before government appointed bodies and parliamentary committees. But he and his sons could also be difficult for government to work with, to get facts and figures from. The Irvings considered it a waste of valuable time to appear before official inquiries. Given this background and the ever-increasing growth of bureaucracy, Irving's answer might have been anticipated when Prime Minister Diefenbaker asked him to preside over a study of the civil service and government functions. Diefenbaker was put out, however, when he was turned down. "I'm not qualified," Irving said, and that was that. If the study had ever come to pass, it is not difficult to suspect the conclusions would have been an exercise in mutual dismay.

Everything Irving got, he fought for. He fought for the Chignecto Canal, and lost. He came to believe that the goal came closest in that 1957 chat with C.D. Howe and felt a Howe back in office would have had the power and the vision to see that the canal was built. But Howe went down to personal defeat that year, retreated to his summer home in St. Andrews, N.B., and told friends, "I'm just another beaten politician."

Even so, it was in the Diefenbaker years that the Chignecto Canal campaign reached its height, with Irving at its centre. He served on a committee dedicated to the cause, as he had on one that laid its case before the previous Liberal cabinet. He appeared at public functions, usually as a silent but potent presence. He even made a Board of Trade speech, an event so rare that not everyone who wanted to could get in. He tramped and flew over the Chignecto area, poked about the remnants of an earlier dream, an abortive, nineteenth-century project that partially built a ship's railway where a canal would be.

He converted Fredericton publisher Michael Wardell to the cause, encouraged him in his close ties with Diefenbaker, and saw him become a zealous advocate. He financed an office and a study by two economists who in 1960 spelled out why a canal was feasible and the benefits it would bring. He got to know the background of a proposal history had caressed and thrust aside.

As far back as 1686, an Intendant of what is now New Brunswick had recommended it. In 1783, the year the Loyalists arrived in their thousands, a British engineer touted its advantages. In the backroom bargaining over the terms of Confederation in the mid-1860s, it was held out as bait to get Maritimers to agree. A flux of reports, studies, and speeches proclaimed it sensible.

Building on all this, the two economists said a canal had been declared by a royal commission to be technically and climatically feasible. They accepted this, and reinforced it with arguments Irving would use himself. The canal, they noted, would open a shipping passage between the Bay of Fundy and the St. Lawrence heartland hundreds of miles shorter than the existing sea route around Nova Scotia. It would cost, engineers had estimated, $90 million, yet would stimulate a permanent $280-million increase in annual production of the Atlantic provinces. It would be a natural extension of the new St. Lawrence Seaway, "linking it with a sheltered route for Atlantic coastal shipping," extending for hundreds of miles the range of Great Lakes-type ships, "which would be cheaper to build and to operate than the ships normally used in ocean travel." It would present no obstacle to potential tidal power developments in the Bay of Fundy and would foster trade down the east coast of the United States. The revenues it would generate could more than offset the net cost to the country. And it would directly create more than $105 million in new industries in the Fundy area.

No greater or more immediate argument surpassed the last, and Irving was almost exclusively its source. It arose, recalled Dr. W.Y. Smith, then economic adviser to New Brunswick's Premier Flemming, during a discussion of tactics. Irving, he said, passionately wondered "how I can put this thing across. We've allowed ourselves to be pushed around. A canal was promised to us. Now how are we going to get it?" The problem, Smith told him, was that they didn't have the dollars. "If we say we're going to put up some money, it could help convince Ottawa." Wardell volunteered Irving's help and, after initial hesitation, Irving went along.

Out of this came his pledge to invest $100 million in industrial development if the canal was built. It made headlines, but its impact was curbed by two factors. Only $5 million more was pledged by other sources, and this tended to put the focus on Irving as the chief champion and chief beneficiary. Secondly, he never said publicly what industry he would build.

Still, it attracted Diefenbaker, that Saskatchewan populist who, more than any prime minister of the past, favoured federal spending to bolster the outlying regions of Canada. He was said to be very impressed by Irving's sincerity. How many times, he asked someone, "have you seen the Maritimes promise to spend money if government money is spent on them?" A Maritime journalist who knew him well said Diefenbaker indicated to him that he came close to building the canal, but would never say why he didn't. Hugh John Flemming, who became a Diefenbaker cabinet minister, told much the same story.

There were probably various reasons why Diefenbaker didn't. They included the opposition of Halifax, the concentration of support largely along the Fundy coast alone, and the attitude of Maritimers who feared that the costs of a canal would lessen their chances of getting other things. But the major reason was probably a report presented to him by Public Works Minister David Walker, a close friend and confidant. It was written by a native Maritimer, Dr. Ernest Weeks, who, at the government's request, made a lengthy study and came to a simple — and devastating — conclusion: the canal would not generate the shipping and other economic activity that would justify its cost.

The campaign for the canal suffered another blow in 1961 when Irving abandoned his $100-million pledge. He got into a fight with the City of Saint John over another matter entirely and said the frustrations of doing business there were so great that he had considered pulling up stakes altogether. In any event, his offer to invest in industrial expansion was cancelled.

When Diefenbaker was questioned, he said no specific commitment from Irving had come his way. Irving promptly wrote to the deputy minister of public works to explain that it would have been unwise to spell out his plans. He added: "If and when the government decides to build the canal, I shall be glad to review, in the light of the circumstances then existing, my plans for industrial development." Eight years later he told a Commons committee that his pledge "still stands, but time is running out as far as I'm concerned."

For the canal, in fact, time had already run out. The fight sputtered on after the government rejection, but it got nowhere. Irving never did say publicly what industry he would have built, but there were various hints. In 1976 his son Arthur said a steel mill and other industries would have sprung up around a canal, and Irving himself once said privately he'd have built a flour mill in Saint John to take advantage of the western grain brought down by Great Lakes ships. He came to regret his 1961 cancellation of his pledge and to suspect that it might have damaged the cause unnecessarily. He also said he did once privately tell Diefenbaker what industries he would build.

Even after hopes for the canal vanished, he kept the faith. In 1963 he told an interviewer that opponents "can't envision the great change" a canal would work in the economy. When, in 1975, he was given an award as New Brunswick's Developer of the Year, he said, "I could only be more gratified had a federal government with vision built the Chignecto Canal in my lifetime." A year later, when he was made an honorary life member of the Saint John Construction Association, he said it was needed "if we are going to regain our former dominant position in water transportation."

By then the government's fat file on the canal had disappeared into the obscurity to which history had condemned it. But in the 1980s something happened that reinforced its advocates' belief that, if it had been a central Canadian project, it would have been built: Ottawa cancelled a debt worth well over half a billion dollars for a St. Lawrence Seaway that had never paid its way.

One of the imponderables of Irving's life and times lurks in the question of whether Ottawa and the Maritime provinces missed a rich opportunity when a Chignecto Canal was rejected. For the most intensive aspects of the campaign coincided with probably the most dynamic phase of his career.

As he neared and entered his sixties, he pushed his oil business to new horizons, built the oil refinery he had wanted for years, used it as a springboard for expansion into allied fields, bought a shipyard and went into shipbuilding, expanded his pulp production into a new line, planned a newsprint mill, bought into New Brunswick's last English-language newspaper that he didn't already own, got into mining on a major scale. Whatever talents, momentum, and genius were inherent in the man, they came to flower then. Saint John became known nationally as a boom town, and he was the heart of the boom. He dealt with international corporate giants, making pacts with two of them. He fought a third in one field, then made a pact with it in another. Even without the projects his $100-million canal pledge might have produced, he did striking things. What further impact he might have had if a canal had been built will never be known.

CHAPTER EIGHTEEN

❧

The Refinements of Oil

"No matter how dirty your hand was he'd take it."
– *CONSTRUCTION FOREMAN EARL EMENEAU REMEMBERING THE*
YEARS HE WORKED FOR IRVING IN NEWFOUNDLAND.

AS IRVING REACHED THE SIXTIES AND A TIME OF DRAMATIC
expansion, his commercial and industrial involvement in
his adopted city was overpowering. By 1960 Irving was
responsible for well over half of the $144 million that was being,
or just had been, spent on new projects. He had done much to
make Saint John the twelfth or thirteenth industrial city in Canada.
On a per capita basis, Saint John ranked very near the top: Toronto
and Montreal did not exceed it and Vancouver stood well behind.

When Irving opened his oil refinery in Saint John, it was the
culmination of a long dream, of long, complex corporate bargaining and thirty-five years of building a network of outlets that
would sell what it produced. The number had grown from two in
1925 to 3,000. They were so numerous in the Maritimes that one
American visitor remarked that his filling stations, with their red,
white, and blue colours and the Irving name prominent, more
than anything else made her feel she was in a different country.
They were, in fact, selling just about as much oil and gas as Imperial in the three provinces, and there were scores more in Newfoundland and Quebec.

Irving had renewed his interrupted invasion of Newfoundland with its return to competition on entering Canada, and construction of a section of the Trans-Canada Highway across its rocky ribs made it a more attractive place to be. When construction foreman Earl Emeneau started to work in Newfoundland in 1953, "Irving had nothing there, so we started building, and we built steadily." Emeneau was there for ten years, living in a trailer, supervising as many as thirteen projects at once, with more than 100 men. In each community, he said in his Lunenburg County accent, he did what he did for twenty-five years with Irving: he found out what the going wage was, and paid it. Irving never complained, never said a word. "He'd leave it to me."

Emeneau's men built bulk tank farms in Cornerbrook, Botwood, Gander, Stephenville, St. John's, and Harbour Grace. In the first, Imperial Oil beat Irving to a lot he wanted, and he had to cut off the top of a hill to get another. In St. John's Emeneau's crews used reinforced concrete to erect tanks "right on the side of a bank" over the water. Emeneau got to know key Irving men. There was young Charlie Van Horne, "a damned nice fella," who spent hours poking through official records so he could acquire land. He remembered live-wire Harrison McCain, Irving Oil's sales manager, who'd "come around laughing and light-hearted." Later Jack Irving took charge of construction after working with Emeneau and others "on a shovel, with sand and cement."

Emeneau came to be fond of all the Irvings. Irving himself was frequently around. He once noted a heavy jacket Emeneau was wearing in the summer heat, and asked if it wasn't too hot. Emeneau said he hadn't been able to get a lighter one big enough. The next time Irving came around he brought one with him. He once clambered up a scaffold being used by someone who told this stranger to get off because he didn't want an accident. Later, he was introduced to a grinning Irving who said he'd done the right thing. To Emeneau, "You couldn't want a nicer man. If I said something was going to be tough to do, he'd say, 'Gosh darn, Earl, have you tried it?' He'd let you use your own judgment. He was a man you could reason with, a very reasonable man. And no matter how dirty your hand was he'd take it."

Irving sought business from pulp mills, fishermen, construction companies, in towns and villages and cities. He made a friend of

Premier Joey Smallwood. He acquired a lot of land and, said Emeneau, "When he wanted it, he wanted it. In Stephenville he paid a lot more for it than I would have. The price didn't bother him. If Imperial had a station on one corner and he wanted another, he got it." In Cornerbrook he moved "a thundering big house" to get a station built near the big Bowaters paper mill. On the acquired sites, over miles of rugged country, service stations arose. Some in filled-in bogs. Some hanging out over the sea, propped up by steel and concrete. "I suspect," said Sid Grant, another construction foreman, "the Irvings would build them in the Atlantic if they thought they could sell gas."

In Quebec, Irving embarked on an aggressive expansion policy. For some time, colleagues said, he was opening a service station every three weeks in places like Sherbrooke, St. Hyacinthe, and Granby. He took aim on Montreal but would find in time that he was better off expanding elsewhere. His national rivals had too big an advantage. To the east and north, however, from Trois Rivières to the Gaspé, along the north shore of the St. Lawrence, in the Lake St. John country, he did become a major factor.

He bought a small retail firm called Les Petroles de Québec, used both its name and his own for a time, then combined them into Les Petroles-Irving de Québec. He sold through other acquired firms, Gaz Oullette, Domestic Petroleum, in gas bars. He found time to inspect every building site for himself, to the despair of those who thought he should delegate power more. He sought new locations as close as possible to a church and a post office because experience showed that was the best place to be. He faced gossip, opposition. The priest in one small town bade his flock not to buy from him. Then when an Irving tank sprang a leak the priest joined others in mustering jugs and cans to gather up the oil.

That sort of thing was minor, however, compared to the opposition from Imperial. They warned him in the 1950s that if he persisted in his invasion of Quebec they would refuse to supply him with the products he'd been buying since 1930. Typically, that only made him more determined. He went to Imperial's American owner, Standard Oil of New Jersey (Esso, later Exxon), and got from them what he was about to be denied by their Canadian subsidiary. Standard, *the* giant among oil's most powerful corporations, had things to sell, and they didn't hesitate to exploit a market when it was available. But the episode only increased Irving's determination to have a refinery of his own.

How K.C. Irving got the oil refinery he had dreamed of for so many years is a story in itself. He knew he lacked the expertise to build it. He needed a major partner to provide management and research facilities to keep him abreast of technological change. He looked in various quarters before he found what he wanted. His early contacts with Imperial had come to nothing. Now he went back to Standard of New Jersey, only to find that they were unwilling to go that far. He began to look elsewhere, and things began to happen.

For weeks in 1955 representatives of British Petroleum, another giant, were around Saint John. Rumours began to circulate among Irving workers that a refinery was under discussion, and BP was going to build it. BP might well have — Irving even made a public announcement — but something happened at the last minute.

There were long negotiations. Said Irving: "We had the price of crude set. We had the grade set. We had it all worked out." It came down to the last act, the signing of an agreement, and he was all set to do it when he sat down to examine a final draft prepared by the BP lawyers. It contained a clause that said BP would have the right to purchase Irving Oil in the event of his retirement or death, and he said "No way."

He kept trying. He sent off wires and letters. "I tried but I couldn't change their minds, and finally I said it was all off. They said I was an awful character to have wasted their time. I said, 'You were insisting on something we never discussed.'" The deal was dead. But another was soon in the works. In 1956 W.H. Beekhuis, vice-president and treasurer of Standard Oil of California (Chevron), came to Saint John. A bank had referred him to Irving, in his quest for an oil company to be associated with in Canada. Standard, he added, would like it to be Irving Oil.

The company had a surplus of oil from its wells in the Middle East and was looking for ways to sell it. Irving liked Beekhuis, and he liked what he said: that Standard would supervise construction of the refinery under a joint venture, would provide crude, research advice, and top management but leave control of the partnership in Irving's hands. It was a deal much like that he had worked out with BP, but there was no offending clause about a future takeover. It offered Irving a pact with a company known for its excellence in research, a company with the know-how and resources he needed.

An agreement was soon in the making, only to run into another last-minute problem. This time it was an international crisis. Britain, France, and Israel struck with military force at Egypt and when the clouds cleared the Suez Canal was out of business. It was through the Suez that Standard had shipped its crude, and Irving hesitated. "We have an agreement," he said, "but how are we going to get our crude now? If things clear up in a satisfactory way, I'll sign."

Things did, though ships henceforth would have to go round South Africa's Cape of Good Hope to reach Saint John, and the era of the supertanker took shape. But now the deal was signed. It gave Standard 51 per cent of a new company, Irving Refining Ltd., Irving 49 per cent. But under a joint agreement Irving kept 51 per cent of Irving Oil, the controlling company, and Standard got the rest. In later years those deals were changed and the Irvings achieved majority ownership of the refinery as well as Irving Oil. Still later, with Arthur Irving as president, the family purchased all shares held by Standard, which by then had become the Chevron Corporation.

It was, K.C. Irving said years later, "about the best deal I could have made. We've had our difficulties but overall Standard proved to be an excellent partner."

By 1958 the refinery was under way, but it wasn't long before Irving found himself reacting to a new problem. He appeared before a federal Royal Commission on Energy in response to the possibility that Ottawa would give Alberta oil exclusive access to markets east of Montreal. What he said then, in 1958, would sound strange twenty years later when Alberta was fighting to get its prices up to world levels driven sky-high by the Arab nations. But at the time Alberta's prices were high, out of line, and Irving wanted no part of them. He argued that his refinery should not be compelled to purchase Canadian crude oil at prices higher than those for which imported crude was now available. Federal policies should not be allowed through artificial prices to further burden the Atlantic population by regulating or restricting free trade in crude oil.

As things turned out, the Ottawa River was chosen as the boundary for the sale of Alberta oil. From there east Irving and others were left free to get their crude where they wished. Thus, as his refinery was building, he knew his deal with Standard was secure, that Quebec remained open to him but that his hopes of penetrating the Ontario market had been thwarted by the Ottawa River boundary line.

In the construction of the refinery itself, on hundreds of acres he had been quietly buying for years, more tales gathered about Irving's name. There is one he would laugh at, without confirmation or denial: Five large storage tanks were proposed for a prominent position, easily visible to those who drove by on Loch Lomond Road, but he said, "no, not five but six." Six with the letters I-R-V-I-N-G boldly etched on their steel hides. The letters are there to this day, lit at night beside the bewildering array of apparatus that makes the refinery a giant still turning out a wide variety of the petroleum products that allow civilization to run on wheels and engines.

To the men who know the oil business, Irving's influence is apparent in a more unusual way. Refineries are usually built bunched up, in depth. His elongated, eventually stretching a mile in one long, thin line, because that's the way he wanted it — it would make expansion easier and would help in fighting fires. But people close to him say he had another reason: he saw the refinery as a showplace, a perennial essay in publicity.

In the construction, too, he had his own ideas. He stepped in when he saw the plans for a bridge over the Little River in the valley just below the refinery, believing them too elaborate and costly. He called the river "that darned brook" and said it was about as formidable an obstacle as the ones over which he had seen lumbermen build far simpler bridges in Kent County. He got a simpler, less costly bridge, and the fact that John D. Park, Jr., Standard's project manager, agreed with him about this and other changes helped convince him that he should hire Park for other things.

But perhaps the most imposing aspect of his impact came in yet another way. Some of the mix of interlocking companies he had been building for years now found a major single outlet. What was done in constructing the refinery was done as much as possible by Irving firms. On a huge sign at the entrance thirty names were listed as "contractors employed," and seven at least belonged to him. J.D. Irving Ltd. was there, as were Ocean Steel, Thorne's Hardware, Commercial Equipment, Steel and Engine Products, Harbor Development Ltd., and Saint John Drydock Co. Ltd. The conglomeration of machinery J.D. Irving now had at its disposal was packaged in a new subsidiary, Irving Equipment, and it was present with all sorts of things. Overall, it was an industrial feast so varied, so widespread that it was said to have amazed Standard Oil people and other outsiders who had never seen anything quite like it. To Irving, it was only a logical thing to do.

At last the job was done. The installation could refine 40,000 barrels of oil a day, gave birth to varied offshoots, and had ultra-modern machinery that would end Irving's long years of dependence on others. The refinery would grow to twice its original size and five times its original capacity. Eventually, it would become the largest oil refinery in Canada.

In the refinery construction, Irving Equipment took the shape of a powerful unit in the Irving mix of companies. Because of the refinery, Kent Line expanded and modernized its fleet. Because Kent, and others, needed ships, Irving built them in the shipyard he had only recently acquired. To see that the ships, and woods camps, got the supplies they needed, Irving Chandler Sales was formed. Because ships needed tugs, Atlantic Towing Ltd. came into being, in time handling all ocean-going vessels coming into Saint John and ranging far out to sea. Because the refinery produced propane gas, among numerous other products, Irving bought up companies that sold it and began to market it himself through such firms as Speedy Propane. Because of the refinery, he built within a decade a floating dock called Canaport a mile or so off the Saint John waterfront, one in water deep enough to handle the supertankers that came from the Persian Gulf with the crude the refinery turned into other products. To carry those things, Irving established his RST (Road and Sea Transport) line and equipped it with enormous trucks.

That a Chignecto Canal link to the St. Lawrence Seaway would have made the impact even greater is obvious. With it, there would have been easier and more direct access to the rich markets of the heartland of Canada. With it, Irving once said, the advantages Halifax had over Saint John would have been reversed. Without the canal, he added, it would have made more economic sense to build the refinery in Halifax. Indeed, he would claim that for some years he'd have been better off and made more money if he had not built it at all. The $50 million it cost was substantially more than that of any other project he had undertaken. He shared it with Standard of California, raising his own share with an issue of bonds. It was a mark of his progress that one bank he didn't deal with told him that if he needed money all he had to do was ask.

If the refinery did cost him some profits, it didn't inhibit him. He expanded it twice and by the mid-1970s it was one of the six largest in North America.

When a writer asked him why he built it where he did, given the advantages of other sites, he replied simply: "Because I live in Saint John."

CHAPTER NINETEEN

≈

Sideshow in Lancaster

"He kept coming back until he got what he wanted."
– A DESCRIPTION OF K. C. IRVING'S NEGOTIATING STYLE.

WHILE IRVING WAS WORKING OUT HIS AGREEMENT WITH
Standard of California, he was working out another
with the Kimberly-Clark Corporation, the big international firm that made Kotex, Kleenex, and other paper tissues.
Standard sent key men from their San Francisco headquarters,
and both groups took suites at the Admiral Beatty Hotel. Said a
witness to the proceedings: "Every day Mr. Irving met the Standard men until six o'clock and every night he was back meeting
the Kimberly-Clark people until two or three a.m. And then every
morning sharp at nine a.m. he was the first man in the hotel
lobby."

Kimberly-Clark wanted a special kind of pulp, kraft, for a new
manufacturing facility that would arise next door to Irving's pulp
mill. The deal they made in 1957 gave them 35 per cent of the
ownership of Irving Pulp and Paper, and the responsibility of providing top management. To Irving's sulphite mill would be added
a sulphate process — all crowded together on that nub of land
beside the Reversing Falls. But before it was built, and after, there
were battles.

145

Irving undertook to negotiate a tax agreement with Lancaster and a water agreement with Saint John, which handled water supply for both neighbouring communities. "He kept coming back until he got what he wanted," is the way one observer described his negotiating style. What he got from Lancaster was a fixed tax of $10,000 for three years, a $15,000 tax for the next twenty-seven. What he got from Saint John was an agreement to provide 25 million gallons of water a day at a graduated fee — a cent for each thousand of the first 9 million gallons, half a cent for the rest — and payment of $35,000 a year to help meet the cost of new pipelines from reservoirs to the east of the city.

When the enabling bill reached a committee of the Legislature, Irving's lawyer A.B. Gilbert urged its passage and defended the concessions. The mill, he said, would employ some 100 highly paid workers. Other communities, notably in Quebec, he added, had offered inducements to attract the project, and he cited examples of large concessions to major industries elsewhere. He testified that the new venture was risky, and the risk could not be incurred without security. He said much harm could come to a community if industry was not encouraged to locate and keep operating, and added that many old, established firms in Saint John had very low valuations.

Lancaster's solicitor and two councillors backed the bill too, but Mayor Parker D. Mitchell opposed it, although a majority of the city council had approved the tax contract. He supported any new industry for Lancaster but he believed it should pay certain portions of the costs it caused. He suggested a tax rate geared to the city's budget or to future dollar value, and called for protection against inflation and further increases in city spending.

On behalf of a group of Lancaster citizens, lawyer George O'Connell said he didn't object to tax concessions but felt the thirty-year arrangement was too long. Moreover, he argued that the Saint John area was a natural site for a pulp mill because of its good rail and water shipping facilities. Irving intervened to point out that much of Lancaster's current prosperity was due to tax concessions given a few years earlier to Irving Pulp and Paper, thereby placing a large payroll in the city. Back in the 1930s, he said, the province and municipality joined to back a bond issue to keep the mill running during the Depression. "We are not asking that today," he went on, "but consideration for fixing taxes for the new industry we are bringing in." And the mill would not go to Saint John unless they got concessions there too.

The bill passed the Legislature with one significant change: the tax agreement was cut from thirty years to fifteen, with an option for renewal "if approved by legislation." But there was a sequel. Saint John soon found that it had underestimated the costs of fulfilling the water agreement, and when a new council was elected Mayor D.L. MacLaren urged Irving to modify the agreement. Irving didn't budge; a contract, he said, was a contract. This eventually brought the statement that the city considered the contract invalid and would "take no further steps under it." When that got nowhere, the council decided to go to court to break the contract, arguing that Irving's payments should be at "a fair industrial level." Its claim was that the contract was illegal because it should have been made with the city's assessment department rather than with the council itself. By 1963 the Supreme Court of Canada had joined the two lower courts in rejecting the argument.

Meanwhile the kraft mill had been running for some time, and Kimberly-Clark was a valuable consumer of what Irving produced. Its next-door tissue factory was, in fact, an important customer of a mill turning out 500 tons of pulp a day, ten times its 1946 production rate, and it would continue that way despite changes in the 1957 agreement. One arose from Irving's steady, keen, and knowing interest in the mill. Eventually he became dissatisfied with the way it was being managed: "You can't be happy about something that is not right. Whatever an agreement says, I insist that it be carried out." There were meetings. Irving asked that the merger agreement be changed, and Kimberly-Clark finally suggested that he put his own manager in charge. Irving men have run the mill ever since.

CHAPTER TWENTY

ஓ

Location, Location, Location

"I'll sell it for $5 million or $6 million — if there's any damn fool who would pay that much."
  — C.N. WILSON PUTTING A PRICE ON THE
   SAINT JOHN DRYDOCK IN 1958.

K.C. Irving: Mr. Wilson, have you sold the land around your drydock?

C.N. Wilson: No, but I have an offer and I have given an option to buy.

Irving: By gosh, it will ruin your drydock if you sell that land. You have to have more facilities, and it will never be able to grow.

Wilson: I don't need that land.

Irving: If you are not interested in using it, and you are going to sell, would you sell the drydock, land and all? Is there any reason why you can't?

Wilson: No, I could cancel the option. All I have to do is send a wire to say it's no longer for sale.

Irving: Would you sell to me? Tonight?

Wilson: For a price, yes.

Irving: How much do you want?

Wilson: For the whole thing, $4,500,000.

Irving: I accept your price, Mr. Wilson. Then we have a deal?

Wilson: For $4,500,000 we have a deal.

Irving: That is fine. You have sold it. I have bought it. You will cancel the option? Right away?

Wilson: Yes, by wire tonight.

Irving: Thank you, Mr. Wilson.

Wilson: Thank you, Mr. Irving.

That mid-evening telephone conversation in 1958 signalled dramatic changes in Saint John's old, down-at-heels drydock that many observers believed was on its last legs. It gave C.N. Wilson a handsome profit on the business he had purchased thirteen years earlier for $400,000. It paved the way for conversion of the drydock to a state-of-the-art shipbuilding yard, and it would herald the return of Saint John as one of the world's great shipbuilding centres. Eventually, about a quarter of a century later, it saw the start of the greatest shipbuilding program in Canada's history as the Irving Yard captured a multi-billion-dollar contract to build frigates for the Canadian Navy.

It all started almost by chance when K.C. Irving overheard a conversation in a room at the Admiral Beatty Hotel. It was there, as Irving recalled, that he heard a remark by a man who knew the politics and machinations of the back rooms. The man said outside interests were going to buy unused land on the grounds of the Saint John Drydock Co. so they could erect a newsprint mill on Courtenay Bay. To Irving it was exciting and disturbing news. He had ships that needed periodic refits but he considered the Saint John Drydock unsatisfactory. Consequently, he had to send his ships to Halifax and the United States to get the service he needed. That bothered him and he had initiated quiet inquiries about buying the drydock, but nothing had come of them. But now he had another reason to be concerned. For years he had been planning a newsprint mill. It was, in his mind, a natural extension of his timber operations and pulp mill. Now that plan was in jeopardy.

He was soon on the phone to Charles N. Wilson, like himself originally an outlander, a native of rural Albert County. Wilson was something of a scrapper. He had started out as a bank clerk and ended up buying the drydock for $400,000 in 1945. He had done well in other business ventures and was prominent in the community. But the drydock wasn't doing much in 1958 and there was no question that it had seen better days. There were fewer than 200 employees on the payroll, and the plant and the nineteen hectares it didn't use were "an expensive luxury." He had been told that he might get $5 million or $6 million for the works. Wilson was amazed by those figures and told an emissary that he would sell "if there is any damned fool who would pay that much." From Irving himself, Wilson said, had come an offer of $3.5 million, which he turned down. He said it was $1.5 million short.

When Irving agreed to pay $4.5 million Wilson went away happy, still amazed that he had found someone who would pay that kind of money for a drydock that had fallen on such bad times that the new owner himself wouldn't even use it to have his ships repaired. But for Irving it was just the beginning of a new and challenging phase in his career. He got the money by approaching James Muir, president of the Royal Bank of Canada, with the details of his aims hand-written on yellow sheets of paper. Muir pondered them, then told Irving the funds would be available when he wanted them. In time, his purchase of the dry-dock emerged as one of the best business moves he ever made — for himself, for the drydock, and ultimately for the people of New Brunswick. Eventually, it would employ over 3,000 workers.

Irving had a use for a ship-repair and construction plant in Saint John, especially now that his refinery would strengthen his position in the oil business, but he didn't think much of the dry-dock as it was. He wanted a place to repair and build ships, to help him stay in the shipping business. He had other ideas as well. He foresaw the day when the shipyard would need the adjoining property for expansion, but he also wanted desperately to stay out front in the race to build a newsprint mill in southern New Brunswick. If Wilson had sold off adjoining property it would not only have inhibited future growth of the shipyard; it would also have paved the way for others to get a jump on him in establishing a newsprint mill.

Irving's creation of a company named Irving Pulp and Paper was an early notice of those intentions. He had no paper plant when it was established in 1951, but for years he had wanted one. He saw it as the apex of what that particular line of business was all about. By 1957 he had found a partner who shared his views in his friend Lord Beaverbrook, a man who shared a habit with

Irving himself: he asked more questions, one after another. Beaverbrook was also the publisher of two newspapers in London, consumers of huge amounts of newsprint.

Irving spent months mapping out plans for a joint project, studying every aspect, and seeking and finding markets. He picked St. George, some forty miles west of Saint John, as the site for the mill. There was one crucial and unresolved problem. He needed crown lands to make it a paying proposition, and he had to go to the provincial government to get them.

It was at this stage that he heard that those other interests were planning a newsprint mill in Saint John. His purchase of Charlie Wilson's drydock threw a monkeywrench into that by securing the land those interests thought they had. But the battle was just beginning. It confronted Irving with a man as stubborn as himself. Leslie Forster and he had met before, and against the same background as that from which the newsprint struggle sprang. It involved Sogemines, a subsidiary of the Societé Générale de Belgique, a world-embracing financial colossus. Headquartered in Belgium, and big in African mining, Sogemines were looking for new investment opportunities. They found in Forster the man they felt they needed in Canada to search these out.

Forster was an urbane, unflappable Briton who drove a 1959 Bentley sedan so lordly that it attracted stares wherever he went in Montreal. He was driving it during this battle in the late fifties and early sixties; he was still driving it in the 1980s. He had spent years away from his homeland. As a British Army colonel and engineer, he had worked to block wartime Nazi Germany's desperate ambitions to seize the oil wells of southern Russia. He had watched, rejoicing, one night as the violence of deliberate flame destroyed major elements of them even as German forces approached. In peacetime, he had headed Shell Oil in Venezuela and searched for oil in various lands before coming to Canada to join a Toronto investment house. There Sogemines found and hired him, put $5 million at his disposal, and told him to make it work.

Forster put it to work in cement, chemicals, and glass under the corporate umbrella of what became known as Genstar. Because of Sogemines' initiative, a new oil company, Petrofina Canada, came into being and it sought an established chain of gasoline outlets. Irving had such a chain. Discussions started but, said Forster, they got nowhere on a first attempt in a Montreal hotel room; Irving was so busy on the telephone that there was no time to talk. They resumed in Irving's home where, Forster said, a lady called and said she had no oil, and Irving took the time to arrange for it to be delivered to her. They came to a conclusion after a pleasant lunch at the Admiral Beatty Hotel, when Irving said "I have three sons and I want to keep this business for them." They parted on good terms.

Leslie Forster's quests were by no means over. Sogemines asked him to find a newsprint operation, preferably one already established. He looked around the country but found nothing worth buying. So he started looking for a mill site, and lit on Saint John as nearly ideal. It had a sea position, low-cost wood, and power cheaper than Sogemines could produce.

Forster realized at the time that Irving was a powerful man on his own turf, but underestimated just how powerful he was. His first awakening came with Irving's drydock purchase and, with it, the site for his mill. The drydock Sogemines didn't need — though Forster says they were going to buy it anyway — but land they did.

With the chosen land gone, Forster went to Fredericton and received both bad and good news. The government's Electric Power Commission had a site near the drydock that would have done admirably, but it wouldn't sell. Nevertheless, Forster got encouragement from a Flemming government anxious to welcome a new industry to Saint John. With that, Forster set about seeking a new site around Courtenay Bay. He got some access from the National Harbours Board, some from the Joseph A. Likely business interests, and an option from a government department that owned more. But he still didn't have enough forest lands to supply the first paper mill to be built in Canada in years.

Enter Dr. John S. Bates, a consultant in the pulp and paper business who was acting as an adviser to Forster. Bates came up with an idea. He knew Fraser Companies Ltd. had a large swath of forest on southern New Brunswick's Canaan River, far from their own mills in the north. The answer was to get them involved. The key man was Roy Joudrey, a wealthy, homespun Nova Scotian industrialist who was on Fraser's board. Joudrey had long been associated with Fred Manning, whom Irving had tangled with before.

Bates caught Joudrey by telephone in Denmark. He had just had breakfast, and he was interested. Forster's people soon had

Fraser on board, paid them $3 million for their land and got them to put it into the new company. For $10,000 they also got an option on another 11,207 square kilometres of timber limits owned by F.E. Sayre Ltd. They would get more from the government. Now they had the land they required. They had involved not only Sogemines and Fraser, but British, German, and American interests. They got a private bill worked out to incorporate Rothesay Paper Corporation, and seemed to be on their way.

It was when the bill came before the Legislature that Irving's views surfaced in public. When it went before a committee, he was there with his lawyer, Adrian Gilbert, to hear Rothesay spokesmen say they would employ 700 to 800 men in a $30-million, two-year construction job. Once in production, the mill would provide work for 200 with an annual payroll of $3.5 million. When his turn came, Irving said he wanted to make it clear that he was not trying to prevent an industry from coming to Saint John, but he believed there should be protection to prevent it interfering with industries already established. He said there had been difficulty in getting information about the size of the mill, and he wanted to know whether Rothesay paper would be controlled from outside Canada.

Norwood Carter, Rothesay's lawyer, observed that outside interests were involved in Irving's refinery and pulp mill. Irving retorted that he held the major interests in both. Carter said that the company had a head office in Montreal, that the new industry would complement Irving's own, and that they were interested in co-operation. Gilbert, in turn, sought assurances that Rothesay's powers of expropriation would not be allowed to affect existing industry. Irving said then and later that if Rothesay could expropriate they might be able to do so from him. He feared there wouldn't be enough wood available. He foresaw complications and damage to installations on the St. John River if a Rothesay drive were added to his own in those days before the Mactaquac Dam ended all drives. He would call Rothesay's foreign investors "ghosts." When Carter told him Rothesay had no intention of trying to expropriate Irving properties, he retorted, "I wasn't born yesterday."

In the Legislature, Opposition leader Louis Robichaud spoke on Irving's behalf. He said he was pleased a new industry was coming into the province but it should not prejudice already existing industries through powers of expropriation. Further, he said, the government Power Commission had requested — and been given by amendment — protection from "nuisance" caused by Rothesay but Irving had been denied it, and this was wrong. Premier Flemming said the government could overrule any private expropriation, and "you must trust the government."

Robichaud then read a lengthy telegram sent to all members by Irving, arguing that the bill did "not provide the protection existing industry is entitled to." Irving said he found "it impossible to understand why the protection granted to a government-owned industry should be denied to a privately owned industry operating on the same river. Am still fearful of expropriation rights to be granted to company, the control of which has not been disclosed." The expropriation rights given Rothesay had caused an uproar on radio and TV and there were so many people concerned with the bill that Robichaud felt it should be referred back to the corporations committee for more study.

Attorney General Gordon Fairweather retorted that Rothesay had given assurances that "not one square foot of land" owned by Irving would be expropriated. Indeed, the common law provided that it couldn't expropriate from a company that itself had expropriation powers. Fairweather suggested a jointly owned boom-driving company could settle the problem of the drives. He said Irving had rejected a proposal accepted by Rothesay that it would give up its "nuisance" powers if he gave up his too.

The bill was passed, with Robichaud abstaining on the final vote.

To all this, Leslie Forster later added an ironic footnote. He said Rothesay had no intention of driving logs anyway. What he wanted was the equivalent of any powers Irving had — and he got the right to drive.

For his part, at the time Irving saw what he did as a legitimate attempt to shield his own interests, and they still included a newsprint operation of his own. A year later, in the spring of 1960, he went to Flemming to discuss plans for a mill that would produce 500 tons of paper a day with a work force of 500. His plans, in fact, had grown. His main problem was an adequate supply of wood. Much of the forests he already owned were many miles away, and he felt he needed more resources closer at hand. He had his eye on crown lands in Charlotte County, where his mill would be. He was assured, he later said publicly, of assistance in getting what he needed. Indeed, he said, Flemming "advised and recommended I tell my associates I felt certain the required lands would be made available to us."

But the Flemming government, after encouraging both Rothesay and Irving, was at that time contemplating an election. It was called for June 27. Even after eight years in power, the premier was confident he would win. It didn't work out that way. The thirty-four-year-old Liberal leader, Louis Robichaud, had grasped an issue and made it stick. To get access to state-provided hospital care, citizens had to pay a special premium, $25 for single individuals, $50 for families. It wasn't much but it rankled. Robichaud said he would abolish the premiums and pay for hospital care out of general revenues without raising taxes.

On June 27, 1960, he became the first Acadian ever elected premier. Irving still did not have those woodlands he wanted for his proposed newsprint mill but the stage was set for a new approach.

K.C. Irving and Louis Joseph Robichaud started out as friends. It was a friendship that soured, and eventually Irving found it impossible to find a single good word for this small, turbulent, and spellbinding figure who shared his rural Kent County background. Robichaud came from a large French-speaking family, started learning English at twenty, and even in college had identified himself as a future premier of the province. It was not long after his election that Irving was talking publicly about new plans. At the christening of a small ship, the first built in Saint John since 1954, he was asked if shipbuilding could be brought back as a major industry in New Brunswick. His answer: "Yes, definitely." As chairman of the board of the Saint John Shipbuilding and Drydock Ltd., he noted that there were about 6,000 people employed in shipbuilding in Nova Scotia the previous year, about the same number in Quebec, and only 243 in New Brunswick. To improve this situation, he said, he was prepared to go ahead with a huge expansion program. He needed land to proceed, and if he got it he would.

At a special fall session of the Legislature, he got what he wanted after Robichaud made a stunning move: he took from Rothesay 36.8 waterfront hectares they had acquired for their second site. Construction of their mill had not started. Now, again, they lacked a site to start it.

Robichaud's takeover, said Leslie Forster, came without warning when Rothesay Paper was about set to go ahead: "No notice was given. No reason. We were simply told the land was needed for another industry." The industry, Robichaud revealed to the Legislature, was Irving's drydock. The purpose, he said: to allow Irving to fulfil a promise that, if he got the required land, the 36.8 hectares, he would expand it and provide 1,000 additional jobs.

The explanation given for the government's proceeding as it did was that actual ownership of the land was vague and shadowy. The government believed, said Robichaud, that the owners were the heirs of three men who had died a century earlier, but no heirs could be found. To cover any possible claims that might arise from individuals or corporations, and to protect itself, he said, the government had obtained from the drydock firm a twenty-year bond of indemnity. In other words, Irving would underwrite any costs that might arise from such claims. But Robichaud also revealed something else: he said the Flemming government had, in 1958, given to "a corporation" — obviously Rothesay — an option not only on the 91 acres but on a total of 300, and that apparently even former Attorney General Fairweather didn't know about it. Certainly, he said, the Liberals hadn't.

Said Fairweather: "I didn't know the extent, or the terms . . . I think anybody in New Brunswick on either side [of the Legislature] knew of the option." Argued Robichaud: "If it was feasible at that time to give an option . . . it is still feasible to . . . do whatever we want with the property." Asked whether Rothesay had indicated what the loss of the 91 acres would do to their plans, he said the company had stated that it would not build a mill in that area; even with the 85 hectares remaining it could not build. Even so, the government contended that assurance of the employment of approximately 1,000 men at the drydock transcended the mere possibility that Rothesay would establish a pulp mill in the area. Robichaud doubted that they intended to start within the next twenty-five years. According to him, "They had a pulp mill that was designed to the last bolt in 1958 and there's still no indication that they wanted to build, and that was two years ago." He added that he'd heard the company wanted to sell their rights, or option, and timber limits, meaning that they were no longer interested in building a mill.

Fairweather suggested the land be put up for public tenders. Robichaud said it was better to get 1,000 jobs than to take the chance that some other company would get it and keep it in reserve for years. His job figure was questioned. He'd said expansion would raise drydock employment from 1,700 to 2,700. A Conservative said drydock president John D. Park — Irving had hired him from Chevron — had informed him there were 1,200 men on the payroll and that expansion would add another 450 to 500. Robichaud now said there had been 1,932 at work but the figure was down to 1,200, and the 1,000 new jobs would be added to that. The Conservatives said they were pleased to welcome any new employment, but one of them saw the bill as a forerunner of laws that could place the people of the province under the "legal control of a dictator."

The government, said Robichaud, was acting in line with precedents. It was acting, said Opposition leader Cyril B. Sherwood, through a public bill when a private bill would have been preferable, because then all interested parties would have been able to testify in committee. Though everyone was anxious to see drydock expansion, he, too, thought that protection for claims arising from the takeover should be written into the bill itself, not left to a bond of indemnity alone. He moved an amendment to that effect. Robichaud rejected it because, he said, the point had been considered and legal opinion was that the bond was preferable.

Fairweather said that besides options to Rothesay from the provincial government and the National Harbours Board, someone had given an option on about 1.4 hectares of the 37, and he was concerned about this. Robichaud said he had assured the latter that if he had any right, title, or interest, it would be fully protected under the bond of indemnity.

The bill was passed but with a late amendment by Robichaud to make sure, he said, that anyone would have time to put forward claims. To do so, he provided that it should come into force on a date to be fixed by proclamation.

Meanwhile Irving was already forging ahead with his modernization program. On drydock property, adjacent to the 37 hectares, a long, wide building was taking shape. It was one of the initial steps that would soon enable management to say it had the most modern facilities of any shipyard in the land. It would house an assembly line and magnetic equipment to draw designs on long, thin flats of steel, to be cut as required, for the building of ships. From that building the steel would be rolled on for the next stage of construction.

The legislation gave a body blow to Rothesay Paper at a time when, behind the scenes, there were blows enough. Money, said Forster, had become a problem, and he was having trouble raising capital. Sogemines kept stalling on purchase of the 188.5 hectares of the Sayre forest property. Its option, given in the name of Sogemines Consultants Ltd., was originally scheduled to end on October 16, 1959. Instead, it was amended and renewed several times. On March 31, 1960, it was extended for the last time, to February 28, 1961.

With Robichaud's legislation, it appeared for a time that Rothesay might never have use for that land. But within weeks counterattacks were forming. In December Joseph A. Likely, a prominent Saint John businessman, urged the Board of Trade to take steps to help revive the industry. He was apparently the individual Fairweather had mentioned. His firm, Likely said, had given Rothesay an option on any rights they might possess in certain property for a building site. "We entered this agreement," he added, "not for any great capital gain but with the hopes that a large independent industrial development of this nature would balance the growth of our economy and forestall the tendency towards a 'company town.'" He was faced, he said, with the fact that the transfer of land to Irving was of a type that "does not stipulate any payment for lands so deeded," and he considered it "very questionable that there is little or any legal protection against the drydock for third parties."

Meanwhile, Likely argued, the legislation, not yet proclaimed, "hangs like a sword over our heads." If it became law, he felt "no other major concern will consider this province and particularly our city for development unless they wish to subject themselves to Mr. K.C. Irving's will." He said that "Mr. Irving certainly plans on making a profit and we should, above all, hold the door open for all those who are willing to invest here and share some profit with us." Likely said that Rothesay Paper was still prepared to build a mill. He appealed to the board to try, with the "utmost delicacy (but with firmness)," to help prevent the Robichaud legislation from being proclaimed.

In fact, Robichaud was already off on another tack. He sought the best of both worlds, both Irving's expansion *and* a Rothesay mill. On November 18, ten days before he stated that he had doubts that Rothesay planned to build one, he informed Rothesay Paper, as Forster recalled to him in a letter, that he still wanted to see a Rothesay newsprint mill built and would be willing to provide an alternative site.

On January 18, 1961, Forster stated that Rothesay was prepared to start building by June 30 on the original site if it were made available by February 23. Or it would build on an alternative site next door if the government prepared it and made it available on terms that would mean no increase in cost of site preparation. T.C. Higginson had copies of Forster's letter to Robichaud and others on January 31 when he made his farewell address as Board of Trade president. Without quoting Forster, he said that though Saint John was known as a boom town, unemployment was rising and he cited what Rothesay was still prepared to do and what it could mean economically.

By February the Conservatives in the Legislature were urging action to get Rothesay started, and on February 21 Robichaud made a consoling statement. By vesting the 37 hectares in Irving, the government had not prevented or precluded the establishment of the proposed paper mill. Other nearby land was suitable for Rothesay's purposes. Negotiations had started and were continuing. They involved both levels of government, the two companies, and the National Harbours Board, and Robichaud was optimistic they would be fruitful.

About this time, Robichaud met with Irving and Forster in an effort to resolve their differences. There are differing versions of what happened. What is known is that it was a meeting doomed to failure, and it did fail. Robichaud said both Irving and Forster left the meeting angry. When they'd gone, Robichaud said: "I wept. I was not only frustrated, I was heartbroken. I wanted a reconciliation between two great men, and I failed." Forster said Robichaud did look as though he had been stabbed. Irving, when Robichaud's story of weeping was told to him years later, snorted in ridicule.

Whatever the facts, Robichaud did move to make the Rothesay project possible. He met Forster with news Forster found hard to believe. The premier asked him if Rothesay would accept the New Brunswick Electric Power Commission land they had already found admirable and been refused. Forster made a show of phoning his engineers, and then said reluctantly that they would accept. He was, in fact, delighted.

On April 4, 1961, the government announced that Rothesay would build its mill, and a bill was introduced to transfer the necessary land. Two days later the bill was passed unanimously.

Irving had not objected to the bill, but in other ways he was busy and on the move. When Rothesay's last option on the Sayre property expired at the end of February, he bought it. When the Power Commission built a pipeline to Rothesay's site through the 37 hectares he had obtained from the government, he objected and eventually sued. He feared it would disrupt his plans for dry-dock expansion, and the pipeline was moved. When the question of water for its mill came up, Rothesay got involved with another Irving fight with Saint John's common council at a time when its lawsuit to break the 1958 contract with his pulp mill was still before the courts.

In that same year Irving obtained a lease from the city on the watershed of the Little River. He wanted it as a backup water supply for his oil refinery. He was to pay $1,000 a year for the privilege, but in 1961 the cheque, by some oversight, was not sent. The city promptly cancelled the lease, apparently believing this gave it a new bargaining chip in the dispute over the pulp mill contract. But Irving sued and, for emphasis, said that his $100-million Chignecto Canal pledge was off. The city, he said, was repudiating agreements with two of his industries after he had built them. It was, said Irving, no way to do business. It was not the way he did business. Irving never denied that he was a hard bargainer, but once a deal was made, whether it was by a handshake or a 100-page legal document, he expected both sides to stand behind it. Now, the two agreements he had made with the city, both for water, were being retracted. Worse, in his view, the city was reneging after he had made his investments, after he had gone ahead with projects based on those agreements. He was bitter and in no mood to proceed with further industrial development in Saint John. "How can you conduct business dealings in such an atmosphere?" he demanded.

Mayor Teed called it all a misunderstanding, and another fight petered out. The New Brunswick Water Authority had suggested use of the Little River watershed, a mile from the site, for Rothesay. Irving got his own lease back, agreed to let Rothesay have half of its supply, and Teed publicly congratulated him for his co-operation in making the new mill a reality. As a final footnote, the price it paid for water was considerably higher than Irving paid under his 1958 pulp mill agreement.

Still, even as the Rothesay plant took shape, Irving had not given up hope of a newsprint mill of his own, but he faced complications. In March 1962 he said publicly that it was not yet an impossibility but that he was unable to meet the wood requirements. If they had been met after Flemming's assurances in 1959, he said, the mill would now be nearing completion.

He later met cabinet ministers and said he was convinced of their interest and determination to see him proceed. But he added that the only sizeable holding of crown lands that could be used as a basic source of wood for a new mill was tied up by an agreement with Rothesay. He added something else that indicated he was angry that he had not received from Robichaud's government the sort of help promised by Flemming, and given to Rothesay. "In some quarters," he said, "there seems to be a reluctance to see any further expansion of my interests in this province. One member of the government has recently said my interests are too vast. It does not seem to matter how vast the interests of outsiders are. Too much of this thinking can cause New Brunswickers to become outsiders." His statement prompted Tory leader Sherwood to ask who had said Irving was already too big. "No government member, to my knowledge," said Robichaud, "ever entertained such language."

On May 22, 1964, the new Rothesay mill opened. Irving was there. The plant meant business for him, and his equipment had shared in the construction. His oil fed a Power Commission unit that provided its electricity. Irving Pulp eventually met some of its needs. Irving tugs would tow the barges that took Rothesay newsprint down the coast to American markets.

Irving looked to the future in other ways too. During the long and bitter debates over the property and crown lands he had argued there was not enough wood for two mills, and while his views were greeted with some scepticism, he himself was growing more and more concerned. The 1957 start of his reforestation program was designed to ease shortages of the future and he kept on buying woodlands, from the Blacks of Sackville, the Hickmans of Dorchester and Rothesay, and from others.

He was also determined that the properties he acquired would operate more efficiently. The changes did not always go down well, and soon after he purchased the Sayre property the Irving broom stirred strong reactions in the little town of Chipman.

As Irving men tell it, the Sayre workers had been accustomed to easygoing management, to taking advantage of it, and to drinking on the job. They resented the sterner measures that came with change, and hot-tempered Jim Irving took drastic action. First there were firings and then he called in one of his northern New Brunswick woods foremen to whip things into shape.

The foreman, Armand Côté of Grand Falls, said he didn't want to go. It was far from home, he was French-speaking, and he correctly anticipated that he would be resented in English-speaking Chipman. Still, under pressure, he went. He brought in men from the north and elsewhere. He put them to work in the Chipman sawmill and in the woods, and local resentment grew. One night the lines were cut on the booms that held logs driven down the Salmon River. It took days, says Côté, for imported river men to round them up. But gradually he began rehiring men from the Chipman area with the stipulation that there be no drinking or taking advantage on the job. In time, he said, those woodsmen turned out to be the best he ever had, and soon things were going so well that Irving built a modern sawmill for the Chipman operation.

ε∂

For his new drydock, Irving had another able man, John D. Park, Jr. They couldn't have been more different. They came from different worlds and lived different lives, with nothing in common except that each in his own way was a builder. Kenneth Colin Irving was trim, wide-shouldered, and looked like an oldtime boxer from the era of John L. Sullivan, like a grown-up version of the bareknuckle fighter he'd been as a kid. John D. Park, Jr., looked more like a Sumo wrestler. All he needed was the ceremonial sash and G-string; he had the weight. He was tough, enterprising, and calculating.

Irving looked you straight in the eye and you knew where you stood with him. Park also looked you straight in the eye, but it was a mischievous look with the twinkle of a riverboat gambler. He was gregarious, articulate, supremely confident. Irving was an entrepreneur, a seat-of-the-pants flyer who rolled up his sleeves and made it his business to know everything about his enterprises — more than his engineers, financial advisers, lawyers, technicians, carpenters, even more than the men who poured the concrete. Park was a brilliant, innovative, ambitious engineer who dreamed big and built big. He was a salesman who believed he could talk his way out of hell.

Construction of the Irving Refinery in Saint John brought them together and the drydock extended their unlikely relationship because Irving put Park in charge. Years later Jim Irving recalled how Park handled situations when K.C. Irving was upset. "He knew my father was obsessed with detail," Jim Irving remembered, "and whenever he sensed that my father was upset about something he would arrive for a meeting with a bundle of blueprints under his arm. He would place the blueprints on the boardroom table. Then he'd ask my father if the plans were in keeping with my father's understanding of the project. That was all that was needed. They could spend two hours going over the plans and never get around to the problem Park had been called in about. It worked for a while because my father couldn't resist examining every detail of anything that was being built, but it didn't take him too long to realize the game that was being played and that was the end of that."

In the Irving operations there had never been anyone quite like John Park, and there would not be another like him for a long time to come. He had been sent to Saint John by Standard of California to head up the refinery-building project and Irving soon recognized his genius. Irving's mistake was in believing that he could work with Park — or, perhaps more correctly, that Park could work for him. It was an arrangement that was doomed from the start. It was only a question of how long it would last. But while it lasted, Irving and Park were an awesome combination and there were fast and dramatic changes at the old drydock.

Typically, Irving was determined to revive and rebuild. The yard became a customer of Irving Oil, building ships to carry its products. It purchased supplies from other Irving companies. It had work done by Irving Equipment. In tough times work for Irving companies kept it going. But it needed more than that to survive and grow. It needed work from outside firms that wanted ships built and refitted. Soon there was a long-range plan to turn it into one of the top shipyards in Canada. It was at this time, in the early stages of the planning and rebuilding program, that Irving decided Park was the man to provide the on-the-site drive so badly needed. He was put in charge, and things would never be the same again.

Park had the energy and managerial skills, and his performance in the construction of the oil refinery had met Irving's demanding standards, but for all that, it did not prove to be a popular appointment. Managers at the drydock thought he knew too little about the work he was directing. They told stories of his keeping an eye on things with binoculars from his distant office window. They told other stories of extravagance and high living. But Park was also a doer, and for a time he seemed to have an inside track with Irving.

It was under this unusual duo that the drydock improvements started and a new era took shape. By 1960 Irving had planned to extend the shipyard over neighbouring property, the site of the Municipal Home for Indigents. His purchase of the property provided Saint John residents with a chuckle: now Irving even owns the poorhouse.

The drydock was being fitted up to be the first automated shipbuilding yard in Canada. Many of the new employees were skilled craftsmen from Clydeside in Scotland. The shipyard went on to become the largest single manufacturing industry in New Brunswick, the pride of cabinet ministers boasting of what the province could do. It faced stormy labour problems, union struggles, and increasing competition from foreign yards fortified by subsidies larger than the Canadian government provided. With Irving and then his son Jim in charge, it accepted what subsidies there were but called for a long-range government shipbuilding policy. It had its ups and downs, but it benefited from a core Irving policy: every cent of profit it made would be plowed back into operations. In a country without enough of the required skills, it trained its own workers under the management of the Americans, Swedes, English, and Scots. It built ferries, naval ships, tugs, and ships for other oil companies, and it provided the Irvings with a modern fleet of tankers. It also built the long, low Great Lakes grain carriers, and when one was launched Irving did not resist one more appeal for a Chignecto Canal. With it, he said, lakers could sail into Saint John, be repaired there, or even built there — all of which would contribute to a more lucrative life for the city.

Irving would soon interest himself in another big cut in the ground.

?

CHAPTER TWENTY-ONE

A Hole in the Ground

"I should have raised hell."
– K.C. IRVING'S LATE-LIFE COMMENT ON BRUNSWICK MINING'S
*TROUBLE-PLAGUED DECISION TO BUILD A SMELTER AT
BELLEDUNE.*

WHEN MATTHEW JAMES BOYLEN WENT TO IRVING IN MAY 1961, just as the Rothesay fight was coming to an end and the drydock and oil refinery had got moving, it was at the suggestion of Premier Robichaud. For Irving, it was a rendezvous with fate. Robichaud had called and asked him to lend a hand in a new project. The province wanted to see ore bodies developed in northern New Brunswick. Robichaud thought the enterprise required a builder like Irving rather than a promoter like Jim Boylen. What Boylen wanted to discuss turned out to be the most galling and disturbing episode of Irving's life, but notwithstanding later disappointments and bitterness, it was his involvement that triggered the development of the greatest mining operation in the province's history.

Boylen was a former trapper, prospector, and promoter who in 1952 had discovered enormous base metal prospects near Bathurst. Armed with a pledge of $500,000 a year for three years from a New York syndicate, Boylen had spent only a fraction of the money when, after drilling eleven holes and finding nothing, he insisted on trying just one more. By doing so, he hit fabulous pay dirt around the site of a defunct iron mine, triggering a frenzy of staking, speculation, and greed.

Boylen had struck lead, zinc, silver, pyrite, and copper. New Brunswick would now be an important mining province, and experts calculated that it was almost certain that eastern Canada's long-awaited zinc smelter would become a reality. Over miles of rock, trees, and poverty between Bathurst and Newcastle, outsiders swarmed to stake claims. The names of big companies soon became involved in the activity and speculation. Politicians and newspapers joined in rosy anticipation.

But seven years later not much had happened. St. Joseph Lead of New York, a major international mining company, had bought into the New Brunswick Mining and Smelting company only to run into troubles that added up to an impasse. They spent a long time and $9 million seeking without success an economic way to extract lead and zinc from a difficult ore. They launched a 100-tons-a-day pilot mill at one ore-body, No. 6, and sank two shafts at another, No. 12, 9.6 kilometres away. In 1956 they encountered a slump in world prices, fired a 175-man work force, and waited for better days. The deposits had become a reserve. They were still a reserve when Robichaud came to power.

His election platform had promised action. "When I become premier," Robichaud had said, "I will see that a smelter is built and the mines will go into production." He had said other things, had attacked Boylen for promoting mining stocks that "bounced up and down on the stock market like a yo-yo," leaving many New Brunswickers with heavy losses. Two mines had closed only shortly after publicity had lauded their potential. Boylen, expressing surprise, had said he could not understand how the publicity began. "Who," asked Robichaud, "did he think he was fooling?"

This, Boylen told a reporter, was "a pack of nonsense. I never took a quarter out of the area and was a heck of a lot richer when I went in than when I came out." At this, Robichaud scoffed again, but he kept a foot in the door of the future: "If Mr. Boylen will renew activity . . . if he will fully develop the large ore deposits he controls, then I will be the first one to commend him."

Though Boylen was reportedly angry, once Robichaud was in power things did change. In 1960 Sogemines and St. Joseph Lead decided to build a 2,000-tons-a-day mine and ship concentrates overseas. Sogemines would manage the project; Boylen would be out as president, and because only high-grade ore would be used the stock of Brunswick dropped to a point that made him even unhappier. So Boylen went to Robichaud and said he'd bring a mine into production if the government would provide a financial guarantee for a smelter. Robichaud agreed, saying that not a pound of ore would be shipped out of New Brunswick unless a smelter were built.

Now Boylen went to St. Joseph Lead and found they were still not interested in a smelter, though Robichaud was telling them they must either develop the ore body or make way for someone who would. Boylen formed East Coast Smelting and Chemical Co., and offered St. Joseph $10.5 million for their interest in Brunswick. He was given forty-five days to raise the money. After no success he went to Irving. According to Boylen's account of what happened: "After a few minutes, he said, 'Yes. To what extent do you want me in this?' I said I was perfectly willing to put up $5.5 million and I was looking for the other $5 million. I asked him for $3 million. He didn't blink an eyelid, and accepted."

Boylen, wanting a mining company involved, next went to E.R.E. Carter, a former Saint John man living in Toronto as Canadian head of Patino Mining Corporation, another big international company. From Patino he got the last of his $10.5 million on the last of his forty-five days. St. Joseph sold its 40.6 per cent interest in Brunswick, Irving putting up $2.5 million to buy a 24 per cent interest in St. Joseph's 1.6 million shares, Boylen's Maritimes Mining Corporation Ltd. 46 per cent and three Patino companies the balance. Carter would be president.

The property was back in the hands of Canadians, but the market for lead and zinc was lower than for many years and Boylen was faced with the problem of raising $20 million to put the mine into production. He finally asked Irving if he had any ideas. Irving had.

Irving went to Henry Blaise of Sogemines, the very firm he had fought over Rothesay Paper, the firm whose original plan of producing concentrates and shipping them to Belgian smelters had now been thwarted by Robichaud. Though Sogemines were still against a New Brunswick smelter, Blaise agreed to advance some $12 million for first mortgage bonds to get the mine into operation and provide the concentrates Sogemines wanted. Irving put up another $8 million on the same mortgage basis through a new firm, Engineering Consultants Ltd., which would provide management services under John D. Park, build a 3,000-ton concentrator, and arrange for a 35-kilometre railway and for shipping services on the north shore. The New Brunswick government chipped in with a guarantee of the $20 million. They were on their way. In November the throne speech opened the Legislature with a statement that the way was clear for "the orderly development of an integrated mine, mill, smelter, and chemical complex" that would "place New Brunswick in the forefront of mineral development in Canada."

There was nothing orderly about the debate that followed, especially after an admission by Robichaud. Prodded by the Opposition, he said he had wrongly thought the security for the $20 million was the $51 million expected to be spent overall rather than the $20-million estimated cost of a smelter. In long committee sessions, there were arguments, amendments, and compromises in discussions about the wide powers Brunswick sought: among others, expropriation rights, freedom from nuisance claims, the right to divert watercourses, and exclusive rights for the smelter to produce in the province. Irving, saying financing was "a tremendous problem," appeared to add that, though he would be delighted to see the smelter in Saint John, due to the orebody site it had to be in northern New Brunswick. Boylen testified that there might be 150 million tons of ore available — press reports had already said they could be worth more than $3 billion — and that in the next ten years it was hoped the complex would number five or six units.

By the end of the year the Legislature unanimously backed the government guarantee, a reincorporated Brunswick, and East Coast Smelting and Chemical, a Boylen concern that included Irving as a director and in due course would turn over to Brunswick, for 600,000 Brunswick shares, all its shares and exclusive rights to build a smelter. Under the government guarantee a smelter had to be started by December 1963. In the meantime, Brunswick would develop a mine and build a concentrator to turn the ore into powdered lead and zinc ready for smelting. For five years, Brunswick's directors agreed in June 1962, the concentrates would go to Sogemines smelters overseas; once their own smelter was going, Sogemines would receive any surplus for another seven years.

On a site 35 kilometres south of Bathurst the first sod was officially turned for the concentrator on June 13 and Irving's Mace Ltd., the general contractor, began additional clearing, grubbing, and excavation. By late July a shaft was being deepened into the No. 12 ore-body by Mindecon Ltd. By the end of the year it reached a scheduled depth of 560 metres.

The smelter was another matter. In the search for the best method it might use, the company obtained the advice of Singmaster and Brayer, a prominent New York engineering consulting firm, who recommended the so-called Imperial process. But when samples were sent to Britain for Imperial testing, they were not exact samples of the ore Brunswick would use. The tests showed acceptable results, but they were the wrong tests. The mistake was prophetic, but it was for more important reasons that Irving was soon having second thoughts.

Twice in 1963 he tried to convince Robichaud that the smelter should be delayed. Twice he failed. In Irving's words, spoken in 1971:

> The construction of the smelter was started without adequate planning, even before the design was available, and without adequate financing. The company was forced to proceed prematurely by political pressure from Robichaud: He had told the company to proceed or someone else would.
>
> In early 1963 E.R.E. Carter, John D. Park, and I went to the premier and asked for a delay. He refused. In September 1963 I again tried to impress upon him the possible consequences. Again he refused to agree to a delay. By this time there was a report from Singmaster and Brayer that the smelter should be built at Saint John. The then premier said despite the report the smelter had to be built on the north shore. I did not disagree, provided there was time for proper planning, but the then premier insisted on a premature and what was to be a disastrous start. That was the beginning of the problems, and the man responsible was Louis J. Robichaud.

On October 31, 1963, Robichaud announced that Belledune Point, on the shores of the Bay of Chaleur some 61 kilometres from the mines, would be the site of the smelter and a chemical offshoot, and that the concentrator's capacity was being enlarged. On November 20, he turned the first sod for the smelter, to be built in the name of East Coast.

Despite cold weather, it was a festive occasion. The chairman was Boylen, now dignified by two honorary degrees from New Brunswick universities. The audience included Irving, and in speaking he mixed praise for Robichaud with a reminder that it was Robichaud who had refused the request for a delay in the smelter project. Beyond that, Irving said, they hoped that, with the co-operation of the provincial and federal governments, Belle-dune would become a year-round deepwater port. As for the smelter, it "had long been the dream not only of Premier Robichaud but of many New Brunswickers. This dream is about to be fulfilled, and more, no doubt, will follow."

He made those conciliatory remarks, he later said, because he thought he must be wrong in opposing the start and didn't think things would turn out as badly as they did. So the smelter began, with president John D. Park's Engineering Consultants Ltd. supervising, with an international staff, with cost-plus contracts, and with Irving's mix of companies involved in every way possible. It involved him in what was, for him, an unusual — and fateful — situation: he had only a minority ownership position of the whole Brunswick development. It bore comparisons with the CPR's huge, integrated Consolidated Mining complex in Trail, B.C., but there was a crucial difference: Cominco had taken decades to do what Brunswick now proposed to do in a few years. Experts in later years observed that there was a much more logical way to do it: go slowly, build a mine, a concentrator, pay for them from profits, accumulate capital and experience, and take a long time to study and decide just what sort of smelter would serve best.

Logical, it might be, but New Brunswick had waited for twelve years for a base metals payoff. Its people had elected a government hell-bent on industrial growth. So, quickly, without adequate planning or financing, and with a process whose international acceptance would dwindle, the smelter proceeded, with Irving growing increasingly concerned that it was being built at all. His apprehensions were soon reinforced by Desmond Bayley, a widely experienced metallurgist who had worked as development superintendent for Cominco, who had recently been a consultant in erection of an

Imperial smelter in Zambia and found it hadn't worked very well, and who doubted that the process was suited to the Canadian climate. When Bayley joined Engineering Consultants that year as chief metallurgist he concluded that what was being done was crazy.

Years later he would say that he and Irving would ask each other why it *was* being done. Years later, too, Irving would say, "I should have raised hell." Instead, the smelter went ahead — straight into trouble.

CHAPTER TWENTY-TWO

❧

A Matter of Wages

"He was all right, that man."
– K.C. IRVING RECALLING CLAUDE JODOIN, PRESIDENT OF THE
CANADIAN LABOUR CONGRESS IN THE EARLY 1960s.

BY THE NOVEMBER DAY IN 1963 WHEN THE FIRST SOD WAS
turned for the Brunswick smelter, Irving had been
embroiled for two months in what would be the longest
and most significant strike of his career. It was, at the same time, a
gauge of his progress. With the involvement in his life and the life
of New Brunswick of such international corporate giants as Standard of California, Kimberly-Clark, and Sogemines, there came
the claims of an international union that the time had come for
Irving to pay wages not at the local but at the national level.

The strike began in September 1963 and lasted six months; it
affected 145 employees of his three-year-old refinery. But this was
only part of the problem. Another supporting strike began over a
different issue in January 1964 among 150 men who delivered the
refinery's products out of fifteen Quebec communities. In Saint
John things became nasty. In Quebec they became ugly. For Irving
they became a preoccupation.

In launching a major industry, he had come up against a major
foe. The Saint John union, Local 9-691 of the Oil, Chemical and
Atomic Workers International Union, mustered both local and

powerful outside muscle in coupling its demand for national standards in wages and fringe benefits. Irving and his lawyers counterattacked. Montreal lawyer Yves Pratte, a key participant, said Irving was "convinced, honestly, that he couldn't afford it" and that "what he did was for the good of New Brunswick." The union, in turn, would come to claim that what happened was a watershed, even though, on the face of things, it lost.

The story, as Irving recalled it, went back to a deal he made with the local's leader when the refinery was built: he would not, apart from management, follow a customary oil industry practice of bringing in trained men to run it; he would bolster local employment by hiring men from the area and training them on the job. In return, the local would accept that its men would not be paid full wages until they were trained, until their merit justified them. By 1963, however, that leader had departed and the local, egged on from outside, said it wanted national or "industry" pay levels.

An Industrial Inquiry Commission probed the conflicting positions and in August Alan M. Sinclair reported that the refinery, by itself, did not have finances that could meet most of the union demands. With rates ranging from $1.85 to $2.15 an hour, he said, it was paying not much above local levels, but Irving had proposed a merit scheme that over the next few years would raise the rates of most of the personnel to a much higher level. Sinclair recommended wages from $1.97 to $2.55 and a further merit scheme that would take them as high as $3.08 after six years' experience. He cited top wages for crude-division operators in five refineries across the country at the time as ranging from $2.97 to $3.22.

Irving's response was, in effect, a rejection. He stood by his original offer of a two-year contract with a fifteen-cent-an-hour raise, an incentive plan that could double this, and a provision to reopen discussions in April 1964. Employees, he said, had been promoted at a much faster rate than in longer-established refineries, and he maintained that many had already reached pay scales equal to the highest paid in industry. The union counter-proposed a thirty-cent increase and a plan for workers reaching certain standards to receive industry rates after six years on the job under a program subject to grievance procedures. The company refused. The strike began.

It began with picketing of the refinery, service stations, and other Irving plants. Crowds of strikers milled around cars attempting to enter the plant; rocks and sticks were thrown, as well as many harsh words. With court injunctions, Irving soon blocked the secondary picketing and cut the refinery pickets sharply. There were continuous attempts at sabotage and harassment, such as shooting power-line insulators, and anonymous phone calls to staff wives.

Inside the refinery, Irving imported bunkhouse trailers and cooks, and men from his woods operations who operated boilers. Some seventy-five staff members kept the refinery going. Among them were men who supported him and others who would be forced to resign if they refused to work. As professionals, with help from others, they kept the refinery going more efficiently than it ever had, and Irving dropped in at times to lend moral support. Standard of California, his partners, didn't become involved at all.

Bedevilled by their own mistakes, the union did not fare well. National wages were $84.67 a week, New Brunswick wages $64.26, which many New Brunswickers accepted realistically; there were always considerably more job seekers than jobs. Then, too, the nearly automated refinery was not very vulnerable to labour trouble. When the 145 union members walked out, Irving's manager, William Forsythe, instructed clerks and bookkeepers to start watching the knobs and dials. In 22,000 man-hours per month they accomplished what the previous work force had done in 46,700.

As the strike entered its second month, public interest had begun to subside. Saint John was not much inconvenienced, and Irving saved more than $10,000 a week on payroll costs. On a November night the union staged an outdoor rally and hanged and burned Irving in effigy, along with the provincial minister of labour, K.J. Webber. Many in Saint John who respected if they did not like K.C. Irving were offended, especially since they suspected the bonfire had been engineered by outside agitators.

In January, Claude Jodoin, president of the Canadian Labour Congress, came to Saint John and spoke to a rally in support of the strikers. But his speech also ended the union's hopes of sympathy strikes at Irving's other businesses. Jodoin said he did not consider a general work stoppage necessary then.

By this time Irving's truck drivers in Quebec had struck against a plan to hire private truckers. Becoming violent, they slashed tires, smashed car windows, damaged trucks, harassed Irving employees, and released thousands of gallons of oil. They lost their strike too, and some of them faced court charges.

It was against this background that Irving intervened publicly a week after Jodoin spoke, giving a talk on his own radio station — the first and only time he had done so. Yves Pratte suggested some changes in what Irving was to say. Irving rejected them, and went ahead with a speech he had prepared himself. He gave Jodoin a tactful blessing, and then called on him to "call the national and international officers of the union to account."

After four months of attrition, the Oil, Chemical and Atomic Workers International Union sought a compromise. It was willing, it announced, to accept the wage adjustment offered originally by Irving. But on Irving's offer to raise all workers to the maximum wage as fast as they qualified, the union demanded a clause in the legal contract. Furthermore, if there was any doubt whether a given worker had qualified to move to the maximum through the long ladder of sub-qualifications (it could take five moves and five years), the union insisted the decision should not be left solely to Irving Refining, but also to a union nominee and someone from outside the company. If Irving denied a merit promotion to any worker who had earned it, then the worker and the union should have the right to file a grievance.

Irving was unyielding that cold winter. Even the legal two-man picket teams were often absent from the road outside the refinery. In March the union settled for almost everything Irving had offered in September. His wages were accepted and there was to be a right of arbitration on grievances only in the case of "discrimination," a face-saving word that neither side elaborated on. It ended a strike that had boiled over into politics. In the Legislature, Opposition members criticized the Robichaud government repeatedly for its failure to bring about a settlement, urged the premier to intervene, and sought the resignation of a beleaguered labour minister. A former Customs official, Webber had brought the parties together at least five times and said he had no legal power to compel a settlement. One union outsider said Webber wouldn't know the difference between a credit union, a labour union, and the Soviet Union. But what Irving liked to remember was the day he heard the same outsider say what a dreadful place New

Brunswick was, and Webber telling him never to say it again in his presence.

The settlement statement was signed by Irving and his refinery manager and five union officials, and it said the highest rates provided were "in line with those generally paid in the industry." In later years unionists would claim it as a breakthrough, a step towards the future national pay rates. They also said that for the first time Irving had taken them seriously.

As for Irving, he singled out Claude Jodoin for praise: "He didn't say a thing wrong. He said 'Sure, we can settle this,' and we got it settled. He was all right, that man."

CHAPTER TWENTY-THREE

❧

Portrait of a 65-Year-Old

"This man's gone mental. He's running everything."
– *Union leader J.K. Bell talking about K.C. Irving*
in the 1960s.

WHEN *MACLEAN'S*, THE NATIONAL MAGAZINE, PUBLISHED Ralph Allen's three articles on Irving in the spring of 1964, it was the most detailed and penetrating look any journalist had taken at him, even though Allen confessed that he initially approached the task with trepidation.

By the time they appeared Irving was sixty-five and showed no signs of slowing down. Allen undertook the assignment with the "same twinge of apprehension with which I had embarked in 1961 to do stories on Moise Tshombe in Katanga and Hendrik Vorwoerd in South Africa and, in 1962, on Fidel Castro in Cuba." Irving dominated New Brunswick "to a degree unknown in Canada since the long-vanished days of Lord Selkirk in Red River and Sir George Simpson in Rupert's Land. . . . I was warned: even enemies are loath to discuss him except in private, among themselves, like *Maquisards* hiding out in cellars."

When he got to Saint John, Allen raised the estimates of Irving's worth to $400 million. Yet the corporate aspects of the man "did not begin to match his personal aspects. He is a lean man, very hard and wary. He looks like a print of an English bare-knuckle fighter, a James Figg or a John Broughton or a Cheshire Hero. He is six feet tall, with wide shoulders and a narrow waist. He is as bald as an iceberg, his eyes are deep and gray, his jaw is square and strong and his aquiline nose is a little off-centre, as if he had been hit with a lucky punch. His manners are phenomenally inconsistent. With his subordinates and his casual acquaintances he shows the natural, old-fashioned courtesy of a boy who was brought up to be polite. Irving helps people on with their coats and calls everybody Mister. . . . But with those in a position to fight back he sometimes pounds tables and stalks out just like [Soviet premier] Khrushchev."

Usually, Irving wore conventional business suits but sometimes a checked jacket or "a hound's tooth as sporty as a bookmaker's." He had by this time moved his headquarters to a Golden Ball building converted to offices and "inhabited an office a third of a block long, loaded with Madison Avenue broadloom and panelling. Away down the room is a boardroom table. To the left was the only painting, a reproduction of one of the Graham Sutherland portraits of Lord Beaverbrook. The one other decoration was a small, three-cornered pennant saying *Irving Oil*.

"Behind the desk is the master set of a private network that is connected to all his plants and stores and ships and the homes of his senior employees. His four private planes and three automobiles are on the network too so that no Irving man . . . is ever far out of reach." Irving swivelled around constantly to use the network: "Golden Ball to Bouctouche store. How are you, Mr. Smathers? It's nice to hear from you."

In one of the studies in the Irving home there were more phones and microphones, and "hard as it is to believe," Allen found, "the first book you see is by Horatio Alger, Jr., the one entitled *Helping Himself or Grant Thornton's Rapid Rise in New York*."

Allen found that people who thought well of Irving were as unwilling to declare themselves as people who thought badly. A taxi driver told me he had once been stalled in the street in a blinding blizzard and that Irving, on his way to the theatre, had come along, pushed him to the nearest Irving gas station, filled his tank and paid the bill himself. Allen asked the driver if he would give me his name. "Nobody gets my name," he said nervously. "The union is mad at me already because I've run their picket line."

About Irving, with "monotonous — and after a while frightening — regularity," Allen got the same reaction, even from prominent businessmen in New Brunswick, Montreal, and Toronto. "The same phrase kept coming up, 'I'll have to ask you not to quote me, but . . .'" One other cab driver was an exception. "There is only one thing I know about Mr. Irving," said Raymond Gallant of Moncton, "and that's that he's very kind. Fifteen years ago I was broke and my wife was sick and I couldn't find a job anywhere. A man I knew gave me a note and told me to take it to Mr. Irving. Mr. Irving gave me $25 and told me to get on a train and see a construction man he knew here. It was as good as saving my life."

Irving, in fact, baffled not only Saint John and Fredericton but Montreal's St. James Street, Toronto's Bay Street, "and occasionally the financial thoroughfares of Paris and Brussels, Berlin, London, New York and Rome." It left him vulnerable to the kind of second-guessing that affected a famous medieval cardinal. The cardinal dropped dead and an emissary hastened with the glad news to his closest rival. "Dropped dead, eh?" said the second cardinal thoughtfully. "I wonder what his motive could have been."

One of Irving's American managers said, "There's nothing mean or dirty about him, but he knows the rules and expects you to know them too, and if you don't you'll get bruised. With him, business is a contact sport. He is the most amazing man I've ever met. I simply can't understand what he does. Almost against my will I began to like and admire him. There are two things that have impressed me most. First, his sensitivity to people. It's absolutely acute. Second, the loyalty he will return to the other man's loyalty."

To union leader J.K. Bell, "This man's gone mental. He's running everything."

A senior politician pointed out that "We haven't got a democracy in New Brunswick in the ordinary sense of the term. It's not a case of being corrupted in the way of money or favours. When the Conservatives were in power in the late 1950s, Mr. Irving got some of his new businesses moving and we all knew the province had begun to move. Then the Liberals got in but if the Conservatives had voted against him or any of his things it would have looked as if they were opposing progress and opposing their own performance."

As for an Ontario financier: "I like K.C. I like and admire him and what he has done not only for himself but for his part of the world. But when I am in a business transaction with him I find it well to keep my elbows up."

A Standard of California executive who "has not lost his astonishment at finding so sinewy and successful a man flourishing in so unlikely a portion of the hinterland" said, "I don't know if he indulges in introspection or self-evaluation. But I do know one thing. He's dedicated to building up this province and his determination has kept him going. The only quarrel a clear-thinking man could have with him is on the ground that industrialization is bad for this area. If industrialization is wrong, he is wrong. If it's right, he's right. The wealth is not on top of the ground here. It takes a very strong man to get it out."

According to Allen, Irving was not even "a distant cousin to the twentieth century entrepreneur or to the Harvard Business School executive with his sacred first command: 'Hire good men and give them their head.' He is not interested in being a boardroom genius and the only place he was ever known to give any man, however good, his head, it was tucked under his arm, accompanied by a one-way ticket to Chicago." By "instant, fingertip control" of everything he owned, by rarely selling stock, by freeing himself to make instant and unilateral decisions, he had been able to "conduct his affairs with the proud and sometimes ruthless independence of the last of a breed of kings." Even when he entered partnerships, he had in all but one case arranged to be the largest owner, and even in the one exception (Brunswick) he was the most influential member of an inner group of four.

He showed no signs of giving up work. When Allen asked if he had ever thought of retiring, Irving said carefully: "Well, of course, everyone figures he must get out gradually. But one advantage of having a small organization is that you don't have such rigid rules about retirement and such things." His toughness was demonstrated in the refinery strike, in his reactions to Rothesay Paper, his quests for concessions and other matters, and in his use of the courts.

"He is the most litigious man in the world," one lawyer said. "Normally a lawyer tries to get his client out of court but Irving wants to fight everything through to a finish. Once he had a really difficult case and he was advised to settle. 'I don't believe I asked you for a verdict,' he said to his lawyer. 'I was inquiring whether you'd care to represent me.' He went to the Supreme Court and won."

The admiration Irving inspired, said Allen, "is frequently tempered by a sort of *yes-but* syndrome. 'Yes, but if he weren't so bloody big.'" Or a kindred statement voiced by many, high and low: "K.C. Irving is the greatest thing that ever happened to New Brunswick. It's too bad we haven't got four or five (or six or seven) more like him. . . . It would be much greater for everybody if there were a few other Irvings to cut him down to size."

Yet Irving showed no inclination to be cut down to size. The tougher the competition, the more he seemed at home. When a Canadian Oil official claimed his was the only Canadian-owned oil company operating in the Maritimes, Irving issued an outraged statement saying that his was not only Canadian-owned but Maritimes-owned. "Let's not forget," he said, "that in some cases Upper Canadians are the worst type of foreigners."

Allen said it was "almost never safe to guess what Irving is thinking or is apt to do," and he had a personal experience that proved it. On his arrival in Saint John, Irving said he would not be interviewed. Then he granted four interviews with no hint of an explanation for his change of mind.

"It was true that he told me almost nothing, but even in his most guarded moments he fell far short of the advertised figure of the icy, arrogant feudal lord. . . . Even when I brought up matters which he clearly believes are nobody's business but his own, he was polite. His personal manners bear so little resemblance to his corporate manners that some of the people who have seen him lose his temper or heard him hurl his clipped insults . . . have put it down to business tactics rather than to blood pressure."

In the interviews, Irving refused to comment on his wealth and denied that he was the power behind the provincial Liberal party or got excessive concessions. When Allen reported the widespread impression that Irving maintained "such close personal control over your enterprises and delegate so little authority that they couldn't possibly carry on without you and no one can possibly ever succeed you," Irving said: "In my absence the senior men in the overall organization are my sons in the order of their ages."

Allen asked how many companies he owned. Irving said, "That gets to be something that doesn't mean anything. It sometimes gets to be kind of silly. I think sometimes the more foolish you are the more companies you have. But that's not necessarily so. However, the number of companies you have is no measuring stick for anything."

And how many employees did he have? Irving: "That figure will take a few days to obtain." Later Allen was told: "Our employees are estimated to number between 12,000 and 13,000," about 8.5 per cent of the provincial total.

CHAPTER TWENTY-FOUR

☙

Bad Chemistry

"In the final analysis K.C. Irving was right."
  – NEW BRUNSWICK PREMIER LOUIS J. ROBICHAUD, RECALLING
  IRVING'S PREDICTION THAT THE DORCHESTER CAPE CHEMICAL
  PARK WAS DOOMED TO FAIL.

K.C. Irving: "Is that before or after depreciation?"

New Brunswick Government Official: "Before or after what?"

Irving: "Depreciation. You know what depreciation is, don't you?"

Government Official: "Yes, of course I know what depreciation is."

It was a tense, somewhat testy exchange as politicians and government officials attempted to convince Irving that a fertilizer plant at a proposed chemical park would be a viable project. Irving was seething, but his voice was low, under control. He was being lectured and patronized by people he was convinced did not know what they were talking about. On this day his patience was sorely tested.

The Robichaud government was determined to forge ahead with the chemical park at Dorchester Cape, 35 kilometres south of Moncton. A key component of the park would be a fertilizer plant. The government saw it as part of a huge industrial complex with unlimited economic possibilities. Irving saw it as a colossal, ill-conceived, ill-timed blunder.

He repeated the question: "You say the project will make millions of dollars even in the early years. Is that before or after depreciation?" Another pause. And then the reply: "I'm not sure . . . I don't think I checked on that."

Now it was time for Irving to blink in disbelief. The man who knew everything about balance sheets and taxes and depreciation; the man who would pause to pick up a ten-cent piece on a busy street, the man who shined his own shoes all his life, looked at the young expert on the other side of the table who a few moments earlier had been speaking with such confidence on the merits of the government-backed project. He shook his head in despair and wondered if he had heard correctly.

A thoroughly exasperated Irving recalled later that the young man did not seem to comprehend that the profit or loss figure would change by hundreds of thousands of dollars, perhaps millions of dollars, as it moved below the line of depreciation on a project of this magnitude. On top of all that, Irving was convinced the project was doomed to fail and that its proponents were blinded by business ignorance and political expediency.

"Well, thank you for that information," said Irving. "It tells me a lot."

Then the meeting got rough.

It took place in the 1960s in a government office in Fredericton, and it turned into a bitter confrontation and became one of the incidents that would drive a wedge between Irving and Premier Robichaud.

As for others, the 1960s were to become the most controversial decade of his career, a turning point in his life, a time of frustration, boardroom battles, confrontation with government, and in the end, a time of extreme bitterness. In his view it was a time of deceit, backroom intrigue, and conspiracy. It was also, he felt, a time of vindictiveness and stupidity, when ordinary, reasonable people were blinded by hate, distrust, and greed.

At the centre of much of the many-sided controversy was what many saw as New Brunswick's golden gateway to the future — the huge Brunswick Mining development on the outskirts of Bathurst. Irving thought of that great ore body as New Brunswick's heritage, something to be nurtured, developed, and controlled by New Brunswickers. He would never forgive those, notably Robichaud, who played a pivotal role in bringing in outsiders to run it. To Irving, that act alone was a stab in the back.

And of all those involved, all those on the Brunswick board who favoured the action and all those who played roles in bringing about the takeover, Robichaud, in Irving's eyes, remained the villain. Irving held him responsible. Never again was there an accommodation between the two men. It was, in fact, the culmination of a number of controversies between the two men. For in the 1960s the flamboyant Robichaud was a man on the move, a man of action and high energy. He made little attempt to hide or disguise his love of the good life. He would party hard and long, and often would be at his best on the hustings or as a dinner speaker while fueling his rhetoric with a nectar that was not purchased at the corner grocery store. For Robichaud, the 1960s were a time of hectic activity, turmoil, change, controversy — and paradox.

It was, after all, he who in 1960 spoke warmly at the opening of the Irving Refinery, who gave Irving those 36.8 hectares of land to expand the Saint John Drydock. In 1961 he initiated the move that got Irving into Brunswick, and in 1962, under his government, the long Beechwood conflict was settled. But he was proud, and the initial friendliness changed as controversies and collisions grew. He did not want anyone to think he was an Irving man — an Irving yes man. It was in this changing atmosphere that he sought to do what Hugh John Flemming before him had started with Rothesay Paper: broaden New Brunswick's industrial base and in effect balance Irving's power with the power of others.

He opened the way for Rothesay Paper to get into production, refused to countenance delay in construction of the Brunswick smelter, refused to grant Irving the crown lands he wanted for a newsprint mill that, he later said, would have given him an almost complete monopoly in southern New Brunswick. He appeared to Irving to be threatening his tax concessions. He brought in foreign interests for forestry development and launched government-sponsored projects that Irving opposed or would have nothing to do with. He brought in outsiders to take over Brunswick. By 1967 there was only bitterness between them, but it had been years in the making.

Not long after the Beechwood matter was settled, Robichaud's government started to build another major St. John River power

development, the $120-million Mactaquac dam that brought the log
drives to an end. The New Brunswick Electric Power Commission
authorities said there was no practical way for logs to pass through
the dam. One provincial official said Irving had indicated he realized
the era was coming to an end anyway. Irving himself said he felt a
flume could have been provided to allow the drives to survive for at
least another ten years. When it wasn't, he closed his Saint John
sawmill and moved its equipment hundreds of kilometres north to
Estcourt, Quebec, lamenting the loss of an industry and great quan-
tities of Maine wood to Saint John, claiming the city, which had
been the site of many sawmills, had been shorn of a birthright.

Irving was involved as well in at least one more Robichaud
move into industry. A study headed by John S. Bates had reported
that hundreds of thousands of cords of overmature wood were
going to waste each year in the watershed of the Miramichi and
that the best way to avoid this would be to build pulp mills to
exploit them. The Flemming government had not acted on the
report, but Robichaud did. He called together representatives of
the firms that held timber rights in the area, Irving among them,
and urged them to build a mill he said had been promised to the
Miramichi for years; they could do it any way they wished but it
had to be done. Irving offered to combine with another company
to do it, but the plan did not go ahead. Various company spokesmen said a mill would be uneconomic; Robichaud accused them
of dragging their feet, of keeping lands as bank collateral.

Robichaud made a deal with Italy's Cartier del Timavo to build
a $15-million groundwood pulp mill under the name of South
Nelson Forest Products Ltd. In return for a licence to cut wood,
much of which was to be exported in a semi-processed state, the
company would be obliged to buy as much wood from small
woodlot owners as it sent overseas.

To make the deal possible, Robichaud reallocated crown lands in
the Miramichi area, giving South Nelson sufficient stumpage to
make the mill possible. He was soon caught up in a political storm.
In the Legislature, the Progressive Conservatives accused him of
giving away 2,590 square kilometres of choice timberland, favouring
foreign interests, and offering to build roads and provide cheap
power at the taxpayers' expense. He replied that this was the first
phase of a three-stage project worth $45 million and that the initial

steps would involve 1,500 jobs. The Tories argued that most of the jobs would go to Italians; they called for a judicial inquiry and suggested that the whole thing was a public scandal. Robichaud charged them with being against outside capital and industrial development.

The arguments came to a head in an election campaign. Sensing an opportunity, Robichaud caught his enemies off guard by announcing an election. After a bitter fight, Robichaud won. On April 22, 1963, he took thirty-two seats to the Conservatives' twenty, without ever disclosing just what he had promised to the Italians.

The campaign was viewed by Irving in public silence. He didn't oppose the South Nelson project vigorously, but he was opposed to it. Robichaud saw this as one more step in the deterioration of their relations. Publicly, too, Irving had little to say about another development, but in private he expressed indignation. It was the brainchild of Frederick Gormley, a Nova Scotian-born engineer who had come up from Texas to head the provincial government's Development Corporation. In his thirst for jobs, Robichaud accepted Gormley's recommendation to usher New Brunswick into a new age by building a chemical park that would, it was trumpeted, lead to numerous industrial offshoots and to thousands of jobs. It was this project — the chemical park and a fertilizer plant — that was under discussion the day Irving asked questions of people he became convinced didn't know what they were talking about.

For political reasons, under pressure from cabinet ministers from that area, the park was to be built in the south of the province, somewhere near Moncton. Gormley was assigned to find a site, and found it on a weekend trip that took him to the shores of Shepody Bay, that inlet of Fundy, in Albert County. With binoculars, he looked across the waters and saw what was to become widely known as Dorchester Cape, though it was known locally as Cole's Point. It was low, treed, rustic, and empty, on ground just below where the Petitcodiac and Memramcook rivers surrendered their brown, muddy waters to the bay. This, Gormley decided, would be the site, and there the project started.

The Brunswick Mining development already was committed to one large fertilizer plant and Irving couldn't believe that the province was about to become involved in the creation of a second. Irving's assessment of the project was cold, blunt, and negative. He said it wouldn't pay. He cited facts about what it was to produce, said the site was wrong, that his ships had sailed carefully through these waters for years; he knew what silt and mud could do, and with two rivers contributing them to the bay at that spot he had grave doubts about the location. Furthermore, and most significantly, a government-backed chemical park, he said, would make as its major product fertilizers that would compete in a limited market with those to be produced by the plant to be built as part of the government-backed Brunswick complex, a plant it would be tough to make pay.

Robichaud denied it, but Irving said the premier reacted violently. Irving's version was that the premier "gave me the goshdarndest lecture you ever heard. Said he didn't want to hear this terrible talk. He was mad as a porcupine. He got red in the face. He banged the table. I got two or three fits of the damnedest tirade. He just raved on and on." Whether Irving liked it or not, Robichaud said, the park would go ahead.

When the meeting was over, Irving said, Finance Minister L.G. Desbrisay of Moncton came over to speak to him and to ask whether he realized that the government had consulted a number of experts and found them agreed that the project was feasible. It didn't change Irving's mind, but he thanked him. In any event, the chemical park was built, with rosy predictions of a varied economic payoff for an area badly in need of stimulation, with plans to defeat the mud, silt, and troubling tides with a floating dock linked to the land. The story goes that the captain of the first ship that appeared with cargo refused to dock, and sailed away. Soon, for various reasons, the whole project was a disaster, its structures abandoned, the rails that linked it with the main CNR line a few miles away left to rust. Never one to miss an opportunity, Irving had built the floating dock. He eventually purchased it and towed it away for possible use another day, in another project. The dream that turned into a nightmare had cost the taxpayer millions and it was, Robichaud admitted publicly, a mistake, the only one he ever acknowledged.

"In the final analysis," he said years later, "K.C. Irving was right. It was a failure. Gormley felt strongly about it, and he was wrong. But the whole cabinet agreed to go ahead despite Irving's objections. I later told the Legislature I wasn't happy to admit it, but I did: it was a blunder."

CHAPTER TWENTY-FIVE

❧

Irving and Noranda

"The committee was stunned. This legendary figure overwhelmed us. It was the first time he had personally said publicly 'I don't approve.'"
– *FUTURE PREMIER RICHARD HATFIELD DESCRIBING K.C. IRVING'S APPEARANCE BEFORE A LEGISLATURE COMMITTEE.*

FOR IRVING, WESTMORLAND PARK WAS NOTHING MORE THAN an irritating incident when compared to the long and bitter struggle he endured through his involvement in the destiny of Brunswick. Originally he had been a vital linchpin when the premier recognized that a builder was needed and M.J. Boylen sought Irving's financial help to create the huge mining complex near Bathurst. Yet the same men who sought Kenneth Colin Irving's help to provide financing, stability, and credibility would in time, in his own harsh and unforgiving judgment, betray both him and New Brunswick.

But the bad times and the bitter ultimate confrontations were still in the future in January 1964 when Brunswick president Erskine Carter reported to shareholders that construction on the No. 12 mine and the concentrator was on schedule and that, under Irving's Engineering Consultants, the work had been carried through well. The concentrator should be ready to ship concentrates to Belgium by May. Results of extensive metallurgical tests were good. No. 12 had exposed a larger ore-body than anticipated — enough, indeed, to last at least twenty years. The directors, Carter

190

said, had agreed to boost the concentrator's capacity to 4,500 tons a day, to construct the $24-million smelter and an associated refinery to be ready by July 1, 1966, and to build a sulphuric plant. To raise the $30 million necessary to meet these costs, the company faced complications because its assets were already mortgaged. It proposed to do it with first mortgage bonds, $20 million of them guaranteed by the government, and with a $2-million advance from Engineering Consultants if the bond sale and an additional $4 million were not enough to pay for the smelter. Carter added that they proposed to increase authorized capital to 10 million shares from 7.5 million.

That summer the confidence and high hope found expression in another way. At Irving's shipyard in Saint John the largest ship in the Canadian merchant marine was christened — a 30,700-ton ore and oil carrier built at a cost of $9 million. Its owner, Canadian General Electric Ltd., had leased it to Engineering Consultants for charter to Brunswick. It would take concentrates to Belgium and return with oil for Irving's refinery. The christening ceremony was a gala affair, with a proud Jim Boylen and a large group of friends present as his wife named the ship the *M.J. Boylen* — a name Irving eventually would have removed from the ship's hull when relations between the two men ended in bitter controversy over the future of the Brunswick mining development.

In August Brunswick shares were attracting buyers at a price of $10.25, perhaps on word of the company's cashing in on high zinc prices. Then came much larger news: on October 26 Robichaud went on television to announce a $117-million steel, mining, chemical, and fertilizer complex. All this, Boylen said, would make Brunswick a $200-million complex. Arrangements had been made for virtually all of the $117 million expenditure without diluting shareholders' equity, and even this was not all. Already, he said, Brunswick was thinking of further steps.

Within a week it was reported that Irving now controlled Brunswick; he owned 1.7 million shares of Key Anacon. His Kent Line was also buying $900,000 worth of Anacon debentures, which could be converted into 900,000 shares to make Irving 47 per cent owner of Anacon. With the Brunswick shares Anacon owned and with those he already had, Irving would have about 38 per cent of Brunswick, Boylen 29 per cent.

These developments raised a question that vexed Irving then and later. It was true that he had been buying Brunswick shares wherever he could find them, and that he sought majority control. Boylen said he needed money and Irving provided it in return for shares in various Boylen properties and, with them, Brunswick shares they owned. But "I never had control of Brunswick," Irving would say repeatedly. To him, control meant at least 51 per cent and preferably more, the sort of control he was used to, the sort that would have let him delay the smelter and prevent what eventually happened.

By that summer he knew the smelter was in both financial and technical difficulties. But he was getting nowhere in urging reconsideration, or at least a slowdown. In June Robichaud snipped a ribbon at the formal opening of the first mine and the first concentrator, announced a $22-million ammonia plant, and then made a pointed remark that the time had come for other mining companies to follow Brunswick's lead in developing their New Brunswick properties or to face government action.

Profits were reported excellent, the mine was employing 500 and once construction projects were in full stride there would be 3,000 people at work. In July improvements had been made to the smelter's Imperial process and modifications had been authorized that would increase its capacity by 80 per cent and its cost to $32 million.

But all was not well and the black clouds of trouble and conflict were forming. In fact, Irving said he eventually got information that Boylen had told an accountant that he wanted the accountant's firm out of Brunswick, that they were captives of Irving, that he was going to run the company and Irving could resign if he didn't like it. On a trip to Finland, Irving said, he refused to sign an agreement with a Finnish firm for construction of the steel mill despite the urging of Boylen and Gilbert Kerlin, a key Brunswick director from New York: "They chased me all around the hotel."

On August 20 he wrote to Boylen — now president after the resignation of Carter — to warn him that the company was heading into financial trouble. On September 2 he wrote to Kerlin in concern about Brunswick's debt and urging that they "develop a completely new program in respect to both the timing and extent of building of the plant."

Certainly the work was having difficulties. The smelter was being designed and redesigned during the building program. Changes and expansion had to be worked in. Designed to handle zinc, the Imperial process had to be modified to refine lead too. The close proximity of the lead and zinc refineries caused problems, as did key sintering equipment that would set the pace of production.

For Irving, John D. Park proved to be a headache too, but that one he did resolve. He ended his association with Park in October, bought out his minority shares in Engineering Consultants and ended what many had considered a strange mismatch of two entirely different management styles. It was a cold parting, the culmination of varied difficulties. Irving refused to say publicly what prompted it, but he did indicate it had nothing to do with Brunswick. He denied reports that it stemmed from Park's close social contacts with Robichaud, but there is no doubt that Irving resented the latter, nor was it any secret that Irving was concerned about the effect Park's high-flying lifestyle might have on Robichaud. He did confirm that Robichaud tried to get him to reinstate Park, and that he refused.

Before Park's departure, Irving had had another rebuff from the premier. Plans for Brunswick's steel mill had prompted him to go to Fredericton to seek a $50-million government guarantee of bonds to finance it. If given one, Irving told a Legislature committee, "we'll gamble the rest of our money on all the projects associated with it." He didn't get it. Robichaud was said to be surprised by the request, and he refused to make any guarantee without more information. Irving was unhappy. The project was shelved, and there it remained.

By now there was open and bitter dissension on the Brunswick board as costs continued to escalate. At a meeting of Brunswick directors in New York, Irving repeated once again that the smelter was costing much more than had been planned. He asked the meeting to hear a report from Eugene Estes, the American who was now heading Engineering Consultants, but he got cold comfort. Carter, he recalled, said he had to leave on a trip. Kerlin left the room, and Boylen didn't want to listen.

The strains at Brunswick's top level were now as apparent as they were paradoxical. On one hand there was Irving, arguing that the start of the smelter construction had been premature and urging a slowdown. On the other side was Boylen, who wanted to push ahead but claimed that the real problem was the number of Irving companies involved in the construction, making more and more money the longer the smelter job lasted. Yet despite this, Irving was blowing the whistle on the project, fighting for a delay that would have halted construction.

While Boylen and Brunswick had become thorns in Irving's side, what provoked his public wrath in December 1965 was news that the provincial government was about to place before the Legislature its proposals arising from the Byrne Report.

As chairman, Edward G. Byrne, a prominent Bathurst lawyer, and four other men were appointed by Robichaud in 1962 to a royal commission asked "to evaluate every aspect of municipal government in New Brunswick, the financial and other relationships between the province and municipalities, and the division of functions between the two levels of government." Its recommendations, made public in 1964 — in a document of 834 pages plus a smaller volume of appendices — urged changes that would markedly enhance the scope and power of the provincial government and thus inflame political debate.

Among other things, they called for elimination of traditional county councils and assignment of local matters only to local bodies. Concentrated in Fredericton would be power over education, health, welfare, and justice. Appointed commissioners would assess and collect all real property taxes at uniform rates. There would be equalization grants to municipalities, higher salaries to attract more able people to the public service, abolition of the poll tax, to be replaced by taxes on personal property ranging from hens to cars, a new tax on motor vehicles, and an increase in the provincial sales tax from 3 per cent to 5 per cent. The report called for a uniform educational system to consolidate schools and wipe out hundreds of one- and two-room schools, eliminate most local school boards, and make teachers provincial employees at salaries set by the province. Multiple-member political constituencies would be replaced by single constituencies, timberlands would be more equitably taxed, and tax concessions granted to industry by municipalities eliminated.

Late in 1965 Robichaud announced his policy, "Equal Opportunity," in a long speech and in a white paper. The commission had recommended its report be accepted as a package. The government rejected the proposal that social services be run by appointed boards. It also proposed to raise the sales tax to 6 per cent to bring in an estimated $20 million a year to help meet the costs of change. Otherwise, it very largely set out to do what the commission had urged it to do.

In an impoverished province with a scattered population of 626,000, one-quarter the size of metropolitan Toronto or Montreal, this coincided with Quebec's Quiet Revolution and it became a sort of unquiet, unrestrained parallel that shook New Brunswick's English–French relations to their depths.

The government sought quicker passage for its assessment act than for its other bills so the program could be launched by January 1, 1967. That bill was sent to a new law amendments committee for public comment, and it was there that Irving made an appearance, abandoning his silent ways and launching a devastating attack on apparent proposals to do away with existing tax concessions to industry.

"Nowhere," the report said, "is the lack of uniformity in real property taxation more glaring than in the case of exemptions and reliefs from the tax levy. The present chaos is the result of generations of indulgency by provincial governments in the face of the vociferous appeals of municipalities, industry and others. Score upon score of concessions have been made in a haphazard fashion, and now it is virtually impossible to count them accurately let alone estimate their cost." It had identified more than eighty-five private acts and eleven orders-in-council providing for special tax arrangements, and at least seven more that existed without apparent legal authority. Its recommendation: "That all existing exemptions and relief from the taxation of real property granted to commercial and industrial concerns be cancelled and without the payment of any compensation."

In the cabinet's first drafts of legislation, it accepted this proposal. Then it said it would not. But the bill presented to the committee didn't say so. To Irving and others, it indicated that the government did intend to abolish existing concessions. A cabinet minister of the time said the bill "was honestly capable of two interpretations," a fateful factor he attributed to differences of opinion in Liberal ranks.

The second background factor involved Irving's reaction to things Robichaud had already done, ranging from Rothesay Paper to the refusal of crown lands and the seizure of others, from Mactaquac to the Westmorland Chemical Park and the refusal of delay in construction of Brunswick's smelter. A storm was brewing, and Irving's impassioned appearance before the Legislature committee blew it into a hostile gale.

As committee chairman, Attorney General Wendell Meldrum faced a hectic task only three months after being elected to the Legislature. A former solicitor for the university town of Sackville, and a future judge, he was at forty-one a solid, brawny man who liked to play a round of early-morning golf before work. He believed in the report's findings. But on the first day of committee hearings he was in a difficult position because the cabinet had left doubts about its attitude to the tax concessions. Moreover, there was an agreement that committee members would not argue among themselves or with witnesses.

Robichaud was away that day. Municipal Affairs Minister Norbert Theriault was present, and listened for hours to Irving and others before making a final statement of the government's position. Into that vacuum controversy stalked.

What the bill itself said was that "Notwithstanding any private or special Act, where no other provision is made under this Act, the Municipalities Act or the Schools Act, all provincial, municipal or local taxes or rates on real property shall be calculated and levied upon the whole of the assessment or assessments made under this Act."

That was the first thing Irving's lawyer, Adrian Gilbert, noted in a submission on behalf of three companies that had special statutes related to the assessments. Irving Refining Ltd. had been granted one by the County and City of Saint John and other bodies in 1958, "provided the Company proceeds to construct a petroleum refinery . . . within three years." For five years it would pay $51,000 a year, then $65,500 for the next ten, then a maximum of $75,000. "Without such tax agreements," Gilbert said, "no refinery would have been constructed." Again, under a 1959 statute, the company had built a causeway that became a highway link across Courtenay Bay on the agreed understanding that the 118 acres north of the causeway would be assessed at not more than

$100 an acre until they had been reclaimed by filling and put to use. In 1951 Irving Pulp and Paper Ltd. was granted a concession if it expanded its plant and built a bleached sulphate mill. In 1961–62 J.D. Irving Ltd. obtained a special assessment in Madawaska County: provided it constructed a sawmill, it would be exempt from municipal taxes for five years and pay only an annual $500 school tax. In 1963 that company erected a sawmill at Chipman and got from the County of Queens an exemption from tax during construction, then faced a tax of $5,000 a year for ten years. If these agreements, made in good faith, were killed, Gilbert said, it would have ruinous financial results for the three companies.

It was in following up that submission that Irving himself delivered his "blast." People who sat near him say he was shaking in fury as he awaited his turn to speak.

He was, he said, "gravely concerned" about the "breach of faith." As things now stood, the government would have the power to destroy agreements. He also understood that the suggestion had been made that broken agreements might be renegotiated, that "the government may, if it wishes, grant some industries the right to remain in existence while retaining the power — a power morally wrong if not illegally seized — to force other industries out of business." Was the government under the impression that New Brunswick's relatively few industries would be able to provide the great costs needed to launch and sustain the report's program? "Gentlemen, you cannot get blood out of a stone, nor can you find food in an empty cupboard."

Since he took it over in 1946, he said, his pulp mill had operated at capacity, but without the concessions the operation would not have been possible and expansion would not have been undertaken. Over twenty years, in fact, the mill had had a net operating deficit of $4 million. In the last five years it had an operating loss of over $7 million. "Do you honestly think the government is going to assist the economy of New Brunswick by breaking a tax agreement with this mill?"

He expected those tax agreements to be honoured and, he said, "We are alarmed that anyone would propose legislation which would deprive industries of their contractual rights." Yet, as he understood it, the bill would give the government the authority to do so. It was "trying to stuff this bill down our throats," but it should understand that "some industries are liable to choke to death. Others may have to pull back on expansion plans. . . . Surely the government does not expect to attract new industry, or even retain existing industry under such terms. Where are we going to place our trust?"

Irving's speech shook the committee. To Conservative member and future premier Richard Hatfield, it went beyond that: "He did it with such force, strength and power that it permeated the whole province. It was the first time I ever saw power being manifested in such a personal way. In capital letters. And the impact it had! The committee was stunned. This legendary figure overwhelmed us. It was the first time he had personally said publicly 'I don't approve.'"

It was not until Robichaud returned to the city that the government answered Irving and the other critics who testified. In a prepared statement, Norbert Theriault said, "There is no provision in this act whereby existing tax concessions can or will be broken. Nor is there any intention by the government to break such agreements. The government believes it has a moral obligation to honour these agreements and it fully intends to do so." This, the minister said, had always been government policy; it thought that policy was reflected in the legislation, but it would revise the bill to make the intention even clearer.

In the Legislature later, the Opposition accused the government of trying to smuggle in the relevant clause. The cabinet retorted that the clause was inserted so that industries that wished "voluntarily" to have their concessions removed could do so. Whatever the explanation, Irving had made his point and seen it take effect. But most significant of all was the broad meaning of his words. Explicitly, it was unstated. Implicitly, it was clear. The break with Robichaud was irreparable.

⁊

The fight over Equal Opportunity went on for weeks in a growing crescendo of animosity that descended into hate. The Byrne Commission had had little success in getting public reaction at its hearings. The government's legislation provoked it in virulent and multitudinous variety. Members and newspapers were flooded with letters. There were widespread accusations that the more prosperous English-speaking areas were to be taxed to pour money into a French-speaking population that comprised close to 40 per cent of the provincial total. A Protestant minister asked if it was "right to rob Peter to pay Pierre," and the words became a rancid slogan. English-speaking teachers criticized the educational proposals; French-speaking teachers favoured them. English-speaking Fredericton, said to be expected to raise $600,000 a year through higher taxes, became a cockpit of rancour. It was a trying time for the premier, the pressure all but unbearable. The legislation was called the most extensive program of reform in provincial-municipal administration in Canada. He also knew — whatever history's ultimate judgment — it would be the most important legacy of his political career.

J.S. Rioux, a well-to-do Acadian resident of Fredericton, led a self-described non-partisan committee, stumped the province with a petition demanding withdrawal of the assessment act, and said his main concern was that a vicious anti-Catholic, anti-French whispering campaign was producing an Acadian backlash; the Opposition, he said, was opposing governmental centralization, not the French.

The ultimate focus of struggle, the Legislature, sat until late February 1966 in the longest session in its history, passed a revised assessment act, then resumed the fight at a new session in March. Progressive Conservatives led by Cyril B. Sherwood filibustered for an election and opposed the teeming legislation every step of the way.

Irving's name came up when Labour Minister Webber claimed Irving had protested against possible renunciation of tax concessions for his own benefit. Webber said he was going to bring in a wage bill that was "going to hurt Mr. Irving and others. And when you hit the pocketbook it hurts." When the Rioux petition surfaced with 31,000 signatures — less than a third of the 100,000 it sought — the Opposition demanded withdrawal of the assessment act. Robichaud laughed it off. He said he would not budge an inch from his objectives, though he would allow for amendments when improvements could be anticipated.

By the end of 1966 the battle over Equal Opportunity was over. Its legislation was passed, and on January 1, 1967, it began to take effect. It left the government with the task of working out the details of enhanced power and enhanced and costly responsibilities, left county shiretowns without the official functions they had had for decades, left bitterness, changed political loyalties, English–French cleavages, and anticipation that more fighting was to come.

To some, Robichaud had courted political death in tackling Irving. There was speculation, too, that Robichaud's relations with Irving had not been helped by his friendship with John D. Park. Since Park and Irving had parted, Park was seen as a rising industrial power. He had become a director of Atlantic Sugar Refineries Co. Ltd., a rapidly diversifying company backed by the Gairdner financial interests of Toronto. Its Canadian Tuna Corporation had announced plans for a $1.5-million fish plant in a new government-backed industrial park at a time when Irving was reportedly interested in getting into fish processing himself. Moreover, Atlantic Sugar had also gained control of South Nelson Forest Products and hoped to build a newsprint mill.

But it wasn't over South Nelson or John D. Park or Equal Opportunity that the final break came in Robichaud's relations with Irving. It was over Brunswick Mining and Smelting. On the New Year's Day Equal Opportunity began to take effect, things were happening at Brunswick Mining and Smelting.

The smelter was up, a complex of rugged, handsome structures near the Bay of Chaleur. It looked good. The buildings were of structural steel, most of them with walls of prestressed concrete slabs. The automated plant had for its basic unit an Imperial smelting furnace, only the eleventh such to be built in the world.

Jim Boylen told shareholders in late July 1966 that it would be operating by the end of the year, with annual sales revenue close to $76 million, and that operating profit before depreciation writeoffs and taxes could reach $29 million. But that anticipated profit, from processing and selling concentrates, could be doubled once the company had facilities to produce iron sinter and sulphur and to recover additional zinc, lead, silver, and copper still being lost in tailings. These, however, awaited expansion, and expansion depended on prices and the raising of money.

Brunswick's president and chairman said No. 6's open-pit mine would be in full production and the No. 1 acid plant in operation by the end of the year, with the No. 1 fertilizer plant starting up a year later. The ammonia plant, the steel rolling mills and chemical plants were for the future, but even without them Boylen could foresee sales revenue of $162 million, approximately 34 per cent of the gross value of all manufactured goods in New Brunswick in 1965. A first dividend could be paid by 1969 or 1970.

That July the *Northern Miner* said that the smelter would start operating in the third quarter of 1966 and that an increase in its estimated metal capacity — for zinc from 31,000 tons to 52,000, for lead from 31,000 to 54,000 — had increased the capital cost of the plant to an estimated $62 million but "will raise profitability." A second July article reported that the smelter was "getting very close to the start-up date." The equipment for sintering had already been run in. The acid plant was about 99 per cent complete, the furnace building was well along, and the zinc and lead refineries were not far behind. The new $62-million estimate of total cost, the *Miner* explained, included $17 million for the fertilizer plant. As late as January 7, 1967, it reported that running up of the smelter was "proceeding satisfactorily" and that its general manager was "very pleased" with the way things were going. In fact, rising costs, vanishing profits, swelling animosities, and continuing technical problems were heading the world's eleventh Imperial smelter into terminal trouble. Metallurgist Desmond Bayley couldn't get his pace-setting sintering process working adequately and, behind the scenes, two rival forces were making moves in the face of a baleful prospect: that Brunswick was in serious danger of going broke unless something was done, and that its ores and concentrates couldn't make money as fast as the faltering smelter was swallowing it.

Against that background, the two forces moved in mutual secrecy into corporate drama. One was Irving. As his warnings of a premature smelter start took on brutal reality, he offered to buy Boylen out of yet another mining company, First Maritime, whose Brunswick shares could give him majority control. He had already turned to his oil allies, Standard of California, and acquired from them an engineer to manage the smelter. Then he got them to send in an expert to see what could be done to make it work properly and to consider whether their company should get involved as part of its subsidiary role in mining. He made arrangements to raise $63.5 million to bring about Brunswick's rescue.

Standard's men came to Belledune and worked quietly. So did their rivals, metallurgists, engineers, and accountants from Noranda Mines Ltd., a powerful Canadian company with headquarters in

Toronto. They, too, were there by invitation. Jim Boylen and at least one other Brunswick director, with the blessings of the Robichaud government, had invited them in. A race was on.

Noranda's people came, saw, and reported, but for a time there was a lull. Then came a call: "Help, help, you've got to help us." Brunswick was close to going bankrupt. Noranda's two top men were in Barbados. Executives flew down and they made a decision that was put into contract form on a plane on the way back: they would offer to take Brunswick over. They knew the company was in deep trouble over its smelter, but they felt its massive ore-bodies justified what they proposed to do and they were confident they had the know-how that Brunswick lacked.

They won the race. In Irving's words, he ran out of time. His bid to take over Boylen's shares in First Maritime was frustrated, colleagues said, because Boylen held up a meeting until it was too late. Irving's offer of $63.5 million, one he would refer to repeatedly in years to come, was never made clear to them, Brunswick directors and cabinet ministers said, until that was too late, too. But other factors influenced the outcome of this multi-million-dollar struggle for control. Boylen was against him. Other Brunswick directors were against him. Robichaud's government was against him, and it had a crucial weapon. Brunswick had asked for another $20-million guarantee and, as government-appointed director E.G. Byrne put it, there would be no guarantee unless Noranda was brought in.

Boylen announced Noranda's involvement on March 21. The directors, he said, had voted unanimously to bring Noranda in, indicating that Irving had accepted it because, as he later said, he saw no alternative. The second and final step was taken in June, at a special five-hour meeting attended by sixty-eight shareholders. Noranda's takeover was approved after the chairman, Erskine Carter, spent three hours fielding questions. Carter cited frustrations including revised, higher construction costs and wage rates, a labour shortage, inflation, lower base metal prices, difficulties in start-up operations at the smelter and acid plant, the tight money situation. He predicted that Noranda would provide the money to make Brunswick viable.

Thus, for $50 million, Noranda assumed control of Brunswick ore-bodies, mines, concentrators, the smelter, the works. It did it by purchasing 100,000 $5-par preferred shares and $49.5 million worth of ten-year income bonds. Together, they could be converted into 10-million common shares. With the money, it paid off $33 million in first-mortgage Brunswick bonds, including the $8 million worth owned by Irving's Engineering Consultants. The balance it used for capital.

With 10 million shares, Noranda gained majority control. Brunswick, said Boylen, now would have an authorized capital of $20 million of which $19,676,279 would be outstanding, thus giving Noranda 51 per cent. A new fifteen-man board replaced its nine-man predecessor, with eight of the seats held by Noranda, and Irving among the other seven. At the June meeting the company president, W.S. Row, said, "Nobody, should be unduly critical of production delays at the smelter. We know it takes up to four years to work a smelter up to its full potential."

The takeover came as a surprise to several involved Irving men; they said they thought they'd done a good job. One called it a shock. Desmond Bayley said he could have gone all the way if he'd had another year. Irving indicated he might well have closed the smelter down if he'd taken over, but he also suggested he might have given Bayley his year.

As it was, his companies were swept off the scene they had dominated for six years and his contract to ship concentrates to Belgium was cancelled, leaving him angry and bitter. It was an anger that lasted for years and to which he would return again and again in conversation. But he was far from through with Brunswick. He kept his shares and he kept adding to them for the same main reason that had attracted Noranda: those massive ore-bodies it owned. Besides, they gave him a ringside seat to watch what Noranda did, and he had rough things to say about that.

❧

Noranda! The mere mention of the mining giant's name caused Irving to bristle for years. He spent the rest of his life convinced that there had been a conspiracy against him and the people of New Brunswick, because he believed the province had been deprived of control of one of its great natural resources.

Although Irving called it a conspiracy, those who opposed him said it was simply a bailout for a company in deep trouble. The huge Brunswick project, on the verge of bankruptcy, needed the expertise that Noranda could provide, they said. The building was burning and it was time to call the fire department. Premier Robichaud rang in the alarm, and Irving, who said he had been ready to man the pumps himself, to pour many more millions of dollars into the project, never forgave him.

Irving would insist that political expediency, undue haste, and improper planning, all due to pressure from Premier Robichaud, had condemned Brunswick's trouble-plagued smelter to certain disaster, to the very brink of bankruptcy — and straight into the hands and control of Noranda. On only one point would they ultimately agree: Irving had sought delays and Robichaud had insisted on an open throttle and full speed ahead.

Two public statements of the time reveal both the widely divergent views of what brought about the Noranda takeover and the animosity of those who once had been friends. The first was made in 1971 by Senator Charles McElman, Robichaud's former assistant and a Robichaud-appointed member of the Brunswick board. As part of an attack on Irving's ownership of the New Brunswick media, McElman charged in the Senate that New Brunswick press stories and editorials "would lead the public to believe that the Irving groups are the aggrieved parties" in the Brunswick debacle when the "truly aggrieved parties" were those small shareholders who had suffered losses.

Irving's papers, McElman said, had remained silent even though Boylen had said publicly that mine-concentrator costs had exceeded estimates by $8 million and "related that fact directly to the multiplicity of Irving companies which were in total control of the physical development." The smelter was originally supposed to cost $25 million; with expansion, costs were estimated at $35 million. Yet the Irving companies "led it from problems to chaos and finally to near disaster for the province as well. . . . Instead of being within the limits of the outside estimate of $35 million, the cost was slightly in excess of $70 million. Dr. Boylen and other major shareholders were screaming mad, and they said so publicly. The smelter was supposedly ready to go on stream at this point, but it was a mess and it just would not work. The economics of it had become a catastrophe. . . . The stock of Brunswick had plunged on the market to somewhere in the range of $4 to $5 a share. No real information was given to the public in the news-papers of New Brunswick. There were no editorials." Yet Brunswick was bankrupt, its capital structure "largely destroyed because of the outrageous overrun in construction costs at mine, concen-trator and smelter." Under the circumstances, McElman said, "drastic action was necessary and drastic action was taken. . . . The province literally had to force the Irving group out of control so the project could be salvaged."

Responding to McElman's statements, Irving said some of the statements "presumably were true. Some were half-truths; others were misleading and incomplete, and some were false." It was untrue that he had ever controlled Brunswick. It was true that his Engineering Consultants had been given a management contract for the smelter, but it was the East Coast board that gave it, and the contract specified exactly how expenditures had to be approved by directors. Boylen, he said, had headed that board.

Irving said McElman "attempted to create the impression that the Irving companies, and myself specifically, were responsible for all the problems associated with the smelter construction." Perhaps, he added, he had been silent too long "because someone must take the responsibility for what has happened to what is probably the great-est natural asset within the boundaries of New Brunswick."

It was then that he told the story of his attempts to delay smelter construction, of Robichaud's refusals, of his warnings to other directors, of being forced to go ahead without adequate planning or money. "If the shareholders who have suffered finan-cial loss because of these events wish additional information or verification of anything I have said they should urge the provincial government nominees [on the board] to call for a public inquiry at which the full story will be disclosed."

Robichaud told a reporter a public inquiry would be beneficial; he would be happy to testify, and to have Irving reveal the names of his companies that profited from the smelter's construction. He agreed with Irving's statement that delay had been sought: "He wanted to delay and delay," but the government wanted it to go ahead. "And we said if you won't build it we know someone who will."

Robichaud's later version of what happened was that the gov-ernment decided it must obtain know-how Brunswick did not have: "It's not that we fired Irving. It was that the board didn't have the expertise to operate a smelter." Yet at first "we hadn't foreseen that we would have to have experts in. It was a gradual process. We kept getting reports from our two directors that things were not getting better. It became obvious to them that we had to bring in expertise." It was "a known fact that Noranda were experts and we were delighted when they accepted to rescue the operation." Robichaud asserted that he was not aware that Irving was "very unwilling to proceed" with the smelter, and added that John D. Park was "very instrumental in wishing to proceed." As for McElman's speech, he said he didn't know what the senator was going to say "and there were some things he said that I wouldn't have said myself."

No public inquiry has ever been held, though Irving later in 1971 accused Robichaud of refusing to "listen to reason" and of adopting "a political damn-the-consequences attitude" towards smelter construction, and said it was unfortunate that the Conservatives, by then in power, had not ordered one. Louis Robichaud said that when he asked Irving in 1961 to get involved in Brunswick the response was a "very gracious" acceptance. By the time Brunswick's management changed hands in 1967 all graciousness was gone from their relations. Robichaud had told Irving to get elected if he wanted to run the province.

Soon after the premier's 1966 statement that "we have no place for those who claim personal or political power by divine right," Robichaud was accused of planning to run an election campaign on an anti-Irving platform. Robichaud promptly denied any war with Irving. But the presumption of inevitable collision remained. It was encouraged by a report that one of his key advisers had told Liberal supporters "we are going to get that bastard Irving." It was encouraged far more when Charlie Van Horne came home from California and took aim at the provincial Conservative leadership that was slipping from the hands of Cyril B. Sherwood. Van Horne, a human tempest, a former member of Parliament and a former Irving executive, was seen as a political maverick who might well be the man who could remove Robichaud from office.

As the rumours flew, another aspirant for Sherwood's job emerged. He was thirty-five-year-old Richard Bennett Hatfield, a cultivated man with politics in his blood, in the very name he bore.

His father, Heber, a well-to-do Hartland businessman, had been a member of Parliament for years, and the son had spent many hours around the House of Commons, later working as an executive assistant to Tory leader Robert Stanfield. He'd been elected to the Legislature in 1961, and he entertained fond hopes of becoming premier. One of his first steps, he decided, would be to see if he could get Irving's support.

When he sought an interview, he was well aware of the reports that Irving wanted Van Horne and he must have known that many Conservatives felt he himself didn't have the fire in the belly that would give his party the opportunity "to fight Robichaud with another Robichaud." That, it was generally conceded, was probably Van Horne's greatest strength. Hatfield went to see Irving anyway and was surprised to find himself bewitched by an experience that left an indelible imprint on his mind.

"When I went to Saint John, it was taken for granted in the province that Irving was supporting Van Horne," he recalled. "People told me I didn't have a chance, but I decided I wanted to meet him. I didn't like fooling around with second-hand information.

"He invited me to his home and he literally gave me a history of his life. I was there for purposes of my own, but I found myself fascinated by what he said. It was beautifully put. I was shocked at how well he expressed himself. He told me of how he reached a point where he could no longer support premiers of the past. He went on and on, fascinating, and I will never forget what he said when he came to Van Horne. What he said was, 'I gave him nothing but discouragement.'"

The sentence captivated Hatfield, not because of its significance for himself, but because of the way it was put. It marched in his mind. He kept repeating it to people. He was still repeating it years later. But Irving told him something else too.

"I said," Hatfield recalls, "I would appreciate his support. I would have appreciated financial support or even a word from him, but he said he was out of politics. He wasn't going to get involved." Hatfield said he left that meeting with no illusions. He still suspected that what Irving said about Van Horne was true, "but I also suspect that he did support him financially." Van Horne returned to New Brunswick from California in October, after Sherwood's resignation, and he was soon up to his cowboy hat in a drive for the Tory leadership. He was a curious mixture of constructive talent and wild, dramatic intemperance. He came from Campbellton, was fluently bilingual, the son of a French-speaking mother and a father of Dutch descent. He served in the army in the Second World War, in the RCMP, became a lawyer by taking a correspondence course, and was from 1955 to 1961 an MP. There, his speeches were so unrestrained that the Speaker finally refused to let him speak. In 1960 Van Horne sent Robichaud a wire congratulating him on his victory: "Be assured," he said, "of my wholehearted co-operation." It was a strange message from a Tory to a Liberal, but it may have stemmed in part at least from the facts that Van Horne had been illegally, deliberately, and defiantly serving liquor in his Campbellton hotel and that Robichaud had promised to bring the province's liquor laws into the twentieth century, which he did.

Charlie got things done. He had, as an MP, been credited with getting a bridge built over the Restigouche River from Campbellton to Quebec, and boasted of how he did it: he got federal officials to come see the ferry service on the one day in the week when it was really busy. He had demonstrated talent for impressing people by getting a top executive position with the people who ran the Place Ville Marie skyscraper project in Montreal. That didn't last long and by 1966 he had been in real estate in California for some years.

Soon after Van Horne began to campaign for a November 26 party leadership convention, a large newspaper advertisement urged support for him and, among other things, quoted "one New Brunswick industrialist" as saying "Charlie Van Horne is probably the best project organizer in Canada." People assumed the industrialist was Irving, but he said: "I had nothing to do with bringing him back. He came to see me but I didn't get him to run. I did give him a little money — you give to both parties — but it wasn't any great amount." Other Irving people said Van Horne was a delight to work with in earlier years when he was associated with the Irving companies. "He was," said Sam Roy, "the most likeable fellow I ever knew." Irving himself said Van Horne was an able real estate man: "He did some excellent jobs for us. He was a terrific worker, and he did things as fast as they could be done. He was worth two or three average men. He did a good job as an MP."

If Irving had a qualification about Van Horne personally, it was one he expressed to Sam Roy: "He has no brakes." Brakes or not, Van Horne crushed Hatfield and another candidate on the first ballot of a leadership convention some said was packed. On February 6, 1967, he walloped his opponent in a Restigouche by-election fought in bitter weather against the costly assembled might of the Liberal government. After the Throne Speech, Robichaud retorted that Van Horne's maiden oration betrayed such an ignorance of provincial politics that it "can almost be described as a case of indecent exposure." It was obvious that two feisty, driving spellbinders had locked horns.

Van Horne was soon calling for an election. Everybody knew one was coming, and there were reports that, through Michael Wardell, Van Horne's troubling bills of the past had been paid, and that money was being made available for his personal and election campaign expenses. Robichaud attributed Van Horne's election as Tory leader to "the remote control centre at Phoenix Square [home of Wardell's *Gleaner*] and others."

Then came the showdown at Brunswick, and with it new considerations. Irving was telling people of his anger at Robichaud. He was quoted as saying he was a Liberal "but I don't know what I'm going to be now," that he was a Liberal "but not a Robichaud Liberal." Soon after his September announcement of an October 23 election Robichaud came closer than anyone had since 1939 to making Irving an issue. He never named him, but he left no doubts. "If there is a man who wants to run this province," he cried, "let him present himself to the people." Before a roaring audience in Bouctouche, he linked it with "this man who has his home not far from here, this man who wants to run the province."

Irving himself kept public silence, though he did attend one Van Horne meeting. However, with son Arthur in open support, Irving money, Irving cars, and Irving employees were thrown into the fray. It was, said one executive of the time, war. On the other hand, Irving's newspapers stood on the sidelines, neutral. Even Wardell's *Gleaner* remained neutral.

Van Horne toured the province under the slogan "Charlie Cares," sometimes in a handsome car-trailer, sometimes in a Cadillac. He handed out white stetsons, spent money lavishly, had Don Messer and his fiddling-singing Islanders rouse audiences, and made flamboyant promises from a 113-point program. Still, he failed to penetrate the government's armour on any major item, and he could shake his backers. Before one speech, he was told there were two things he should not do or say. He did and said them both, then explained that he got carried away.

Because he did get carried away, the Liberals portrayed him as irresponsible. Robichaud fought with the skills and rhetoric of a veteran gut-fighter and extolled Equal Opportunity as a launching pad for a better future. Equal Opportunity *was* the real issue, and Liberals sensed that opposition to it was dwindling: the Tories were saying they would alter it if elected but had indicated that most of it would remain.

On election night the Liberals took thirty-two seats, the same number they had won in 1963, with virtually the same percentage of the popular vote. To a larger Legislature, the Conservatives had elected twenty-six members, compared to twenty in 1963. The Liberals swept predominantly French-speaking ridings. The Tories won twenty-six of the thirty seats in which mainly English was spoken. The split between the province's two peoples was documented in elementary and melancholy form. Yet, said one political analyst, it was essentially a standpat election.

Van Horne lost his seat. Hatfield was re-elected after spending most of the campaign in his own riding, because he felt "extremely uncomfortable" under Van Horne. On election night he told friends a new era had come to New Brunswick. He saw the result as a historic turning point in that Robichaud now had "the authority to proceed with Equal Opportunity." But to Hatfield it went beyond that. The provincial government now had access to the larger budgets that came with centralization — which would soon soar — and it had the power that came with being the largest employer in the province.

❧

Back at Brunswick Mining and Smelting, Irving's other *bête noire*, the 1969 annual meeting was tension-packed. Present were unionists who had been told that the big shots from Noranda, the huge Canadian mining giant, were out to get the Irvings and that, somehow, in the process workers at the shipyard would suffer. The workers had been given voting shares in Brunswick, the day off, and a paid trip to Bathurst from Saint John. The workers believed their jobs were in jeopardy because of cancelled contracts and Brunswick's refusal to pay money owing to Irving companies. A boisterous group that became known as Irving's Rent-à-Crowd, they caused a great deal of confusion before the day was out.

Whether Irving himself was responsible, or whether it was someone else's idea, was not clear and was, in fact, irrelevant. The point being made was that labour, in an uncommon show of solidarity with Irving, was prepared to take on "the outsiders" from Toronto, to fight for New Brunswick and for their own jobs. They would stand with fellow New Brunswickers, shoulder to shoulder with management, and, yes, shoulder to shoulder with K.C. Irving.

It was an unusual day and a strange, rowdy meeting. For Irving, leading the attack on Brunswick and Noranda, it was all-out war and it was not a confrontation that was confined to the hotel room where the meeting was held. As the meeting broke for lunch, a big man in overalls sauntered up to Noranda president Alfred Powis and dug him in the ribs with his elbow. Sure he had the company president's attention, he said: "You sure know how to do it, Mister!"

"Do what?" asked Powis.

"You know," came the reply, and then as Powis and others looked on, the big man from Rent-a-Crowd went into a shovelling motion.

Powis looked at him, perplexed. "I don't know what you mean," he said.

"Oh, you know all right. You just don't want to say it. It's horseshit," said the man with one voting share. "Horseshit," he repeated. "You sure know how to shovel it."

Irving himself did not see that encounter but if he had, it is doubtful that he would have objected or criticized the dockyard worker. He was that bitter. He did not like to lose, and he did not know how to quit. He never learned to acknowledge defeat, only momentary setbacks.

Yet if he was bitter about Noranda, he still wanted Brunswick to succeed. He had much at stake, including his own multi-million-dollar investment as a shareholder. He was also concerned about small shareholders, some of whom had invested in Brunswick because he was involved. He was determined to see that Noranda lived up to its claims that it had the expertise to deal with the problems that had plagued the smelter construction program. He continued to charge that those problems were related directly to a premature start, the result of ill-conceived political pressure. But now something much more personal was bothering K.C. Irving, something he saw as an attack on his personal reputation.

Noranda was refusing to pay bills from Irving companies. There were claims that they had made handsome profits, that there were too many of them at the job site, and that they were responsible for many of the troubles during construction of the smelter.

Irving reacted sharply. He was not going to listen to rumours, gossip, whispered accusations, and innuendo. If anyone had anything to say about him or his companies they had better be prepared to say it in court. He launched thirty-one lawsuits. He claimed he was owed millions of dollars for work done by his fifteen companies, Engineering Consultants, Irving Oil, Kent Homes, J.D. Irving Ltd., Mace Ltd., Commercial Equipment, Thorne's Hardware, Kent Line, Industrial Security Ltd., Ocean Steel, Saint John Shipbuilding, Irving Oil Transport, Marque Construction, Silica Sand Ltd., Steel and Engine Products, some of which involved subsidiaries of their own.

In amassing evidence to back their suits, Irving's lawyer Adrian Gilbert was at first thwarted by a lack of records. Then he struck pay dirt. He asked engineer Del Reeleder if he knew anything about the unpaid bills, and Reeleder said he'd have to consult his diary. "You mean," Gilbert asked, "that you kept a diary?" As assistant general manager of Irving Equipment, a subsidiary of J.D. Irving Ltd., Reeleder had. From his diary poured the information Gilbert needed. In it, Reeleder had recorded day by day everything he saw going on.

Irving also called back Eugene Estes, former head of Engineering Consultants, from Honolulu to prove the bills were legitimate. He went beyond that. As Noranda pored over confounding mounds of paper, making audits and supplementary audits, he descended upon two Brunswick meetings with Rent-a-Crowd, but also with lawyers, company heads, executives. Even his old union adversary Angus MacLeod was there, and Joe McLeod, head of the drydock's largest union, who recalled, "We had the executive of all five [drydock] unions; we even took the grievance committee."

He enjoyed it, McLeod said, though he felt Brunswick president W.S. Row tried to get rid of them. But they remained, trading insults with Row and Noranda lawyers and frustrating them with procedural details amid scenes of tension and bedlam. McLeod, who never claimed to be an Irving fan, said nevertheless he enjoyed watching Irving take on the Noranda big shots.

The unionists were there to protest the cancellation of Irving's contracts to carry concentrates to Belgium, and the replacement of his ore-carriers with foreign ships. Angus MacLeod accused Brunswick of sabotaging efforts to build a Canadian merchant marine and he found it wrong to oust ships that had been built by New Brunswick workers to carry a New Brunswick resource to market. Unionists charged Brunswick with trying to hold down workers by denying payment to the companies employing them. They went down to defeat on various demands, among them one for a royal commission, which Irving said he'd support. But they were heard. They told Row there was no way they wouldn't be.

Row retorted that the costs under the original ore-carrying contracts were "nowhere near competitive." The Irving response was that they were fair and that they ensured a firm level of costs in a volatile shipping world.

Irving attacked on that front and on others. He said his companies were owed more than $10 million. What, he asked, "are you trying to do, spite business? Because if you are you are not going to succeed." Powis said the matters in dispute were very complex and "we certainly have no objective of putting Mr. Irving out of business, and if we did we certainly could not succeed." Accounts would be paid, he and Row said, once they were verified.

Noranda's men faced the protests of one Irving executive after another. Hans Klohn said Ocean Steel had been placed "in jeopardy" because it was owed $1.6 million. Kent Homes said it had had to close down. Others joined in. Arthur Irving suggested that Brunswick be nationalized — "Let the people of New Brunswick have it" — and said, "Somebody up top is making a policy that nobody associated with Irving is going to be paid." Untrue, replied Row, but Irving himself said one company after another had been placed in financial straits.

It was the Irving team in full cry, and it paid off. By 1971 the last of the bills was paid. Only one case actually went to court before Noranda settled. Irving had won this battle. Even if he would not win the all-out war with Noranda, he was far from through.

CHAPTER TWENTY-SIX

༈

K.C. Goes to College

*Lord Beaverbrook: "You don't drink. You don't
smoke. You don't wench. What in hell do you do?"
K.C. Irving: "I work."*

EVEN AS BRUNSWICK'S FIGHT WAS UNFOLDING, POLITICAL dissent was flaring through the world, shedding blood and shaping protest into revolutions. A black revolution destroyed whole sections of American cities. An anti-war revolution took America out of Vietnam in bewildering and unprecedented military defeat. A Quiet Revolution shook Quebec. A Third World revolution sought a sunnier place for developing nations, out of the shadow of the industrial world, and the Arabs turned the oil industry in which Irving operated upside-down .

Caught up in the drama of a changing society were issues concerning marriage, law, the church, business, the way people behaved, authority, and the structures and purposes of politics, not to mention the public predominance of men. A youth revolution, at a time of the greatest affluence the country had ever known, questioned the virtues of material satisfactions and acquisition that had made it so. All this was spurred on by drugs, extolled in music, dramatized by sit-ins and love-ins and eloquent rage.

This tumult came to New Brunswick with youth rebellions of its own, one of them on the University of New Brunswick campus where Irving sat as a member of the senate and later the board of governors. But what colleagues there remembered was his calm voice of reason, as student dissent grew louder. They saw, in fact, something very few people had ever seen: the sight of Irving wrestling with problems, debating, discussing, suggesting, not seeking a dominant position, but simply as a member of a group of some two dozen equals. Not all his colleagues united in unstinted praise, but a majority seemed to. Even a member long active in leftist politics was impressed that at a time a union for non-academic staff was under discussion it was Irving who stilled voices against it, deciding the issue with the quiet statement: "In any large organization you have unions, and of course you recognize them; they can make life easier."

Irving was naturally at his best in discussions of finance and construction at a time when the university, like others all over North America, was expanding rapidly. He was, said Dr. Colin B. Mackay, president from 1953 to 1968, invaluable not only in board meetings but in private discussions on matters Mackay had to decide.

Dr. Alfred Bailey, a noted historian, faculty member, and administrator, remembered being assigned by Chancellor Beaverbrook to work with Irving in making plans for an elaborate and eventually abortive project. Beaverbrook was going to build an archive to house papers of the great — of British prime ministers Bonar Law and David Lloyd George, of R.B. Bennett, himself, and others. In fulfilling his task, Bailey came up against Irving's penchant for the specific. It involved shelves. Irving wanted to know what sort they would be, how big, how deep, and they ended up in the university library with Irving using a tape measure so he could tell exactly what an archive shelf would be. The experience convinced him, Bailey said, why Irving was rich and why he would never be.

Mary Lou Lynch, a lawyer who had done a lot of work for Irving in Saint John, bought land for him, then went to Ottawa as a member of the National Parole Board, recalled Irving especially for a contribution to the physical attractions of the hillside campus. At issue was the location of a new headquarters for the teachers of New Brunswick. It would be placed in a dominant position, she said, and it would clash with the prevailing architectural design. It was Irving who intervened, said it shouldn't be allowed, and carried colleagues with him.

Fred Harrison, a former vice-president of the Canadian International Paper Company in Montreal, had special memories of Irving leading two campaigns to raise millions for the university. What he remembered best of all was setting up meetings with the élite of Montreal's business community and having Irving fly up to make presentations. "He didn't seem to realize," said Harrison, "how important he had become, or what an impact he would have." He received warm greetings from men obviously as impressed with meeting him as he was with meeting them. He was pleased, too, by the pledges he got.

It was in 1968 that the sixties rebellions spilled over into the campus life of U.N.B. Trouble found its flashpoint in a physics professor, Dr. Norman Strax, who led students in strident protest. The administration ruled that students must present an identification card if they wanted to take books out of the library. Strax and his supporters refused to accept it, kept piling up books at the circulation desk until the library was ordered closed, then carried on their protests in campus revolt. Engineers led a counterattack. The university bristled with rancour. Placards taunted. Editorials preached. Hostility grew until finally the protesters seated themselves in the building where the board was meeting, filled the hall outside the meeting room and waited, grumbling, chanting, citing the infamies of an oppressive regime bent on the removal of Strax.

Irving, colleagues said, never seemed to take the whole thing seriously, though many did. Nor did he seem to have merited notable mention on placards or in outbursts against the administration who lent it support. The day of the sit-in he emerged from the board meeting and saw the assembled, abusive students blocking passage and he asked Mary Lou Lynch what she was going to do. She replied: "I'm going to walk on their hands — and dig in my heels at every step." Irving told her he couldn't do that. A picture in *The Brunswickan*, the student newspaper, showed him moving slowly, carefully through the students, a campus policeman at his side.

Strax was barred from the grounds through legal action, and Colin Mackay, who took the action, soon resigned as president, a weary man. Some felt he was driven out and wanted to invite him back, but Irving was among those who said the resignation should be accepted. Though Irving liked and admired the ailing man, he thought that Mackay had the best interests of the university at heart. Indeed, it had its own sequel. With Mackay about to go, Irving did what he had done when Allison Dysart left politics. He resigned after eleven years on the board.

As for Mackay, he bounced back quickly, his health improved and he went on to a long and distinguished career in higher education in Canada and internationally. Among other positions, he served as an adviser to the Canadian International Development Agency on the development of higher education in Botswana, Lesotho, and Swaziland. He visited Africa frequently, called on the Canadian government to make more spaces available for foreign students in Canadian universities, opposed apartheid, and championed more education for blacks in Africa and through bursaries at universities in Canada.

❧

It was Lord Beaverbrook, as chancellor, who had got Irving to join the U.N.B. Senate, and it was because of Irving's admiration for Beaverbrook that he stayed as long as he did. The combination of the mercurial Beaverbrook and the quiet, reserved Irving was an unusual friendship, but one that grew stronger with the years. Strangely, Irving, who had an exceptional memory, did not quite remember when it started, but it was sometime during the postwar years. Irving could not recall any direct contact with Beaverbrook during the war even though it was during this time that Irving was driving production twenty-four hours a day at Canada Veneers in Saint John to produce veneer sheets from which the famous Mosquito bombers were built. Earlier, Beaverbrook, as minister of aircraft production in Churchill's wartime cabinet, was credited with a decisive role in producing the Spitfires and Hurricanes that won the 1940 Battle of Britain.

The two came together during those years when Beaverbrook returned to the New Brunswick roots they shared, when he spread benefactions among its people and became chancellor of U.N.B. in 1947. It was the beginning of a long friendship, and more. If Irving had a hero, friends say it was probably Beaverbrook; Beaverbrook, in turn, liked and admired Irving greatly.

There passed between them the peer vibrations of power won and held, the shared experience of great achievement and of their rural Presbyterian backgrounds. The Beaver read a great deal and quoted things he'd read. Irving read very little. Beaverbrook was fascinated by what Irving had done, in a province thin on hope and short on progress, by the combination of steely drive and unassuming personality. Irving was impressed by the things Beaverbrook had done in a larger sphere, by his sophistication, worldliness, and dynamism, though he was sometimes taken aback by the coarseness that went with them.

Beaverbrook found in Irving the friendship of the biggest figure in a province whose élite had spurned him in what he'd call his "feckless" youth. Irving found in him the central link in a chain of friendships reaching out to the Maritime greats who'd gone away — to Bennett and Dunn and Killam, to Andrew Bonar Law, that son of a Kent County Presbyterian minister who had, with the help of Beaverbrook's machinations, become the only British prime minister born abroad. Beaverbrook told him tales of these men, and of Churchill, Roosevelt, and Stalin. Irving would repeat them himself. When they went to Halifax together, the Beaver got him to drive out to the former home of William Stairs, the businessman who put trust in him as a young bond salesman, who "made me," as Beaverbrook would write. They sat there in the street, just looking at the house, with Beaverbrook remembering and telling of the remembering — of Stairs steering prosperity his way, of the young Max Aitken trudging the many miles from Halifax to Yarmouth, peddling investments all the way.

In some ways Irving puzzled him. "You don't drink," he said. "You don't smoke. You don't wench. What in hell do you do?"

"I work," Irving is said to have replied with simple accuracy.

Beaverbrook wanted Irving to call him Max. He would ask others why Irving would not. It didn't change anything. Irving always called him Lord Beaverbrook. Yet their friendship prospered. At the Beaver's request, Irving did something he had never done before and would never do again. In 1961 he joined the board of directors of Price Brothers, the Quebec City newsprint firm in which Beaverbrook had a large interest. He eventually quit because he didn't like some of the things the company did, and had no power to change them. He became interested in the splendid Fredericton art gallery that bore Beaverbrook's name, and the Beaver is said to have groaned in mock dismay — "Kenneth, you have no soul!" — when Irving once asked the price of almost priceless things and, joking, wondered how much pulp they'd buy. Irving acquired the land for The Playhouse, which the Beaver wanted to build just across the street from the art gallery for dramas and other entertainments. He bought the land and supervised the construction of the Beaver's gift to Saint John of a rink, and perhaps amused the mischievous peer by establishing an Irving service station immediately next door.

Beaverbrook could be a bully. Once, in front of others, he grossly abused a U.N.B. president for refusing to give an honorary degree to a woman recommended at the last minute by Sir James Dunn. The president walked out, telling his wife he'd had enough. Wait, she said. The Beaver, as she expected, invited them to dinner. It was a splendid affair, attended by those who had seen the president rebuked. The Beaver was lavish in abuse of himself for what he'd done, and in his praise of a president who was, he purred, everything a president could possibly be. In an ecstacy of redemption, the president told him it was the most handsome apology he had ever heard and, if there was ever anything he could do, the good chancellor had only to ask. "Give that woman an honorary degree," the Beaver purred. It was done, eventually.

Sometimes Beaverbrook needled or challenged Irving. He didn't attack him head on, as was his habit with others, but teasing, challenging, and ridiculing was Beaverbrook's way and no one was ever spared completely. One exchange with Irving occurred at a dinner the Beaver gave for some of Fredericton's élite. He heard a muffled comment about a former Conservative premier and wanted it repeated. What was repeated was hardly flattering and Irving spoke up in the premier's defence. He had always found the premier all right, he said. This, of course, was just what Beaverbrook wanted — a lively exchange at the dinner table. The more controversial the better. He interjected to disagree with Irving. In fact, he couldn't see how anyone could speak well of that premier. He had been a completely ineffective politician. His face colouring, Irving said just as firmly that he took people as he found them and he had always found the premier all right. And then there was silence.

Beaverbrook had a thing about punctuality, the majesty of scheduled time. Irving was known as a man who told underlings to be available at given moments, then let them wait for hours, even days, because something else had captured the immense concentration of his mind. When they flew together the Beaver could despair. Once when they landed in New York he bellowed, "Now don't let him get away. Don't let him near a telephone." And when Irving did vanish at length into a booth with that instrument that was like some projection of his being, Beaverbrook stalked about in profane and incandescent indignation.

Beaverbrook brought into New Brunswick, and into Irving's life, that Brigadier Michael Wardell who, in mischief, he insisted on calling captain. It was Wardell, a patch over one eye, whose one-time sweetheart, the flamboyant American actress Tallulah Bankhead, called the swain of his day in West End London. She also said he had lost his eye not in a hunting accident but on his sword in bending over to pick up a lady's handkerchief. Wardell had been high on the staff of Beaverbrook's *Daily Express* and, on his own, had made a lot of money in buying, building, and selling a magazine. He was about to go to South Africa with the funds he had to invest, only to be convinced by the Beaver, on a fishing trip to the Miramichi, that he should choose instead the small, conservative, and unprepared capital of Fredericton. He remained for years, a puzzling, bewitching, controversial, outspoken, and not infrequently damned figure. He would sink much of his fortune and fragments of the fortunes of Beaverbrook and others in grandiose plans for books, a magazine, a modern printing establishment, and the weary and shaken Fredericton *Daily Gleaner*. This dashing figure from Fleet Street in time came to have a love for the province and an unbending respect for K.C. Irving and all he did.

Beaverbrook twitted both of them. He amused a U.N.B. dinner with some of it. He said he had been touring the north shore of the province, a region almost mystical in his mind, and had come to a place where he wanted to go down to the seashore to refresh nostalgia. He sent his driver to ask the owner if he could trespass on his land, and the man said no. The Beaver sent the driver back to emphasize who he was. The owner still was not impressed. "I don't give a damn," he said, "if he's K.C. Irving." Apocryphal perhaps, but it brought down the house.

That was in the days, from 1956 to 1968, when Irving was a member of the university senate, later the board of governors. He was, a number of colleagues said, a dedicated and valuable member, but there were times when he felt out of place and wondered aloud one day what he was doing there when he didn't even have a college degree. Beaverbrook — who didn't have one either — heard him.

"I'll tell you why you're there," he answered. "You're there because I put you there and I damned well want you to stay." Irving stayed, and Beaverbrook would call him "the best thing that ever happened to U.N.B."

One of the most memorable events of the Beaverbrook–Irving friendship occurred just as the shades were about to be drawn on the life of Beaverbrook, who had been such a controversial figure in British journalism and politics for more than half a century. It brought together at the Dorchester Hotel in London giants of the newspaper industry, business, finance, and politics. For Irving, it was an unforgettable experience — a spectacular dinner that honoured Beaverbrook on his eighty-fifth birthday on May 25, 1964. The host was a proud and beaming Lord Thomson of Fleet, another Canadian of humble beginnings, who smiled in later life as he recalled that he had once been known in Northern Ontario towns, where he scratched out a living selling radios, as the fat fellow with the shiny pants.

He also knew that he had not always been one of Beaverbrook's favourites and that the Beaver had referred to him not too many years earlier as "a little fellow . . . he owns a lot of little newspapers." Now the little fellow had scaled heights that had been beyond even his wildest dreams. Not only was he the owner of a lot of little newspapers, he had acquired the prestigious *Scotsman* in Edinburgh, Scottish Television, the *Sunday Times*, and the one honour he had sought with unabashed zeal and even impudence, a peerage.

Now, at the zenith of his career, Thomson wanted to preside at a dinner that would go down in history, and it was generally agreed that he brought it off. Yet it was an event that almost did not happen. In fact, it would not have happened if it had not been for Beaverbrook's personal determination to put in an appearance despite the fact that he was gravely ill with cancer. He knew this; most of the audience did not.

On the morning of the dinner his doctor told him he could not attend. It was out of the question. Beaverbrook, weak and frail, finally agreed. He would not go. Instead he would send a taped message so that at least his voice would be heard that night. His son Max would sit in his place at the dinner.

But then he found he could not record his speech. His voice was weak. He didn't want to talk into the damned machine. He *would* go. Somehow, he would be there, he would manage. And he did. Not only did he arrive at the hotel at the appointed hour, he brushed aside the suggestion that he be transported to the head table in a wheelchair. He would walk through the ballroom to a standing, table-thumping ovation from old friends, old rivals — and some old enemies.

In his never-to-be-forgotten speech, Beaverbrook recalled that it had been said his boyhood town of Newcastle was too small for him. He had gone to Halifax, and the Nova Scotia city, they said, was too small for him. So it was on to Montreal, then a city of a quarter of a million, but Montreal was too small. London was his next stop and London, it had been said, was too small for him. But never fear, soon he would go to hell. The audience roared, but the Beaver hadn't finished. Eyes sparkling and grin spreading, the old man said: "Hell will be too small, too."

Irving, sitting in the first row of tables directly in front of Beaverbrook at the head table, marvelled at his strength, for he knew that Beaverbrook was seriously ill. Irving, like others, was transfixed by the old man's sense of humour and the mischievous curiosity with which he faced the future and what he referred to as his next apprenticeship.

Fifteen days later Beaverbrook was dead and within the month Irving stood in the town square in Newcastle to give a eulogy to the Little Canadian who had grown up in the Manse in that small New Brunswick town where his father, the Rev. William Aitken, had been the Presbyterian minister. The date of that sombre gathering was June 24, 1964, almost a month to the day after that glorious dinner in London. Irving paid tribute to the man he remembered as New Brunswick's "greatest friend and benefactor." Beaverbrook had been an inspiration to youth. He had provided university buildings, recreation facilities, and scholarships. For young people, he had opened the doors of learning "and for this he will always be remembered."

And so it ended. Beaverbrook's death also forestalled a potential partnership in a New Brunswick newsprint mill that would have fed the roaring presses of Beaverbrook's Fleet Street newspapers. But the break was inevitable. Beaverbrook was twenty years Irving's senior and time simply ran out.

ða

How much money Irving made and how much he gave away were subjects that were discussed, argued, and speculated on for years in New Brunswick. Contributors to campaigns — whether for the United Way, a community rink, or a university building — inevitably asked: How much is Irving giving? It was more than idle curiosity. Some contributors wanted to give more. Others were determined to give less because, they reasoned, he had more money and therefore should bear a larger portion of the burden.

If Irving knew this, it is doubtful it bothered him or influenced his own contributions. From his earliest days in business his respect for a hard-earned dollar never wavered. His personal goal — and for him it was an obsession — was to develop industry, create jobs, make a profit, and reinvest that profit in new ventures. That was his way. Nothing, in his view, was more important to a family than a regular pay cheque. He provided those cheques and with rare exceptions left the fund-raising to others.

This did not mean that he ignored worthy causes. He gave away millions during his lifetime, but just how many millions will never be known. What is known is that for some people — and especially for his critics — it was never enough.

For years he was a substantial contributor to the United Way of Saint John, yet there were many in his home town who resented his reluctance to commit all of his companies to the payroll deduction plan. They said other companies did it, so he should too. In the early days of the United Way some of his companies were on the payroll plan, but many were not. This changed over the years as Irving executives and companies became more active in the United Way and other community events, but it was no secret that he did not favour payroll deductions.

His reason was as simple as it was straightforward. He believed far too much money was taken out of workers' pay cheques — too much by governments for taxes, too much for other reasons, and too much in voluntary deductions. He knew, from long experience and bitter exchanges in union negotiations, that the take-home pay was what really mattered to the workers and their families. Those workers, he said, needed every cent that was in their pay cheques.

Other factors influenced his attitude toward charities and community projects. He himself worked hard and long for everything he achieved or acquired, and he believed that many of the well-meaning and usually dedicated volunteers who came to him for contributions were not nearly as committed to their own businesses as he was to his. As a result, he was not greatly impressed when he was solicited by a successful businessman who, he knew, would spend the weekend on the golf course or cruising the river while he would be working.

There was also the need for money for his own companies. No matter how much his businesses produced, they always needed more — for expansion, for new businesses, for the opportunities that would arise. And he never forgot his mother's lectures about the sin of waste and the value of a dollar. Yet, though he did not flaunt it, in many cases not known, or perhaps simply ignored, he could be generous. In every section of New Brunswick there were those who had stories of significant contributions, made quietly, usually without public knowledge, and almost always with little public fanfare or recognition.

Of course, those seeking gifts from Irving or those who wished to determine the extent of his largesse — or, conversely, the tight grip he kept on his purse strings — often faced problems. The tales were as interesting as they were varied. One collector said he did learn how to get money from Irving, but he'd be damned if he'd tell anyone else how he did it. Another said he left with nothing but had never been treated so courteously in his life. A third said Irving made a pledge, accompanied him all the way to the front door of the office building, and beckoned a car to take him home. It turned out that the car was driven not by an Irving employee but by a customer. The customer did it anyway.

In St. Stephen, N.B., former mayor Whidden Ganong recalled the time the town needed an Irving property for a traffic circle; Irving donated it free, but said he didn't want the fact publicized. In Antigonish, N.S., the town wanted land on which an old Irving station stood; Irving himself came down to soothe critics, charmed the council, was presented with a gift, and made the land available. In New London, P.E.I., he bought a property that included the birthplace of *Anne of Green Gables* author Lucy Maud Montgomery. He gave the house to the government as a historic site. An Irving station stands next door. In Quebec City he owned one building so old that the government wanted it for a historic site too, and got it.

It was a sign of Irving's overwhelming stature in Saint John that Dr. Richard Bonnycastle, long headmaster of Rothesay Collegiate School, attended by Irving's sons, recalled going to him alone for a donation. He went alone because the other two on a campaign committee, both businessmen, begged off. A blithe, likeable, and humorous man, Bonnycastle approached Irving successfully more than once, and found him "very gentle, approachable, and interested in our affairs. He helped take your coat off. He saw you to the outer door. He seemed pleased to see you."

He was also, in Bonnycastle's opinion, generous. He gave R.C.S. some $100,000 for new buildings. He suggested the school get an architectural consultant's advice on design, arranged it, and flew Bonnycastle to North Carolina for consultations. On one approach for money, Bonnycastle says, Irving met him with his three sons: "They still called me Dr. Bonnycastle." The father asked the size of the largest donation already pledged. "We had one good one and I was happy about that because Irving said immediately: 'We'll match it,' and did. Once he said, 'If you need a little more, don't hesitate to come back.' I did, and he simply wrote out another cheque."

If Bonnycastle was pleased with his success, the Université de Moncton was stunned by its own. The French-language institution was founded in 1963 and embarked three years later on a drive to raise funds. Two emissaries assigned to see Irving were told they just had to get at least $25,000. They got the customarily gracious reception in Irving's office. They were greatly impressed by his detailed explanation of one of his projects. He left the room briefly to talk with his sons, came back and said he would pledge $500,000 over a period of eight years, and wished it could be more. It was a campus legend for years.

It was only one of numerous Irving kindnesses to Acadian and Roman Catholic causes, and at the time it was thought to be the largest single contribution he ever made. It was the largest ever made public — there was in this rare case an announcement — but he himself indicated there may have been bigger ones. "I have contributed to a number of universities," he said. "I wouldn't think," he added, "that the donation to the Université de Moncton was the largest."

It was much larger than the one New Brunswick's Mount Allison University got, but it was pleased too, and the representative who went to Irving delighted in telling the story. He was the Rev. William Godfrey, a perky man with celebrated skills in separating corporations from some of their money. Seeking a contribution for an athletic centre, he figured he was up against two forces in his approach: the natural reluctance of any human being to part unnecessarily with money and the fact that the Irvings remained Presbyterians after the big fight in the 1920s over whether that denomination should join the Methodists in the new United Church.

Mount Allison was a United Church adherent for years and still has its representatives on the board, but when Godfrey went to Saint John he suspected that, to the Irvings, it was still too much of what it once had been, a Methodist institution. Irving later laughed at this, but it was in Godfrey's mind. So, in what he called his recitation, Godfrey went into the background of his mother's people, Kent County Presbyterians, Camerons from up near Rexton, working to arouse his friendship. Irving listened attentively. He hardly said a word through the whole thing, but Godfrey kept going: "I gave him the works, and he sat there and he never took his eyes off my face. You talk about steel! Granite! The toughest fellow I ever met. The most interesting man I ever interviewed. I enjoyed him. I admired him. I liked him."

Godfrey left with a promise of $25,000. He was elated, and so was the university: "amazed that I got anything." When he thought it over, he decided that what did the trick was what he said about the Presbyterian Camerons from around Rexton: "I think that was the convincing point." But he'd never know for sure.

Irving's gift to the Université de Moncton belonged, like so much else in his life, in a larger picture. Presbyterian Scots-Canadian though he was, the most intriguing aspects of his contacts with religious and ethnic groups were those he had with French-speaking Roman Catholics.

He once told a priest he found Acadians his best, and most dependable workers. He employed them in the thousands. Largely to him is attributed the fact that in his lifetime the French population of Saint John multiplied steadily. They came in ever-increasing numbers to work for Irving companies and he continued to praise them as excellent employees. In Irving's soul there was real affection for them as a people. He said publicly that in his youth Acadians taught him much of what he knew, and that he never forgot. He formed then an admiration for what priests did for communal morality and authority. In a village without police, he saw them as bulwarks of law and order and, yes, decency. It was a place of unlocked doors and unstolen property, and he saw the priests as a major reason why. Their names he never forgot. Their influence, he thought, permeated the community.

Numerous priests knew and admired him and received gifts from him for their pursuits. They tell of a gift for this, a gift for that, money for a rink at St. Leonard, money for festivals, construction materials, a Hammond organ for a residential seminary near Grand Falls, others. The ebullient Rev. S.A. Dionne of the Parish of Our Lady of La Salette, Sheila, N.B., told of going to Irving for funds for a rink at Tracadie, of facing so many questions that "I thought I was in front of a court tribunal," of being told the project "is what youth needs at this time to keep out of mischief." He got both advice and a major contribution.

Irving and his wife were there as honoured guests the day the rink was opened. In turn, Irving often invited priests to ceremonies of his own. "He feels at home with us," said a monsignor. "He has all the qualities we find in a Roman Catholic. He's religious. In his heart he is a good man, and he likes the way we practice religion."

With no priest was Irving more at home than with Monsignor Desiré Allain. Allain first served in Bouctouche as a young man and remembered buying a pair of skates from Kenneth Irving and thinking he'd never make a salesman because he was so shy. Years later, long after Irving left town, he became parish priest and set about building a stone church so impressive local wits called it the Kent County Cathedral. To help out, he got gifts from Irving that he estimated cost $100,000 — oak pews, an altar, lockers, confessionals. And bells. The story of the bells is core Irving. When Allain broached the subject, Irving got deeply involved, learned a lot about bells, and got architect Sam Roy to help out. Irving even flew with them to Boston and Philadelphia to listen to bells, and to make a selection. Then on a trip to Europe he heard a carillon and decided Allain's church should have one too.

He tracked the priest down in Quebec City, and flew him off for more investigations, put him up at a hotel Allain found so lavish that, after Irving left, he went to the desk to ask who was paying the bill. It was Irving, and he had told the staff to take good care of his guest. The carillon joined the bells in the great tower of the church. But the sound proved so thunderous that it provoked complaints, and from then on it was rung less often.

Irving's friendship and admiration for the French-speaking people of New Brunswick, said Yves Pratte, was a broad one that extended to the people of Quebec. Pratte did a lot of legal work for Irving, but the first time they met his English was poor, and what struck him was that this didn't matter to Irving, then or later: "Language was, to him, a matter of communication, not principle." Probably because of his youth in an Acadian village, Pratte thought, Irving understood and accepted the aspirations of Quebec's French Canadians during the Quiet Revolution and its stormy sequels: "He has a much better understanding of them than, say, Westmount."

Others said Irving loved Quebec City, enjoyed being there, bought and refurbished a motel there. Quebec meetings of Irving company officials were conducted in French, even with Irvings present. His own working command of the language and his employment of thousands of French-speaking people have also had a lasting effect on his family. Of his sons, Jim speaks it best, but Irving's grandchildren have studied it formally, and have worked in Quebec to perfect it.

Irving's respect for priests and his affection for the Acadians of his youth continued throughout his life, but the Roman Catholic Church did not have his exclusive attention. His ties with the Presbyterian Church in Saint John revealed another side of his generosity. He attended services rarely, but lawyer Hugh McLellan said his own father described Irving as its financial angel. Irving's comment: "I haven't sprouted wings yet." It was not true, McLellan said, that Irving kept the church going but he was generous, and when the time came to rebuild the church, he made it possible — in his own way. Irving strongly disagreed with the building site; it was too small and crowded, with virtually no parking space. For that reason, he wouldn't contribute to the construction, but he did arrange to pay the minister's salary for some years. When a receipt was sent to him, it said it was for donations to the new building. Irving sent the receipt back. The money was not, he said, for the new building.

In 1960, the year Irving opened his oil refinery in Simonds parish, a Saint John peewee hockey team called the Simonds Oilers won the local championship and the right to compete in a big tournament in Quebec City the following year. The team was run by LeRoy Vincent, an Irving drydock official, and salesman Jack Ingraham. Vincent would tell how Ingraham did something he would never have thought of doing: they needed help and he went to the Irvings to get it.

Though they had nothing to do with the team, the Irvings said they'd fly it to Quebec City in their own aircraft. When that was blocked by government regulations, they chartered an Air Canada plane, bought the players cowboy hats and new uniforms, flew a contingent of twenty-five to Quebec City, and put them up at the family-owned motel. By the time the Oilers had won two games before enormous crowds, K.C. Irving showed up to cheer them on, told them to buy what they wanted at a gift shop, on him. When they lost in the semifinals he put on a banquet for them, three other Maritimes teams, and the host team from Quebec City, then flew the Oilers home. They all wrote him letters of thanks, and he replied to all of them. "To this day," Vincent said many years later, "those players of 1961 still talk about it."

Another aspect of Irving's attitude to fund-raising and his personal desire to avoid public attention for his contributions came to light during Saint John's campaign to restore its old Capitol Theatre in the centre of the city.

By this time Irving was in his mid-eighties and no longer ran the Irving business. "The Boys" were in charge, but when something involved him he could still cut to the core of a problem and snap out a decision; this was one of those occasions. The promoters of the program decided they wanted to honour Irving by having his name associated with the restored theatre. The suggestion was made to the sons; and although they would make substantial contributions of money and land to the project, it is doubtful they were enthusiastic about the idea of having the Irving name on something they would not own and control. Still, it was their father's decision to make. Arthur broached the subject.

"The Bi-Capitol people want to name the theatre after you," he told his father.

"They want to do what?"

"They want to name the new theatre after you — to call it the K.C. Irving Theatre."

"Do they want some money?"

"Probably."

The older Irving looked at his second son with that hard stare that had been his trademark. The thoughts of those who wished to have his name on the theatre were probably honourable. They most certainly were well-intentioned. Still, it was not his theatre. He hadn't planned it. He wasn't in charge of the project. He hadn't supervised it. In truth, he knew very little about it. It might be a very fine theatre and then again it might not. It simply wasn't an Irving building. His response was unequivocal: "Well, give them some money on the understanding that they keep my name off it."

CHAPTER TWENTY-SEVEN

K. C. Goes To Ottawa

"I've been treated as if I were a member of the Mafia."
  – FREDERICTON PUBLISHER MICHAEL WARDELL IN APPEARANCE
        BEFORE DAVEY COMMITTEE ON MASS MEDIA.

IT WAS OFTEN SAID THAT IRVING, THE INDUSTRIALIST AND entrepreneur, should not be in the newspaper business. A man with so much power should not also control the press, especially in a small province like New Brunswick.

In fact, his critics maintained, it was obvious that he was simply buying protection, control over the media so that his vast business and industrial interests would be free of criticism, and so that he could dictate what appeared in the press, and what didn't. His media executives scoffed at the idea, claiming that if he bought newspapers for protection he didn't get much of a return on his dollar.

What was ignored in this long-running debate and was seldom if ever mentioned was that Irving had been in the newspaper business long before the time of his greatest growth as an industrialist. It was not a case of his becoming an industrial giant and then deciding to acquire all the English daily newspapers in the province. He was involved in daily newspapers from a very early stage in his career — when he was in his mid-thirties in the Depression years, and long before his great acquisitions and successes.

By the time Irving was seventy years old he owned all the English-language daily newspapers in New Brunswick, but it was an ownership that brought him a raft of criticism, showered him with black ink from the newspapers themselves, had him summoned to appear before a Senate committee examining ownership of the press in Canada, and landed him in the courts where his newspapers faced charges under the Combines Investigation Act.

Yet there were times, in lighter moments, when he could laugh at it all, and at himself. Once, during the combines court hearings in 1972, he had just finished several hours on the witness stand and was asked, while relaxing with his lawyers outside the court, if he was through buying newspapers, or would he acquire more in the future? What if a newspaper were available tomorrow?

"Why," he said, chuckling, "that would be just like tossing raw meat in front of a hungry dog." He laughed a self-deprecating laugh, a little unsure of whether he should be joking about so serious a subject but determined, through it all, not to lose his sense of humour.

He first got into the newspaper business in 1936. For years it would not be generally known that he provided the capital for a Saint John newspaper called the *Citizen*. Official inquiries in later years spent months delving into his media ownership without finding a mention of it. No one asked him, and he obviously saw no reason to divulge it.

Behind his first media venture was a man named Charles Munro who ran a weekly publication devoted to reporting what was coming up in radio broadcasts. Irving persuaded him to go daily, bought him a modern press, and provided money to underwrite development. Its original publisher, listed as The Broadcaster Publishing Co. Ltd., later changed its name to The Citizen Ltd., with Munro as president, but men who worked on the paper say the real boss was Gordon Daley, a Halifax lawyer associated with the *Halifax Herald*. Irving got him to come to Saint John regularly to oversee the operation.

The *Citizen* was a bouncy, perky newspaper, costing one cent in Saint John, two cents elsewhere. It inked its name in red, proclaiming itself "A Newspaper in Public Service" and urging readers to become New Brunswick-conscious, to buy New Brunswick products. It also called for a Chignecto Canal, for making Saint

John a free port, and for the Maritimes to be put "on the air map." In a full-page display at the beginning of 1938, it declared: "It will be our aim and desire at all times to give to our readers a fearless and fair presentation of all matters of general interest." It urged port expansion, improvements in education, fishing, and agriculture. Its editorial-page comments tended to be bland, but those it ran, under two-column headings on the front page were brisk and varied, ranging from calls for a better deal for fishermen to taking the provincial civil service out of politics.

The editor was A.W. Thorne, a young man named John Fisher its feature and editorial writer. Fisher, from Sackville, had a way with words written or spoken, and his later eulogies earned him the title "Mr. Canada." Other good men were on staff: Bob Hanson, who would later do well on the *Montreal Star*; Charles Lynch, who became a national columnist in Ottawa; Doug Costello, a future sports editor for the *Telegraph-Journal* and in later years an award-winning journalist in Maine and Pennsylvania; Bert Burgoyne, who became a mainstay on the *Telegraph-Journal*. In summer holidays it hired college student W.Y. (Bill) Smith, later an economic adviser to government.

Lynch spurned college, went to work at the *Citizen* at age sixteen for $7 a week, and was soon the top feature writer. He recalled his *Citizen* days as the happiest of his working life, though there was one time when he had his doubts. In red ink, the paper cried that "SOMETHING MUST BE DONE to alleviate Saint John's wretched housing conditions," and it relied on Lynch's revelations to prove it. But his articles on slum housing were so graphic in their description of sordid conditions that they aroused not only landlords but the slum dwellers themselves; they threatened to hang him.

The *Citizen* had other problems. For one thing, it could not afford to obtain the services of the Canadian Press, the news-disseminating co-operative owned by dailies from coast to coast. The *Citizen* subscribed to International News Service in the U.S. and went its own ambitious way. Daley brought over circulation expert Barney Archibald from the *Herald* and had province-wide goals. Then one day in 1939, without warning, at a time when staffers were buoyant, a statement was pinned on the notice board of the Canterbury Street office. Signed by Daley, it said publication was ceasing immediately.

"Nobody said goodbye," said Lynch, and he grieved for days over the bereavement. Years later the New Brunswick poet-author and newspaperman Alden Nowlan recalled a meeting of weekly editors at which three former *Citizen* men toasted it as the best newspaper they had ever known.

Irving never said why it was closed. Even in his eighties he was hesitant about discussing the whole thing. But in the *Citizen* a pattern was set. He never went into the office or called the editors. He didn't know them and they didn't know him. He was a silent, invisible owner.

He did get back some of his money in the sale of the newspaper press he had bought only three years before. He sold it to a one-time radio salesman who was trying to scratch his way into the newspaper business in Timmins, Ont. His name was Roy Thomson, later Lord Thomson of Fleet.

&a.

For Irving, the years ahead would be equally exciting, challenging, and rewarding as he built an industrial empire in which newspapers would be almost incidental to the scope and value of his vast holdings. He would acquire the *Telegraph-Journal* and the *Evening Times-Globe* in 1944, the *Moncton Times and Transcript* in 1948 and the Fredericton *Daily Gleaner* in 1968. These media holdings were insignificant when compared to those of Thomson, who specialized initially in small newspapers in small towns, and the Southams, who owned many of the daily newspapers in Canada's larger cities. But in later years it was Irving who was frequently under the microscope of public attention as his newspaper ownership was challenged.

The questions persisted. What about the Irvings? What about K.C. himself? Did he buy newspapers to control the news in the province where he owned and controlled so many other businesses? What was it that he wanted — was he looking for dominion over the province and its people? Did he dictate the editorial policy of the newspapers? Did he actually decide what would and what would not appear in the news and editorial columns?

The answer to the question of editorial policy was yes, according to Ralph Costello, longtime publisher of the *Telegraph-Journal* and the *Evening Times-Globe*: "He did dictate editorial policy and it was as simple as it was brief. He said, 'Publish good newspapers, the best you can, in the interest of the people of New Brunswick.'"

The answer to the second question — did he decide what would appear in the news and editorial columns? — was equally simple and clear, according to Costello. It was no. "He never knew what was going to appear, never asked and never spoke to the publishers or editors on news reports and editorials once they had appeared."

"So," said Costello, "the publishers and editors of the New Brunswick newspaper did what they always had done: they made their own decisions, went their separate ways and published the best newspapers they were capable of producing — for the people of New Brunswick.

"Those are the facts. That is the way it worked — but isn't there more to it than that? Why did Irving buy newspapers?

"Like others, I can only speculate on what was in the mind of this driven man half a century ago — back in the grim Depression years, back when he himself was still in his mid-thirties. My guess is that in the beginning Irving did see the *Citizen* as much more than an investment. He was deeply involved in politics, in the Liberal party, and a friendly newspaper was a necessary tool of a political party, *because*, and this is important to understand, that is the way things were done in those days. That is how newspapers and political parties operated. They were not strange bedfellows, as they are today. Rather, they entered into what were long-term marriages or sometimes just affairs of political convenience.

"So was Irving's first venture into the newspaper business politically motivated? The suspicion and the circumstantial evidence would lead to that conclusion — to the belief that, like so many others who were involved in politics in that period in history, Irving recognized the need, and decided to do something about it.

"That being the case, or presuming that to be the case, wouldn't it be natural to assume as well that his purchase of the *Telegraph-Journal* and the *Evening Times-Globe* in 1944 had a similar, political motivation?

"Well, yes — or perhaps more accurately, maybe. But if that was in the back of his mind when he acquired the two Saint John newspapers, there was to be at least one major flaw in his plan: it just didn't work.

"And, more importantly, he didn't do anything to make it work. Speculation, suspicion, assumptions, and accusations aside, Irving did not use the Saint John newspapers for political purposes, for personal or corporate glorification, or for any other purpose.

"Or, put another way, if he did, he somehow managed to bring it all off like Mandrake the Magician, with smoke and mirrors and phantom reporters and editors, because anything that was done was accomplished without the knowledge, co-operation, or, as would have been necessary, the collusion of the publishers, editors, and reporters."

Not everyone agreed with Costello's version of Irving's hands-off relationship with the newspapers he owned. Some experts said even if Irving stayed away from the newsroom and editorial offices, his chief lieutenant would know his wishes and would see that they were carried out. Editors and reporters would be cautious in handling Irving stories. The newspapers, experts said, would not take an aggressive role in investigative reporting when Irving companies were involved.

These views surfaced in testimony before the Davey Committee in 1969, again when media experts were called as prosecution witnesses in the combines trial in the 1970s, and once more when the Kent Royal Commission on Newspapers toured Canada in 1980. Irving's first public appearance as a newspaper owner, and his firm defence of that ownership, took place at the Davey Committee hearings in Ottawa. It was a day that would not soon be forgotten.

ᕦ

The time was 11:30 p.m., the date December 15, 1969. K.C. Irving was sitting on the edge of a large double bed in his room at the Chateau Laurier Hotel in Ottawa, reading the statement he had prepared for the Special Senate Committee on the Mass Media. He wanted to be certain he said exactly what he meant when he appeared before the committee the following day.

Irving had flown to Ottawa that evening from Saint John with copies of the statement for the committee and the press, but he wasn't quite satisfied with it. A word or a phrase was bothering him. His appearance was scheduled for 2:30 the following afternoon but he wasn't going to bed until he was satisfied with every word in his prepared statement. In Saint John, standing by in case there were any changes, were Winnifred Johnston, his secretary, and Bob Bonnell, the advertising manager of Irving Oil. If there were changes, Miss Johnston would make them, arrange for copies to be run off, and Bonnell would fly them to Ottawa the next morning to be distributed when Irving started his testimony.

Finally, one or two minor word changes were made, telephoned to Saint John and Irving said he thought it was time to go to bed. It was a few minutes past midnight in Ottawa, a few minutes past 1 a.m. in Saint John.

L. McC. Ritchie, seventy-five, recently retired from the Federal Court, and back as a legal adviser to Irving, agreed, but Brig. Michael Wardell, publisher of the *Daily Gleaner* of Fredericton, thought the group should hear the statement he would make the following day.

Ralph Costello, as publisher of the *Telegraph-Journal* and the *Evening Times-Globe*, said it would be better if Irving didn't know what the publishers were going to say. They would be speaking for the newspapers and he had no involvement in the newspapers. It would be better, he said, to keep it that way.

Irving quickly agreed, but Wardell was anxious to go over his statement. He wanted someone to listen to it. Perhaps, he said, he could run through it with Costello. Wardell would like to have his reaction. Costello said he'd rather not know what Wardell was going to say. At this point Ritchie brought the discussion to an end. He said: "Well, I'm going to bed. I'll see you all in the morning."

He left the room followed by Wardell and Costello. Wardell was disappointed that no one wanted to know what he would tell the Davey Committee, but Wardell would have his day in court that afternoon — and it would be a long, lively, and at times disjointed harangue by a bitter man.

No one had asked what Costello intended to say. Irving, preoccupied with his own statement, didn't know that Costello would be saying anything. He didn't ask and Costello didn't tell him. Wardell, Costello suspected, never gave a thought to anything other than his own statement.

On the afternoon of the hearing Costello arrived at the committee room shortly after 2 p.m., about fifteen minutes prior to the scheduled start of the afternoon session.

Borden Spears, a former editor of the *Toronto Star* and the executive consultant to the committee, was already there and Costello asked him about the order of appearances.

"What do you mean?" he replied.

"Which newspaper is to appear first?" Costello asked.

"You're all on together," he said. "It's the Irving group."

That didn't sound very good to Costello. He had a vision of half a dozen Irving executives sitting as a panel, all with different personalities, different ideas, and different perspectives — and the Senate Committee taking pot shots at the group, up and down a line of sitting ducks.

"Are you sure?" Costello asked. And then added: "I think we should appear separately."

Spears nodded. "Okay, but you'll have to check it with the chairman. He'll be along in a minute."

He was right. Senator Keith Davey breezed into the meeting room a few minutes later. He was a smiling, affable man wearing a blue blazer, a large puff in his breast pocket and a screamingly loud polka dot tie — something of a trademark for him at the time.

"Senator," Costello said, "Borden tells me the plan is for the New Brunswick group to appear together. I think we'd prefer to be heard separately."

"Fine," he answered without hesitation. "We'll start with Mr. Irving, then the *Telegraph-Journal,* and then the Fredericton newspaper. Will that be all right?"

"First rate," Costello replied, "and thank you."

In truth, Costello would have preferred to have led off as he had been there before, on the opening day a week earlier, as president of the Canadian Daily Newspaper Publishers' Association. That would have given Irving and Wardell an opportunity to see the committee in action before appearing themselves. But at least they now would appear separately and that was his main objective. He decided not to press his luck. And it was just as well, because the batting order worked out well. Irving made a strong presentation, answered questions carefully in his own scrupulous, deliberate style. Costello, as the middle witness, was more aggressive, and the brigadier came on with guns firing in all directions as the final witness of the day. It was, some writers said, a day to remember.

When it was over the press converged on Irving in the hallway. After answering a few questions he returned immediately to the hotel, and none too soon. As his son Arthur recalled later, "We were walking back to the hotel and Dad started staggering. He couldn't walk straight. I had to take his arm to steady him." Within the hour he was flying to the Lahey Clinic in Boston, where his problem was diagnosed as an inner-ear infection that affected his balance.

Arthur Irving found it possible to chuckle in later years about what the public reaction would have been to his teetotalling father staggering through the Parliament Buildings, but there was little to smile about on that December day when Irving appeared before the committee.

Irving himself was grim-faced, serious, and controlled. That he felt resentful was obvious to anyone who listened to his statements and the charges he levelled, in a voice that crackled at times with anger. From the outset it was clear that the New Brunswick newspaper executives were there to fight. They saw the committee as an accuser, prosecutor, judge, and jury.

There was another side to Irving's indignation. He had been accused of using the newspapers as a personal shield for himself and his companies. The paradox was that he felt those same newspapers were often harsh, even unfair, in how they handled news about Irving companies, but he owned the newspapers and he couldn't complain as others would. What he said in private was another matter. One of his senior executives recalled once seeing him so upset by a news story that he muttered that he was thinking about suing. A lawyer with him for years said that if he'd been the owner he'd have raised hell over some of the stories published by the newspapers. One morning the *Telegraph-Journal* carried a story at the bottom of page two about an oil spill in Courtenay Bay. The guilty party was not Irving Oil. If it had been, rasped Arthur Irving, "that story would have been on page one."

The Irvings' attitude was summed up by K.C. Irving at one stage in the prolonged combines court case when he denied that he got preferential treatment from the editors of the newspapers he owned.

"Have you," a lawyer asked, "been treated any better than any other business or enterprise in New Brunswick?"

"I would say a little worse," Irving replied.

"Why would you say that?"

"I think they lean over backwards to put me in black ink just to keep their skirts clean."

None of this made any impression on Senator Charles McElman, the one-time executive assistant to Louis Robichaud.

Charles McElman, a determined, combative man who came from the Fredericton area and was once a bank teller, had entered the political milieu in 1954, in the McNair years, and became a backroom political strategist, a key figure in Robichaud's first two election wins. During his years in the Senate McElman was consistent in expressing admiration for Irving as an industrialist — and vehement in his belief that he should not be in the newspaper business. He was convinced the newspapers were under Irving's thumb, tools to protect and support him.

There were newspapermen in New Brunswick — some of the best of that time — who understood McElman's views on Irving's media ownership even if they didn't agree with them. Fred Hazel, then the managing editor of the *Telegraph-Journal*, was one of those who heard McElman's charges more in sadness than in anger. Hazel knew McElman well and was one of those newspaper veterans who recognized and respected his political skills. "Charlie was a backroom politician," said Hazel. "He was the one who crafted policy and strategy, wrote speeches for the Liberal members of the Legislature — and always sought the political advantage, always played the political angle. That was his game and he was good at it. He used all the political tools at his disposal and if there was a friendly newspaper, or a friendly reporter, that was fair game, too. Charlie just couldn't imagine a politician or anyone remotely interested in politics doing otherwise."

There was another factor that Hazel thought influenced McElman's perception of the newspapers in New Brunswick. After years of quietly observing the passing scene while perched carefully on the political fence, the New Brunswick newspapers had undergone a dramatic change.

Wardell had arrived in New Brunswick in the 1950s, bringing with him not only a Fleet Street brand of sensational and provocative journalism but also a partisan political point of view that had him cuddled up to his friend, Progressive Conservative premier Hugh John Flemming, during the 1950s and then bitterly opposed to Robichaud when he came to power in 1960.

"The other change," said Hazel, "was at our own newspapers in the early 1960s, when T.F. Drummie retired as publisher. He was seventy-five and very cautious. His retirement opened the door for us to face up to our responsibilities as a newspaper, and we did it in both the news columns and on the editorial page. We were more aggressive in our coverage of the news and more opinionated on the editorial page.

"Charlie McElman lived through those changes and what he saw were newspapers, docile for years, that now were questioning and challenging just about everything the government did. He probably thought a wild dog had been unleashed against Premier Robichaud, but that is not the way it was. What happened is we were given the opportunity, as reporters and editors, to start doing our job. We did it as best and as honestly as we could.

"In fact, and in retrospect, Louis Robichaud's successor, Premier Hatfield, got a much rougher ride from the press of New Brunswick than Robichaud did."

By way of illustration, Hazel recalled Alden Nowlan's assessment of the evolution of the *Telegraph-Journal* from when he wrote of it as "a newspaper whose editorial policy could be summed up as 'no comment'" to one which became so critical of the government that Premier Hatfield would say, only half-jokingly, that Costello's motto was: "If there's a government here, I'm against it."

That, of course, was Hazel's assessment of the changing face of journalism in New Brunswick, and it was not one McElman shared. He was convinced that the Irving-owned press was being used and that this was bad for the province and, closer to home, bad for Premier Robichaud and the Liberals. Yet McElman had good things to say about Irving even as he assailed his press ownership. His first attack was made on a limited front in a Senate speech on March 11, 1968. A new Canadian Radio and Television Commission was being established, and he said there was a situation in New Brunswick "which cries out for corrective action." Besides his four newspapers and broadcasting station, it was "a rather poorly kept secret that the Irving interests have repeatedly endeavoured to purchase the only other television station in New Brunswick," CKCW in Moncton.

McElman hastened to add that "I have nothing but commendation for Mr. Irving and his corporations, for the great faith he has displayed in his native province by continually expanding investments." McElman wished that there could be at least six more Mr. K.C. Irvings in New Brunswick to make it go ahead even more rapidly — and, incidentally, to create more competition.

What did bother him was that it was "most undesirable" that, owning so much, Irving should also own so much of the media. The Irvings themselves "might be most meticulous in maintaining a 'hands-off' policy towards their papers, but when their interests were involved I suggest that balanced news coverage might suffer." The new CRTC should, in the public interest, suggest Irving sell control of Saint John's CHSJ radio and television stations and, if he declined, refuse to renew his licence.

McElman's second attack coincided with the 1969 establishment of the fifteen-member special Senate committee "to consider and report upon the ownership and control of the major means of mass communications in Canada, and in particular . . . to examine and report upon the extent and nature of their impact and influence upon the Canadian public." Senator Davey, a Toronto advertising executive and the architect of numerous Liberal election campaigns, cited as one example of monopoly the fact that "there is one entire province, New Brunswick, in which the press is controlled by a single owner." More than half of Canada's 107 dailies, he added, were controlled by chains; each had extensive broadcasting holdings, and so did seven of the fifty-two independent newspapers.

He was pleased, McElman said, that the CRTC had denied a cablevision licence in Saint John and that CHSJ's radio licence had been renewed for only one year. He was confident that Irving now would never get control of CKCW-TV, but he was not pleased to discover that he controlled the *Gleaner*.

McElman cited the "strange silence" Irving papers maintained about Irving industrial pollution of rivers, cited "many situations . . . which have cried out for media coverage" yet got little or none "because of the danger of involving an Irving interest." Then he revealed that he had asked the federal government to undertake an investigation of Irving's media control, and "if the evidence shows an improper monopoly," to apply the anti-combines law.

Irving retorted that "I make no apology for the ownership of newspapers, and I will not apologize to anyone as long as these newspapers are operated properly by people who have a great deal more concern for this province than Senator McElman has ever demonstrated." He lauded his newspaper executives as professional people who were known and respected, made their own decisions without consultation with him, and had every reason to resent the allegations. He asked if McElman believed "that Canada would be better served if the news media were foreign owned and controlled? I have had many opportunities to sell the newspaper properties over the years, but it has been my view that they should be operated by New Brunswickers, not by some company with a head office in Toronto or some foreign country."

By the winter's day that Irving was to appear before Davey's committee, combines investigators had made raids and seized documents from his newspapers, his home, and the homes of his top media executives. The night before his December 16 appearance he happened to meet Harold Shea, Ottawa correspondent for the Halifax *Chronicle-Herald*, at the newsstand in the Chateau Laurier. Shea asked him how he felt, and he quoted Irving as saying "I'm mad as hell."

The sixteenth was a tense, high-strung day in a packed room, with chairman Davey himself perhaps a bit nervous as he introduced the star witness as Kenneth *Charles* Irving. For a week the hearings had been tranquil. If the committee did nothing else, said columnist Charles Lynch, "it should take a bow for giving the nation its first direct look at our most legendary tycoon."

The electric anticipation was rewarded. Charles Lynch saw it as a bitter confrontation, "with Irving saying he was there only because he had to be," saying he had not come to make accusations, then accusing Premier Robichaud, and scarcely raising his voice, in Lynch's words, "as he put the lash to McElman." With Michael Wardell, very British, very angry, snapping "I'm damned well on trial here," with both Costello and Wardell demanding McElman's withdrawal from the committee.

It was a hectic, memorable day, and when it was over William Wardwell of the *Montreal Star* made Irving his story lead. "He sure can fight," Wardwell wrote. *Maclean's* said his appearance had "the smell of raw power."

At the beginning, Irving handed out to reporters that written statement detailing his media ownership. He said he held 25 per cent of the voting shares of K.C. Irving Ltd., and his family owned the rest. K.C. Irving Ltd. controlled the New Brunswick Publishing Co. Ltd., which owned the two Saint John papers, and it had as subsidiaries the Moncton Publishing Co. Ltd., with its two dailies, and the New Brunswick Broadcasting Co. Ltd., owner of CHSJ. The *Gleaner* was published by University Press of New Brunswick Ltd. in which K.C. Irving Ltd. owned a majority of shares.

"No salary, remuneration or expenses in any form have ever been paid to me or any member of my family by any of the newspapers, the radio or television stations. No dividends have been declared by New Brunswick Publishing Co. Ltd. during the twenty-five years . . . since its incorporation. All profits and cash throw-off resulting from [their] operation have been reinvested in New Brunswick endeavours.

"You have asked whether it is 'socially desirable for conglomerate corporations to include among their holdings interests in the communications media.' It is my contention that no individual or company or group of companies should be denied the right to publish a newspaper or a group of newspapers in a free society."

Irving then added a statement as to why he diversified his interests: "Almost any New Brunswick corporation subject to national or international competition must, if it is to survive successfully, either diversify its activities or itself become national or international in scope. If the latter happens, the head office will no longer remain in the Maritimes. I prefer diversification. Call it conglomerate or what you will, in New Brunswick it contributes to survival."

In testimony, Irving accused Robichaud of trying to destroy Wardell, and McElman of meddling in the CHSJ franchise. He said the premier had taken government printing from Wardell as an "economic reprisal" for his support of Conservative leaders, that he "failed in his effort but not because he did not try." As for McElman, he had the right to call for an investigation of Irving's media holdings, but he had also indicated to friends that CHSJ-TV would lose its licence, that "he could be of assistance in Ottawa should someone be interested in obtaining the television licence." The comments had been heard by others, said Irving, and he hoped the senator would have "the good grace" to acknowledge them. McElman retorted that the statement attributed to him by an unnamed source was "patently false."

Questioning probed Irving's methods as they had never been probed before but made no deep penetrations. Senator Harper Prowse, an Alberta Liberal and former reporter, asked him why he bothered to own newspapers when he left their management and profits in their own hands. Irving said there was great difficulty in getting capital into New Brunswick, that its people had to build up their own industries, and this possibly affected his ownership. It might seem strange elsewhere in Canada, but that was the only way New Brunswickers could retain control of their own enterprises. His media profits, he said, were invested in new buildings and plants and in New Brunswick ventures.

Clarifying his position on his responsibilities as an owner, he said if he thought some of his media were not being run properly, he would speak to the president of the publishing company about business management but not editorial policy because he knew nothing about it. What, asked Prowse, would he do if one of his papers advocated nationalization of industry? Amid laughter, Irving replied that he could think of instances where nationalization would be the lesser of two evils. He added that he would be inclined to step into more than his newspapers if something harmful to New Brunswick interests was threatened.

Prowse then asked if anything that hurt the province would also hurt Irving, and vice versa. Irving at first agreed, then said "I am not sure of your reasoning. I think we are kind of grasping at straws." But if New Brunswick was prosperous, all would prosper there. Prowse turned to Irving's purchase of the *Gleaner*. Irving said he had "made a certain arrangement" with Wardell on May 15, 1968, but resisted questioning: "I would prefer not to go beyond that." Then Prowse asked if any Irving company was a shareholder in Moncton's CKCW-TV. Irving said he was not a shareholder, controlled no shares, but had an obligation of a party that did own those shares. "However, I do not hold those shares as collateral." When Prowse asked if he had ever considered offering media shares to the public, Irving said he had but did not see how to do it successfully.

Under questioning by committee counsel Yves Fortier, Irving said he had "purchased companies and started companies to create activity, not necessarily to make money. They might never make money, but they would create a certain amount of activity." Fortier said he was "genuinely curious about your reasons for acquiring newspapers. . . . Why do you?" Irving said he would "have to ask myself the same question."

When Senator Douglas Everett of Manitoba asked what he thought of a suggestion that up to 50 per cent of any newspaper should be owned by citizens of the community, Irving said that would be impractical in New Brunswick. It would take a long time to explain but his was a province where money did not flow freely. He had developed a pattern of control for good reasons. "Why change something that works all right? Leave it alone."

What was important, said Everett, was that the committee had not been able to probe Irving's vast holdings in New Brunswick "or your feelings as to how New Brunswick should be run." He came back to "financial return." That, said Irving, was not a phrase that matched his intentions: "I believe that the newspaper business and newspapers, if well run, are good business. So I am interested in them from that standpoint and, too, seeing that good people are in charge." He told Fortier that he treated the purchase of newspapers like any other commodity.

Davey asked to what extent Irving might be concerned about concentrated newspaper ownership. Irving said he'd be concerned if one person owned all the newspapers in Canada, and lived in Toronto.

"Would you," asked Fortier, "be concerned if someone owned all the newspapers in Manitoba, or in Ontario, as you do in New Brunswick?"

"That," said Irving, "would depend on the owner, on the motives."

Fortier asked if he had bought New Brunswick papers to prevent them from falling into the hands of outsiders. "Yes," said Irving, "that was one of the reasons."

The questioning of Irving had lasted for an hour and a half. Although intense, the interrogation had been quiet and courteous, ending still on the question of his reason for ownership and his interest in a financial return, with Senator Everett putting this question: "So, then, we can say that you are interested, albeit in the long range, in the long range financial return?"

Irving: "Yes, I am."

Now the atmosphere of the hearing was about to change. One reporter wrote: "It was when publishers Wardell and Costello testified that the tempo, the mood, shifted from fencing to slugging."

In their written briefs, both deprecated government interference in the media. Wardell said freedom of the press was freedom to run it without such intrusions, and he linked the combines investigators' raids with his statement that he had faced "a degree of insult, harassment, and attempted intimidation never before, I believe, applied to the free press of any country under democratic government." He argued that the newspaper industry needed no policing, saw no need for a suggested press council, and no advantage in publishing the names of principal owners and managers of the media.

Costello said it was far more desirable to have a system that permits group ownership of newspapers than to have any government attempt to dictate who could publish one. The first step by government might not destroy press freedom but it could lead to others that would. The public, he said, was adequately protected by libel laws and journalistic standards. Moreover, group ownership had yielded benefits for the public in that it had given many newspapers financial stability and a high degree of integrity and professionalism.

Under questioning, Wardell said it was "utterly indefensible" that a biased McElman should remain on the committee after his attacks on the Irving press. Costello said McElman should withdraw because "the validity of these hearings surely is open to question if our accuser and prosecutor is also to sit in judgment." Wardell cited McElman's speeches as support for his statement that he had been harassed. He linked McElman with the combines raids and said, "I've been treated as if I were a member of the Mafia."

Davey sought to have him concede that the committee aimed at an impartial inquiry and said McElman had no advance notice that it was to be set up. Wardell said he would regard a committee inquiry as admirable, but when it was combined with other events the whole seemed to be "a direct attempt at intimidation and harassment." It would not, he assured the members, intimidate him. Davey regretted any feeling of persecution or accusation: "No one is on trial here." McElman, he said, was but one member of the committee, and it was "graced by his presence."

In less heated moments, Wardell praised Irving for his achievements and linked McElman with general applause for Irving's accomplishments. It was, he said, about the time that McElman went to the Senate that Irving became the object of hostile acts and public criticism. Noranda's takeover of Brunswick Mining was "like a booby trap" opened on Irving, and the Robichaud government had given Irving scant support to retain control. Shocking things were said publicly, with Irving portrayed as a financial ogre who exploited the poor.

Irving, Wardell said, had never tried to interfere with the way he ran the *Gleaner*. Nor had he himself ever allowed distortion or suppression of the news. Elaborating on Irving's statement about Robichaud, he said the premier had taken away his contract to print the official *Gazette*, and liquor companies were told it was illegal to advertise in the *Atlantic Advocate*. Later, outside the committee, Wardell said Robichaud had ordered that no more liquor ads were to be published, and estimated that the premier's acts had cost him $1 million. He found this "a most monstrous injustice."

Costello said, "If an honourable member suggests that a newspaper is giving a story a wide berth because of its owner's interests, or that labour might not be given a fair deal in a dispute, and if the senator makes the statement often enough, like the relentless drip-drip of the Chinese water torture, then some people are going to believe him."

Costello asked the committee what it was seeking. If it was looking for an ideal newspaper it would be disappointed, "and you certainly will not create it by any form of government legislation or regulation." He cited weaknesses in his own and other newspapers, but presented exhibits of news stories that he said showed improvements in his publications. McElman, he said, had accused them of failing to fight against river pollution, had suggested that they were inhibited by the fact Irving owned mills. Yet, said Costello, other North American newspapers had not campaigned against pollution until recently. Nor had McElman when he was executive assistant to Robichaud.

McElman intervened to say the Saint John newspapers had opposed the Robichaud government from the day Irving attacked it on the tax concessions issue. Prior to that, he said, there had been "a honeymoon period." Costello dated the opposition from the introduction of Equal Opportunity; the papers believed the program was too expensive for the province.

When the four-hour session was over, McElman told reporters it had reminded him of "three elephants trying to trample a flea. They rather got their feet entangled." Davey said he did not see the session as a partisan affair, but there had been a tendency to confuse strife between McElman and the Irving newspapers with the basic inquiry. "Personally," he said, "I feel it was a very useful day."

❧

When the Davey Committee issued its report — exactly one year after the start of the hearings in Ottawa — it was anything but kind to the New Brunswick newspapers. In fact, it branded New Brunswick and Nova Scotia as "journalistic disaster areas." It spoke of some news departments as being the graveyards of broken dreams, and when it got around to New Brunswick it accused the newspapers of seldom extending journalistic enterprise beyond covering trout festivals. It said they had not annoyed anyone of importance in years.

Those statements, Costello said, were false. He said the Saint John newspapers had so infuriated some people of importance as to leave them virtually incoherent. As examples he said "The *Telegraph-Journal* didn't think it was a trout festival when we fought the centralization of what we believed was too much power in Fredericton, when we warned that school boards and hospital boards would become rubber stamps under the program of Equal Opportunity, when we said New Brunswick would suffer from the loss of regional representation when county councils were killed."

Other examples of an aggressive press were cited by the New Brunswick newspapers but the Senate Report was now part of the public record. Protests from the aggrieved newspapers would do nothing to change that.

As for the report itself, it came in three volumes and called for such things as a government-appointed Press Ownership Review Board "to represent the public interest in future mergers or takeovers of publications" and a government Publications Development Fund "so that the loudest voice in town won't inevitably become the only voice in town." It also called on the media to establish a Press Council as an ombudsman, a watchdog on quality and the public interest. "You do have something besides profits to protect."

Perhaps it was that curl-of-the-lip tone that did the trick. In any event, press councils soon were organized across Canada and continue to provide a court, short of the law courts, where people unhappy with the press can vent their anger and get a judgment on whether they have been treated fairly or unfairly. Newspapers in turn agreed to publish the findings of the press councils.

In dealing with the New Brunswick newspapers, the Davey Committee felt much of the criticism of the *Daily Gleaner* was justified, but quoted pundit Dalton Camp as saying Michael Wardell had at least turned it from an outrage into a reasonable facsimile of a newspaper. It said New Brunswick was "the outstanding example of conglomerate ownership," quoting Beland Honderich, publisher of the *Toronto Star*, as saying, "Mr. Irving has in effect created a private empire of New Brunswick, complete with its official press." But it also quoted Camp as defending the New Brunswick newspapers warmly, as saying concern about them was excessive and that their number was remarkable. The Davey Report added: "The man is dead right. New Brunswick *does* have more newspapers per capita than anyplace in Canada, except P.E.I. We don't think they quite qualify as 'diverse and antagonistic voices.' But it is at least arguable that the province is better off with a home-owned media monopoly than one controlled from Toronto or Winnipeg."

While the Davey Report drew hot retorts from the Irving press, its central recommendations lived and died without changing much of anything. A decade later, concentration of ownership had gone so far that it provoked yet another government inquiry, this time by a royal commission.

It was during debate on the report that Senator McElman made his most virulent attack on the Irving media and interests. To him it was "regrettably but totally accurate" that the Irving conglomerate had flagrantly abused the public trust and had "a suppressive effect on the quality" of its newspapers. Now Wardell was about to depart for Britain after years of stirring up "racial disunity, hatred, prejudice, malice, bigotry, and mistrust" and McElman wished him "God speed and good riddance."

McElman turned his anger on the *Telegraph-Journal*, saying the paper had bilked the public to protect other parts of the Irving empire. Never had it editorialized against "the inequitable and iniquitous" tax deals Irving in particular had with municipal governments.

The primary purpose of financial-industrial tycoons who owned newspapers, said McElman, "is to grasp power and more power. They want the power to choose and appoint publishers and editors who share their philosophy." An owner did it by hiring pawns. "He can then testify publicly, or even before committees of Parliament, that he has never interfered with the operation or editorial policies of his newspapers. He can even appear mystified to explain, under questioning, just why he ever bothered to buy up newspapers." He also had "the power to decide what will and what will not become public issues."

Yet, McElman said, he respected and admired K.C. Irving personally. "He is courtly, courteous, and almost gentle in his relationships. He has displayed incomparable genius in assembling a powerful and great corporate empire in a part of this land that has been historically and chronically undeveloped. I know of no person who could or would have done it so successfully, and great benefits have flowed from that to the people and to the province.

"That is the man, but the corporate empire is something else again. It displays none of the gentle or considerate attributes of the man. Its thirst for power and more power is insatiable. That corporate empire operates with the power of a lion, the appetite of a vulture, the grace of an elephant, the instincts of a barracuda, and the principles of an alley cat. It is for this reason that I desperately want to see the media of New Brunswick separated from the ownership and control of that collossus. . . . A free and independent press in New Brunswick would become an integral and major part of the necessary system of checks and balances that must curb the excesses of the Irving corporate empire."

This time there were reactions in Ottawa. Senator David Walker of Toronto said he had submitted the Senate to "a filthy afternoon." Tom Bell, Saint John Progressive Conservative MP, called McElman's remarks "venomous," while Hugh John Flemming praised Wardell's "definite and most outstanding contribution" to New Brunswick.

The *Moncton Times* argued that McElman had failed to distinguish between press ownership and control, said conglomerate ownership has its dangers, and called on the senator either to demonstrate real abuses or stop shouting. The *Gleaner* quoted Wardell's rebuttal, a brief and general one charging McElman with "bitter personal bias," and ran a long editorial in his defence. The *Telegraph-Journal* said it could hardly improve on Senator Walker's comments.

Irving himself said he found it difficult to take McElman seriously, and quoted from the Bible, Matthew 5:22: "But I say unto you, whosoever is angry without a cause shall be in danger of the judgment. . . . But whosoever shall say, thou fool, shall be in danger of hellfire." To this he added, "I'm wondering who let him out."

Fred Hazel, who had held every position on the Saint John newspapers from cub reporter to editor-in-chief, said, "I'm convinced that Charlie McElman believed every word he said about the press in New Brunswick. It wasn't true. That's not the way it worked, but that's what Charlie believed — because that's the way it was done in the past and that's the way politicians would have done it if they'd owned or controlled newspapers.

"That," he added, "is as good a reason as any why politicians shouldn't be the ones to decide who should own the press."

CHAPTER TWENTY-EIGHT

❧

A Tale of Two Ports

"The naive are those who say he is naive."
– PREMIER RICHARD HATFIELD COMMENTING ON K.C. IRVING'S
POLITICAL ASTUTENESS.

THE DAVEY COMMITTEE RECOMMENDATIONS GATHERED dust, but the controversy over the New Brunswick newspapers would continue for years even as a new political era left little more than an angry echo of the turbulent sixties. A Conservative government came to power in 1970 under Richard Hatfield, son of a well-heeled businessman-politician, a lawyer with business experience, a skilled politician, and a man of the world given to frequent travels to far and exotic places. Under him the province entered a period of public tranquillity in the relations between the government and the Irvings.

Hatfield didn't share McElman's worries about Irving ownership of the provincial English-language newspapers. "I don't care who owns them," he'd say, "but they must be vehicles for the exchange of local information in a community." Irving had told him in 1966 that he had never told any of them what stand to take, and Hatfield believed him: "No one has ever been able to prove he misused them." In his own experience, he said in the early eighties, their editorials didn't tend to coincide, "except when everybody is against something."

Moreover, Hatfield said he didn't believe in "taking on industry as such; you get nothing out of it except a little bit of bravado." He admired Irving: "He has an ethical discipline that governs his business habits." He said, "I have never met anyone who made the impact he did; you felt this is a man who has it all together." He also called him "a very, very reputable businessman. I go into homes and find people keeping calendars with his picture on them. He has outwitted people, but I doubt that he ever did it dishonestly. I'd want a lot more evidence to make me think otherwise."

With that sort of philosophy, Hatfield assumed in 1970 the powers Louis Robichaud had gained through Equal Opportunity, those powers that made the government the largest employer in the province, and he left them intact. He enjoyed using them, unabashedly enjoyed being premier. He had his own perilous experiences with state encouragement of industry; his government brought in budgets that sent expenditures soaring, making it an economic factor even more significant than the Irvings' own.

He did nothing about Irving's call for a judicial inquiry into what had happened at Brunswick Mining. His government was sued by the Irvings over a tax measure, and did something else about taxes that was linked in the public mind with one of the most stunning moves in Irving's life. But, overall, he exercised power for years according to the terms he had sensed on that election night in 1967 — terms that, as he saw them, made Irving and his sons no longer an outsized force in the political life of the province.

One of Hatfield's cabinet ministers recalled Irving coming to Fredericton not long after the 1970 election and making a strong case about a tax matter. He remembered being awed in the great man's presence. "Then, when he finished, the premier said quietly, 'Thank you, Mr. Irving. We need the revenues and we are going to proceed.'"

That Irving appearance the minister had witnessed involved one significant difference he had with Hatfield's government, and it came to have a fascinating history of its own. Hatfield proposed to tax Irving's Canaport oil storage facilities. He did, and Irving sued, and for three years the case was fought in the courts. Irving won the first two rounds but finally lost when the Supreme Court of Canada ruled that Canaport's tanks were structures for the storage of "movable property" and therefore taxable. Then, in

1980, with back taxes amounting to more than $1 million, Hatfield did a surprising thing: he brought in legislation that waived the right won at substantial cost. He said the company was important to the province and that he was honouring a government understanding reached with Irving when Canaport was built. He later said the Irvings had come back to him and argued that they were having difficulties with the supply of crude oil, that the Supreme Court was wrong, and that the Robichaud government had given an undertaking that the facilities involved would not be taxed. Said Hatfield: "You have to honour a previous government's commitments."

Hatfield later expressed admiration for both Irving and Robichaud, those pivots of controversy while he sat in opposition. He said Robichaud surprised many people, including himself: "At first I thought he was a joke, a zero with the ass out of his pants. But he learned to be premier very fast, and I came to have a great admiration and respect for him." He paused, grinned, and added, "I'm also very proud to have beaten him."

He differed, however, with Robichaud's assessment of Irving's approach to politics. Robichaud once told someone Irving did not understand politics, that he saw his way as the right way to serve the best interests of the province. Hatfield, on the contrary, said he found Irving "an extremely competent politician. The naïve are those who say he's naïve. He's one of the few businessmen I've ever met who knew when he came to you that he was not dealing with the premier but with the people. He knew how far he could go in the area of public opinion, and how far a premier could go. If he thought you'd gone too far, he'd say so."

Still, Hatfield had to live with the Irving mystique. "Some people," he said, "are never going to believe he doesn't order provincial governments around." Personally, he doubted that Irving ever had: "I have no evidence but my guess is that from the thirties to the sixties his political influence was far more indirect than real. I don't believe he ever snapped his fingers and had premiers jump. I do believe that people were afraid of him. They believed that whatever he wanted he got." That was still a popular assumption in the 1980s.

He recalled Irving's 1965 explosion against the removal of existing tax concessions, but he said he personally had never feared the man after that 1966 interview in which he unsuccessfully sought support for the Tory leadership: "It touches me that he goes to funerals; my Dad did, too." In their own relations, he said, he had found Irving "firm and forceful, but he never attempted to give me orders." In part, he felt all the Irvings had "understood that a change had come" with that 1967 election, and that they would be treated by government with the respect that was their due as important businessmen, but no more. Nor, he said, had they asked more. As corporate citizens, they had "virtually shut down nothing. They would do anything rather than lay people off, and if they do, it is because they are at the end of their rope."

❧

The Canaport that led to Hatfield's curious tax decision was opened the year he came to power. It became one more Irving addition to the economic realities of his home town and one more element in the controversy about its future. In this case, he made his views and intentions stick. In an earlier case, he hadn't.

In the early 1960s he had found himself in the centre of a raging controversy over plans to erect a combined harbour bridge and a throughway in Saint John to link up with major provincial highways. The throughway would arise in what is known locally as "The Valley," in the heart of the city. Irving thought the plans were crazy, and in muted form said so publicly. He admired the way the Loyalists had laid out the city. "By gosh," he'd say, "they did a good job," and he was certain the proposed bridge-throughway would do anything but.

In 1965 he advocated that an expressway and river bridge be built in a more northerly and relatively undeveloped part of the community, a second bridge and a badly needed central street system in the harbour area. It would prevent valuable land from becoming worthless. In his view, Saint John was missing an opportunity to become a large and prosperous city of 200,000. He made no bones about the fact that the $18-million estimated cost of the proposed harbour bridge alone — it had jumped from $10 million — would make it the only toll bridge in the province and hurt businesses, including his own.

But as much as anything he fretted over what would happen to Saint John's harbour. He feared, correctly, that the harbour bridge's low clearance would block shipping from the waters above it. He said it was possible to build a dam across the St. John River above the Reversing Falls, catch the fresh water coming down, stop the current and the tides, and allow the harbour to be markedly extended rather than restricted. He argued that a higher, cheaper extension bridge over the harbour would help make this possible. He had plans for industries that would have become possible with a Chignecto Canal and a larger harbour.

Nor was he alone in his opposition. A Community Growth Committee emerged belatedly but vociferously to champion the views he held. It consisted of businessmen, professional people, and others: Irving's son Jack was a prominent member. The committee managed to delay the plans, even temporarily halted construction already under way, but it could not change the will of both the provincial and federal governments, which were to contribute millions. Mayor Dr. Stephen Weyman said Irving "set us back on our heels." Weyman also acknowledged Irving was "a very astute man" with the interests of the city at heart, but in the end city council and the supporting governments went ahead with their own plans.

In 1966 the *Atlantic Advocate* published an article that said the bridge would stand as "a monument to controversy," and only future generations would be able to tell whether it and the throughway "signify intelligent foresight or the complete reverse."

Years later there were still opinions both ways, and the Saint John newspapers were still bemoaning the existence of New Brunswick's only toll bridge, whose deficits mounted year by year. As for Irving, he never changed his mind. "I knew," he said, "they were wrong."

But as the bridge and throughway were rising, he was off in pursuit of another dream. To explain it, he would drive people out to a treed and lonely spot at Mispec Point, only a few miles from downtown Saint John. The tides of Fundy lapped at its shoreline. Time gnawed its rust into the remnants of a wartime coastal artillery base. Gulls wrote beauty into the sky. Here, Irving would say, he planned a major development, a first for North America.

On June 18, 1968, he revealed it publicly, announcing that he was prepared to proceed at once with construction of a $14-million deepwater facility for the docking of supertankers bringing crude oil from the Middle East. He had applied, he said, for a

$4.5-million grant from the Atlantic Development Board, that government body established by Ottawa to channel millions into backup projects for industrial development. If the grant were forthcoming, work would start that summer on a terminal that would bring closer the expansion of his oil refinery, which in turn, he said, could be expected to stimulate shipbuilding and ship repairs.

Plans, Irving said, had started a number of years earlier, and studies had been completed. The location was suitable. The largest tankers in service or planned would be able to dock — tankers six times the size of those then bringing oil to the city. Saint John would benefit from new business and new prestige. The city could become the oil distribution centre for much of this section of Canada and the northeast United States. Because of rapid, recent changes, he said, Saint John could benefit uniquely if it constructed the first terminal facilities of this type on the eastern seaboard. Already, he added, he had a contract to supply crude oil to an American refiner.

But he emphasized the need for haste. Similar developments were being planned and constructed by major European ports to take advantage of the era of the supertanker. He was ready to go ahead with a contract with Canadian Bechtel Ltd. of Toronto that would open the way for an average of 45,000 barrels of crude to be supplied daily to his own refinery and another 50,000 to be exported to the United States.

He hoped, Irving said, that the Atlantic Development Board would deal promptly with his application for a grant. Delays could not be afforded because they could weaken the beckoning advantages. Moreover, he thought chances for a grant had been "greatly improved by the position taken by both major party leaders in the [recent] federal election campaign, and by the latitude allowed the A.D.B. in providing grants to the four Atlantic area cities which had been excluded from the federal government's incentive program for designated areas."

He had, in fact, sought that expanded latitude for some time for Saint John, and now it was available. Now, he said, the A.D.B. had recognized the potential of the type of development he had in mind by teaming up with other government agencies to give aid to a new refinery in Nova Scotia. New Brunswick's own Department of Economic Growth had been kept informed, and its minister, Saint John lawyer Robert Higgins, had helped greatly in getting Saint John made a designated area for federal aid.

His own refinery, Irving said, had been built to permit expansion if Saint John became a terminal for supertankers. If it did, he implied, he would double the refinery's capacity, provide up to 3 million man-hours of labour, and give permanent work to many more than its present staff of 200. As it was, the refinery had stimulated construction of five tankers in his shipyard in the last six years. Given the terminal, there would be more.

His announcement made news across Canada, and the Halifax *Chronicle-Herald* said it saw no reason why it would prejudice another deepwater terminal envisaged for Nova Scotia's Canso Strait; there the British-American (later Gulf) oil company, with federal aid, was to build a large refinery and docking facilities for supertankers. Nor, said the paper, did it seem to be a threat to less developed plans for Halifax to become a container terminal for general cargo. The Saint John newspapers observed that the Irving statement was only one of two exciting announcements within a week about the development of deepwater terminals in the Saint John area. It was true, and it was more than a coincidence. It was a story within a story.

Just three days after Irving's statement, the Robichaud government announced it was going to have a deepwater port of its own at Lorneville, a few miles west of Saint John. Planning, said the premier, would take about a year.

Behind the news there lay another difference in Irving's contacts with the Robichaud administration. In short, Irving wanted no part of the government project. He would build his own terminal where he wanted it, and he would build it on his own timetable to meet his own needs, to fulfil his own vision. His plans did not go down well with the government and once again there was tension and bitterness in the background. Even in the names of the two proposed terminals there was a ring of rivalry that was no accident. The government's was to be called Canport. Irving called his Canaport.

Canport was part of a broad design for industrial development mapped out by James Addison, the successor to the Frederick Gormley who had fathered the ill-fated Westmorland Chemical

Park and paid for it by losing his job in 1965. For more than a year after that, the New Brunswick Development Corporation had no chief. Then on January 1, 1967, Robichaud named Addison its president.

A native of Scotland, he had been managing director of an international engineering, manufacturing, and trading company based in South Africa, and more recently of a group of companies owned by Courtaulds, famous international chemical and fibre manufacturers. Once a fighter pilot in the Battle of Britain, Addison was urbane, handsome, persuasive, and at times arrogant, capable of treating politicians with disdain. Armed with a ten-year contract, he set about winding up the Westmorland debacle and laying plans of his own that soon had him eyeing Irving's Saint John stronghold as a logical place for development.

Given that background, given Irving's own plans and the emphasis Brunswick had added to his determination to control whatever he was involved in, and given his attitude towards active government intervention in the economy, not to mention his lone-wolf character, there was little reason to expect that Irving would have much enthusiasm for participating in Addison's plans. What's more, new events had added to his irritations. Soon after launching the Italians on their doomed plans on the Miramichi, Robichaud had brought in another infusion of foreign capital, that of the Landegger interests of New York, and given government support to promote a $70-million hardwood pulp mill at Nackawic, 64 kilometres above Fredericton on the St. John River.

Into this context stepped James Addison, with his grand designs and his belief that Irving's co-operation was necessary, even vital, if they were to get off the ground. In February 1968, he outlined those designs in broad sweeps in an article in the *Atlantic Advocate* entitled "Develop or Die — the Industrial Challenge for New Brunswick," and four months before Irving's announcement of Canaport, it listed a superport or deepwater harbour as a major objective.

Working with Canadian Pacific Railway, Addison wrote, he sought to establish a super deepwater port to handle ships up to 800,000 tons deadweight, requiring thirty metres of water, large areas of sea for manoeuvre, and large areas of low-cost land for a reception and distribution terminal. The aim was to provide reciprocal facilities for similar ports in Malta and Rotterdam, Holland. There was also the possibility that they could be established jointly with Maine and become an international free port.

Other developments anticipated were a multiple light-industry complex (multiplex) that would take eight years to build, require $250 million in capital, and employ some 20,000 people in forty to fifty firms or processes, including two major fish docks to improve processing, packaging, and marketing, and a plan to settle about a dozen German farmers on some 4,047 hectares of land to sell their produce abroad through a co-operative.

As Addison later told the story of his superport and what happened to it, foreign names with billions at their command tripped off his tongue. The Rothschilds were interested, he said. The CPR saw his superport as a place to dock great ships that would take coal to Japan and return with Arabian oil. Continental Oil (Conneco) was interested. So was an important independent company. The Arabs talked of building a refinery.

But, said Addison, he still saw Irving as the key. So did the interests he hoped to attract: "They were all asking what he was going to do." Irving had his refinery; pipelines could take crude to it from Lorneville. Irving had a healthy cash flow. Irving was wooed and invited to a Miramichi fishing lodge for a crucial Sunday meeting.

Irving asked if he could bring his three sons, and they all came. The virtues of Canport and of Lorneville, were extolled: its ice-free location, its relative nearness to Europe, its access to railways, its support by government, the great wharves it would have on shore, preferable to the floating dock of Irving's Canport. It would, it was said, become an "energy city" such as the east coast of the United States could not match because it had no comparable location. It would be good if Irving got involved.

Irving listened and said, "Let me consider it," and with his sons he went away. Addison kept pressing him. Never, he said, did he get a decisive no. What he did get was Irving's request that he be alloted 405 hectares and that no other oil company be involved. It was a demand the government would not meet: "It was all very polite but we didn't get one yard."

Irving's announcement of Canaport confirmed his rejection of Addison's proposal, and Robichaud's announcement would become an epitaph. Years went by, years of struggle with local residents over the expropriation of thousands of acres of land, with the federal government over costly pollution standards, years of more expenditures before the fate of Addison's Canport was finally settled in the mid-seventies: It was abandoned. So were most of Addison's other plans, among them the proposed Saint John multiplex concept.

It was, Addison believed, Irving's decision to build his own deepwater terminal that was the breaking point for Canport: "I really believe that if he had come in with us it would have worked. But he wanted no separate development he couldn't control."

That was hardly surprising after Irving's experience with Brunswick Mining and Noranda, nor was it surprising that Irving paid a political price in what happened to his application for a government grant for his own terminal. It was approved by the Atlantic Development Board and recommended to Ottawa's Area Development Agency, which controlled funds to be allotted to regions covered by the broadened terms for designated areas. But by late December 1968, Ottawa was dubious about whether Irving's proposal fitted into its terms of reference. Furthermore, there were doubts that Canport really needed government support.

Irving was prepared to make further representation to the board. He thought approval could easily be justified within the existing terms of reference. But in the end the application was refused, and Irving had his own version of why it was. He was convinced that interference came from "some of the backroom boys in the Liberal party." He said he knew of one Liberal power-broker, with clout in both Ottawa and New Brunswick, who had said, "There's no way Irving's going to get that $4.5 million."

He went ahead on his own, with his own plans, his own timetable, and his own money. On a windy September day in 1970 his Canport was officially opened, with due ceremony and celebration, with the 212,000-ton supertanker *H.J. Haynes*, a giant one-fifth of a mile long, tied up after a 20,800-kilometre voyage from the Persian Gulf, the first of many great ships to moor at a doughnut-shaped, green-and-yellow monobuoy 1,250 metres offshore.

The terminal itself was a floating dock, a buoy moored to the sea floor 36.6 metres below. Through underwater pipelines the oil moved ashore from tankers to a tank farm, a cluster of great white receptacles with a capacity of not less than 2.5 million barrels. From these, in turn, it moved through an overland pipeline to the refinery.

Irving tugged a cord to unfurl a Canadian flag and a blue Irving pennant. Behind him, on a rocky, windswept hilltop, stood the white tank farm into which the *Haynes* was already pumping her millions of gallons of crude. There were ten tanks in all, six of them flaunting the letters I-R-V-I-N-G, each equipped with a floating lid that would ride up and down with the level of the oil it contained, thus allowing no air space, no evaporation. Gleaming silver pipes led from them to the refinery; mighty pumps were there to bring the oil ashore and propel it on. And already, said Arthur Irving, they were planning to build three more tanks twice the size of the first ten.

The site was equipped, too, with its own fire-fighting equipment and was graded so any oil spill would be directed into a holding pond. People could stand on an observation platform and look out at the monobuoy, 16.7 metres in diameter, heated, fitted with lights and a foghorn, with gear that allowed it to be controlled from shore. They could see a new 20.7-metre, Irving-built vessel, the *Irving Tamarac*, whose task was to help tankers moor and to ferry supplies and workers. They could press a button and hear a recorded story of what Canaport was all about. The site in fact, was a tourist attraction where visitors could park their cars and picnic and watch the great ships that had made it cheaper to carry oil around the Cape of Good Hope than it had been to take it over a shorter route through the Suez Canal in conventional tankers.

Arthur Irving saw Canaport as far more than a tourist attraction. He called it a catalyst and an economic multiplier. Because of what it made possible, he said, the refinery was being more than doubled in size, its daily production capacity boosted from 50,000 barrels to 120,000 at a cost of up to $30 million with 800 men at work on construction. Work would also be plentiful for the Irving shipyard on tankers that would take much of the crude arriving in Saint John down the coast to American refineries. In one stroke the Irvings had become both importers and exporters of oil.

Lord Beaverbrook (centre) is greeted at the Fredericton airport in 1960 by (from left to right) publisher Michael Wardell, K.C., Dr. Colin Mackay, president of the University of New Brunswick, and Fredericton's mayor William Walker.

K.C. with Irving Oil super salesman Arnold Payson in the 1960s.

Arthur addresses an Irving Oil sales convention in the 1960s as K.C. beams approval.

TELEGRAPH-JOURNAL

K.C. with Jim, Jack, and Arthur at Canaport deepwater site in 1968.

The atmosphere was cool when K.C. met Senator Keith Davey at the media hearings in 1969.

CANAPRESS PHOTO SERVICE (CHUCK MITCHELL)

Right: K.C. speaking at a christening at his shipyard in 1969.

&

Below: The industrialist was declared amateur bricklaying champion in 1969 — and presented with an honorary membership in the union.

TELEGRAPH-JOURNAL

TELEGRAPH-JOURNAL

K.C. and his wife Harriet in the twilight of their years together.

GARY PRIDHAM

Above: K.C. marks the planting of the one hundred millionth tree in 1977.

ﺽ

Left: Measuring the growth of the trees he planted was one of K.C.'s passions.

ﺽ

Below: When K.C. was named New Brunswick's honorary chief forester, it inspired this drawing by editorial cartoonist Josh Beutel.

K.C. is inducted into the Canadian Business Hall of Fame in 1979 by Royal Bank president Rowland Frazee.

K.C. discusses construction plans with sons Jim, Arthur, and Jack.

K.C., wife Winnifred, and K.C.'s cousin and lifelong friend Leigh Stevenson, in Bermuda in 1988.

K.C. and Winnifred enjoying a summer day in New Brunswick in 1992.

CHAPTER TWENTY-NINE

☙

Tussles with the Boss

"Working with Irving was frustrating, maddening,
stimulating, and gratifying."
– PROJECT ENGINEER EDDIE SHEEHAN RECALLING HIS WORKING
RELATIONSHIP WITH K.C. IRVING.

F ew people said it as clearly, as bluntly, or as honestly as
Eddie Sheehan. The fact is, few people had the nerve, but
Sheehan was a gutsy, outspoken Irishman who found that
working with Kenneth Colin Irving could be sheer hell.

As Sheehan told it, Irving interrupted, delayed, stuck his nose
into everything, and created nightmares for those working with
him and for him. It was not something Irving denied, even though
he saw his involvement and his hands-on approach from a very
different perspective. Simply put, it was his way. From the very
beginning, from the earliest days in Bouctouche when as a six-
year-old he had started his first business venture and bossed ten-
year-olds Leigh Stevenson and Addie McNairn, he had run
things, supervised, directed, and yes, interfered. In his seventies, he
was not about to change.

That put a terrible strain on his relationship with Eddie Sheehan,
a consulting engineer and project boss during one more expansion
of Irving's pulp mill in Saint John. But what was most striking
about the explosive association of these two men was that when it
was all over, when the scars of personal conflict had begun to heal,

Sheehan realized something he would never have believed possible. He liked the man. He admired him. He respected him. And, to his utter surprise, he learned that Irving liked, admired, and respected him too.

At this point in his career, Irving was still doing what he had been doing since he was old enough to make money and stuff it in the family clock: he was expanding. At seventy, he announced the $40-million expansion that would double the capacity of his oil refinery. At seventy-one, he opened Canaport, started expanding his pulp mill, announced he was going to expand his drydock, and saw his forestry operations expand with the construction of a sawmill at Estcourt, Que. At seventy-two, he was lean and stepped briskly, his cheeks pink and unwrinkled, his eyes alert.

It was at this stage of his life that Irving worked with Sheehan. They came into frequent contact — and conflict — because Irving was back at his Saint John pulp mill, fussing, fuming, intruding, but above all else, directing and supervising one more transformation designed to make it produce more, a remarkable twenty times more than it had when he bought it a quarter of a century earlier. His aim: to boost its daily capacity from 500 tons to 800 in the largest expansion of its kind in North America at the time. He wanted to do it as he had done it before, without a halt in the rumbling, roaring work it did twenty-four hours a day, seven days a week. And Sheehan was the engineer he brought in from Boston to oversee the job.

Irving had always had ideas — one engineer had said they were those of a man whose knowledge he would compare to that of a trained mechanical engineer — and never hesitated to express them. Sheehan was the same way. Irving called him "a good guy, very intelligent, reliable, and honest." He was also able, blunt, determined, at times comical with the wit of the Irish. He called Irving "the last of the rugged individualists," and he described what it was like to do business with him in succinct terms. It was, he said, "frustrating, maddening, stimulating, and gratifying."

Sheehan had direct experience of Irving's methods. He sat down one day in the 1980s and put it on paper, page after handwritten page of it. Of all the men who have worked for and with Irving, no one went into the details, the warts-and-all, day-to-day complications as Sheehan did. This is his story:

Some time during 1967 Mr. Irving retained the services of Charles T. Main, Inc., engineers of Boston, to design and construct a new pulp-drying installation for his mill in Saint John. After what we considered a short time, he was not satisfied with the progress we were making so he fired us. He then formed his own engineering company and hired an experienced engineer from a paper-making company as project manager. About halfway into the construction stage Mr. Irving again became dissatisfied with the progress, so he fired his own engineering company, disbanded the organization and instructed the project manager to continue the job to completion. This, of course, was not humanly possible, and the project ground to a halt. Charles T. Main then received a frantic call to send people to Saint John to save it.

Up to this point I had no knowledge of the previous or present project, and least of all of Mr. K.C. Irving. All of the personnel associated with the original work had been reassigned and were no longer available. My boss asked me if I would go to Saint John, talk to Mr. Irving, and find out exactly what the problem was. At that time we had had nothing to do with the project for two years.

Mr. Irving sent his plane to Boston to pick up one of our electrical engineers and myself. On landing, we met with the project manager. He asked if we could talk before our meeting with Mr. Irving. The manager explained that he was very concerned with the structural steel bracing that Mr. Irving demanded be removed from the building because he did not like its appearance. My first meeting with Mr. Irving was scheduled for 6 p.m. at the mill. It eventually got under way at nine. It is, in fact, not the least bit unusual for him to be two to four hours late for a meeting with people at our level.

Present at this meeting were all the Irving sons, the general manager of the mill, the production manager, the project manager, and we two engineers from Charles T. Main. The most significant part of it was that Mr. Irving did all the talking. It was my job to learn about the problem and report back to my boss, who would then decide whether we wanted to pick up this mess or forget it. Mr. Irving asked us to look at the construction that had taken place. We stood in a group on the cold, silent ground level and the question was, "Now, Mr. Sheehan, if Charles T. Main had designed this job, you would not have steel bracing in all these places, would you?" I said, "Mr. Irving, if Main had designed this job we would have bracing in there where you have taken it out, and I suggest that you do not take out any more. Under the present conditions, you will not be able to run your dryer because of the bracing you have taken out. The dryer is now holding the building together, and the bracing must be put back in place."

Well, everybody kind of moved away, wondering who does this guy think he is, talking to Mr. Irving like that? Mr. Irving himself stood for a moment, thinking, and then he said, "We're paying for expert advice and I guess we'd better take it. Replace the bracing."

Now he started to give all kinds of instructions as to what Charles T. Main, Inc., would do and should do. I think I deflated him when I said, "Mr. Irving, I haven't said Main wants this job." But we had now developed a better understanding of him, so my boss and I decided to assign a crew to do it. We picked up the loose ends and at this point we learned that both his engineering firm and his project manager had done a very good job. The project was completed to the satisfaction of everyone.

One year later they came back and asked me to become project manager for a large expansion of the mill. This was rather flattering. We were asked to increase production to 800 tons a day from 500. This required many surveys and studies. We eventually came up with a suitable program and it was prepared as a bound report. It was presented in Mr. Irving's office, with Jim Irving in attendance along with many Irving staff people. "Now, before my father comes in," Jim said, "let's plan a time, scope, etc." I said, "Jim it's all in the covering letter in the front of the report." He said, "Oh, fine," then glanced at the letter, looked across the table at me with piercing eyes and said, "$55 million; we said $50 million. Thirty months to completion; we said eighteen months."

"Well, Jim," I said, "that's the way the numbers add up and the pieces fit together."

"You wasted three months of my time and money to give me a worthless document," he said. "If you can't do the job for the amount we can afford and in the time we want it, you can get the hell out of here and we'll get someone who can." With that, he heaved the book across the room. So I got up and said to my two colleagues, "Well, gentlemen, let's get out of here."

Just then Mr. Irving entered the room very gracefully and sat down. So did we. Mr. Irving said, "Oh yes, the Charles T. Main report, that's fine," and opened the book. "It's no deal, Dad," Jim said, "they want $55 million to do the job and they are going to take thirty months." Mr. Irving slowly closed the book and said, "Well, of course, that won't do. Now Mr. Sheehan, I'll tell you what you are going to do. Go back to Boston and review this report very carefully, and when you have a mill we can afford and in the time we say then come back and see us."

"Mr. Irving," I replied, "if I agree to do that I have to admit that what I have in this report is wrong. What I have in this report is not wrong and going back to Boston to review it is not going to change anything."

He charged out of the office to call my boss and tell him how unco-operative I was. Things marked time for three months — until Mr. Irving had to face the fact that cutting several million dollars out of the project meant giving up some of it. The expansion was then reduced to 600 tons. We refigured the program, came up with an acceptable outlay of capital and resumed design work. Two problems soon became obvious. For one, Mr. Irving still wanted the job finished by the original date. That now gave us fifteen months, and there was no conceivable way a plant of this magnitude could be built in less than thirty; the schedule was a source of constant battle throughout. For another, here we were designing an expansion to 600 tons only to find that Mr. Irving had never given up his ideas for one of 800 tons.

On many occasions he would craftily sneak in an addition or a larger piece of equipment. He would, for example, ask me many times if I thought the three new digesters would turn out the necessary production. I would explain that, considering the tight, strict budget he held us to, three digesters would be just adequate, absolutely nothing to spare but just adequate. This question would come up every so often and we would say, "Mr. Irving, we are trying to hold to the budget."

"Oh yes, yes," he'd say, "of course, by all means." But by then I knew him well enough to know that once he gets onto something he hangs on like a bulldog. He did. At a meeting in the mill, with its operating people present, he brought the question up again. Now naturally the operating people would have liked to have an extra digester; it would make life less hectic for them. I said, "Mr. Irving, you can have all the digesters you want, but you have to pay for them."

"Well," he said, "we would hope they wouldn't be too expensive." Just then he was called to a phone in another office to talk with Jim, who was phoning from London. When he returned he said Jim wanted to talk to me. I talked with him, then came back, and found things had been happening in my absence. "Now Mr. Sheehan," Mr. Irving said, "while you were on the phone we decided on an extra digester."

"Mr. Irving," I said, "if you want four digesters that's fine with me but, as I've said, you'll have to pay for it."

"Not four, Mr. Sheehan. Five."

"FIVE?"

"Does that bother you, Mr. Sheehan?"

"It sure as hell does. Do you know what that fifth digester is going to cost you? One hell of a bundle of cash. The end of the digester house will have to be torn down, the elevator replaced, the railroad track moved and the chip feed system replaced."

The room went tomb silent. Then Mr. Irving broke into a hearty laugh and that was the signal for everyone to laugh.

From there he went on to increase the six-ton chlorine dioxide generator to eight tons, added an extra deck to the pulp dryer, put in a bigger cylinder forming machine, which was too big so he added two more sections to the dryer. And so on and on.

Mr. Irving wanted the location of the expansion, really a new mill, planned so that there would be no interference with production. He wanted everything bunched together because he thought he would save operators this way. This was not true. The number of operators would be the same in any location. Completely in line with his stubborn nature, he managed to move the new pulp mill up against the old one. There was a railroad siding running the entire length of the mill that had to be retained, and what he wanted to do meant that the mill had to be bridged over the track. Mr. Irving never liked this, even though he created it. He would refer to it as "Sheehan's tunnel."

After moving the mill, he set to work on moving the recovery boiler and evaporators to the opposite side of it. This turned into quite a battle. It ended up in Mr. Irving's office with a staff of eight men putting it to a vote. There were nine votes in favour and two against, Jim Irving and me. It was just about as democratic as a Soviet election. The move was not sensible, and it added considerably to the cost because we literally hung the structure out over the Reversing Falls.

Our people did a masterful job of structural design, but when the cost of all the additions and changes in plans was presented to Mr. Irving he hit the ceiling and charged out of the office like a raging bull, saying something like, "Jim, you don't have that kind of money. Get it out of here."

Well, we moved along pretty well. The foundations of the new mill were in and most of the structural steel had been erected when Mr. Irving noticed how close the mill was to the woodroom where the logs come in. He didn't like this, so he asked us to move the mill twenty-five feet south. At that stage, this was utterly preposterous; if carried out, it would result in a major disaster. We explained that the woodroom was slated to be torn down in the near future anyway, and I fought Mr. Irving bitterly over his idea because it was a downright unnecessary piece of foolishness.

So now we go back to the voting table, with Jim Irving and the same group of staff men. I explained all the problems the move would create, the excessive cost, the lack of necessity, but I knew I was doomed to defeat. Mr. Irving passed out his little paper ballots. "If you favour moving the mill, vote yes," he said. "If you favour not moving it, vote no."

I wrote no on my ballot and tossed it on the table. "Mr. Sheehan," Mr. Irving said, "you are disqualified. I can see your vote."

"Mr. Irving," I said, "my vote is no secret." Some of the staff started asking for a better definition of the vote, and Jim Irving said, "Let's start again. Simply vote move or don't move." I marked my ballot, folded it, and tossed it on the table.

Mr. Irving marked his, folded it, then marked the outside K.C.I. I said, "Mr. Irving, you are disqualified. Your ballot has your name on it."

"Well," he said, "I think we will cancel each other out."

The vote was nine to move, two against. Jim and me. "Well, Mr. Sheehan," said Mr. Irving, it looks like you lose. The mill will be moved." It was a Friday, and I had to go home. I seethed with anger all weekend. I could not believe that responsible people would make such a profound decision based on silly little ballots marked by a bunch of Irving employees who knew absolutely nothing about the consequences. I was determined not to let this happen because the physical and financial upheaval were well beyond verbal description. Monday morning I told my secretary to locate Jim and K.C. Irving and set up a conference call. When we all got together on the phone, I said, "Mr. Irving, that was a very bad decision that was made on Friday."

"Well," he said, "I thought we had all agreed to it."

"Not all," I said. "I didn't agree to it." I told him I had made a very careful study of the problem and that it would cost at least $500,000 to make the move and create a chain of never-ending problems. I also stated that I would have nothing further to do with a project run in this manner.

"Jim," he said, "did you hear that?"

"Yes," said Jim, "I heard it."

Then K.C. said, "If what you're telling us is true, then we won't move the mill. Do you agree, Jim?"

"Yes," said Jim, "I agree," and in his gentlemanly style Mr. Irving said, "Well, Mr. Sheehan, we certainly thank you for bringing this latest information to our attention. We're very grateful."

He had difficulty visualizing a new manufacturing facility. This is not unusual for a lay person, but he wouldn't believe that we engineers could visualize a final arrangement. So he would have a model made. He would have a lot of fun moving everything around. The only trouble was that the plant was under construction, and it was too late for tinkering. However, we made every effort to co-operate; after all it was his plant and his money.

I did try to explain that models have a limited use. The main problem is that, as a person, you can't scale yourself down to the size of the model. I would say, "Mr. Irving, that big pipe at the level of your eyes will be 90 feet up in the air. It will not look the same. The model also has transparent floors and walls so that everything is visible to the observer." This got us into trouble with Mr. Irving. We had a series of seven pulp washers. Each washer had two air duct pipes connecting to fourteen fans. These fans were all located on a mezzanine floor above the control room completely concealed behind a blank (not a transparent) wall. We arranged all the pipes in the visible operating area in a symmetrical pattern from the washers to the wall. Inside the wall they had to run at random to a particular fan.

Now Mr. Irving, using the model, could look through the transparent wall, and he wanted all those pipes run in a neat and orderly manner. I said we had two choices: make the invisible pipes neat and orderly or make a mess out of the visible pipes. He said, "the whole damned business looks like a devil's bunk chain."

"What," I said, "is a devil's bunk chain?"

"It looks like hell."

"Well, we can't settle this on the phone. I'll be at the mill tomorrow afternoon."

"Tomorrow is too late," he said. "Be here tonight."

The last plane to Saint John had left Boston, so the designer of the air duct system and I chartered a single-engine plane and got to the pulp mill about 6 p.m. We waited and waited. I made several phone calls trying to locate Mr. Irving, without success. I got the mill manager and he said, "I didn't know you fellows were in town. I'll be right down." Finally, about 10 p.m., he located Jim Irving, and I told him his father had insisted we be there that night and asked if he was coming to the mill.

"No," Jim said. "My father is in Montreal, and I'm going home to bed."

Next day K.C. came barging into the mill office and said, "There's the man I want to see. Your damned elevators are no good." I said, "I want to see you too. Where were you last night?"

"Never mind that," he said, "I'm talking about elevators." What had happened was that he had tried to use them, they wouldn't work, and he had had to walk. He was in a special complaining mood that day. We walked through the mill and he pointed out one devil's bunk chain after another. One in particular. I said, "Mr. Irving, at a meeting in Boston we called that condition to your attention and said it would cost $8,000 to fix it, and you said 'Don't change it.'"

He stopped short. "Don't tell me what I said," he said, and punched me on the shoulder.

"I'm damned sick and tired of your perpetual complaining; I don't care to listen to any more of it," I said, and walked away. He came after me and in a more subdued tone said there were other things he'd like to look at with me. I said, "I'm not interested." He said maybe my boss would be, and I said, "He may be, but I'm not." He realized what he had done and was trying to make it right, so when he came after me again I decided to allow him to maintain his pride, to call a truce and listen to some more complaints. That night we discussed those pipes behind the wall in a very rational manner. He accepted our logic and the discussion ended without a change.

That's the way the job went. I learned that if I was going to confront him with a difference of opinion I had to do my homework very thoroughly, be straightforward and honest, and never back down. In the whole master plan of his widespread and diversified operations, he could see the broad picture but he was also a stickler for details. He could be so strong on a small detail that he could lose the big picture. It was during these sessions that I had to keep the big picture in mind and not give in to him because substantial damage could be done to the master plan. Doing business with him was an exercise in mental gymnastics, but I am glad I had the opportunity. I am proud that I finished the job to the satisfaction of the Irvings and still remained in their good graces. Years later I still miss the everyday challenge of doing business with Mr. Irving.

There was a footnote to all this, which brought out the lighter side in both men — and more. It brought, in effect, a witty but serious engineer's response to Irving's dislike of devil's bunk chains, those things he saw as intrusions upon neatness and industrial order. Sheehan had learned from an associate that Irving thought he was a good process engineer but lacked a flair for the aesthetic. To refute this he once sent a facetious letter to Irving, signing himself "Edward Sheehan, United Artists Guild," and later sent a group of pictures of the house he had designed and built for himself.

One of their arguments during the expansion had concerned overhead lights and helps explain part of Irving's answer on December 7, 1971.

"Your home," he wrote, "is very nice indeed. It reminds me of a composition I wrote in the ninth grade. It was rather imaginative and verged a bit on the writer being made the hero of the happening. Mr. Robinson, my teacher, had known me for only two or three months. After reading my composition, he said, 'Kenneth, you had help.' Such a lovely group of pictures of your home makes me wonder if Mrs. Sheehan was not somewhere in the background.

"You have a lovely home, but I am sure you would not believe I was sincere in my remarks unless I did make some comment. Looking over one of the booklets showing the first five pictures of the bedroom causes me to believe you are a good sleeper and that you go to bed for that purpose. Otherwise you would have the lights at the head of the bed a little lower. Am I right?"

CHAPTER THIRTY

&

The Hands-Off
Monopolist

"Irving had a perfect right to buy the Gleaner. . . .
*Newspapers should be freely acquired and freely
sold, despite any risks involved."*
 – DALTON CAMP, TESTIFYING AT NEWSPAPER COMBINES TRIAL.

JOHN J. ROBINETTE, QC, WAS ONE OF CANADA'S MOST
talented lawyers, a distinguished servant of the bar, a man with
silver hair and a silver tongue. For almost sixty years he captivated judges and juries with his mastery of the language and the law,
especially press law. He was the son of a lawyer, born to his calling.
Known as a lawyer's lawyer and acknowledged as the dean and master of his profession, Robinette had excelled in law from the day in
1929 when he graduated as gold medallist from Osgoode Hall. Now,
in K.C. Irving, he was meeting a very different man.

In late December 1971, these two giants were about to meet for
the first time. Irving had flown to Toronto and the meeting was to be
in Robinette's office in the Toronto Dominion Centre in downtown
Toronto. Robinette was a senior partner in one of the most prestigious law firms in Canada, but he worked in a relatively modest
office, not unlike the type of office that Irving had occupied for so
many years in Saint John.

Irving was there to discuss the future of the English-language
newspapers in New Brunswick, all owned by Irving, and all under

attack in recent years by the Senate committee, individual senators, the Combines Department, and, potentially, the courts.

A devil's advocate painted the most difficult case that could be anticipated from the Combines Department. Irving listened intently, impatiently, with anger in his eyes. He didn't like what he was hearing, and he had difficulty in accepting, or perhaps understanding, criticism of the New Brunswick newspapers. It didn't matter that the comments were put forward as a worst-case scenario.

When it was over, he turned to Robinette for his reaction. Looking directly at Irving, he said: "You've got a good case in law." That was all Irving wanted to know. "Will you represent me?" he asked.

Robinette: "I'd be pleased to."

It was going to be a landmark case, and Robinette knew it would end in the Supreme Court of Canada in a final appeal. The two men rose and shook hands.

Irving had two of the best lawyers in Canada to represent him — Donald Gillis, QC, of Saint John, another country boy from a small town in New Brunswick who had one of the most respected legal minds in eastern Canada, and John Robinette. In general, Gillis would do the fighting in the courtroom. Robinette would be his background adviser, and the lawyer who would make the defence's final argument in the Supreme Court.

The battle lines were drawn.

That month the federal government set out to prove in the courts that Irving's media ownership violated the Combines Investigation Act. Four charges of forming mergers or monopolies were laid against K.C. Irving Ltd., New Brunswick Publishing, Moncton Publishing, and University Press. Irving, Wardell, and Costello were listed as parties to the alleged offences but were not charged.

The Crown went into battle with a mass of documents seized in 1969 and 1971 raids on Irving premises and those of his executives — 3,855 pages of them. Later, a judge of the New Brunswick Supreme Court ordered the search warrants quashed and the private documents returned. The Crown complied, but first made copies of the seized documents. In that form they became accepted as evidence.

The Combines Act itself was dubious fighting ground. No prosecution under it had yet succeeded in ending an alleged

K . C .

monopoly. Anti-combines chief D.H.W. Henry had told the Davey
Committee that the courts had held that "competition must be
virtually stifled before the merger can be struck down under the
law," that the Act was "too blunt an instrument to deal with
concentration in its incipiency and probably too inflexible to deal
effectively with the real issues involved in continuing concentration in mass media."

Because the Act was part of the criminal code — the courts
had thrown out a predecessor, based in civil law, as a violation of
provincial jurisdiction — the Crown had to prove its case "beyond
a reasonable doubt." Because of this, too, Irving had to pay the
entire cost of his defence, regardless of the outcome.

Years later, the government sought a tougher, more effective
Act, and met stiff resistance from business. But in 1971 it went
into the Irving case with the law it had. By July 1972 it had won
the first round: after hearing twenty-three witnesses for the
Crown, Provincial Court judge C.F. Tweeddale ruled there was
"amply sufficient" evidence to warrant a trial in higher court.

The government had for its counsel William Hoyt of Fredericton, a future judge, a newspaper buff, an unsuccessful Liberal candidate in the 1970 provincial election — and a man who had gone
skiing with his friend Jack Irving shortly before ordering the 1971
raids. Both Hoyt and Gillis knew that Senator McElman's request
for prosecution was the culmination of years of Irving conflict
with the Liberal government. Both saw the selection of a judge as
important. Gillis wanted the only Conservative-appointed judge
in the province's Supreme Court, Mr. Justice Albany Robichaud
(no relation to Louis), a former MP who had served on the bench
for fifteen years. Hoyt made a show of resistance, but said — before
he went to the bench himself — that he didn't want a Liberal-
appointed judge either; he believed Robichaud was a judge who
could be moved by argument and evidence, and would not necessarily come out of a case with the opinions he took in.

A dismayed Robichaud got the case. As he said in his judgment, he "almost pleaded" with Hoyt and Gillis "to relieve me of
this burden." He had, he said, three reasons. He was the judge
who had quashed three of seven search warrants for the raids. He
was convinced, from reading the evidence at the preliminary hearing, that "some political undertones would be aired during the

trial. This made my position, as presiding judge, difficult." Finally, he was annoyed that the trial involved "a racial question rather delicate for me to deal with" because he was a former member of the board of directors of the newspaper *L'Évangéline*, and the paper was an issue.

Having failed to sway the lawyers, he began the trial in Fredericton that October, then moved it to Moncton. He soon had new reasons for apprehension. He was flooded with 11,104 pages of documentary evidence, most submitted by the Crown, plus another 5,900 pages on newspaper circulation. To these would be added 1,673 typewritten pages of testimony.

The Crown, as Robichaud saw it, had to prove two things: that there was a monopoly, and that it operated or was likely to operate "to the detriment or against the interest of the public."

Hoyt launched his case by stating that Irving's purchase of the Fredericton *Gleaner* was "merely the icing on the cake" of a monopoly that already existed, which prevented public opinion informed by a "diversity of news available to it." Moreover, the situation was "even more apparent and more serious because of the ramifications of the economic interests of one of the accused." Irving's monopoly had been used, Hoyt charged, in an attempt to put the French-language *L'Évangéline*, the province's only other daily, out of business.

L'Évangéline was the beleaguered, Moncton-based voice of French Acadia, subsidized, and in chronic financial difficulties. As one former member of its staff later put it, "We didn't fight Irving editorially. We were too busy fighting ourselves, just to stay alive."

Gillis refused to make Irving a witness, so Hoyt did. They both questioned him in June for the preliminary hearing and Hoyt found him "very polite but obviously angry. The name McElman really rankled him."

That month the Irvings announced that the five papers had come under new ownership. John E. (Jack) Irving now owned outright Moncton Publishing and University Press. James K. (Jim) Irving and Arthur Irving each owned 40 per cent and K.C. Irving Ltd. 20 per cent of New Brunswick Publishing. Jack Irving disposed of his interest in K.C. Irving Ltd. and his two companies operated independently of New Brunswick Publishing. In other words, the Moncton and Fredericton papers were controlled by

Jack Irving personally, and would be completely separate from the ownership of the Saint John papers.

In a sworn statement for the court, Irving said that Michael Wardell called him in 1968 to say he had received an offer for the Fredericton *Gleaner* from the Southam chain, and he explained why he bought control — 55 per cent of University Press to add to the 25 per cent he already had. Later Wardell told him, in one of the letters seized in the raids, that Lord Thomson, head of the Thomson chain, "is very anxious to buy the *Gleaner*, will top any figure, and offers to make a secret deal for the duration of my life," and that Wardell had said, "nothing doing."

Irving was shown a record of a telephone conversation with Wardell in May 1969 in which Irving said, "Possibly we should not make this deal until after the hearing." It could have been a reference to the Senate hearing, he said; he did know that McElman was "up to something" at the time.

In addition to Thomson, Irving said, Sir Max Aitken, son of Lord Beaverbrook, had indicated a wish to become involved in New Brunswick papers. He did offer to sell "to some Maritimers" but the outsiders' bids by Thomson and Aitken "I did not take seriously. I would not consider it." Irving did not identify the potential purchasers, other than as "Nova Scotians" and a "Mr. Cameron," apparently the professor and writer Donald Cameron of the provocative *Mysterious East* who had told the Davey Committee the *Daily Gleaner* was "a dreadful newspaper" nicknamed the *Daily Wiener*. He said he called Irving with "a facetious but quite genuine" offer to buy it; businessmen associated with "a political party out of power" had promised to put up the money. Irving was very courteous, he said, and asked him how long he'd lived in New Brunswick. Cameron said three years. Irving said he'd lived there seventy-one and that he was not interested in selling anything: "I'm looking to buy more things in New Brunswick."

Irving was asked if he had ever been advised by Ralph Costello — whom he called his "only contact with the newspapers" — "that you should divest yourself of your newspaper holdings." Said Irving: "On one or two occasions he [Costello] said I was crazy to take the abuse I was taking. Irving had replied that "I wasn't going to deprive them of their favourite whipping boy, and

I would stick to it." He was asked if he would "be in favour of a political party having an interest in or control of a newspaper in New Brunswick." He said, "It would be a step backward. I wouldn't recommend it."

Gillis showed him a seized document recording a conversation with Wardell shortly before Irving appeared before the Senate committee. In it, said Gillis, was a reference "which I am going to suggest was a threat by a politician that he would nail the hide of a publisher to a barn door, or words to that effect." Irving said Wardell was the publisher, and Premier Robichaud was the politician. "I could tell you what he [Robichaud] said. He said he'd tear his [Wardell's] insides out and I don't know what he wouldn't do to him. . . . He'd ruin him financially too, if he could."

"How?"

"Cutting off advertising and so forth, anything bad that he could say in at least one or two meetings, and it took him quite a few minutes to express himself."

Using McElman's word, Gillis asked Irving if he considered Costello a pawn. "A stupid remark," he said, "a derogatory, cheap remark about a good man." Wardell was no pawn, either. He was "a very strong character. Very." He cited what had happened at the *Gleaner* since his takeover: Some $250,000 had been spent on plant and machinery and "if it hadn't been for this affair" there would be a new building under construction with "new equipment and new machinery and new plant." This prediction was fulfilled a few years later when the *Gleaner* moved to a new site, built a new building and equipped it with state-of-the-art equipment.

Hoyt's charge that Irving's papers had tried to put *L'Évangéline* out of business was called by Gillis "a very serious statement, which we challenge." Gillis said Hoyt had "overstated the case" and trusted he would apologize if the evidence did not support him.

The evidence produced some revealing remarks from Irving and others. Irving used it as a takeoff for comments on his feelings about Acadians ever since his youth. In Bouctouche, "with the exception of my father and perhaps George Weeks and one or two others, everything that I learned was taught me by the French people. . . . I remember a saying that if you treat a dog well in hard times, he remembers it in prosperous times, and in that way a dog is different than a lot of people who don't remember in the same way. So I guess there is a bit of dog in me, and I have never forgotten what the French people did and have done for me."

With that, he talked about *L'Évangéline*. In the early 1960s, he said, Premier Robichaud and others had come to him several times to ask him to help that paper get the right to carry *Perspectives*, the French version of the *Weekend* supplement used by his Moncton and Saint John papers. Because his newspapers had been original investors and had taken initial losses to establish *Weekend*, they had contracts for New Brunswick distribution. They could block any such move in their circulation area, and did.

Twice, Irving said, he went to his Moncton publisher, Jack Grainger, to urge that *Perspectives* be made available to *L'Évangéline*. Twice he was told no, that Grainger "couldn't very well agree to that based on the economics of his operation." Still not satisfied, Irving went to Costello, who agreed with Grainger that it would be against the financial interests of Irving's own papers.

Robichaud and others came back at him, Irving said, but he told them of his efforts and that they would have to deal with the management of the Moncton papers, "that I could not and would not interfere further." Gillis asked if it later came back to him "somewhat in the nature of a threat" that there would be other "ways and means to get what they wanted." That, said Irving, "came very definitely to me," but not through those who had made representations.

In related testimony, Costello said he had told Irving that to allow *L'Évangéline* to publish *Perspectives* would be like making space in an Irving service station for a rival's pump. He said the newspaper was subsidized by the Roman Catholic Church and the government of France, that Moncton was too small to support three dailies, and that it would have been better for *L'Évangéline* to be printed in the heart of a French-speaking region. Costello also disclosed that in 1970 growing French–English tension in Moncton led to withdrawal of the objections to *L'Évangéline* getting the weekly supplement: "We felt that whatever the economics of the situation we should stop any opposition." Even so, *L'Évangéline* had never used it, but a letter from its head said this was not due to any opposition from the Irving papers. In another move, Costello said, the Moncton papers had agreed to allow

L'Évangéline to become a member of the Canadian Press, the national newspaper co-operative, for a $500 fee rather than the $25,000 then required by CP by-laws.

Grainger denied that they had ever tried to put *L'Évangéline* out of business. "We've certainly been rivals," he said, "but we've been friendly rivals."

When they summed up their cases, Gillis and Hoyt presented opposing views. Gillis said Hoyt's charge was "unfair and over-zealous." Hoyt said the Saint John and Moncton papers had shown profits of $10.5 million from 1957 to 1970 while claiming they were threatened economically by *L'Évangéline*. But even during the trial itself it became apparent that his charge had boomeranged. As one of numerous prominent Acadians who had tried to keep the paper virile, Judge Robichaud indicated that Hoyt's accusation did not square with his own knowledge, and his judgment rejected it.

The trial went on for seventeen days over a period of two months, but without Irving on the scene, wrote Richard Wilbur in the *Financial Post*, it became "a fizzle." For Costello, it became an ordeal; he was on the stand for five days. He said he resented what the trial had done to the image of the papers and their staffs: "Do I object to this prosecution? Yes." Hoyt had called him as a witness because, again, Gillis wouldn't, and now he found himself trying to have Costello declared a hostile witness so he could be subjected to cross-examination. Judge Robichaud refused the request. He had been, he said, "very favourably impressed by Mr. Costello's demeanour on the stand."

As overall head, until the June change, of all three Irving publishing companies, Costello said he could not recall "any editorial critical of Mr. Irving" or any of his companies. Costello had played no part in day-to-day operations of the Moncton and Fredericton papers but did discuss such matters as subscription rates, policy towards TV stations, and competition from *L'Évangéline*, and occasionally commented on editorials. Costello said federal tax policies prompted group ownership of newspapers because they made it difficult for individuals to retain control. Group ownership provided financial stability that prevented constant sales to pay estate taxes. More and more dailies were being absorbed by chains, but group ownership was not necessarily bad; some of the best dailies in Canada were owned by chains.

He produced numerous copies of Saint John news stories on labour and other matters to refute charges that Irving interests were shown only in a favourable light. Irving's pulp mill, he said, was named as one of the biggest offenders in pollution, and in 1970–71 there was a series of articles and editorials about the sinking of two Irving-built fishing boats, and an inquiry was finally ordered.

Costello was asked about Irving's statement that his papers leaned over backwards to avoid favouring him. "I don't know," he replied, "that he's treated any blacker than others. But it would be the position of the papers to lean in that direction if there was any suggestion we were giving him favourable treatment." He denied that any story had been killed or played down to protect the owner. The one order he had received from Irving was to produce better papers, and he held that all of them were better than they had been twenty-five to thirty years earlier. None had ceased to publish in a period when newspapers in general were fighting for their lives.

If, said Costello, the papers had not criticized Irving editorially, they had not criticized other prominent New Brunswickers either. It was not their function to harass people, but they did have a responsibility to keep their readers informed of all developments. In recent years the Saint John papers had been strongly critical of provincial government policies, especially the abolition of county councils and the centralization of power. Irving papers, he said, sometimes differed editorially. Editorial writers in Moncton were not allowed to read Saint John editorials before deciding what to say.

Costello maintained that, because of TV and radio competition, "it is no longer possible for daily newspapers in New Brunswick to monopolize the news. . . . The situation is much more competitive than it was thirty to forty years ago." As a result, the Irving papers were far better than they had been.

Financially, Costello said, the Saint John and Moncton morning papers had sustained heavy losses but were kept going as a public service. The *Atlantic Advocate* had lost up to $40,000 annually for many years. An associated printing plant had suffered similar losses, though they had been cut by new equipment installed since the Irving takeover. The semi-monthly *Maritime Farmer* lost $10,000 to $15,000 a year. Under Hoyt's questioning,

Costello said the two Saint John papers together had a net profit of $261,000 in 1970.

All told, Costello said, the Irving dailies had a circulation of 108,000, and they competed with one another in various ways. The *Times* had become "much more aggressive" since Irving bought it, had doubled its circulation in some areas at the expense of the *Telegraph-Journal*, and now outstripped it on the north shore. The Moncton papers had campaigned editorially for Maritime Union; the Saint John papers had not. The Saint John papers had favoured a new, central airport for southern New Brunswick; the Moncton papers opposed it. The Moncton papers had supported most aspects of Equal Opportunity; the Saint John papers had opposed them.

There were clashes over the seized documents, with Gillis suggesting that political pressure from Senator McElman was behind the raids that produced them, with combines officials denying they themselves had anything to do with McElman. Though Judge Robichaud had ruled earlier that the 1971 seizures were made with defective warrants — the 1969 seizures were made without any warrants at all — it was revealed that Hoyt had ordered the documents copied before they were returned, an act Gillis called incredible. Hoyt said there was nothing in the court order that prevented the copying. Over Gillis's objections, the documents went into evidence, though the judge said he was "disappointed, to say the least, that in disregard of my order, copies were made." The Crown, having failed to find in them any real evidence of Irving interference in his papers, called a number of journalistic experts to bolster its argument that his ownership was a bad thing, in turn rebutted by Gillis with his own set of experts.

Dalton Camp, a columnist and former president of the Progressive Conservative party, said New Brunswick's dailies had "improved qualitatively more in the last ten years than any other comparable group of newspapers in the country." Irving, he held, had "a perfect right" to buy the *Gleaner*; the principle of free ownership had to be inviolate if there was to be a free press. Newspapers should be freely acquired and freely sold, despite any risks involved. He was against broadcast outlets in any community being owned by the same person who owned the newspapers, but he noted that it was the federal government that had made this possible for Irving in Saint John. It was only, Camp said, when the Irving papers began to express opposition to government policies that they were labelled a monopoly.

In all, thirty witnesses testified, and when the lawyers made their final arguments they swapped vivid charges. On the key point of whether Irving's ownership constituted detriment, Hoyt argued that it did. Earlier combines cases had established that "to lessen competition unduly" was by definition "to the detriment and against the interest of the public." The prohibitions in the Combines Act could not be evaded by good motives. The mere fact of common ownership of the five papers constituted a restriction of competition injurious to the people.

Newspapers, said Hoyt, were still the dominant source of news in New Brunswick. There was abundant evidence that direct Irving control was exercised over all five dailies. Staff members did not need a memo to know what to do. Control could be exercised through selection of staff, selection of news, in job assignments and promotions. "No one is suggesting," said Hoyt, "that K.C. Irving should be muzzled, but there should be other voices in New Brunswick. By the existence of this monopoly, other papers are prevented from coming in."

Gillis argued that the Crown had failed to establish that the Irving papers were operated to the public detriment. On the contrary, Irving control had provided a better and a beneficial press. The Crown had failed to establish beyond a reasonable doubt that a monopoly situation existed. "And if it exists," said Gillis, "it has not been proven that the papers are operated or are likely to be operated to the detriment of the public." Circulation and advertising rates were among the lowest in Canada. There was no lessening of competition, no papers were closed, no central control was exercised. Irving interests were treated no better than any others; there was evidence that they were treated worse. The papers themselves had improved. Though some witnesses felt it would be socially desirable to have other owners, this did not necessarily mean the situation was detrimental to the public.

Robichaud delivered his 129-page judgment in January 1974. It was heavily laced with quotations from prior judicial findings, both Canadian and American. He had warm words to say about Irving, called him "a great New Brunswicker and an impartial citizen," but found the accused companies had established a monopoly, combine, or merger whose object was "the prevention or lessening of free competition" in violation of the Combines Act. The result, he held, had operated or was likely to operate "to the detriment or against the interest of the public."

He pronounced, as well, on two other issues. He said his apprehension about political undertones in the trial had proved to be right: "The evidence and material before me did reveal that political pressure and interference lay behind the facade of these proceedings. It is a fact that political undertones, as well as overtones, were noticeable at the hearing." But, he added, "as these considerations cannot in any way . . . influence my decision, I prefer to ignore this side issue."

He rejected the Crown's argument that Irving papers had tried to put *L'Évangéline* out of business. As one "personally well acquainted with this paper's struggle for survival," he said he had heard this charge with "great amazement." Yet if it could be proved it would indicate detriment to the French-speaking people who made up 34 per cent of the provincial population. In fact, Robichaud found, the Irving papers in Moncton and Saint John had lost money during the first three or four years they carried *Weekend*, and their opposition at that time to *L'Évangéline* getting *Perspectives*, its French translation, was "a purely business and quite understandable decision." He was favourably impressed by Irving's own evidence on this issue and by his "noteworthy admission" about his feelings towards Acadians. Actions spoke louder than words, and Irving "lived up to his avowed affinity towards the French-speaking public of New Brunswick by doing his utmost to facilitate *L'Évangéline*'s bid to obtain *Perspectives*." Nor was management's opposition in any way based on any "racial or linguistic reasons." There had, in fact, been an *entente cordial* between the English and French Moncton dailies, one reflected in assistance and co-operation. "The circulation of *L'Évangéline*," he said, "is far from being what it should be. As deplorable as this may seem, it is not due to the absence of *Perspectives*." The Irving papers had withdrawn their opposition, and that absence was "certainly not attributable" to them.

As for Irving's own papers, Robichaud found "overwhelming" evidence that he had never influenced or tried to influence the publishers and editors: "I find, as a fact, that [they] have complete editorial autonomy and the owners have never cast over their columns any editorial shadow whatsoever." Nor had Irving interfered with advertising or "other important segments" of publishing.

The judge found no detriment to the public in the papers' circulation and advertising rates, and noted the improved quality and quantity of news after the Irving takeovers. He acknowledged that newspapers encountered competition from TV and radio, but said they remained "a most important cog in the machinery of properly informing the public. . . . The press still mans the front line in the bastion of our liberties and civil rights."

And, he held, even the papers' editorial autonomy and the lack of Irving interference were not sufficient "to eliminate what is meant by 'control' under the act. . . . Even if, as it appears, the direction of the acquiring company saw fit not to exercise this right, this prerogative of control, yet the potential was always there to be exercised at any time, and the likelihood that such control could be exercised was always present. It was never extinguished." Moreover Costello, as Irving's "right-hand man," had exercised control over the papers.

The evidence "clearly discloses," Robichaud said, that complete and total ownership was established. There had been a "virtual monopoly" even before the *Gleaner* was bought. Once it was, the door became completely closed to any competition in the field of English-language newspapers in New Brunswick. Free competition therein was absolutely stifled. The structure became monolithic.

The defence had argued that Irving's ownership "rather than being a detriment had actually resulted in public benefit" through new buildings and equipment, the continuation of losing properties, and in other ways. Robichaud said prior court decisions blocked him from considering economic advantages. He rejected other defence arguments in concluding that the Combines Act did apply to newspapers, that the relevant market was not the "distinct and individual" ones for each paper as the defence had said but the province, that the Crown had established beyond a reasonable doubt that a monopoly existed. Since it was the "policy of the law to encourage trade and commerce," an "agreement or arrangement designed to prevent or lessen competition, to restrain trade, or even tending to take it out of the realm of competition, must be considered to be against public policy and consequently illegal, even although it may not appear to have actually produced any result detrimental to public interest."

The prime question of fact he had to decide was whether the monopoly amounted to undue prevention or lessening of competition in violation of the Act. He found that it did and that, in law, it was detrimental.

On July 10 Robichaud fined the four companies a total of $150,000 and, to strike "as I must, at the root of the evil," he ordered Irving to sell the two Moncton papers within a year. The Crown had proposed a fine of $500,000, but the judge said such a sum would "savor of persecution." He cited benefits arising from Irving's ownership and again paid tribute to him:

"As a New Brunswicker born, bred, and educated in our small province, I must profess again my great esteem and admiration for Mr. K.C. Irving, who has done so much to develop and enhance our economy. How many times have I heard over the years the remark that New Brunswick would be a much better-off province from an economic standpoint had more of our former successful businessmen and financiers followed Mr. Irving's example and not only continued to remain and work here, at home, as long as possible, but to reinvest their profits in New Brunswick enterprises."

Still, Robichaud said, it "becomes my duty to remain within the boundaries set by comparable Canadian cases." Hoyt had argued that the transfer of the five papers to Irving's sons did not dissolve the monopoly. Robinette had on the other hand argued that because of the change there should be no divestiture order, that it should be sufficient to prohibit K.C. Irving Ltd., formerly the parent company concerned, from any repetition of the offence. Gillis had argued that the transfer of the papers to the Irving sons had occurred before the trial, and said the Crown's persistence in prosecution was but another indication of the involvement of political "undertones and overtones."

The judge said court proceedings had started before the change. He agreed with Robinette that the divestiture order suggested by the Crown was "a most extraordinary, drastic, offensive, and vindictive document." It would be "absolutely unjustifiable" for him to accept it. What the Crown had proposed was that the order should apply to the Saint John papers. But there had been no monopoly involved when they were bought, Robichaud said. A "virtual monopoly" was established only when Irving bought the Moncton papers.

Robichaud said he personally had seen "the noteworthy improvements" Irving had made in the premises of his Saint John papers. The papers themselves had been praised during the trial. Their readers were satisfied. "Why, in the name of reason," the judge said, "should I order their sale?" But he had a duty to perform and he had found that "the planting bed of the Irving monopolistic tree" lay in his purchase of the Moncton papers four years after he bought those in Saint John. "This is when and where the offence of forming a monopoly . . . actually took root." He agreed that transfer of ownership to the Irving sons did not amount to a dissolution.

Simultaneously, he paid tribute to the Moncton publisher, Jack Grainger, and to Jack Irving, the new owner, who "with his brothers and his famous father . . . shares in my admiration as New Brunswick's best public-spirited and most successful home-grown businessmen."

He had, Robichaud said, "endeavoured to discharge my duties throughout fairly and conscientiously, in accordance with the well-known old saying 'Do your duty come what may.'" He also was convinced that in the trial he had faced "the longest, hardest, and most exhausting" case of his career.

It took a heavy toll. Mr. Justice Robichaud died that fall, and a curious thing happened when he did. His family asked Irving to be an honorary pallbearer at the funeral, and Irving accepted.

❧

That autumn Irving's lawyers took the newspaper case to the New Brunswick Appeal Court to argue that Robichaud had erred in his interpretation of the Combines Act and was against the weight of the evidence. By September Robinette maintained before three judges that any monopoly was dissolved when the Irving sons took over the papers, that Robichaud had no jurisdiction to order Jack Irving to sell the Moncton dailies when he had not been charged, had played no part in the trial, and had had no hearing.

But his main point was that the Crown had failed to show that a monopoly, such as K.C. Irving was alleged to have created, was against the public interest and therefore detrimental.

The combines law, said Robinette, required proof of public detriment, and the judge "did not find actual or likely detriment." He had in fact based his decision solely and wrongly on evidence that monopoly control had been achieved. Even then, he argued, a newspaper monopoly was impossible because of radio and TV competition.

Hoyt again argued that newspaper competition was vital to free public opinion. He held that transfer of the papers to the Irving sons did not constitute the dissolution of a monopoly as required by law. The three men had close common interests. Jack Irving could have testified at the trial if he had wished. A conviction would be meaningless unless the monopoly was ended. Elimination of competition was detrimental itself, Hoyt said, and Judge Robichaud had found this to be so in a decision "sound in facts and sound in law."

The result was a unanimous decision read by Mr. Justice R.V. Limerick in June 1975. It ignored the issue of Irving's transfer of the papers to his sons. In rejecting the Robichaud findings, Limerick said that judge had erred in ruling that "there was a presumption arising out of the requisition of the controlling interest in the five English-language dailies by one owner that detriment in the law followed automatically and that there was or would be a lessening of competition which would be detrimental to the public.

"No such presumption is created by the Combines Act," Limerick said, "or if such presumption is created it is rebuttable." The Crown had to establish that under Irving's control the newspapers operated or were likely to operate to the detriment of the public, and this was a question of fact. "There is," Limerick said, "no evidence of detriment to the public relating to this indictment let alone a reasonable doubt thereof, nor any evidence of any lessening of competition or likelihood thereof." On the contrary, the evidence "disclosed a more competitive effort on the part of the acquired newspapers in the areas of competition after the acquisition and that each paper operated independently of each other."

The journalistic experts called by the Crown had testified "that it was not only possible for commonly owned newspapers or chain-owned newspapers to operate independently of the owner but that such actually occurred" in the Southam and Thomson chains. The Crown experts also admitted they had made no study of newspaper conditions in New Brunswick and knew nothing of the operation of the Irving newspapers. Robichaud had found that those papers operated autonomously. Nor had the possibility of a sixth daily being established been altered by Irving's ownership.

Limerick found, too, that the long list of prior cases relied on by Robichaud were not applicable to support Crown arguments. In leading up to his summary, he agreed that a monopoly existed. He agreed that a newspaper was an article or commodity of trade but said the Combines Act "was not intended to control or restrict the expression of ideas, editorial comment, or editing of news." None of the Crown experts had been able to point out a single example of editorial control by Irving. On the contrary, the publishers and editors were told only to run good newspapers.

Once Irving took over, Moncton Publishing became more competitive. All five papers continued as separate entities without interference. They had had money to replace outmoded plant and equipment. They were among the last in Canada to raise their price to ten cents. Their advertising rates were not above average. Their editorials at times expressed opposing ideas or came into direct conflict. They carried news articles unfavourable to Irving interests and editorials critical of Irving pollution. During the 1963–64 strike at Irving's oil refinery, the Saint John papers carried fifty-three items originating from the union and only two from Irving management. According to Costello, the papers leaned over backwards against Irving interests.

Judge Robichaud had said Costello's advice to sell the *Gleaner* went "to the real root of the question" and expressed the view of "the most important newspaperman in New Brunswick." But Limerick said it "was written from the viewpoint of a devil's advocate, not as expressing his opinion but to raise all possible arguments" that Irving might face.

Limerick said Robichaud "was largely influenced by the wording of a charge, 'have operated . . . or are likely to operate' to the detriment of the public." He had disregarded facts and gotten into "the realm of theory" about the likelihood of Irving control once the potential was there, had erred in his interpretation of "likelihood" because the word "likely" in the Act meant "will probably" not "may possibly." In Limerick's view, "we can only judge the likelihood of future conduct on the basis of past performance," and Irving's past performance was one of granting the papers editorial autonomy.

The Crown, said Limerick, "relied on the sole ground that there was a lessening of competition" under Irving ownership and the trial judge had agreed that this was so. But there had been no evidence to support it.

By October 1976, the Crown was appealing the Limerick decision to the highest court in the land. The Supreme Court accepted the case and all nine judges listened to two days of legal argument, then came to a unanimous decision of their own. On November 16, seven years after the first seizure of documents, Chief Justice Bora Laskin rejected the appeal.

With a touch of scepticism, Laskin skirted the question of the relevance of editorial content. Limerick, he noted, had made a point of "separating the newspaper as a physical object . . . from the expression of ideas therein, its editorial content and editing of news; and he held that although as a physical object a newspaper was caught by the combines legislation as being an article of trade or commerce, the legislation would not cover the contents as such. This is not a question that I need to decide here and I leave it open, especially in view of the fact, established by the evidence, that editorial content of the five newspapers was left in the hands of their respective publishers without any attempt at central or other combined direction. At first blush, it seems incongruous that a prohibited merger or monopoly should not include newspapers in respect of their editorial direction but, as I have said, I leave the point open."

Laskin said there was no proof of detriment in fact through Irving control. There remained the question of whether competition was, or was likely to be, lessened, and whether his ownership had operated or was likely to operate to public detriment. The Crown's argument was based on "a mistaken application of the law governing unlawful conspiracies or agreement unduly to prevent or lessen competition." There was no such charge in this case. He reviewed judicial decisions on which the argument was based and said it was not open to the court to "raise a presumption such as is contended for by the Crown" in the absence of legislative direction. An "inference cannot be drawn here in the face of the evidence and the findings [by lower courts] that the pre-existing competition where it existed remained and was to some degree intensified by the takeovers of the newspapers."

The same conclusion applied to relevant previous legislation and to "monopoly" under the current Act. They brought up the question of operation or likely operation to public detriment. Proof, said Laskin, must be adduced. It could not be presumed merely by showing complete control of a business let alone a substantial control. The evidence must go beyond this, and it was not produced.

With that decision, the events touched off by Senator McElman came to an end. At the highest level possible, the Irving companies were found not guilty of the offences they were alleged to have committed. The case had, Donald Gillis noted, seen twelve of thirteen judges find in Irving's favour.

ஜ

The newspaper executives who appeared as prosecution witnesses in the Irving combines trial in the early 1970s had at least two things in common. All expressed concern about the potential for conflict of interest when the newspaper owner was also the province's leading industrialist, and all stressed they had made no study of the New Brunswick newspapers. They were speaking on a question of principle. This picture of hypothetical questions and potential dangers changed in 1980 when the Kent Royal Commission on Newspapers visited Saint John and several former employees in Fredericton and Saint John did say that their newspapers were protective of the Irvings, and never assigned in-depth investigations.

Frank Withers, who had worked for the *Telegraph-Journal* in Saint John and the *Daily Gleaner* in Fredericton, saw newspapers in the hands of the Irvings, Southams, or Thomsons as "a blight on our country." While the *Telegraph-Journal* might appear to be a "lively, hard-working, fair-dealing, and objective news operation," that was not the true story. Those genuine attributes, he said, did exist, but they only obscured the truth because the Irving newspapers did not attack the Irving interests editorially. Other former employees Jon Everett and Julian Walker came forward with similar and uniformly harsh charges. All three complained that the newspapers did not go after the Irvings hard enough.

However, if the Irvings bought newspapers to protect their interests, they made a pretty poor job of it, in the opinion of Ed Larracey who held every position from cub reporter to publisher of the *Moncton Times and Transcript*. Larracey started his career with the Moncton newspapers in 1938 and retired as publisher in 1984. "They just didn't know much about the newspaper business," or if they did, Larracey saw little evidence of it in his forty-six years at the Moncton newspapers, thirty-six of those years under Irving ownership.

"In my view," said Larracey, "they didn't want to use the newspapers for any personal advantage or protection, and even if they had, they wouldn't have known how." Larracey could recall no Irving influence on the Moncton newspapers during the years he served as a reporter, managing editor, general manager, and publisher. "It just wasn't there. It was as plain as that."

When Jack Irving took over ownership of the Moncton newspapers in 1972 his instructions to Larracey were brief and to the point: "Put out the best newspapers you can," he said. "You know how to do it, I don't." Larracey recalled frequent conversations with Jack Irving "but if I mentioned an editorial subject he just cut me off. 'Don't tell me about them,' he'd say. 'I'll read them in the newspaper.' Not once did he ever criticize or even comment on an editorial."

If the Irvings weren't using the newspapers to either promote or protect themselves then what was their angle? "There wasn't any angle," according to Ed Larracey. "It was just another business."

He recalled one occasion shortly after he'd taken over direction of the publishing company and a related printing company. "Some of the Irving companies in Saint John owed us money and we couldn't seem to get payment. Harold Crawford, our comptroller, was after me to do something so I called Jack Irving. I told Jack I wanted to check with him to see if other Irving companies should get any special consideration from us. He didn't hesitate for a second. 'No,' he replied. 'Why do you ask?'"

"Well, we're having trouble collecting some of our accounts," Larracey told him.

"Why don't you get a lawyer?"

"A lawyer?"

"Yes," said Jack Irving. "Why don't you get a lawyer to write to them? Isn't that what you usually do with bad accounts?"

"Yes," said Larracey, "but first I wanted to check to see if they should get any special consideration."

"None."

Larracey said he had the newspaper's lawyer write to the Irving companies that were in arrears and the payments started immediately. "That was all there was to it. We never had any trouble after that."

On the specific question of Irving's involvement, Larracey said he'd like to say that K.C. Irving had never given any instructions about how news should be handled in the Moncton newspapers. However, he acknowledged, that was not exactly true. Not only had Irving told a reporter what he thought should appear in a news report, he had actually prepared notes, which he read to the reporter.

On that occasion the reporter told Larracey he had received what he took to be instructions from Irving on coverage of a fire on Irving property in Bouctouche. The reporter was Peter Crosby, an experienced newspaperman who worked for a number of years for the *Times and Transcript*.

When Crosby arrived at the scene of the fire in Bouctouche, Irving was already there. The fire was under control and when Crosby approached Irving with some questions, he said Irving took an envelope from his pocket and read him a list of names. "Those are the men who fought the fire and got it under control," he said, "and I think you should mention them in the newspaper. They should be recognized. They're good men." Crosby took the names, dutifully reported the incident to Larracey — and, yes, the names were included in his story. "After all," said Larracey, "names make news."

Was that all?

"That," said Larracey, "to the best of my knowledge, is the closest K.C. Irving ever came to saying what should appear in our newspaper."

There was, however, one more thing that Crosby reported to Larracey about his unusual encounter with the owner of the Moncton newspapers. "When I was about to leave Bouctouche to go back to Moncton," said Crosby, "Mr. Irving spoke to me again. He said: 'Thank you for coming to the fire.'"

Brigadier Michael Wardell, who had used Fredericton's *Daily Gleaner* to attack virtually everything Premier Robichaud stood for in the 1960s, was another publisher who was adamant about Irving's hands-off policy at the newspaper. When he appeared in 1969 before the Davey Senate Committee, aggressive and defiant, he said: "Whatever you do to criticize the *Daily Gleaner*, do not blame Mr. Irving or Mr. Costello or anybody like that because he (Irving) has not taken it over." Irving, in fact, by this time did have control of the *Daily Gleaner*, but Wardell's point was that he as publisher, and he alone, was responsible for the newspaper and its practices. He said: "What was done was done by me."

Ten years later, with Jack Irving as the sole owner of the *Daily Gleaner*, and the *Moncton Times and Transcript*, the Kent Royal Commission was given a more restrained view of the role of newspapers and the involvement of the new owner. On one basic point, however, there was no change. Jack Irving, like his father before him, said he kept out of the news and editorial operations.

The *Daily Gleaner*, by this time under direction of publisher Tom Crowther, a former advertising executive and general manager of the Saint John newspapers, continued to be provocative and controversial, but in a province starved for industry, Crowther told the Kent Commission, the Fredericton newspaper had more important things to do than harass industry — whether that industry happened to be owned by the Irvings or others.

CHAPTER THIRTY-ONE

≈

The New Resident
of Bermuda

*"I am no longer residing in New Brunswick. My sons
are carrying on the various businesses.... I do not
choose to discuss the matter further."*
    – *K.C. IRVING, ON TAKING UP RESIDENCE IN BERMUDA.*

WHEN IRVING MADE HIS DECISION TO LEAVE CANADA
in late 1971, it was at a busy, hectic, expanding time in
his life. No final horizon was in sight. Sheehan's pulp
mill job was unfinished. Other challenges, many challenges, were
untested, unfulfilled. But the industry he had built in a lifetime
remained. It was all there, the whole incredible pyramid. The
foundations of the industrial empire he had put together piece by
piece, year after year, building steadily, patiently, brilliantly, were
secure. It was his life's work, a monument to half a century of personal commitment — and, suddenly, he walked away from it all.

Eight years before, Ralph Allen had asked him if he ever
thought of retiring, and he had replied that "everyone figures he
must get out gradually." He didn't get out gradually. He got out
abruptly, and it was news from coast to coast.

He left just before the year died, less than three months before
his seventy-third birthday, and the last person he talked to in
Canada was that mentor of his youth, George Weeks, the man —
now in his nineties — who had taught him how to box, had helped

him buy and sell his first car. He looked Weeks up in Toronto and then he flew south with his ailing wife, first to the Bahamas, then to Bermuda to settle into an entirely new life.

He left as he had lived, with an aura of mystery, and his going startled more than a country. It startled the sons he had groomed to take his place. It startled his wife, who left knitting unfinished when they left. It startled a granddaughter who remembers sitting in her home with the phone ringing and people asking if it was true that he had gone. Her father was away, she told Saint John's mayor one midnight, and she didn't know whether it was true or not.

It took nearly three weeks before it was confirmed, before the Saint John papers tracked him down. Then all they got was this brief statement: "I am no longer residing in New Brunswick. My sons are carrying on the various businesses. As far as anything else goes, I do not choose to discuss the matter further." He did add that "I left last year," and the *Evening Times-Globe* said this was "an apparent reference to the new estate powers of the province, which are to be retroactive to Jan. 1 of this year."

The timing, the abruptness, did indicate that his departure had a great deal to do with coinciding taxation moves: with Ottawa's removal of its estate taxes or succession duties but the imposition of a capital gains tax, and with New Brunswick's decision to tax estates. He left, in good part, because he wanted what he had built to survive. When one citizen wrote that "He won't have to pay our taxes for the profit made and being made on you and you and you," the *Telegraph-Journal* added a note to the letter, saying that the new provincial tax "could break up family-owned businesses. Assets of the companies would have to be sold in order to pay the 50 per cent succession duties. Mr. Irving has not escaped to a hideaway taking tax-free millions with him. Instead, he has apparently left the province to assure that industries will continue to exist and to operate, providing jobs for thousands of New Brunswickers."

Irving himself did not comment further. Years later he said only: "There were a lot of things at that time," and there were. The provincial government proposed to tax the Canaport facilities, which a previous government had promised not to tax. Ottawa was about to level charges against his media ownership. Already it had angered him with combines raids on his offices and his home. Through much of the sixties, he had been in the thick of one storm after another. His wife had a heart condition and could benefit from a more temperate climate. His sons were in or near their forties, and at least one friend had told him that if he was ever going to make way for them, the time was now.

So he left, and a volley of comments erupted. Premier Hatfield said his decision is "one that is regretted." Opposition leader Robert Higgins called it "a serious blow." The president of the Saint John Board of Trade said it was "a tragic loss." Letters to editors both praised and criticized him. Said a critic: "His concern is for himself and his heirs." The *Telegraph-Journal* asked editorially: "Is New Brunswick richer or poorer, not in a financial sense but in every other way, because he has taken his leave? . . . Does the sun shine? Is there water in the ocean? Is it dark at night?"

After Irving left Canada journalists engaged in a game they had played for years: estimating what he had built was worth. Three said $500 million. A fourth said $600 million, and that he was probably the richest Canadian. To Irving, what mattered was that his industry would continue to exist — at a bitter price. He saw himself as what someone called an economic and tax exile. A decade later he would call his departure "just a happening," but if he didn't say more publicly, his face did. When he was asked how he enjoyed Bermuda, he said nothing, but his reaction left no doubt that he would far rather be back where he had been so long.

A year after he left, he was asked if he would ever return. He said he had no such plans. Hatfield, accused of driving him away, said Irving was not among those who had made representations against the provincial estate tax before its introduction. When the government suspended it in 1974, but kept the legislation intact, Irving was asked again if he would return to Canada. He said again he had no such plans.

He accepted what had happened to him. He kept in close touch with his sons, and he saw the reward of his faith in their ability and his schooling of their talents. By the time he left, they had been in training for a quarter-century to take over, and they did, without a hitch. There was no perceptible change.

❧

Despite his frequent visits, Irving's departure left a void, a vacuum in New Brunswick life. Given the social and economic phenomenon he had been, it was inevitable, and into the vacuum flowed reminiscences, stories, amazement, and conjecture. Many of the stories and much of the speculation came from an unusual breed of citizens who were peculiar almost exclusively to New Brunswick. They were known as "Irving watchers" and they had existed for years. The secrecy, the scope, and the successes of the family attracted them. They picked up rumours, gossip, news, swapped stories and filed them in the ledgers of their minds. Given the continuing impact of what Irving had created, it was inevitable that they would keep on doing it — none more so than Saint John lawyer Peter Glennie.

Glennie tracked down statements, gleanings, and legal documents, and he kept in his office a large chart of what the Irvings own. "It started as a challenge," he once said. "Everybody said it couldn't be done." He started and he kept on going, for years, until he had a chart 1.2 metres long and 1 metre tall, intimidating in detail, neat in design: up top the paramount companies, below all the rest slotted into component associations much as an army has corps and corps have divisions and divisions have brigades and brigades have battalions.

Where did he get his information? As an example, he produced a legal document. It was publicly available, because in 1979 five Irving companies formed a partnership "to carry on the trade or business of constructing, owning and operating a vessel or vessels." It was called Irvingdale Associates. So it goes, said Peter Glennie. It was not easy, he said, to keep track: "They keep changing things."

He and Arthur Doyle were friends, and of all the Irving watchers they were perhaps the most devoted. Doyle was born in Saint John but lived for years in Fredericton, where he presided over the activities of the U.N.B. Alumni Association, but as a sideline, he accumulated stories on the Irvings. Given the opportunity in 1990, he jumped at the chance to become publisher of the two Saint John newspapers. He left after two years to establish his own media and public relations company in which he would continue to work for the Irvings.

Doyle grew up near the Irving home. He sold papers at the Golden Ball building. On Halloweens he received treats from the kindly Mrs. Irving. His father, a Saint John businessman, admired Irving tremendously: "He's my kind of man." He remembers driving by the Golden Ball at odd and early hours, his father seeing a light and saying, "See, he's in there, working."

The son, too, admired Irving, though this was by no means true of all Irving watchers. So, for that matter, does Peter Glennie. He said he was numbered among the sceptics until that day in 1964 when Irving spoke out against the strike at his oil refinery. It was the first time Glennie had ever heard him lay it on the line about the difficulties of doing business in New Brunswick. It convinced him.

Among local lawyers, said Glennie, the Irvings "are a favourite topic of conversation." Among newsmen, they are that and more. They watch the Irvings as part of their work, and they are habitually frustrated.

Mark Pedersen worked in New Brunswick for years as a well-regarded, dedicated reporter. He came to see himself as a CBC watchdog on Irving activities. Other CBC reporters felt the same way, that they had a responsibility to balance the scales because the Irvings owned the provincial English-language press. But Pedersen and others at CBC had little success in their efforts to pry information out of the Irvings. Almost invariably they got no comment.

Yet even CBC journalists could become bewitched by what they watched. Newfoundlander Dan Goodyear was one. As a producer of news and current affairs programs, he came to Saint John after Irving left but often returned. He came, he said, with an image of Irving as a J.R. Ewing, the Dallas TV star who stooped to anything to get his way — the "ruthless businessman who rapes the environment and doesn't care for anybody." Goodyear revised his views, he said, and developed much more respect for Irving: "You become enamoured of the man. He's just so unassuming." Goodyear once showed film footage of Irving at the opening of a bank branch, shy, nervous, uncomfortable, courteous in an interview. "Look at him," Goodyear said. "I'm sort of fascinated by captains of industry, and he could be one of the last. You can say a lot about him but he's no J.R. Ewing."

Academics viewed the Irvings through frustrations of their own, given the paucity of public information. Professor Patrick Fitzpatrick of U.N.B. set out to produce a scholarly study of their role in the politics of New Brunswick. He abandoned it before the wall of silence: "All I could find was bits and pieces. So much was anecdotal." Yet, like Goodyear, he said he changed his mind about them. He recalled the days when, to his leftist mind, "if Irving didn't have horns he at least had their buds." Later he deplored government intrusion in the economy; its tendency "to give people a hard time if they are successful." He didn't even fault the Irvings for their secrecy.

His change matched a broader one. On the campus that had seethed with rebellion in the late sixties, his colleague, economist William Smith, would tell of watching a 1980s CBC-TV program based on Peter Newman's *The Canadian Establishment* and asking his students if its portrayal of an economic élite turned them off. One girl revealed the new attitude: "What I want to know," she said, "is how you get in on the action."

If that meant more sympathy for people like the Irvings, academics yearned for something else. They itched to get their hands on papers, files, documents, the working materials for essays, theses, dissertations — and they got none. They had little or nothing on the Irvings to research, little or nothing to teach. Professor Nick DeVos of Mount Allison said its commerce department had no lectures on what they do, what they mean, because so little is made public. It was typical, he said, of Maritime business.

Poets, those iambic gauges of the human equation, didn't seem to care one way or the other. Fredericton's Fred Cogswell, a teacher of literature who published an astonishing amount of verse by scores of them, said he never saw a submission about Irving. Alden Nowlan, the noted poet-journalist, said shortly before his death that though he worked for an Irving newspaper in Saint John for years he saw the man just twice. He never wrote a poem about him because, he said, he didn't write about people he couldn't see.

Invisible he might be to Nowlan, but New Brunswickers would for years tell tales of Irving, would speculate about what he had that drew people to him and kept many of them there for years. These are three such people, and what *they* said:

❧

On the eighty-ninth anniversary of the birth of K.B. Reed, the headquarters staff sang him a wish of happiness in the Golden Ball building in Saint John. When Irving dropped by to shake hands, Reed called him Mr. Irving and Irving called him Reed, which was the way things had always been between them, even though Reed was seven years older and they had shared so many experiences since they came together in 1928. But the most significant thing about that birthday celebration was that for Reed to come down the hall for coffee and cake was quite out of character. He was listed still as president of the SMT bus line, the latest of the many activities he had performed in Irving's name. He came in daily, by taxi, and when, one notably unruly winter day, he was a few minutes late for an early-morning appointment he apologized not once but several times.

Which is the way he had always been. A devoted, able right-hand man, so inevitably and perpetually part of the scene that when he won a sleeping bag at an annual banquet Arthur Irving said, "Now, Mr. Reed, you won't have to go home at all." Such are the varied reactions of human beings that one former underling called Reed a sweetheart and another said he could be very tough indeed. But to one man who had done a great deal of business with Irving Oil, who knew Reed in his prime, he was almost as smart as Irving himself. Why would a man who once dreamed of building up an oil and gas business of his own abandon these aspirations and subordinate himself to another for so many years? What did Irving have that made him do it for so long and so loyally?

When asked this, Reed thought for a bit, temporarily taken aback, and looked out from those eyes that no longer saw as well as he wished they did. Then he said what he thought. "Mr. Irving," he said, in measured words, "Mr. Irving is, you know, a wizard." Then he said it again with emphasis: "A wizard. If he has any weaknesses I don't know what they are."

&

The first time "Scribbie," Miss Kathleen Scribner, sought out Irving's headquarters many years ago, she went, of all places, to the Imperial Oil office in town. Irving had advertised for an experienced lady to take charge of stationery, but she had never heard of him. When she got to the right place he hired her and she, like her colleague Victoria Hallifax, became one of those institutions of corporate life. Both were known for their certainty, Miss Hallifax for the time she placed some figures before Irving, who asked if she was sure they were right. She said she was. He asked why. "Because," she said, "I did them."

Miss Scribner sprang from the same geological layer. She was rocklike, incisive, tart, trenchant. She presided over the purchase and control of stationery with the aplomb of entrenched authority. At times, to make her point infinitely clear, she swore. In trying to make out what made K.C. Irving tick, she recalled something that happened in the later years of her long employment. The man in overall charge of headquarters staff asked her to take on extra duties. She protested that she was already handling all she could. He said they would only be temporary, and loaded them on anyway. They were, she said, injurious to her health.

She was asked, one day after retirement, if Irving would have known what was going on. Yes, she said. Then why didn't she protest to him? Because, she said, she wouldn't bother a man with so many problems. Besides, when told that another long-time employee had called Irving a saint, she said she agreed, and when she was asked what she would do if she heard Irving criticized she said she would tell the critic to go to hell.

☙

Like Reed, Louis McC. Ritchie was associated with Irving for many years as legal counsel and later as an executive. He was a guarded man, and he watched what he said in an interview. But the next day he called back and said there was one important thing about Irving that he hadn't said.

"He's honest."

☙

Tales of Irving's personality were endless. These are some of them:

In the Depression years, Irving and K.B. Reed were driving along a dirt road in Cape Breton when they saw a car with a flat tire, a lone woman beside it. It was raining but Irving stopped, got out and changed the tire for her. She wanted to pay him. He declined. She insisted. No, he said firmly, he couldn't accept money for a thing like that, but his name was K.C. Irving and he was in the gasoline business, and if she wanted to do something for him she could buy what he sold. She said she would, for the rest of her life.

He was almost constitutionally incapable of passing a car in trouble. He stopped many times to change tires or get an engine working, and he rarely said who he was. Only the woman's insistence had made him introduce himself that day in Cape Breton.

Alden Balcom, for years Irving Oil's regional chief in the Annapolis Valley of Nova Scotia, said he once was rushing Irving to an airport when they saw a stalled car. To his surprise, Irving told him to stop. "But you're in a hurry," said Balcom. "Stop." They did, and drove the car's owner to the nearest service station for help.

Irving's pilot, with his permission, once gave a lift to a young, happy-go-lucky girl in military uniform. When she was introduced to him on the plane, she said, "So you're the big cheese." He laughed. "I've been called a lot of things," he said, "but never that."

Irving knew his reputation, both good and bad, and let it be. He was certainly never a distinguished student in school or college. He employed, said his son Jim, many workers with limited education but solid practical skills, and he admired them. One ran a sawmill ably, though he could neither read nor write. Irving admired common sense, and he felt no amount of college training could impart it. "You may be wiser from reading a book," he said, "but you won't necessarily be any more able to solve a practical situation that faces you." In his many tussles with university-trained engineers, he found some of them "bloody fools."

"You don't want to let a college education prevent you from getting the elementary training that will let you know what you're doing," he once said. "Some highly educated people don't have horse sense. A lot of educated people are very clever. They can do a job well, some jobs extremely well, but at the practical end some don't know which end of a wheelbarrow to get hold of. A jackass with a degree is a dangerous man. A jackass without a degree isn't as dangerous. A man who's interested in what he's doing and has average good sense is a good man."

The combativeness of his youth never left him. Sometimes, said a lawyer who knew him well, he would count to ten to avoid slugging someone when he got worked up. He got greatly worked up that December night in 1958 when the "Fighting Fisherman," Yvon Durelle, fought the durable and deadly Archie Moore for the world's light-heavyweight boxing championship at Montreal's Forum. Durelle bought Irving Oil products for his fishing boat.

Durelle was from New Brunswick, from the north shore. Irving knew and liked him, and he flew to Montreal to see what turned out to be an epic fight.

He exulted when Durelle knocked the American down three times in the first round. He watched spellbound as Moore got up and fought back. He grieved when Moore won. He went to Durelle's dressing room and found him battered and weeping. He tried to cheer him up, offered congratulations for a courageous fight, offered him a flight home in his private plane.

But earlier, something else had happened. As he sat watching, writhing with excitement in a ringside seat, Irving heard someone say something derogatory about Durelle. This time he didn't count to ten. Perhaps, he said, the man would care to go outside and settle it, man to man. The invitation was declined, and it may have been just as well. Irving would have been sixty in less than three months.

Waiting was something people who worked for Irving had to get used to. Said Montreal lawyer Yves Pratte: "He had no sense of time. The only thing that was important was what he was doing at the time he was doing it." Irving kept an expensive accountant waiting for two days. He kept a pilot and an executive waiting in New York for a week while he did other things.

People who knew him well differed in their views about Irving's own attitude to the money he made. To his sons, "he never cared about money; he only wanted to put it to work." Once done with fishing, he had no hobby to spend money on: his one recreation was watching trees grow. For years, he bought Hartt shoes because they were made in New Brunswick. He wore them as long as possible. Son Arthur told a visitor to look at the sole of his father's shoe: "See if it has a hole in it." Irving raised his foot, grinning. The visitor said, "No, it hasn't, but there was one in the shoes he was wearing yesterday."

He didn't like credit cards even though he issued them himself. If another firm sent him one, he cut it up. He could blow up over waste, no matter how small. For his eighty-second birthday he was presented with a book about his early life. Golden Ball executives watched him unwrap it, and the care he took to save the paper and the string.

Lesser men could only wonder at all this. "If I had your money," a young executive, Ross Gaudreau, told him, "I'd live it up."

"You're telling tales," Irving said. "It wouldn't be four days before you'd want to be back doing just what you're doing now."

If he ever had any doubts about the remorseless pace he set himself to build and accumulate more, they may have come out one summer in Quebec. He and Ross Gaudreau were standing on a wharf in a small town on the St. Lawrence River, making an inspection, when Irving saw a man sitting there in the hot sun, fishing, a bottle of beer and a can of worms beside him, his face happy — in all, the perfect image of what he himself was not.

He kept staring at the man until Gaudreau asked if there was anything wrong. "No," said Irving, "but I wonder who's right, him or me, and right now I'm afraid to give you the answer."

He often ate in second-rate restaurants. You ate faster there, and he was always in a hurry. He also liked to eat candy: he'd eat Laura Secord chocolates by the pound. He once bought some and paid a cashier, then counted his change and turned to tell her she had made a mistake. She bristled. "You didn't cheat me," Irving said. "You cheated yourself." He gave her the money, tipped his hat and left.

❧

CHAPTER THIRTY-TWO

A Question
of Ownership

*"Irving Oil is a New Brunswick Company and let
there be no mistake or misunderstanding about
that."*

– AN ANGRY K.C. IRVING RESPONDING TO SUGGESTIONS HE DID
NOT CONTROL HIS OWN COMPANY.

A N AUGUST EVENING, 1981. THE FOUR-SEATER AERO
Commander turbo-jet tosses in aerial turbulence as it pre-
pares to land. Arthur Irving looks down into the industrial-
rural face of Pictou County, N.S., and points out a big service
station. He says it sells 1.5 million gallons of gasoline a year. His
brother Jack, his executive vice-president in Irving Oil, corrects
him: 1.3 million, he says.

The Trenton airport lies flat and skinny on a narrow hill, and
when the plane puts down Arthur recalls the time they landed
here in wild winds with a frightened-out-of-his-wits French engineer. They introduced him to the mayor, and the stricken engineer,
his face chalk white, said, "I thought you must be the undertaker.
Where is the nearest railway station?" He left by train, and was
neither the first nor the last to say he would never fly with the
Irvings again.

They have come this time for a public event, to explain the significance of their local attempt to find oil. The search itself is a

sign that they still believe what K.C. Irving said when he opened his refinery: that all he needed now to round out his petroleum interests was his own oil wells. They hope to find them in the Maritime provinces.

With Irving Oil's backing, their allies, Standard of California's Chevron Standard, are doing the exploration. They have an ultra-sophisticated ship working in Northumberland Strait. They have plans to work it in the Gulf of St. Lawrence and the Bay of Fundy. They are probing the land in all three provinces. They have drilled in Cape Breton. For months they have had trucks with seismic equipment travelling country roads, four in line, sending down energy, picking up vibrations from geological structures, reading them, hoping. Now they have found something worth spending up to $5 million on. They have picked a rural area, brought in a drilling rig, and because there is great local interest they have scheduled a public meeting in the firehall at tiny Scotsburn to explain what they are doing.

Across the street is a dolled-up Irving service station. For a week there has been a hassled rush to get it ready for this evening. The meeting starts. The upstairs hall is packed and downstairs there is an overflow. Seven reporters are there, as are Canadian, Nova Scotian, and Irving flags, and pictures of Irving enterprise. Chevron officials speak, low-key: "We are a long way from getting something going." People ask questions about the environment, about who gets what. Government officials say they have found Irving-Chevron extremely co-operative in Cape Breton, even to avoiding areas where bald eagles and blue herons nest. If oil is found, they say, all Nova Scotians will benefit because the province owns mineral rights.

Partly, but only partly, because most of the audience has never seen an Irving, something electric happens when Arthur speaks. He talks machine-gun fast, straight from the shoulder. He praises Chevron, and says the Maritimes, "the best part of Canada," have been exploited too long, and "we are going to do our level best to make you proud again." He tells of the refinery, of the ships that come 17,600 kilometres with $80 million worth of crude oil, the thing they're seeking here. He says Irving Oil has never declared a dividend, always has a bank loan: "We're not clipping coupons. . . . We are looking for oil. We are highly interested, and I'll let you in on a secret: we are going to find it. If it's not here, it's somewhere else. If we don't strike it the first time, we're going to strike it eventually. And I'll also tell you this: if we make a dollar here, it will be spent here."

The crowd loves it, and they love the feast provided by the firemen's ladies auxiliary, the lobster sandwiches, the strawberries and cream, the cookies and coffee. The Irvings move about, chatting, laughing, and when it's all over the service station does much business under bright and happy lights.

☙

The Irving refinery in Saint John, large at the time of its opening in 1960, grew dramatically over the years. Yet it remained neat and trim, stretched out — because that's the way K.C. Irving wanted it. In 1960 the refinery had boasted seventy storage tanks with a capacity of 80 million barrels. By 1990 this grew to 135 storage tanks and production had gone from a daily capacity of 40,000 barrels to 250,000 barrels a day. A new alkylation plant, one component of the refinery, was completed in 1990 at a cost of $60 million — $10 million more than the cost of the entire refinery in 1960 — and the world's largest oil tankers, with capacities of over 350,000 tonnes, tied up regularly at nearby Canaport.

The refinery, on close to 405 hectares of fenced-in soil and rocks, half as much again as it originally had, made numerous grades of gas, fuel oil, stove oil, propane, kerosene, diesel and jet fuels, bunker oil, asphalt, sulphur. This enormous distillery used heat to split molecules of crude in one continuous process, billowing clouds of steam from the millions of gallons of water used every day. It had its own fire brigade, every man trained for an emergency.

By the 1980s there were more than 400 employees at the refinery. Because it was company policy to promote from within as much as possible a good number of supervisors were, in fact, men who had gone on strike in 1963–64.

The Saint John refinery was a fulfilment of K.C. Irving's dream — a world-class facility that competed aggressively and successfully in the volatile international market where experts played a multi-million-dollar balancing act every day as they searched out the best purchase deals for crude oil and then switched to the equally competitive challenge of selling the refined products. Some indication of the company's importance, not simply to the economy of New Brunswick but to Canada's international balance of trade, was disclosed in 1979 when Ottawa revealed it had underestimated foreign trade figures by $500 million because the Irvings had not filed certain Customs reports after the method of reporting had changed. Later reports put the figure at $800 million for eighteen months. Arthur Irving retorted strongly that press reports were misleading, denied any attempt to conceal exports to avoid taxes, and said every shipment had a permit. What had happened was that, through an office error, one of the large number of forms had been overlooked, and even though it was required monthly, Ottawa had not drawn the omission to their attention. The most telling aspect of it all was that it indicated how far they had come since K.C. Irving bucked Imperial in 1924.

Still, there long existed in Saint John a sceptical belief that giant Standard of California really ran the show and told the Irvings what to do. The belief annoyed the Irvings. It was a belief no one who saw what went on inside the refinery would be likely to hold. For years Standard men, by agreement, occupied the top three jobs, but on the question of ultimate authority there was no doubt: the Irvings called the shots.

The Standard men would eventually pursue their careers within its own structure. Here they were Irving men, answerable to Arthur and Jack alone. They did often find the experience strange at first. They came out of a bureaucratic, stratified, hierarchical world into one where there were no memos, no committees, where Arthur Irving in a given day made more decisions, on a wider front, than Standard's boss in California. The men from Standard were schooled in public relations and they had to get used to a lone-wolf company that played things close to the vest. There were differences over the years, and rebukes for some of the Standard men. But both sides said the arrangement worked well. One Standard manager stayed for fourteen years. Another left after five, saying he had learned as much about the oil business as he would have elsewhere in twenty-five.

In the seventies the original arrangement that gave Standard 51 per cent of Irving Refining Ltd. was changed. The refinery, Canaport, and other segments were bundled together, by mutual consent, into a firm called Irving Oil Ltd. Irving owned 51 per cent. Standard owned the rest and continued to do what it had always done — accept Irving control of Irving territory.

Even so, for some years, the chairman of the board was Standard's R. Thornton Savage. He was popular with the Irvings. Then, in 1980, something happened that embarrassed and angered them and that, in turn, showed how things were. Steve Belding, a young reporter with the weekly *Kings County Record* in Sussex, N.B., learned that Irving Oil and Chevron had moved a drilling rig into that area, and set out to get the facts. Belding called a Chevron headquarters number and a secretary suggested he talk to the chairman of the Irving Oil board. Savage said drilling had started in Kings County to determine whether it would be feasible to construct underground reservoirs primarily to store light oil products. But the big news was that Savage *was* chairman.

Once the original story was out, other reporters called Savage too. This time he said Irving Oil was very much run from Saint John; Standard had been involved only in policy decisions. K.C. Irving, he added, had not been involved in Irving Oil's corporate affairs since he left Canada in 1971. From then on, he answered no more phone calls. However, the damage had been done. News reports gave the impression that Standard of California was in the driver's seat at Irving Oil. Irving reaction was not long in coming.

No one was more angry than eighty-one-year-old K.C. Irving himself. He issued a statement declaring that he controlled Irving Oil. It was true, he said, that Savage was board chairman, "but there should be no uncertainty about management and control. I am the beneficial owner of 51.1 per cent of the company and that is not a figure that just happened. This shareholding applies to all of the company's assets. I am not an officer and I am not a director, but I am a shareholder and I speak at the shareholders' meetings, and long before the company reached its present size I took the necessary steps to see that the head office would remain in New Brunswick, that a refinery would be built there, and that control would not be taken over by some national or multi-national company."

There had been reports and statements that "inferred control was actually in the hands of Standard Oil of California." He added that "Irving Oil is a New Brunswick company, and let there be no mistake or misunderstanding about that." He closed on a personal note: "I have been a resident of Bermuda since 1971, but I remain a Canadian citizen and the interests of Atlantic Canada are close to my heart."

In due course there was a further revelation tucked into an announcement that Irving Oil and Chevron were undertaking their exploration program in Nova Scotia. Signed by Arthur Irving and A.B. Bristow, Chevron's president, it identified Arthur as president, chief executive officer, *and* chairman of Irving Oil.

Behind the disclosure lay another incident. The four Irvings had flown to San Francisco to voice their indignation over what had happened. They were received warmly and they came away satisfied. From then on their control was manifest in words as well as deeds. Furthermore, it was control that would become 100 per cent when the Irvings bought out their U.S. partners in the late 1980s.

The ultimate control that K.C. Irving held was through his FMO Co. Ltd. of Bermuda, and this produced an entirely different type of problem — a vexing, time-consuming, high-stakes problem that for years refused to go away. From 1979 on, Irving Oil engaged in a legal battle with Ottawa over its method of buying Standard's crude. Revenue Canada charged that the Irvings avoided full taxes by buying through Irving California Co. Ltd. of Bermuda (Irvcal) and selling at an unnecessarily high price to Irving Oil. Irvcal, it contended, was there simply to inflate prices and create profits for the Bermuda-based company, with tax-free dividends flowing back to Canada as a result.

The Irvings argued that Irvcal was a legitimate arms-length trader, that its price for crude was competitive, not arbitrarily set to yield a set profit, and not designed to avoid Canadian taxes. At stake were huge sums.

The case plodded on for years until 1988, when the Federal Court ruled that the government had erred when it had taxed the Irvings $142 million. It ordered that the money, plus interest, be refunded.

The case then went to appeal, the federal Revenue Department maintaining that Irvcal was nothing more than a sham designed to divert profits to the Bermuda company and then recover the money in Canada through tax-free dividends. Irving lawyer Edgar

Sexton's position was that the money was not made in Canada and therefore could not be taxed in Canada. He estimated the original $142 million would be about $200 million when interest was included. In a unanimous 3-0 judgment the court ruled in 1991 in favour of the Irvings. The court said the arrangement was a "tax avoidance scheme, pure and simple," but it also observed that "everybody is entitled to reduce taxes, as long as he stays within the law." A key and conclusive finding of the court was that the price of crude oil eventually shipped to Saint John for refining by Irving represented fair market value.

❧

When Irving built his oil refinery he got into the propane gas business as an offshoot and soon had a dominant position in the Maritime market. He hired George Urquhart to run it. Urquhart knew the business and had urged a company in which he had shares and a high position to sell out to Irving. He was also deeply involved in politics. He became a rarity in the Irving organization because he kept right on being involved in the Liberal party and in other public functions even though Irving liked his executives to consider business their top priority.

Although colleagues say all the Irvings love to talk politics, Urquhart said he couldn't recall Irving either encouraging or discouraging him in what he did politically. "He never put the screws on me to get in or get out." He said this was true even when he ran for Parliament in 1962 without telling Irving he was going to do it. It didn't stop the *Toronto Star* from calling him "a front man for Irving," or the Conservatives from distributing copies. "It hurt me," Urquhart said. He lost.

Irving did tell him, "Don't be disappointed if you lose," when Urquhart ran for president of the Liberal Association of Saint John. "Don't be disappointed if I win," Urquhart replied, and he did. There was no Irving comment. Because Urquhart went off on trips to golf or curl, Irving said, "We can only afford one sport and that's you." When Urquhart became chairman of Louis Robichaud's Industrial Development Board, there was no comment. Nor was there any protest when he became a key figure in promoting construction of that bridge and throughway in the heart of the city that Irving later opposed.

Later, when Urquhart had left the staff and became a million-aire in Moncton, he chanced upon Irving at a ceremony. Irving came over, grinning, and said just one thing: "Saint John is the only place in North America with a throughway in the city."

The stories of Irving's legal battles could alone fill a book. He won nearly every important case he ever fought, and he fought dozens, often lasting years. He fought governments, business rivals, unions, big people and little people. "He is," said a lawyer, "the most litigious man in the world." Irving took some of his own workers to court for stealing; theft was wrong and apt to be perpetuated. Some cases brought bad publicity, for instance when he prosecuted people who took logs that strayed from his drives. The fact, said lawyer Adrian Gilbert, was that farmers sued Irving for damages after a boom broke and that farmers who helped salvage logs were paid. It was written that four young fishermen were fined for "daring to dip their lines in Irving's private fish pond." They weren't charged with this, said Gilbert, and they wouldn't have been charged with any-thing if they hadn't threatened the warden.

The cases Irving fought poured millions into legal coffers. He had "house" or staff lawyers for day-to-day work. For court combat and complex matters, he marshalled outsiders, at least two of whom eventually sat on the Supreme Court of Canada.

For top advice, he relied for years on the huge New York firm of Dewey, Ballantine, Busby, Palmer. Irving's first contact with it stemmed, like much else, from a Bouctouche background. In the summers of his youth, a young theological student named Alyea came to town to preach and became a friend of the family; Irving's father even thought of sending K.C. to Princeton University with him. Alyea abandoned theology for law and, through him as a partner, Irving made the connection with a firm that had experts in all fields of law, and even ran day and night shifts.

He didn't battle lawyers as he did engineers, trying to implant his own ideas. "The legal side," said one prominent lawyer, "he didn't pretend to know." But he had to know why something was being done, "and he had to have the feeling that it was right. He once told me a contract I'd prepared wouldn't do, that 'if I was the other fellow I wouldn't sign it.' I learned a helluva lot from him."

He had, this and other lawyers found, to understand everything, whether it involved an engineering, financial, or legal problem. A modern manager would look just at the balance sheet; he had to see every piece of the pie. He never did anything on a hunch; everything had to be logical in his mind. Every decision, even the smallest, had to be reasoned. Irving would read legal contracts over slowly, painstakingly going over specifications a foot thick. It could be agony for a lawyer to wait, but when he was done he knew what was in them: it was difficult for him to trust anyone to do it for him; he didn't know how to delegate.

In the legal profession this sort of thing led to another branch of Irving folklore. One Saint John lawyer rejected Irving's request that he represent him in a case because, he said, there should be at least one lawyer in town who didn't; he later headed the committee of admirers who paid to have Irving's portrait painted. Another did a great deal of work for the Irvings but found himself acting for a firm fighting a company in which they themselves had a controlling interest. To the Irvings' expressed regret and even displeasure, he answered simply that he didn't know they controlled the company. In the labyrinth of their possessions, it could happen.

In the maze of Irving's legal activities, two Saint John lawyers probably had more to do with him in the early and middle years of his career then any others. They were Louis McC. Ritchie and Adrian Gilbert. Ritchie was a master of backroom advice, documentation, and preparation. Gilbert was at his best in a courtroom struggle. Ritchie was a Liberal, a party treasurer, a "bagman," and later served on the Exchequer Court of Canada, then returned to take up his association with Irving where it had left off. Gilbert was a Tory, loved to hunt and fish and play golf, and said he once had to pull Irving out of the water after a mishap over one thing he didn't do well — control a canoe. He had capsized.

For a time Gilbert and Ritchie were partners, but they didn't get along. But both were still active well into their eighties, and both kept working for the Irvings.

From Roy (Mike) Lawson, a prominent Saint John car dealer, came the story of a legal fight he and Irving got involved in as allies. They were for some years rival salesmen, but friendly ones. Irving, said Lawson, would drop in on walks to or from work in his early years in Saint John, and they would swap gossip about the trade. In later years, out of the car business himself, Irving helped Lawson overcome local opposition and get established on property he owned on Fredericton's busy Queen Street, selling General Motors cars — and Irving products. One day Lawson got word that the property was about to be expropriated to make way for construction of the Lord Beaverbrook Hotel.

He called Irving and asked what they were going to do about it. "We're going to Fredericton," was the immediate reply. When? "Now," Irving said. "Meet me in five minutes." They flew up the St. John River, but when they got to Fredericton Irving's amphibious plane couldn't put down because the river was clogged with Irving's logs. They flew a few miles south to open water, put down and hitchhiked into town. The man who picked them up found them unlikely people to have their thumbs up, but that didn't bother Irving. "We got into a hotel room," said Lawson, "and he was on the phone to people for a long time, mad as hell."

The matter eventually came before a board of arbitrators, and the chairman asked if anyone could tell him how much Irving Oil would lose per gallon of gas from the expropriation. Some of Irving's executives were there, but none of them had the exact answer. Then Irving spoke up and said he did. He took the stand and said precisely how much, to a fraction of a cent, he would lose, and explained why. The chairman thanked him, but Irving wasn't through. "Then," he added, "there is also the loss on oil."

It took years for him to get what he wanted, but he did.

For his logging operations, Irving had a dam built on northern New Brunswick's Grand River. The gates proved too small to handle an outsized spring freshet, water overflowed farmlands beyond optioned limits, and the owners took legal action to have the dam removed.

Irving went to the area with his son Jim and his lawyer, Adrian Gilbert. They arrived at the attractive property of a gentleman of Scots descent. They had already eaten but he had cake, pie, and coffee laid out and, in the interests of diplomacy, they chatted quietly and ate those too. Then the farmer banged the table and said, "Mr. Irving, how much are you going to pay me for my ruined land?"

"Well now," said Irving, "we are entirely in the wrong; the gates of the dam are too small and we need to buy rights on more of your land. We will pay you whatever you conscientiously think we should pay."

"Oh," said the astonished farmer, "I never expected to hear you say that. I was going to charge you a high price, but if you pay me quick and clean up the flooded land I will sell you the acreage you need for half what I planned."

"It's a deal," Irving said. A cheque was written, a deed was signed and, said Gilbert, as they left the farmer said, "Mr. Irving, you are a fine man. It's a pleasure to do business with you."

The second home belonged to the farmer's brother, and he had phoned ahead. "I hear," the brother said, "you're a good man to deal with." Said Irving: "Not everyone says so." A deal was quickly made — after more food was consumed. So were others. Only one farmer refused to sell rights to more land, but he made another deal. "Mr. Irving," he said, "you clear off the debris after the freshet goes down. I'll plant oats and we'll see what sort of crop I get. Come back in the fall." He had the best crop he ever had, and he did eventually lease Irving more land at a moderate rent.

Irving liked to tell such anecdotes in old age. Drydock veteran LeRoy Vincent told of the time Irving picked Vincent and others up after a funeral in Halifax and fell to reminiscing on the flight back to Saint John. He was going so strongly by the time they arrived over the airport that Vincent said he thought Irving kept the plane circling long enough to finish one of his stories.

Adrian Gilbert said Irving even liked to chuckle over a court case in which he got the worst of it. During the first expansion of his pulp mill a fire caused considerable damage. The mill was insured by more than forty companies, and Irving claimed his loss totalled more than $200,000. The adjuster assigned to assess it came up with a figure well below Irving's. A court case started with lawyer Gilbert, for once, not on Irving's side. He said Irving's claim *was* excessive.

On the witness stand, Irving engineer Frank Lang was asked about a piece of machinery known as a duster which the company's loss claim listed as a major item, worth $65,000. Had he inspected it in the mill before the fire? Yes, Lang said. What did he think of its value or usefulness?

"Do you want my candid opinion?" Lang asked.

"Yes," he was told. "That is what we do want."

"Well," said the engineer, "it was not in use and of no value. I would have junked it."

319

With that, Irving's case sagged, and he settled for a total of about $75,000. When the hearing was over, he went about shaking hands with everyone involved, even the antagonistic adjuster and, said Gilbert, he never ceased to kid Lang about his decisive evidence — for the other side!

At one stag dinner in Saint John's Union Club, Irving was referred to as the "Great White Father." In the forty-six years he lived in the city, he became an overshadowing giant, so powerful that when a yacht club decided his logs interfered with sailing not a single member could be found to make the protest.

He was not, in a normal sense, a citizen of the place. He simply outgrew it. He took no part in civic activities; one former head of the Board of Trade said all the Irvings seemed to feel that if they joined they would only jeopardize it by their sheer size. The city itself developed a love–hate syndrome about him. "Love," one businessman told a reporter, "because his industries put pay-cheques into so many hands. Hate because he sort of dominates it. I guess a lot of it is just plain jealousy." Another said he had two aunts, sisters, who summed it up. One hated the Irvings. One loved them. Both worked for them. In a dress shop across from the Golden Ball building, a woman clerk said five members of her family worked for them, and she appreciated it: "They put bread on the table. I can even stand the smell of their pulp mill."

For years the smell irritated the city. When one man wrote to the newspapers that he remembered the Depression and rather liked the mill odour because it was a smell of work, another retorted that he should "be chained by the neck to the Reversing Falls bridge" to twist and gag in it. Irving himself came out of a restaurant when it was a smothering, fetid blanket and heard someone comment. "Stink?" he asked. "I don't smell any stink." But he spent millions to curb it, for a long time with indifferent success. It became a sort of unholy symbol of Irving enterprise, an exasperating reminder of his presence and his power.

Irving himself, though fully established in residence in Bermuda, continued to keep a close eye on the countless businesses and industries he had started, only now he viewed his enterprises from a different and at times uncomfortable perspective. Now, instead of running everything, instead of calling the shots on a day-to-day basis, his involvement was that of shareholder.

As a shareholder, there was nothing he kept closer tabs on than Brunswick Mining. His association with Brunswick, he was convinced, had encouraged many New Brunswickers to invest in the huge mining development. He felt a deep responsibility for those small shareholders, and he was frustrated that he was unable to do more on their behalf. Yet he was far from through. With Brunswick, and with Brunswick's parent, the giant Noranda, he still had battles to wage — battles for himself and as a champion of minority shareholders.

In 1971 he had accepted a Noranda refinancing plan designed to reduce debt and provide more working capital; it was, he said, either that "or face the possibility of even greater financial losses." He noted that Brunswick shares had dropped from the $7–$8 range to $2.50 since the Noranda takeover, estimated that shareholders had lost millions, and said, "What I predicted would happen, and what I attempted to prevent from happening, has happened." Noranda president Alfred Powis described Brunswick's position as precarious, fundamentally insolvent, but that the refinancing plan was expected to produce a profit by 1973.

But the ill-fated smelter was even then entering a new phase. Noranda announced that it was abandoning the original concept; the smelter was, at a cost of $10 million and the loss of 280 jobs, to be converted to produce lead alone; zinc concentrates would be offered for sale abroad. It was, said a spokesman, becoming more unprofitable to process zinc. Nor was this all; the fertilizer plant was to be shifted from East Coast ownership to Brunswick, then sold to Noranda for $1.5 million, a fraction of its cost.

Irving did not show up for the annual Brunswick meeting in 1972 and 1973, years in which the company's net earnings got into the black. But he was back in 1974, and he was again critical: Noranda, he argued, "has not provided the professional, competent management it promised. How much time do you want?" It had cost 50,000 man-days since May 1972 through strikes and disputes, and its labour–management relations were deplorable.

By 1975 Irving had his first Brunswick dividend; it was ten cents a share, and it meant millions to him. He offered congratulations, but he said the company had "operated far below its originally conceived potential for earnings" and that "there remains a vast area for much greater improvement." He had quoted W.S.

Row as saying the company would have been prosperous if it had never built the smelter, and now he cited figures: it had had profits of $27 million from 1964 to 1966 and losses of $4 million since.

At this meeting W.G. Brissenden, the president, said Brunswick was studying investments of up to $300 million in a zinc reduction plant, improvements to the smelter, and other steps that would make it "one of the great mineral producers of North America." They were feasible, he said, because the company was making a "reasonable profit" — $9.8 million in 1973 and $17 million in 1974 — and could expect to do better.

From Irving came a question: Was more money "going to be poured down the drain" before shareholders were adequately compensated? Moreover, he refused to let the past die. How much, he asked, had the smelter cost since Noranda took over?

A year later he gave his own estimate of that cost: "well in excess of $100 million on a project which I opposed from the beginning, which experts said should not be built, and which was built under political pressure." Brunswick's new president, William James, said it had made money since it was converted, and estimated net losses at $29.2 million from 1968 to 1975.

Irving said he attended that meeting because he felt a responsibility to those minority shareholders "whose early investment made this huge undertaking possible." They had been "treated very shabbily, first by the politicians and later by what I can only describe as the inability of Noranda to fulfil its promises to direct and operate this company efficiently." Brunswick had been built because of their minority shareholders' investments, not "with the money of fly-by-night, get-rich-quick investors" who got stock "at a very favourable price in the early days and then unloaded it at a huge profit when they saw the company was running into problems. They were in a position to take care of themselves and they took care of themselves. I left my money in, and a lot of those who knew me left their money in."

James's predecessor, Brissenden, had said that, in considering a zinc plant, "close contact will be maintained with the government of the province." Was this, asked Irving, an indication that Brunswick is again going to be influenced by government? Would the shareholders once again be ignored because of new government pressure? "This is one instance where history must not repeat itself," he said. James said the zinc project could not be undertaken for at least two years.

But 1976 was notable for more than what Irving said critically. He liked Bill James, and the affable, able James courted him. Irving welcomed him, though he doubted that "anyone at Noranda has given you the story of the political intrigue, the manipulation, and the sellout of this New Brunswick asset." At later annual meetings, James led a round of applause for him, called him "a great New Brunswicker who knows more about creating jobs than anyone else in the province." Irving cautioned him again about political pressure to build the zinc project and other things, but he also complimented him for his "commonsense approach," and for vastly improved earnings in 1979.

In truth, a new, milder, happier era had come, and in part it had a typical Irving touch. He had noted that James's father, a prominent Toronto geologist, "is from New Brunswick and lived as a young man in Saint John." When someone reminded him that the son was, after all, a Noranda man, he replied, "Yes, but he has New Brunswick roots." In this new atmosphere, the Irvings even teamed up with Noranda to seek contracts to exploit New Brunswick's potash deposits. They didn't get any because the government preferred other bids. Brunswick had never developed as rosy, earlier predictions had said it would. The steel mill was never built and for years the Belledune harbour remained undeveloped, which Irving once called "an unbelievable blunder." Belledune itself remained small because workers preferred to live in and around Bathurst. Other plans died. Irving's $63.5-million takeover offer largely faded from public memory, though some people in the area wondered what might have happened if it had been accepted.

It was Noranda that opened the door for a historic sequel to the battle Irving had waged two decades earlier when Rothesay Paper was trying to get established in Saint John. In 1981, soon after it took over the giant MacMillan-Bloedel firm, which had bought control of Rothesay, Noranda sold the shares to the Irvings. Irving himself told friends of the $145-million purchase with great satisfaction. It gave his family the newsprint mill he had long sought, and it rounded out a major episode in his life.

CHAPTER THIRTY-THREE

❧

The Grand Old Man

*"If I'd realized what a nice fellow I would become
simply by growing old, I might well have done it
much sooner."*

– *K.C. IRVING AT HIS 1980 INDUCTION INTO THE CANADIAN
BUSINESS HALL OF FAME.*

KC. IRVING WAS A LOST, FORLORN, AND LONELY MAN AFTER
his wife died in 1976. He had been away from home
often, and often for long periods of time, during their
forty-nine years of marriage. He worked long hours, skipped
meals, and came home late, but in another sense they had been
inseparable. Now there was a terrible void in his life.

In later years, and especially after they moved to Bermuda,
they had travelled together everywhere. Both were in their seventies. Harriet was not well, and they cherished their time with each
other. Irving was not one to discuss his personal life or personal
feelings, but there were times when he acknowledged, sometimes
with a catch in his voice, that everything he had accomplished had
been with her help, with her at his side in person or in spirit.

And then suddenly he was alone. He was in his late seventies,
and it was a difficult time for him until the loneliness was eased two
years later at a quiet ceremony in Bermuda. With his family present and beaming approval, he married Winnifred Jane Johnston,
his longtime secretary. She came from rural Charlotte County on
the south coast of New Brunswick, and she had joined Irving as

his personal secretary after lawyer Louis McC. Ritchie went to the bench in 1955. Ritchie recommended her as a sensible, capable, and collected secretary-accountant. She was unmarried and devoted to her mother who lived with her, and when she was struck by the full force of Irving's work habits, she thought seriously about quitting. "Don't lose that girl," Ritchie told Irving. He didn't.

She became the embodiment of loyalty to him, as numerous people, and especially journalists, could testify. They came up against her for years as the human wall that shielded Irving from their curiosity. She became a bit of a legend in her own right, a legend to men who never saw her.

When the press monopoly case was being heard in Moncton, Dr. George Stanley, a distinguished historian, head of Mount Allison University's Canadian Studies program, and a future lieutenant-governor, remembered most the presence of Miss Johnston as a witness. No lawyer intimidated her. No question confounded her. Her personal feeling, she said, was that "there should be freedom to run businesses according to established ethics. From the evidence I have heard, I would not think the charges are justified."

After their marriage, others called her "Winnifred" or "Mrs. Irving"; he called her "Jane," and she was his constant companion. Leigh Stevenson had urged it, but counselled her not to be overpowered by her husband. She wasn't. During Irving's restless, active version of retirement, she was almost invariably with him when he appeared on special occasions. On a bright June day in 1984 they attended an unusual ceremony in the small New Brunswick community of Sussex Corner, where Jimmy Wade had grown up. The village had decided to honour Wade by erecting a red granite monument in recognition of a hometown flying hero who had gone through many experiences with Irving. Wade's widow, Florence, and his son, Jimmy Wade, Jr., were there and so were politicians and community officials, but the person who had the most personal and intimate knowledge of Wade's heroics as a pilot was Irving.

When it was Irving's turn to talk about his old friend Jimmy Wade, he described him as one of those early wonders of the sky. Wade, Irving recalled, had flown primitive planes long before the days of sophisticated instruments, radar, and landing aids. "He flew when there were few airfields in Canada, and it was not uncommon for Jimmy Wade to search out something that was not much more than an open field when it was time to land."

Despite Wade's reputation for dangerous flights and daring rescue missions, Irving considered him a careful pilot. "He did have his mishaps, as most pilots had in those early days, but Jimmy Wade walked away from all of them." Irving recalled that he, too, had walked away from some of those crashes. Then he told the story of the hairiest episode of them all. It happened at the old Millidgeville Airport in Saint John when there was a problem with the engine on takeoff. Jimmy got the plane aloft but it was soon apparent that it was going to be touch and go at the end of the field.

"We were heading for the trees," Irving said. "I said, 'Jimmy, do you think we'll clear the trees?' He didn't answer. He was too busy, but he did hold his right hand up for a second with his fingers crossed. Almost immediately we both knew we were not going to clear the trees. I said, 'Jimmy, can you get out?' Again, he didn't answer. He just raised his hand, his fingers still crossed, and then we were into the trees." By now the plane was on fire and Irving recalled that "we were nose down and Jimmy, in the pilot's seat, and close to the ground, was able to squirm out through the forward hatch. For me, it was about a 10-foot jump from the tail of the plane."

What Irving didn't mention about the Saint John crash was that he told an airport official to cancel their flight, then went back to his office to work.

ঽ

In 1986 Irving appeared for one more in a series of historic tree-planting ceremonies, this time at Petitcodiac on a site overlooking the Trans-Canada Highway where Irving, now eighty-seven, planted the 200-millionth tree and was praised as the province's first honorary chief forester. It was almost a family picnic, where four generations of the normally private Irvings mingled with employees, urging them to have a good time and thanking them over and over again for coming.

It was also a day of humour.

When New Brunswick's natural resources minister announced that K.C. Irving had been named the province's first honorary chief forester, K.C.'s son, Jim, was prompted to remark: "Dad, when the budworms hear about this, I bet they'll be shaking in their boots." Jim Irving went on to recall his early training under a father who, he acknowledged, had been a hard taskmaster. He said he and his brothers had learned more about forests and general business practices from their father than from any other source.

"One of the first things our parents taught us, very early in life, was that if you are going to do something, you should do it right." It was a lesson that dated back to even earlier times, to the kitchen in Bouctouche when K.C.'s mother had used those very words.

Irving himself said that of all the projects in his life, the reforestation program had been the most important and gratifying. He thanked members of his family for carrying on the program, stressing that "we must do everything possible to leave the forests in better condition than we found them."

One year later he was sworn in as honorary chief forester at a ceremony at the Hugh John Flemming Forestry Centre in Fredericton in a 250-seat lecture hall aptly named The K.C. Irving Theatre. Among those praising Irving on that occasion was Ken Armson, Ontario's chief forester, who said efforts spearheaded by Irving were not only paying off in New Brunswick but served "to guide and stimulate foresters across Canada." Armson recalled that Irving had stood virtually alone when he made his original decision to proceed with a renewal program.

The eighty-eight-year-old Irving listened attentively as speaker after speaker extolled his efforts and his successes. Finally, it was his turn, but it was not, he said, his intention to make a speech. "Now, I suspect that should make everyone happy," he added as laughter rippled through the lecture hall. But he did have something to say and it touched once again on his love and concern for the forests. "In a province like New Brunswick there are few things that are as important as protecting, preserving, and renewing our forests for future generations.

"This is more than an obligation — it is a sacred trust."

❧

As serious as Irving was about forest preservation, there were lighter moments. There was, for instance, the sequel to Irving's long association with Barney Flieger and Flieger's early belief that

Irving's planting of softwood trees on hardwood ridges was destined to fail. This was a story the Irvings loved to recall in later years, but for Flieger at the time, it was anything but funny. It was, in fact, an embarrassment that bothered him much more than his admission that he had been wrong in his early, negative assessment of Irving's reforestation project.

The story was about churches and funerals. In a sense, it went back to Irving's earliest days as a young boy growing up in Bouctouche, back to a time when everyone went to church on Sundays, and to weddings and funerals. Especially funerals.

"It was something you did," Irving would recall. "You went and paid your respects to the person who had died. It was the very least you could do, and it meant a great deal to the family. You sent flowers or a card. You did something personal."

It was all part of Irving's early upbringing and it stayed with him all of his life. Son Arthur would say: "Dad spent a lot of time in church, but mostly it was at funerals." Then, laughing, Arthur or Jim or Jack would tell the story of the one funeral no one would ever forget — the funeral K.C. Irving insisted on attending because the deceased had been "a pretty good chap and I should go and pay my respects."

He was living in Bermuda when he received a telegram from Barney Flieger: "Agerman passed away. Funeral Tuesday 2 p.m." It gave the name and address of the funeral home in Montreal. The deceased was a man Irving had known well as an executive with International Paper Company, and later through his association with Forest Protection Limited.

It was short notice and not all that convenient for Irving to get away but he decided he was going, and that was that. He and son Jack flew to Montreal on the day of the funeral and, as was his custom, he cut the timing pretty fine, arriving at the funeral home a few minutes before 2 p.m. But to his dismay and consternation there was no reference to Mr. Agerman on the board listing those who were resting in the various parlours.

"Jack," he said to his son, "is this the right funeral home?" Jack said it was. There was no doubt about it. "Well, is the funeral at 2 o'clock?" Jack checked the telegram and said it was. They were at the right funeral home and at the correct time. All they needed to do now was find the corpse.

They went to the office. "Could you tell me where we can find Mr. Agerman?" Irving asked the receptionist.

"Mr. Agerman?"

"Yes," he said, "the late Mr. Agerman. His funeral is today."

The receptionist checked her schedule. "No," she said, "I'm sorry. There's no funeral today for Mr. Agerman."

"Are you sure?"

"I'm certain," she said. Then, checking her records, she added: "We had a Mr. Agerman, but he was buried a week ago."

Barney Flieger somehow had got the date mixed up — or he'd sent an ambiguous telegram. In due course he learned what had happened and was mortified. He remembered all those years when he had been cool to Irving's reforestation program, when he'd said he'd eat his textbooks if Irving was right and if the trees actually grew. He said he'd never be able to face Irving again. A few years later, by coincidence, Irving was visiting in New Brunswick at the time of a meeting of Forest Protection Limited. He asked his son Jim if he thought it would be all right if he attended. "Sure," said Jim, "they'd be glad to see you."

Later, when Jim was talking to the Forest Protection office he mentioned that he and his father would be attending the meeting.

"I didn't think about it at the time and my father didn't mention it, but this would have been the first time that he would have seen Barney Flieger since his trip to Montreal to attend Mr. Agerman's funeral."

Flieger, as chairman of Forest Protection Limited, was scheduled to preside at the meeting, but he didn't show up. An official of Forest Protection told why. Barney Flieger, he said, had told him: "I just couldn't face Mr. Irving."

❧

Irving visited more than once in Moncton with Dos Savoie, who had dandled him on his knee as a baby. Dos was in his nineties, white-haired, his eyes twinkling. What did they discuss? "Business," Dos said. "He wanted to know what I knew about properties his father had bought in Kent County, a bit here, a bit there." It was all in Dos's mind. "I wish," Irving told him, "I had your memory."

He had his own memory, and he plunged into it again and again. He was touched when he got a poem from Sam Roy: "I miss the good old Primrose days/ with their nonchalant, trusting ways . . . O joyful days of long ago/ why do we never get to know/ how dear you are/ till you are far away?" He, too, yearned for those days. In the summers, year after year, he and Leigh Stevenson, in from Vancouver, toured their old Kent County haunts, talked of friends, visited people, and many graveyards. When Stevenson was told there couldn't be that many graveyards there, he chuckled, "Oh, we visit some of them more than once. We even visited the Methodist ones."

One day they headed back for the homestead their grandfather had worked, and just as they neared it Irving cried, "Stop, that's the house where I sold my first car up here." On the family land, he met his cousin, George Irving, an old man toiling with horse and plough. They went back again and Stevenson sneaked George a bottle of liquor and told him to keep it out of the sight of the teetotalling Irving. George brought it out of the woodpile anyway. His noted cousin was happy to get a family Bible, and when George retired the Irvings bought the place.

Along with his memories, the impulses, thoughts, and know-how that had made Irving rich and famous remained with him well into his eighties. "They're still in there," he told someone, "but now I have more trouble getting them out." He told Mike Lawson there was one thing they couldn't buy — time. "So let's make the most of what we have left." He did it in his own way. He talked business with his sons. He roamed his forests, pruning trees, measuring growth, took part in ceremonies as reforestation plantings mounted. On one of his trips with Stevenson, he saw an Irving service station property being graded, stopped, took off his coat and supervised. Then he was off to railway tracks where a big tank was being offloaded. He supervised that too. When a company headquarters was being built in Bangor, Maine, he got to know the contractor, poked into and discussed all sorts of things. "That man," the contractor said. "He knows everything!"

વ્ર

New Brunswick started honouring Irving in the 1960s and as the years went by he was summoned back more and more frequently to be recognized and praised by organizations, admirers, and politicians. He was honoured by the Saint John Construction

Association, by the Canadian Forestry Association, by the Canadian Trade and Industry Council, and by many others. He was seventy-six when he was named New Brunswick's Developer of the Year. He was an honorary citizen of that mythical northern Republic of Madawaska that straddles the border of New Brunswick and Maine. One of the first New Brunswick communities to honour him was Bathurst. It had made him a Freeman when the new City Hall was opened in 1961, and in 1967 he took pleasure when the University of New Brunswick named a new multi-million-dollar, five-storey building the Harriet Irving Library, in honour of his wife. In 1965, in a ceremony in Saint John, Irving and his wife had shared an international tribute when they became the first Canadians to receive the Eleanor Roosevelt Humanities Award, with James Roosevelt, eldest son of Franklin D. and Eleanor Roosevelt, making the presentation.

As Irving reached his seventieth birthday there was a lineup of those who wished to pay him tribute. The University of Moncton awarded him an honorary doctorate of science degree, his second honorary degree, the first an honorary doctorate of laws from the University of New Brunswick in 1954. He became an honorary member of the Bricklayers, Masons and Plasterers' Union of America and was presented with a union card at the union's Atlantic Trowel Trade Fair in Saint John. He also won the title of "champion amateur bricklayer" in a competition that union organizer Albert Vincent said was "not fixed — and I'll swear to that on a stack of Bibles." Fixed or not, Irving enjoyed it and returned for several years to successfully defend his title — with Vincent always there at his side as an impartial judge. From the Canadian Forestry Association, the Canadian Trade and Industry Council, from organizations in St. Stephen, Saint John, Bouctouche, and the Miramichi came more honours. But his most publicized honour may well have come one night in 1980 when he was inducted into the new Canadian Business Hall of Fame. When he was first approached about it, he was dubious, made inquiries, then agreed. It turned out to be one of the great events of his career. The whole Irving clan was there, and the ballroom of Toronto's Royal York Hotel was packed by a black-tie audience of 900.

His career was recalled, his achievements praised. In speaking, he added a touch of whimsy that brought the laugh of the evening.

He told of the times he had been "summoned back" for such occasions: "Invariably, someone recites the nice things I am alleged to have done — and very kindly omits all the terrible things I used to be accused of doing. I must confess I like it much better this way, and if I had realized what a fine fellow I would become simply by growing old I might well have done it much sooner."

Looking tanned and healthy, he blinked into the TV lights and found a minute for everyone who wanted to shake his hand. When one Saskatchewan youth came up Irving recalled names from that summer, nearly sixty years earlier, when he had stooked grain in that province. Asked for advice for the young, he said, "You have to apply yourself. You have to be interested in what you do." Was he really retired? "Do you ever retire? I'll answer that question some other time."

CHAPTER THIRTY-FOUR

&

The Boys
Take Charge

"The dogs bark. The caravan goes on."
– *ARTHUR IRVING, BRUSHING ASIDE THE COMMENTS OF CRITICS.*

THE HONOURS THAT WERE SHOWERED ON IRVING LATE IN life didn't change the man, even if he found much of it embarrassing — an embarrassment he would often gloss over with a bit of self-deprecating humour in his acceptance speeches.

Little else changed either.

The huge business and industrial structure he had built went on, run much as he had run it, according to its varied and versatile strengths, only now the sons were in charge, putting into practice the lessons they had taken half a lifetime to learn. Like their father, they were hands-on managers. From the moment their father left there was speculation as to which of the three would emerge as boss. None did so far as the public could see. They worked as a triumvirate, a troika. Each had his own area of command: broadly, with numerous additions, Jim had the whole forestry complex and the shipyard; Arthur, the oil business; Jack, properties, hardware, Ocean Steel, and, with Arthur, Irving Oil. But each knew what else was going on. They met together over spartan lunches. They consulted regularly. Jim once told someone what he hoped to do about a certain thing; next time they met he said it wasn't going to happen: "I was outvoted 2-1."

All three were propelled by and imbued with a deep love and respect for their father, and they dedicated themselves to the continuation and growth of what he'd built. It was as simple as that. There is a story that when he delivered Jim as a baby a doctor said, "There'll never be another K.C." None of the three *was* another K.C., but together they made a formidable team. They brushed off the rain of comments that fell on what they did: "The dogs bark," Arthur would say. "The caravan goes on." But their silence lent itself to conjecture. People would say they *knew* Jim was the boss, the ablest. People would say Arthur was. People would say there was a lot more to Jack — "the nice guy of the family" — than met the eye.

They all had hot tempers. Jim, chunky, solid, loved the forests, was apt to fire people. Supposedly, he once saw several men sitting around the shipyard office and fired them for doing nothing, only to be told they were visitors. Another story tells of him flying low over logging operations, seeing an idle man below and bellowing at him through a loudhailer to get to work, only to find out later that he was a farmer. "When Jim isn't sleeping," said Arthur, "he's working. It's his hobby." But others said he was a skilled fisherman. When he discussed business, he paced the floor, anxious to get onto something else.

Arthur was thin and mercurial, the most abrasive against government and the most talkative. His father once observed, "Arthur, you are more fluent than I am, and you think faster." His father, someone said, would never use a cannon to kill a grasshopper. Arthur did, and loved it. But he could also be devastatingly charming, a supersalesman. He liked to hunt, was lured into Ducks Unlimited, and became its Canadian president. He belonged to an exclusive hunting club in Austria.

Jack was the reader in the family, the one most inclined to open up discussions of public affairs, quiet-voiced, thoughtful of others. He gets worked up over the hungry and unemployed. A friend said his mother felt he was the one who should not go into the family business, but he went, and he enjoyed it. He skied on snow and water, played tennis. He, like his brothers, could chew people out. But Ed Larracey, publisher for years of the Moncton newspapers, said he could look the world over and not find a better boss.

All three long led surprisingly unpretentious lives. As their father did, they had their home numbers in the phone book. They were strikingly different to meet. Their common denominator was work; they were often away, often late — but then, so was their father.

Under the sons, the empire kept growing, and if anything its growth has been accelerated. That was their responsibility and if they got guidance from their father it was not something anyone talked about. When he spoke at company meetings he would stress that he was doing so as a shareholder. Certainly, for years K.C. *was* often around. He was entitled to spend six months less a day each year in Canada, and he kept a calendar ticked off to ensure that he stayed within those boundaries. He kept busy. But still he insisted the boys were running the businesses, and running them well.

"When I quit, I quit," he maintained. "I've never had anything to do since with running the companies, except at shareholders' meetings." Some observers doubted that he could relinquish control, but there was no question that the sons did much more than reign over day-to-day operations. They also broadened their scope.

Once, at a Ducks Unlimited meeting in the United States, Arthur took time out to walk a beach, and he exulted that he hadn't had to bother with business for two days. It was exceptional. When someone asked how he and his brothers stood the office pace, the steady, hectic pounding, he quoted the late American president Harry Truman: "What did he say? 'If you can't stand the heat, get out of the kitchen.' We like the kitchen."

❧

In the early 1970s, Jim Irving wanted an airstrip nearly a mile long built on a cut-over area of New Brunswick's northern woods, and he gave Fred Pelletier a month to do it. That leathery jack-of-all-trades, that "bull of the woods," the typical Irving practical man, had access over a dirt road, and to company men, equipment, and know-how. He brought in tractors, bulldozers, and other heavy gear, as well as gravel, and he and his crew worked 14 to 16 hours a day. Finally, Jim Irving flew overhead in a Cessna and radioed down: "Can I land?"

"Give me half an hour," Pelletier said, "to roll out some big rocks." Then he was ready.

Roughly a decade later a supertanker arrived in Saint John, her belly full of crude oil. A tug inched her towards Canaport, words flowing between ship and monobuoy. An order went out — just too late — and that great vessel bunted, grazed the floating dock, damaging it, and broke the underwater pipeline that carried oil ashore.

All hell broke loose. Arthur Irving, head of Irving Oil, was notified immediately, and a remarkable mix of facilities, talents, companies, manpower, experience, and expertise went into action. Within hours the top expert in North America was on his way by air from Texas to repair the broken pipeline, a barge was on its way from the Irvings' Steel and Engine plant in Liverpool, N.S., to help him do it, ships' schedules were altered to make sure the oil kept moving, men went to work to fix the damaged monobuoy, and legal action was started to try — unsuccessfully — to "arrest" the offending supertanker. It took weeks to get Canaport back into full operation. More supertankers arrived until there were four of them anchored off Saint John, with a third-of-a-billion dollars' worth of crude aboard. Some of it was piped ashore through auxiliary lines. Much was offloaded to smaller ships and brought in. The refinery kept going without a hitch. And someone remembered a weekend when all three Irving sons were on hand, working.

"You work under constant pressure," one employee said, "but no matter how hard you work you know they work harder." Said another: "They want things yesterday. There is always a rush." Outsiders sometimes called it crisis management, reflected in a pell-mell, consuming drive. But it worked. To keep it growing, the sons took on a hardwood mill that made corrugated cardboard in Charlotte County's Lake Utopia; they got it, critics said, for a song, but they also poured in millions to repair, update, and expand it. They built more imposing service stations. They linked some of them to convenience stores selling food and many other things. Their service station restaurants became popular, attracting truckers, tourists, and hometown residents looking for a family-style meal at a low price.

They bought out Standard Oil of California and became sole owners of Irving Oil. They took on the greatest single challenge in company history in 1983 when they got the prime contract to build six frigates for the Royal Canadian Navy — three to be built in Saint John and three, under direction of their shipyard as project manager, in the MIL shipyard in Quebec. Four years later they were awarded the contract for six additional frigates, all to be constructed in Saint John. Total cost of the overall contract was $6.2 billion, but it would run much higher when navy changes and additions were included. This in itself indicated how far the shipyard had come since K.C. Irving took it over.

They got into the food-processing business in Prince Edward Island; they bought a small trucking company, expanded it into a group called Midland with five subsidiary companies doing business throughout eastern Canada; they expanded the drydock, the oil refinery, the forestry operations. They ran a shipping line: perhaps half the shipping coming into Saint John's major harbour was doing Irving business. They bought the MacMillan-Rothesay newsprint mill. Jim Irving said he thought it was a good thing to have it in New Brunswick hands. When VIA rail closed down many of its services they beefed up their SMT line and went after the business. They even got into selling real estate, commercial and car insurance.

They did business around the world, constructing buildings in the United States; their tankers took oil to Turkey, New Zealand, Indonesia. They once shipped a load of lumber to a Middle East port, where it lay on the dock for a long time because the word came back that nothing was going to happen until a certain sum was paid to a certain man. The Irvings said it was a bribe, and they didn't pay bribes. Another attempt was made to convince them that on this occasion, in this country, they were going to have to grease some palms. They stood firm and finally they got their money.

Important changes would come in the 1970s when the Irvings assumed full control of the pulp mill by buying out their partners. The explanation given by Darwin E. Smith, chairman of the board and chief executive officer of Kimberly-Clark, was that his company's needs had changed, principally because of an increasing use of secondary fibres in the United States. The partnership ended without disrupting the business relationship. Kimberly-Clark remained a major buyer of Irving pulp. Then, in late 1987, thirty years after Irving had made his first deal with Kimberly-Clark, the Irvings announced they were buying the plant and henceforth it would be operated by the Irving Tissue Company.

Three years later the next chapter in the tissue mill story was completed with the opening of a $30-million conversion plant in Dieppe's Industrial Park on the outskirts of Moncton. Canada's trade deal with the United States — the very type of agreement that had been abandoned in Canada's federal election of 1911, a move lamented all his life by K.C. Irving — had been a major factor in the decision to proceed with the huge modernization and expansion program. An investment estimated at close to $130 million had gone into upgrading the Saint John plant and building a new state-of-the-art facility in Dieppe.

Robert Irving, one of Jim Irving's sons and now a vice-president and general manager of Irving Tissue, presided at the opening ceremonies in Dieppe. He told his audience that: "It was always a dream of my grandfather's to be able to complete the vertical integration concept in his forestry operations." Completion of the Moncton plant, which produced bathroom and facial tissues, paper towels, and napkins — all under the Majesta label — had achieved that tree-to-tissue objective.

Robert Irving's grandfather had run the business much as K.C.'s father ran the general store in Bouctouche — simply, personally, in immense detail. The sons and grandsons ran it with the same penchant for secrecy. A veteran Toronto financial writer compared them to the Eaton store family in their close-mouthed, private operations, but the Irvings, he said, were more efficient. They liked executives who worked long and hard and came in on Saturday mornings; others were called Monday-to-Friday boys, and didn't get very far. Senior men found it unwise to go to them with a problem and no suggested solution.

The Irvings made the big decisions. They argued for days, weeks, sporadically, about minor details such as the design of a truck's exterior decorations. "Yet I can get a decision in minutes that would take days or weeks in another company," said one executive. Another manager with a major international company said the three were gods around their head office buildings. They didn't like giving titles to senior people, but those people found it worked wonders when they could say "I work for (or with) Jim or

Art or Jack." They didn't like elaborate structures or committees or long memos. They liked to work directly with men in the field. Everything was informal, verbal rather than written. The loose corporate structure, identifiable but not entirely definable, was less complex than any setup of comparable size. They were aware of how different they were. But why change anything that is successful? Providing for family generations, they thought ahead thirty years. Employees got little authority until they earned the Irvings' respect. "Then your word was as good as the day is long," said a business consultant who once worked for them. "You have to know where the boundaries are. You have to be aggressive, but not too aggressive. They test an individual to a tremendous extent, but it's a real education to work for them."

The sons abided to a large extent by a maxim of their father's: "If you get kicked by a mule, it's because you got too close." As time went on they used soothing advertisements in the media to burnish and improve their image: "We're with you all the way." They amazed Saint John by paying their bills a lot faster than in the past.

Their ties with government, and its industrial progeny, were a blend, sometimes smooth, sometimes rancid. Premier Hatfield said they got along on reasonable terms with his administration 99 per cent of the time. Jim Irving did blow up — and so did others — when the government first proposed a radical reorganization of woodlands. But the proposals were altered to put management control, under government supervision, in the hands of major private companies, each responsible for reforestation, for seeing that smaller ones got adequate supplies, and the Irvings accepted a system that took some of their tracts away but replaced them with others.

They looked askance when the government built its first nuclear power plant, when costs tripled and there were cabinet boasts of how much oil it would replace. "New Brunswick," said Arthur, "can't be expected to light the streets of New York." They watched government-backed American Malcolm Bricklin invade Saint John to build cars. They said they never met the flamboyant Bricklin himself, but that his father asked if they'd be interested in participating. Jim Irving said no: "Someone is going to get taken." It was the taxpayer who was taken, for millions. But before the scheme went broke amid rumours of an Irving takeover, Arthur met Bricklin's mother — "a nice lady" — and arranged through her to buy three Bricklin cars. Richard Hatfield found it amusing that at a time when the *Telegraph-Journal* was bewailing what the firm was costing the province, the Irvings were using their three gull-winged sports cars, with "Irving Girls," to promote their own products.

In 1975 the Irvings tangled with Ottawa for an odd reason. They gave their pulp mill workers a 23.8 per cent raise and suddenly found themselves in an unprecedented and uncomfortable position. To fight inflation, Ottawa brought in wage and price controls, and ordered the Irvings to roll back their increase to 14 per cent. Jim Irving appealed. The order was renewed with a $125,000 fine added. It was a stormy time, with a union march on Prime Minister Trudeau's hotel when he visited, and strangely it had arrayed leftists on the Irving side. The Canadian Labour Congress called the government action vindictive, and former New Democratic Party leader Tommy Douglas said it was "tainted with the colour of vengeance."

That same year, chairman Robert Bryce, long a lofty figure among Ottawa's mandarins, came to Saint John to urge the Irvings to co-operate with his Royal Commission on Corporate Concentration. He got a cold welcome from all three. Bluntly, they told him they would have nothing to do with it, that what they did was their own business. They were the only one of fifty companies that said so.

They refused even to comment on factual errors in a forty-eight-page study of "The Irving Group" issued with the commission's 1978 report. Yet it was a study that had numerous complimentary things to say about them, and it made two revealing statements, one about their financial worth, another that threw light on charges that they were an overpowering factor in the regional economy:

1. The group's total size is almost certainly higher than almost all previous statements have made it, and the more accurate picture could well place it in the ranks of the billion-dollar Canadian companies.

2. The main arms of the Irving companies do not operate with overriding market power . . . [Their] aggregate position

poses a facile image of a giant in a region of low growth and industrial pygmies, and to some extent this image is true. But it ignores the more important issue that in the main industrial areas where the Irvings operate, there is substantial competition to the Irving companies. What is particularly striking is that invariably that competition comes from a corporation based outside the Maritime region.

The study lauded K.C. Irving for his skills in building "one of the major industrial enterprises in the country." It called both his versatility and his capacity for detail amazing, his command masterful.

"For years now," it said, "the Irvings have been the butt of criticism, jokes and just plain mischief." But they also got "genuine admiration and respect" and they had a "tremendous capacity to learn new techniques, adopt new ways of doing things in a very short period of time. They kept their word and never reneged on a contract." But the study wondered whether "the time may well have arrived for a basic reassessment of their approach to corporate secrecy and disclosure, if only for the reason that it is better to anticipate voluntarily a situation than to have to submit unwillingly" to potential government action.

One staff member who worked on the study for the commission and later became a business consultant said he went into the inquiry with "fashionable prejudices" against business, and thinking the Irvings were monsters. He came out with his prejudices "quite punctured."

CHAPTER THIRTY-FIVE

&

Inside the Maze

*"If he was a Roman Catholic, they'd make him
a saint."*
— LONGTIME PULP MILL EMPLOYEE JIMMER MCMULLIN'S
OPINION OF K.C. IRVING.

THE CORPORATE STRUCTURE OF THE GROUP OF COM-
panies K.C. Irving built was so complex that Leigh Stevenson kidded Irving that some day the family would buy a
company and find it already owned it, so complex that one of the
sons asked one of the companies about money owing and was told
that it was going, as arranged, to yet another company the son
apparently couldn't remember.

The royal commission study published a chart of them three
pages long with a bewildering sea of names: Grand River Soft-
woods, Grand Lake Timber Ltd., Victoria Forest Products Ltd.,
Boston Brook Enterprises, Harbor Developments Ltd., Brunswick
Motors Ltd., Tidal Chemicals Ltd., Brunswick Book (Wholesale)
Ltd., Avalon Oil Co. Ltd., Fredericton Fuels Ltd., Dartmouth
Fuels Ltd. . . . It included J.J. Snook Ltd., a hardware firm. "Where
else," mused someone, "would you find a J.J. Snook Ltd.?"

Many were small companies taken over in the movements into
propane gas, publishing, and forestry, and kept intact in keeping
with the Irving credo that you could best see how a firm was per-
forming by letting it stand on its own feet. Subsidiaries themselves,

companies such as the drydock, Thorne's Hardware, SMT, and
Atlantic Speedy Propane, had subsidiaries of their own. Many were
owned in varying degree by different elements of the structure. Some
forty alone fell under Irving Oil. Some were no longer active, but
their incorporated status might serve some purpose, so they were
kept there. Some were incorporated federally, some provincially. It
was, said an accountant, a maze he finally fled.

The three core managerial operations were J.D. Irving Ltd.,
Irving Oil Ltd., and K.C. Irving Ltd., each with tributaries feed-
ing into them. In addition, there were holding companies to
which, directly or indirectly, the whole list was connected. The
commission mentioned some of them. It didn't get them all.

The holding companies existed in Bermuda and the Bahamas.
Since K.C. Irving departed they stood at the top of the list, in ulti-
mate possession. There were eleven of them — Irving California
Co. Ltd., Forest Mere Investments Ltd., FMR Co. Ltd., FMO Co.
Ltd., FMW Co. Ltd., FMN Co. Ltd., Fair Isle Investments Co.
Ltd., FMK Co. Ltd., FMX SA, Bayswater Co. Ltd., and FMK
Co. Ltd. But only K.C. Irving and his family knew the whole
structure, and they didn't talk about it.

The Irving companies did a great deal of business with one
another, but where their boundaries met they competed, battling
one another. Some even competed in the marketplace. "Don't let
that rascal get the better of you," one Irving told an executive. The
rascal was an executive of another Irving company.

Given all this, Jack Lamport, a British engineer executive with
Irving Equipment, said he had been amazed at the way they could
work in harmony when the chips were down. Then the loyalty came
out, the sense of family K.C. Irving built into the structure he put
together. Some say the loyalty was typically that of men who never
left the Maritimes, never knew anything else. But you could find it at
its strongest among men like Lamport who came in from elsewhere.

These are some, but far from all, of the parts of the structure
they served, and these are some of the people who made it work,
as seen by a writer a decade after K.C. Irving's sons took over:

❧

The pulp mill stands like some ungainly fortress on its ungainly
site. No one would build it now where it and its antecedents have

stood for decades, in the middle of a city, overlooking a major tourist attraction, on a knuckle of protruding rock so confining that its repeated expansions verge on the astonishing. But it is there and for a generation and more it has fomented some of the most intemperate episodes in the whole Irving story.

It was the second home of Jimmer McMullin, who at seventy-five said he could run up eight flights of stairs and hoped he could go on forever. He loved the place. He had been content there for some sixty years. He arrived early every day, but he didn't call it work. "Work?" he said. "This isn't work." One Christmas morning a colleague picked up Mrs. McMullin to go to Mass, and asked where Jimmer was. "Where else?" she sighed.

It was McMullin who said of K.C. Irving that "if he was a Roman Catholic, they'd make him a saint." McMullin was a man with eight years of formal education who read voraciously, and took offence when asked if he could run the mill. "Run it?" he said: "I did run it for years at night." This bowlegged, hard-hatted man was not retired at sixty-five but was put in charge of incoming chemicals. He studied the chemicals, and became their master. Nor was he alone in this. The Irvings have kept men working into their eighties, then kept paying them when they left.

Through it all, too, the mill has been the focus of varied struggles — over its unlovely smell, over what its wastes do to the river, over what it paid the city for water. Part of its problem was that it did what all chemical pulp mills do. With its multiple, billowing clouds of steam, it did stink. It emitted white substances that foamed and flecked the waters below, descended upon cars and homes. It had, for these reasons, stirred long controversy.

One city councillor suggested it become a shoe factory. One citizen said he and many others had fled to the suburbs to escape "the unholy emissions." In the seventies, when concern for the environment grew rancorous, there were court cases, fines, outcries about the Irvings at public meetings, and government reactions. Ottawa and Fredericton both took steps to have pulp mills and other offenders clean up their acts. The Irvings, said one high provincial official, were by no means the worst of the lot; another said they were "leaps and bounds" ahead of some. But the mill was ordered to control its stench and emissions. Ottawa wanted both air and water cleansed together. Fredericton said it was asking too much, so the mill worked first on the water, then on the smell.

They had never, Irving executives said, viewed pollution in the cavalier way their critics said. In the early seventies they spent millions on equipment that was supposed to help, but didn't help enough. They abandoned their sulphite process, throwing up to 200 out of work. But they said they could not meet rising costs and government standards at the same time. They did more. By 1985 they had spent $30 million to fight pollution. Company officials said the adjacent river had been put in reasonable condition and hoped that the stench would be largely controlled. But the pollution, the criticism, and the expenditure of more millions of dollars continued.

Through it all, the mill rumbled on, a place of ungodly noise so loud that men wore ear protectors. But the days were long gone when most of the work was done manually. Now men sat at long control boards, surrounded by panels of lights and by TV monitors, pushing buttons. When the hard, white pulp emerged from the digesters, the bleachers, the rollers, the chemicals, the liquor, the millions of gallons of water, it was bundled automatically and taken away for markets in many lands.

The mill's appetite was prodigious. It gathered in the equivalent of 2,000 cords of softwood daily, fed by a steady lineup of trucks and a large, cumbersome box-like barge that brought chips downriver. Fed by men like Albert O'Donnell who drove in from the Irving sawmill at Pennfield with massive loads of chips, three times, 480 kilometres a day. It had a woodroom that sucked in logs from the river and turned them, too, into chips, preparing them no longer by water and chemicals that add to pollution, but by shuddering, physical machines.

❧

Late August, 1980. The 38,000-deadweight-ton tanker *Irving Arctic* was at Rea Point, Melville Island, on a historic voyage. Strengthened for ice conditions, she had penetrated farther into the High Arctic's Northwest Passage than any Canadian Coast commercial vessel had ever penetrated before. Behind the Canadian Coast Guard icebreaker *Pierre Radisson*, she had come through some 320 kilometres of ice packs, bearing 100,000 barrels of petroleum products for Panarctic Oil's exploration station. With them all the way had come a tug, the *Irving Birch*.

Arctic's Captain Ken Milburn had been there before. He flew up to see the lay of the land and sea, found a bay choked with ice seven feet thick, with no mooring facilities, no place to tie a line to. Now, in late summer, the ice has vanished, and cameramen for the National Film Board and *Time-Life* in New York were disappointed.

But as the ship emptied her holds — it took thirty-three hours — Milburn was worried. He had run the *Arctic*'s bow against an underwater embankment, kept her engines running to hold her there, using the rudder to keep her perpendicular. He knew the channel was narrow, that there were shoals on both sides of her green and white flanks, and that they could easily trap her. If a stiff wind came up, he'd need help to get her out.

A stiff wind did come up, whipping in at thirty knots, and as the last of the oil disappeared he called for help. He had it with him. The tug *Irving Birch*, his companion all the way from Saint John, took hold and with difficulty dragged the *Arctic* out of there. "I wouldn't have come without that tug," Milburn says. "We couldn't have got out without her."

In July 1981, a year after the *Irving Arctic*'s feat, three Irving tugs led by the 9,000-horsepower, British-built *Irving Cedar* pushed into the Arctic. They were on a unique mission. In 1979 the Bechtel Corporation, acting as general contractor for Canadian Pacific's Cominco, asked the Irvings' Atlantic Towing Ltd. if it could be done. At first Atlantic Towing thought it was a crazy idea, but it bid and, against sixteen rivals, got the job.

The job was to haul a $40-million ore-processing plant some 3,200 kilometres to Little Cornwallis Island, 112 kilometres from the magnetic North Pole. As the mission left Trois Rivières, Que., Bechtel's project manager said it might be the first of many such ventures. En route, the plant — 152 metres by 31, 18.3 metres high — was borne on a barge, and another government icebreaker preceded the three tugs, towing it through the ice. When it got to its destination — in a lagoon, to be drained — Cominco sank both barge and plant into their foundation, and scores of men went to work to concentrate base metals. The voyage cost some $500,000 but it was easier and cheaper than building the plant on the site.

In the half-century since K.C. Irving quarrelled with CNR, their shipping had come a long way. Now it plied the oceans of the world. It had the largest tanker fleet in the country. In place of the ragtag cluster of vessels that did business after the Second World War, it had modern tankers, modern tugs.

The *Irving Arctic* was typical in her ownership. J.D. Irving Ltd. holds thirty-four of sixty-four shares; the rest belonged to five other Irving companies. She was built at the Irvings' shipyard and was paying for herself out of profits she earned.

The hub of their shipping was the Kent Line, agent for the Irvings and for others, its office near the drydock. The Kent fleet included large tankers such as the *Irving Arctic*, *Irving Eskimo*, *Irving Nordic*, *Irving Wood*, *Ours Polaire*, *Aimé Gaudreau*, *Irving Ocean*, *Irving Canada*, and other, smaller, coastal ships. Mainly they carried oil, but sometimes they were chartered out for other bulk cargoes: gypsum, grain, zinc concentrates. On a typical day there were Irving ships due at Gibraltar en route to Genoa, Italy, to await orders, en route to France or to Turkey, just leaving Boston for Saint John, sailing to Newfoundland, leaving there for Halifax, in dock for repairs or inspection. Most of them were strengthened for travel through ice and could go up the St. Lawrence as far as Montreal the year around.

Just up the street from the Kent Line office is the headquarters of Atlantic Towing Ltd., first a marine division of J.D. Irving Ltd., but in 1961 it developed a status of its own. Its manager was Rio St. Amand, a dark, thin, college-educated man who had worked on the log drives, in the Irving forestry operations, and in the Golden Ball. Not a seaman, he had charge of a large fleet of tugs, barges, scows, and dredging equipment. In the early years K.C. Irving was in practically every day, asking, "What's going on? What are your tugs doing? How much wood are you hauling down the river?" At night Irving would call and ask what *did* go on that day.

St. Amand professed to like the work pace, the quick Irving decisions: "You want to spend $100,000? You press a button and ask them a question, you get an answer and away you go." At first, he said, the Irvings had small tugs that could look after river work, but demand kept growing for more and more powerful ones. Now his company did the tug work in Saint John's harbour, had a barge at work in the Gulf of Mexico, and hauled loads to Montreal, Vancouver, and Boston.

He broke off to phone one of his captains, saying, "You are sailing tomorrow afternoon or Saturday morning. You know where you're going," discussed fuel. He groped for a date in answer to a question, laughing, "Time flies when you are having fun."

❧

One evening Jack Lamport of Irving Equipment got a phone call from Saint John's city hall. As projects manager, he had never had a call like this. Fire was destroying a church, and there were fears that the steeple would come thundering down and hurt someone. Lamport was asked if he could do anything about it. He called the duty dispatcher and ordered equipment. He was on the scene when it arrived and he supervised as it butted and gnawed like some prehistoric monster until that steeple came down without hurting anyone at all.

Irving Equipment, a subsidiary of J.D. Irving Ltd., ran like some iron thread through much of what K.C. Irving built. Its headquarters occupied a former airplane hangar that was bought, taken apart, and reassembled on a forested tract of several hundred hectares the Irvings own beside Saint John's South Bay. It was the home and hearth of bulldozers, cranes running up to 300 tons, trucks, transporters with as many as eighteen wheels, diesel engines, trailers, loaders, scrapers, and air compressors. It rented them, with operators, for all sorts of work. Its functions went back a long way, K.C. Irving remembered, but it was when he was building his refinery that it bloomed from two shacks into its present form.

Running Irving Equipment was Roger N. Cyr. With two college degrees, he had more formal education than many key Irving men, and he joked that perhaps he could demonstrate that this was not a handicap. On the phone he might, say, plug the excellence of a massive machine called a Supersucker, which could do in a short time what six men could do in six weeks. He got the first of them second-hand from a British Columbia company having problems in the lumber woods, and he was impressed enough to buy a second. They cost hundreds of thousands of dollars, and he was urging subordinates to tell pulp and paper companies and others that they could be useful in sucking up, vacuuming anything from bricks to oil spills.

Off the phone, Cyr was trying to cope with the ever-rising cost of new things by repairing and rebuilding. He pointed to a sixty-five-ton crane that cost new ten times what it did in 1965; it was rebuilt for much less. He had offices and equipment in four other Maritime cities, and was moving into Newfoundland. One example of many complex jobs: Irving Equipment handled and took in much of the heavy apparatus for New Brunswick's Lepreau nuclear power station, but the supreme test came when it had to put in place, delicately, a 270-ton steam generator that just snugged into that crucial element, the callandria.

He introduced Lamport, his right-hand man, who first came into contact with the Irvings when Jim went to Britain for annual sales of surplus army equipment. Lamport was there as a Royal Engineers major. In 1958, when he was invited to join the firm, he accepted and arrived in Saint John just in time for the refinery construction. The Irvings called him "the major." Jim Irving gave Lamport's name to a giant, low-slung vehicle for heavy loads, which Lamport bought in Germany. Now it was The Lamporter. He had directed equipment in fighting fires, and cleared up problems involving an Irving dredge used on Vietnam's Mekong River — and got blown out of bed when wartime guerrillas blew up a dump in Saigon. For the major, it was just part of the job.

❧

A majestic tree towered amid a stand of spruce in the forests of northern New Brunswick on the old New Brunswick Railway lands. It was bright with numerous ribbons because it was a super tree and the Irvings were looking for them; one wasn't marked well enough and lumberjacks cut it down. J.D. Irving Ltd., "the tree growing company," put out posters offering $100 rewards for finding them, had men out winter and summer looking, told in detail how to identify them by crown, branch, and trunk. The posters: "They are very scarce and valuable for beginning new seedlings from their cones and branches. If you find a jack pine, tamarack (larch), white, red, or black spruce that's at least 10 per cent taller and larger in diameter than all the trees in the stand and meets the above descriptions, first call your Irving district office or the Sussex Reforestation office."

From these super trees, branch tips or scions were collected, taken south to the Sussex nursery, and grafted to young seedlings of the same species. Then the seedlings were planted in an "orchard" to begin a process to produce trees 15 per cent better in quality and quantity.

Irving planes flew overhead, six of them piloted by men who called themselves drivers because they flew so low. They were dropping fertilizer into the ocean of trees. Not long ago they were spraying to curb the budworm. Soon they would spray with herbicides to slay the bushes and infant hardwoods that fight tiny, planted softwoods on soil that has been cleared and crushed by huge machines to make room for reforesting.

It was these programs that made the Irvings a target of those who said the chemicals could well be a menace to human health, that thirty years of it had left the budworm as spry as ever, that spraying should be stopped. In response the Irvings said it couldn't be stopped without decimation of the forests.

For Dr. Bruce Zobel, a U.S. geneticist hired by the Irvings, the longer-range implications were important. Spraying, he said, at least allowed a forest to survive the budworm when an epidemic raged. "There would," he adds, "be no problem if they'd let us use DDT," but DDT is out. To Zobel, the only solution would be a biological agent that would destroy the budworm from within in what he said "has to be the insect headquarters of the world."

On one of K.C. Irving's visits to the site, he expressed concern over yet another insect, the tip-moth. He examined small trees and saw evidence of the insidious work of the insect, which ate the top and made them grow awry. Someone said he was the first to spot this problem. It is scant consolation. The tip-moth, in his view, could be an even worse enemy than the budworm.

He wore a white shirt, the sleeves rolled up, a tie, a straw hat. He drove a van down some of the 960 kilometres of straight, dirt roads, and when son Jim offered to drive he said no, he wanted to get used to the roads again, to stop where he liked. He stopped numerous times, took out a tape measure and gauged annual growth of the trees he planted, now over the 200-million mark. He said the signs that marked each year's reforestation seemed to get fewer every year; one problem is that bears ravaged them. He examined new plantings, old ones.

Irving liked tourists to visit, welcomed their comments and listened intently when they had something new to offer. He also reminisced. At the wheel of the van, he recalled Barney Flieger scoffing when he started planting trees. He recalled the battle he had had with one more engineer who wanted to build roads as they had always been built in the horse-days, and he remembered his own insistence that they be straight, to reduce accidents and to take advantage of tractors. He asked how many accidents there were the first winter they used tractors. Six, Jim said. "I thought," said his father, "there were seven."

He drove on and on, and he asked Jim to call the family lodge and tell the cook they'd be back at 8 p.m. They got back to the lodge after ten, and the cook, knowing from experience, had a chicken dinner ready.

The forest that surrounds the lodge is part of the 1.8-million or so hectares of woodlands the Irvings either own or use with licences for crown lands, an area roughly three times the size of Prince Edward Island. In 1975 Fredericton reported that five Irving companies were working 3,939 square kilometres or 17.4 per cent of its crown lands. In the late seventies the U.S. government made a survey to determine how much land was owned by foreigners. It found that 17 per cent of it, the largest state total, was in Maine, and that the Irvings held most of that: 202,350 hectares. In Ontario's Algonquin Park, for their Canada Veneers plant and a sawmill in Pembroke, they had rights to operate on roughly 61,000 hectares. In Quebec, they had less land of their own. Their aim: to produce twice as much wood in half the time nature would take if left alone.

Through it all the trees grew on, in the long patience of hills.

ಶ

The forests produced Irving logs, which were cut in modern Irving sawmills into Irving lumber. The lumber was piled, stamped with their name, then taken away to supply markets in many lands; foreign orders were the major reason the Irvings became the No. 1 producers in the Atlantic provinces, the major reason they maintained an aggressive sales force headquartered in Saint John.

To sell some of the lumber and other products, K.C. Irving set up Kent Building Supplies. He also used the lumber to make buildings for his own enterprises, and in the sixties the process led to one more company: Kent Homes Ltd., builders of houses and other structures, presided over by Jim Irving and active in the Atlantic provinces and around the world. On the Bouctouche property where he grew up, beside the cemetery where his parents lie — and which he kept up — he erected a plant for the purpose. It replaced the premises where he had made wartime landing barges, and it led to communal improvements, to increased population, to men coming home from the United States and elsewhere to work.

୬

Hans Klohn stood beside an enormous steel triangle, which would shortly be lifted aboard an elongated truck and taken away to Dartmouth, N.S. This roof truss was forty-three metres long.

This was one of the things Ocean Steel Construction Ltd. (OSCO) did, and Klohn was its president, a man whose talents influenced Irving to get into the business. Beside a final bend in the St. John River, he worked in one of several worn wooden buildings dating back to the war. Next to them was a cavernous fabrication plant, a place bruised with noise, and from its concrete walls protruded the ribs that were an emblem of what Klohn did.

Hans Klohn said of K.C. Irving and his sons — Jack was his boss — that "they give you all you can handle and more and they expect you to do it. They get involved if it's not done right." OSCO was started, Klohn said, from scratch with capital borrowed and repaid out of profits. It started in a shack. Then he got the frame of a surplus army building and re-erected it, got equipment in the same way. At first he did work for other Irving companies, then outgrew that market.

OSCO bought steel in Ontario and the United States, stored it in long sheets in a yard, and, as it was needed, electrical cranes picked it up and moved it inside. Computerized equipment cut it, put holes in it with hydraulic machines that sliced it with ease. Other equipment welded stainless steel, bent and set reinforcing steel. Trucks and railcars took the products away for the building of things. The process made the company the largest of its kind in Atlantic Canada, erecting its steel products from Boston to Labrador.

Klohn presided over two other Irving companies. One, Strescon Ltd., incorporated in 1963 and first sheltered in a wartime building, expanded three times into new structures. It now has plants in both Saint John and Halifax, making modern versions of the wall panels that started Irving in the business, but it does numerous other things. Branching out from OSCO when it took advantage of a pre-stressed concrete process developed in Europe, it had three divisions: a pre-cast, pre-stressed concrete plant, a ready-mix concrete plant, and a third for making pipes. It built walls, marine structures such as wharves, parking garages, and bridges. Marque Construction, the third construction firm that came under the direction of Jack Irving and Klohn, did most of its work for the Irvings.

The father of four children, Klohn has an easy grin and an open face, but he can be an aggressive man. His drive made him an Irving favourite. Indeed, he laughed, his wife watched him wipe up crumbs from their table and said he was getting more like the ever-neat K.C. Irving every day. He was like him in another way too. "You just keep growing," he said. "You have to be aggressive. Stand still and you're out."

❧

Universal Sales Ltd. dated back to the early years, when K.C. Irving started putting together an interlocking, mutually sustaining corporate structure. Over the years it did many things. It started out selling cars, acting as an agent for Massey-Harris farm equipment and Ford trucks. It built the early Irving buses. It got into building and repairing trucks and trailers. In the war years it rebuilt engines, made bus and truck bodies, even wooden knees for landing barges. Later it made the first trucks for what eventually became Scot Truck and got into the rebuilding of diesel engines and fuel systems. Now it overhauled the cars Irving firms owned, repaired trucks and vans in Saint John and Dieppe, N.B. In the seventies it went into the repair of electric motors, making peat moss spreaders for the reforestation program, stocking and selling electric motors and mechanical power transmission components. At times, they were busy with work for other Irving companies. Then the pendulum swung, the economy changed; repair work was available from outside firms and they went hard after it.

❧

Like Universal Sales, Commercial Equipment dated back to the early days. When Don Carson joined it in 1951 it was still doing what it had been doing for two decades: providing and distributing automotive gear. A high-school graduate, a wartime army captain, then a car dealer, Carson was hired by K.C. as manager and told to branch out into industrial equipment too. On this double front, Commercial Equipment moved its headquarters from a tired old building in Saint John to modern space, and continued to grow. Stores were opened in cities throughout the Atlantic provinces and Quebec.

. The company became what Carson believed was the largest welding products distributor east of Montreal, probably the largest industrial rubber distributor too. It sold to pulp and paper companies, power stations, a sugar refinery, and to Irving firms, "but I never want to hear that they have to do business with us. We have to earn it, and they are twice as demanding as our other customers." On the other hand, Commercial Equipment competed in certain lines with the Irvings' Thorne's Hardware and Chandler Sales.

Carson was one of those Irving veterans who remembered days when "you never knew when you were going to be helping do almost anything." Once, in 1971, K.C. called him to say one of his tankers was aground on sands 366 metres from the shore of the Magdalen Islands. It was surrounded by ice with a storm brewing. If, Irving said, it was going to be refloated, much of the cargo of oil had to be taken off quickly, pumped ashore — and there was no way to do it with the facilities available on the spot.

It was 1 p.m. Within two hours, by phone, Carson had rounded up 366 metres of firehose from all over Saint John. He told Irving's Saint John Iron Works he needed a flange made to fit the hose to the ship's pump, gave the dimensions, got it, got an air compressor, got a DC-3 Irving cargo plane, and had them on the way. By 6 p.m. the company had the oil flowing through firehose snaking across the pack ice, the compressor boosting it on its way, tanks ashore receiving it. At 3 o'clock next morning the tanker was freed on a rising tide.

Irving called to say thanks. The flanged adapters were stored away in case it ever happened again. Years later it never had, but the adapters remained where they were because the Irvings threw nothing away.

❧

Like Don Carson, Barney McLaughlin did a lot of extra-curricular tasks for the Irvings. He looked after Arthur's prize hound, among other things, while running a big service station. McLaughlin's family had run a tire business, and he didn't like working for the multinational firm that took it over. He went to Arthur looking for a job, and was asked to take on this property in Saint John's valley.

He was there day and night, seven days a week, a brawny man with a face like a map of Ireland. People liked him, and they drove down the hill with houses clinging to it on walls of rock. He ran a 24-hour convenience store, car wash, truck wash, and service department. He served the Irvings with a passionate devotion. From him, as from corporate scripture, comes the language of the loyalist: "The people who run the Irvings down are people who aren't willing to put out."

No Saint John station sold more than McLaughlin; he made his a flagship of Irving Oil. In fact, said Arthur Irving, Barney McLaughlin sold more than any other service station operator in all New Brunswick. McLaughlin and thousands of others made up the Irving infantry, the people in the front line. "That," said K.C. Irving, "is where the competition shows up." That's where the paradoxes of the oil industry show up too. In the front line, people like McLaughlin saw themselves much as soldiers going forth to daily battle, with Imperial Oil as the arch-enemy.

Arthur Irving called McLaughlin a soldier *extraordinaire*. Arnold Payson was another, "a great peddler." Arthur recalled that Payson had wept when he didn't get a contract to supply oil, that he had walked 32 kilometres into the woods to get a contract from a lumber operation.

Payson himself said it wasn't into the woods that he walked. It was, he said, when the government was running the lines for the Trans-Canada Highway in the fifties that he walked 29 kilometres spying out the ground for the best places to put service stations. He and Arthur once crawled, walked, spied in the dew of early morning, wet through, looking for service station sites, and he quoted Arthur as saying, "You can almost smell a good one."

He remembered people, and what they said, and what he said. He remembered the early days and an ornery old man who had four tanks outside his store in the back-country hills of Nova Scotia, and the Irving truck driver saying the old man hadn't let him put a drop of gas in his two Irving tanks for weeks. The driver got Payson to go with him as regional superintendent, and on the way warned that the old man was mad about something and he was difficult, so not to say anything that would make him worse.

The old man was sitting there, whittling, when they arrived. Payson introduced himself, smiling, shining, the personification of the salesman. The old man said he didn't like salesmen. Payson waited, uttered further sunshine, then said, "You know, sir, we're both making our livings in the same way, selling things." The old man grunted. Then he said he didn't like Irving Oil either; they had charged him for a barrel of oil he'd already paid for.

Payson went back to Truro and called Saint John, and got nowhere. Headquarters said the old man hadn't paid for that barrel of oil, and that was that. Payson went back at them a second time. Forget it, he argued, and we could get him back. Finally they did, and he went back to that store in the hills after the old man was informed. He was sitting there, whittling. Not one smile crossed his lips. Not one word of thanks. Not one acknowledgment. But just before Payson left he looked up and pronounced an armistice.

"You'd best get some gas in them tanks," he said. "They ain't much good empty."

CHAPTER THIRTY-SIX

❧

Uses for the Land

"I love the old bastard."
– AN AFFECTIONATE IF IRREVERENT REFERENCE TO K.C. IRVING
BY SYDNEY BUSINESSMAN EDDIE MACDONALD.

IN SYDNEY, NOVA SCOTIA, LIVED EDDIE MACDONALD.
He never worked for K.C. Irving a day in his life, but he saw himself as a friend. MacDonald was tiny, profane, irreverent, and rich. He started out as a taxi driver, got into selling cars, and ended up a millionaire. Then, in his fifties, he sold out his dealership to take it easy, a move Irving said he found inexplicable for one so young, to which Eddie replied that with all his money Irving should do it too.

Instead, they continued to share a common devotion to deals in property. MacDonald was a major reason why Sydney's downtown George Street ended up with so many Irving business outlets that local wits sometimes called it Irving Street. MacDonald sold Irving his car dealership property, and Irving helped lay out the site for a big service station. It flourished next door to an older Irving station, which was kept going too, because the Irvings don't like to close anything they've started, and across the street from yet another property that Eddie steered Irving's way. MacDonald called Irving one day and said the property had on it a business in trouble. It could be bought, and Irving should buy it.

"Why?" Irving asked.

"Because," said Eddie, "it is right next to your Commercial Equipment store, and sure as hell someone is going to buy it and go into competition with you."

Irving bought it. Just as he did in many Atlantic provinces and Quebec communities. And he bought many others in Sydney. Some have houses on them, with tenants paying the Irvings rent on properties that may some day warrant commercial use. In helping Irving accumulate a good number of them, Eddie MacDonald found him "a great guy to do business with." And then, looking at the accumulating ash of a cigar stub, added: "I love the old bastard."

By the eighties the Irvings owned so much land in so many places that one executive said he'd be willing to bet that it alone is worth a billion dollars. It was managed by a number of real estate companies under the direction of Jack Irving, but Irving managers in other lines found themselves looking after much of it. Irving himself kept buying land because he was convinced he couldn't go wrong if a deal was right; it gave him flexibility. When Arthur got angry over something and echoed his father's threats to move out of Saint John, he said they had enough land in Montreal to reestablish there.

Their greatest swaths of it lay, of course, in their forests, the rest in blocks, patches, and pieces. A problem recurred again and again: communities wanted land for development of their streets or other things, and they had to dicker with the Irvings to get part at least of what they needed. In Quebec City, Aimé Gaudreau told Irving in the forties that he should buy a farm on the flats near the river, foreseeing the day a major highway would course across it. In the eighties, the highway was there, and the Irvings had so much land that they built a huge Chinic hardware headquarters on it and still had plenty left to lease to others.

At the eastern end of Moncton, where the *Elkhound* went aground a half-century earlier, there was a steady march of Irving outlets along the main street and beyond, some of them on land Sam Roy had advised Irving to buy years before. In the Saint John area he acquired half the industrial land, and a city official said he doubted that there was a major block in town without Irving possession involved.

Over the years, the city had taken some of it for its own purposes; sometimes Irving asked for other land in compensation, sometimes he said to take it and they could settle later. There were cases, an official said, in which the city used Irving land for years without getting a deed. In the mid-seventies council took advantage of a hassle over an Irving pipeline route to settle up thirty-seven parcels.

One stretch they got is a story in itself. In the late fifties Irving made a deal: he would get 47.8 hectares of mudflats on Courtenay Bay; in return, he would build the city a causeway for general use. He planned to put an oil pipeline across it but never did. He filled in the flats and held it ready for future industrial development. For the causeway another problem arose. If it was to run straight Irving would need property owned by another oil firm. The issue ended up before the common council, with a rival lawyer arguing strenuously against Irving and citing facts about allegedly broken promises. Irving heard him out, then, according to one councillor, proceeded to challenge every argument in a cold, rough rebuttal. The causeway was built, with Irving businesses rising on the reclaimed property behind it.

The mudflats became a problem, too. They had been the scene of the launching of the *Marco Polo* and many other nineteenth-century ships. But what mattered legally was that other businessmen bought an old brick cotton mill across Marsh Creek and claimed that they, not Irving, owned a share of the flats. It went to the courts, with lawyers and the judge nosing through a grant going back two centuries because high and low tidal water was involved. The judge came down on Irving's side, but told him to pay his opponents for loss of riparian rights. In time, Irving bought the old cotton mill, too, and put it to use.

It stood near more Irving property in the heart of the city. He got it in the sixties when the city took advantage of government urban renewal funds and set about cleaning out slums. The city had wanted to lease some of the land. Irving wanted to buy it. He did, and erected new buildings for his newspapers, his TV-radio station and other businesses.

So it goes, from St. John's to Ontario, as Charles Llewellyn recognized. Founder of the Wandlyn Motel chain, he had an acre left over after building a Moncton motel and decided to try to sell it to Irving for not much less than he had originally paid for a much larger property. Irving asked him why he should buy it, and

Llewellyn said because he was going to be around for a long time; and he'd do a lot of business with Irving. Irving bought it and Llewellyn bought a lot of Irving oil.

In 1978, seven years after leaving Canada, K.C. went to Liverpool, N.S., for a funeral, and dropped by the Steel and Engine Products Ltd. plant to see what was going on. A generation after he bought it, he found work being done outdoors in scattered buildings, its marine railway in bad shape and a lot of equipment outdated. He wondered aloud if it couldn't be improved, and when a $3-million expansion took place in 1980 executives and workers attributed it to that visit of a man who at seventy-nine was still thinking about the future. The result: more buildings, new cranes, new equipment for the machine shop and steel plate works, and an improved and lengthened marine railway, 366 metres long, with two cradles, each capable of handling a ship. In the expansion, Stenpro also provoked local controversy, with some people objecting to the blocking of streets and other changes. The company persisted and got its way, partly because its 200 employees made up the largest labour force in town, at work on the construction, repair, and fitting of pumps and tanks.

In 1981 John Marquis sat in his small, trim office building in Bangor, Maine, contemplating big, trim plans. He was a pleasant, affable, and able man whom K.C. had picked in 1972 to head a corporate thrust into the state. He was fifty-six then, with a big job with a major paper company, and friends wondered why he would shift to the Maine-incorporated Irving Oil.

He shifted because he had known Irving for some twenty years, since the days when he went to Saint John to see what Irving could do for the paper company that then employed him. They did business, and Marquis said he came to the conclusion that this was "a really remarkable man, a tough negotiator but a man of his word and one who saw further down the road than anyone I've ever met." He shifted, too, because Irving said "you fit," and because he thought he would like to run his own show.

Irving had already aroused widespread comment in Maine by bidding for and winning large long-term contracts to provide heavy, residual bunker oil to three large paper companies. By the seventies he was planning a major invasion of the state, to establish the same sort of rounded gas-oil marketing setup he had in the Atlantic provinces: service stations, fuel supplies for homes and buildings, diesel oil outlets, the works. He had considered all the angles and he had decided that, backed by his refinery, he had found in northern New England a natural market.

Before the plans could take effect, Irving Oil Corp. was caught up in the consequences of the oil shock. In the face of moves by governments in Ottawa and Washington, the plans were shelved, and Irving decided to hang tough and wait for change. In the early eighties the Irvings were still sitting tight, waiting, but the plans remained alive. Those plans took shape all over the state in the mid and late 1980s. As conditions changed, Irving service stations, convenience stores, and other businesses blossomed everywhere in a dynamic invasion that created controversy and legislative concerns. Those concerns would reach a fever pitch in the early 1990s as the Irvings moved through the state buying up service stations and opening new ones. Small business operators said they were worried and politicians responded with legislation designed to curb and control the expansion-minded family from across the border.

All of this had its paradoxical side because, while the Irvings were criticized for their determination to penetrate the Maine market, they were praised for the high standards they created wherever they went. Their service stations were generally acknowledged to be excellent. Many of them added the sparkling convenience stores and family-style restaurants that had become so popular in Canada.

Ironically, when the *Maine Times* published a special issue on "The Best of Maine," readers voted the Irving stations as the most popular. Ironical? Yes, because the 20,000-circulation, award-winning weekly had been among the most active and critical Irving watchers in Maine.

In the Maine Senate and House of Representatives the bill designed to put the brakes on the Irving expansion was called by its official name, the Petroleum Market Share Act, but elsewhere it was the "Irving Bill." Its intent was clear, its measures oppressive — so restrictive, in fact, that major newspapers in Maine said editorially it had gone too far.

One clause would have placed a two-year moratorium on expansion by Irving or any other refiners in the state, but this was dropped as the bill moved through the legislative process. In its final form it required retailers and wholesalers to disclose fuel sales, and refiners to show which retail outlets they controlled. Refiners were barred from fixing prices of fuels sold by franchise holders. Supporters of the bill said it was not anti-Irving and not anti-Canadian. It was, they said, designed to prevent any giant from dominating the market. Maine politicians said the state welcomed foreign investment and competition at the marketplace. The welcome mat, they said, was still out for the Irvings or anyone else. Maybe so, but there were those who believed Maine had been careful not to take the night chain off the door. As for the Irvings, they said they would continue to do business in Maine — and beyond.

Maine was not the only place the Irvings faced controversy. By the 1980s Irving Oil's business had boomed into the largest of its kind in Prince Edward Island. But it was also in Canada's smallest province that the Irvings have had to buck some of their most active opposition, and it was there that their penchant for growth put them into direct competition with another corporate giant that had emerged in New Brunswick.

The opposition was rooted in that element central to their expansions — land. It was touched off in 1979 when the Irvings purchased a frozen food firm, changed its name to Cavendish Farms, and set about improving things and seeking ways to grow. They wanted to buy thousands of hectares and they found themselves rubbing a raw, historic nerve end in a province that has been touchy about land ever since the eighteenth-century days of absentee British owners.

The direct competition made them rivals of McCain Foods Ltd., the nearest thing to the Irvings themselves as a home-grown New Brunswick phenomenon, a frozen food business launched by two brothers who left Irving executive positions in the late fifties and by the eighties had built it into one of the world's greatest corporations with plants in half a dozen countries.

According to the Irvings, they themselves got into the frozen food business — and more specifically the frozen french fries business — almost by accident when they got involved in a company that needed financial assistance. Soon it was a case of going all the way or continuing to suffer financial losses. They decided to go all the way. They were, they decided, in it for the long haul. Once the Irvings made their commitment to the frozen food business,

Cavendish Farms set about polishing its image, improving its methods, courting markets in Canada, the United States, and Europe. A full-blown publicity campaign sought to make its name a household word. Packaging was spruced up. Frozen foods were stocked in Irving convenience stores, and many others.

In the quest for expansion, the Irvings came up against local opposition. They had 809 hectares around their plant in New Annan, near Summerside, and rented more. They said they needed 2,427 hectares to guarantee year-round supply, to give them a solid economic base, to let them rotate crops properly, and to meet transportation costs and the island's inordinately high electricity bills. Faced by low potato prices three years running, farmers who sold to them protested: "If they buy our lands, we've had it." A National Farm Union spokesman said, "We are definitely scared of a monopoly." Roman Catholic Bishop Francis Spence declared "a land Sunday," sermons encouraged farmers' resistance, and one congregation substituted Biblical passages in singing "This Land Is Your Land." Liberals warned the Progressive Conservative government not to yield. Nor was there encouragement from the government. Premier Angus McLean, elected in 1979 on a "rural renaissance" program, was caught in a bind: he didn't want to chance losing the biggest employer in the province, one said to affect some 1,000 people directly or indirectly, but he also didn't want to offend small farmers. So he stalled, and asked a bipartisan legislative committee to investigate.

Meanwhile, rumours spread that Cavendish Farms might pull out of the island. The Irvings cleared hundreds of hectares in the family's northern New Brunswick woodlands close to a major potato-producing area. They were also close to the McCain Foods' heartland, and the rivalry continued in other ways. McCain charged in Washington that Cavendish was dumping frozen french fries in the United States at less than fair value; the complaint was rejected by the U.S. International Trade Commission.

By the time Premier McLean's committee reported, he had made way for successor James Lee, who quickly said, "We won't allow the Irvings or Cavendish Farms to take control of our lands." But while accepting the committee's recommendations for a ceiling on corporate land ownership, Lee's cabinet left itself a loophole that gave potential buyers a way out, then ordered further hearings.

As the impasse continued, the New Annan plant went on producing, its premises marked by the signs of Irving activity, by their trucks, by corrugated cardboard made in their Lake Utopia, N.B., mill, by buildings with the telltale touches of Strescon Ltd. Inside the low, flat buildings, an assembly line rolled twenty-four hours a day. Island peas went through, carrots from Israel, broccoli from the west coast, corn from Ontario. Other imported vegetables came in frozen and were packaged.

The impact was felt in other provinces too. In Springhill, N.S., another plant froze blueberries and strawberries. In western New Brunswick, Irving-owned St. George Pulp and Paper Co. lands became a gathering point for Charlotte County blueberries to be taken away in Irving trucks, and also frozen. In 1982 Cavendish Farms acquired from a co-operative a lease for 1,027 hectares of blueberry land in northern New Brunswick and expected eventually to produce 350 tons a year at that location, far more than in the past.

The government of Prince Edward Island changed again in the mid-1980s, with Liberal Joe Ghiz succeeding Progressive Conservative James Lee as premier, but there would be no change in the island's preoccupation about its limited land, who had the right to own it, and especially how much.

The Irvings continued their efforts to broaden their holdings, and when Mary Jean Irving-Dockendorff purchased 1,200 hectares of farmland some farmers and the government protested. She intended to grow potatoes on the newly acquired property as part of a company known as Indian River Farms. But she was a granddaughter of K.C. Irving, daughter of Jim Irving, and the government would not accept that she was operating as a private businesswoman. The government said that under the province's Land Protection Act she would have to dispose of the farmland. She protested strongly, later complied, but continued to challenge government policy.

Meanwhile, the media likened the Irvings and McCains to the feuding Hatfields and McCoys of hillbilly legend in the United States. The competition would become known as the "Potato War" or the "French Fry War" and the battlefield ranged far beyond the borders of New Brunswick and Prince Edward Island. At stake was a huge piece of the multi-billion-dollar worldwide market for frozen french fries and a vast array of frozen fruits and vegetables. But primarily, it was a potato war.

While the huge international market was the prize, production capabilities in both Prince Edward Island and New Brunswick posed a problem. Would there be enough potatoes to supply the needs of both families, and who would get first call on those potatoes? And then there was the pride of two determined and highly competitive New Brunswick families. The McCains, of course, were the long-established experts in this field. They did not intend to give anything up, or allow inroads into the lucrative business they had built. It was their mountain and they intended to hold onto it.

On the other hand, they had not been active in potato processing on the island, where the Irvings had established a major presence. Now, in 1989, under prompting and pressure from the Joe Ghiz government, the Irvings were about to build a second multi-million-dollar plant.

That alarmed the McCains. Soon they were charging that government subsidies — benefits that would be available to the McCains as well as the Irvings — would trigger countervailing duties from the United States under a new Free Trade deal. Not so, said the Irvings. They were not going to receive special subsidies. They would receive incentive assistance available to all industries in the Atlantic area. Semantics aside, the argument went on with growing intensity. The Irvings would build a new processing plant on the island. See your plant, and raise you one, said the McCains: they would build a subsidy-free plant.

In job-starved Prince Edward Island, Premier Joe Ghiz thought he had died and gone to heaven. "I can only hope this is going to be a weekly occurrence," he quipped when the McCains announced they would proceed with a plan that would give the island a total of three processing plants.

But that euphoria was not to last. Three processing plants on tiny Prince Edward Island made no economic sense. The Irvings revised their plans. They would proceed with a $30-million expansion of the existing Cavendish Farms plant. The P.E.I. government would build a $10-million waste water plant for the Irvings and a similar, $14-million facility for the McCains. The two companies would pay operating costs to the government.

The next chapter of the saga surfaced in the fall of 1990 in New Brunswick, where the Irvings announced they would build a $50-million potato-processing facility on the border of Madawaska and Victoria counties at Grand Falls, right across the Trans-Canada Highway from the McCains' largest plant. The McCains again charged that government subsidies could trigger countervailing duties against the entire industry in Canada. The Irvings were equally adamant. They would receive no subsidies. The provincial government would provide an effluent treatment plant in an agricultural park, which would be used by the Cavendish Farms and others in the future. Any other assistance would be incentives available to anyone. A year later the argument became academic because the Irvings cancelled plans for the New Brunswick plant, citing unfavourable marketing conditions. But no one believed this was the end of the feud. The rivalry was too intense, the families too powerful, perhaps too proud. Backing off was not their style.

At the height of the public bickering, some observers had sided with the Irvings, others with the McCains. One Saint John businessman said: "Why don't the Irvings leave the McCains alone? Why don't they let them have the potato business? Why do they have to get into everything?" Hardbitten Harrison McCain, himself an accomplished bareknuckle fighter in the international world of business, would have smiled at that comment. He and his brother Wallace fought the Irvings every step of the way, and the Irvings continued to fight back because by now they were completely committed to the frozen food business. For them — as with the McCains — there was no turning back.

Yet, for all that was at stake, both the Irvings and the McCains endeavoured to remain carefully civil in their public statements. When told by a provincial government official that the Irvings intended to establish a competing processing plant not only in his territory but virtually on the front lawn of his largest plant, hard-as-nails Harrison McCain was said to have accepted it like a perfect gentleman.

On an earlier occasion, when the question of rivalry between the two families had been raised, Jim Irving said the Irvings and McCains were the best of friends. Anyone who said otherwise, he was quoted as saying, was looking for a punch in the mouth. He later denied those words but not the sentiment. What he had said, he claimed, was that anyone trying to create trouble between the two families was looking for a punch on the nose. There was a big difference, he maintained. "A punch on the nose is just an expression. But if you say you are going to punch someone in the mouth, that's different. That means you're really looking for a fight."

❧

CHAPTER THIRTY-SEVEN

A Tour
Around a Life

"If Aimé Gaudreau and Frank Lang and I were thirty-five, we'd have something going."
— *A NOSTALGIC K.C. IRVING RECALLING THE EARLY*
DAYS OF HIS CAREER

"**T**HOSE GOSHDAMN PILLS ALMOST RUINED ME, YOU know."

K.C. Irving didn't swear as a rule, unless he was badly upset. Usually, he would settle for "goshdamn," and if his language got any stronger it was time to give him a wide berth.

On this day he was upset. Something short of angry, but still upset. Doctors in Boston had prescribed medication necessary to regulate his heart, but he was convinced there were side effects that had slowed down more than his heart. He didn't like that, and he said they'd better give him something else. They did and he was better now. Not his old self, but better than he had been recently. He was well into his eighties and the years were beginning to take their toll. He could accept that. He didn't like it particularly, but he was prepared to accept it. And everything wasn't bad. Not by a long shot.

He had lived to see his sons assume control of what he had built. His grandchildren were busy, too, taking over the operation of companies — some companies he had started, some that had been started and expanded by his sons. He had long since resigned as president of all the companies and relinquished his directorships. When he had opinions he voiced them at shareholders' meetings. He was meticulous about that. "Speaking as a shareholder," he would say, and then he'd get his opinion on the record.

It was not an opinion that was ignored. In fact, it was an opinion that continued to touch and influence a wide spectrum of economic life in his native province and beyond. His thirst for knowledge, his interest in results, his curiosity, and his penetrating questions abated little with the years. As a shareholder, he said he wanted to be informed. Fully informed. That was the way it was as he approached his ninetieth birthday. And there was much for him to be informed about.

The "Huckleberry" from Bouctouche had come a long way since those early days just after the turn of the century when he had gone into business cleaning basements as a boy of six. He had built a multi-billion-dollar industrial empire so diversified that virtually no one knew how big it was or how much it was worth. His vision in many areas had long since been proven right. The pulp mill that experts said couldn't survive stood as a towering, somewhat grotesque, bellowing, belching, industrial giant of modern technology. The trees that Barney Flieger said wouldn't grow were pushing skyward by the millions. The drydock that C.N. Wilson said he'd sell if he could find anyone crazy enough to buy it was busy with the largest contract ever awarded a shipyard in Canada. Nearby the largest oil refinery in Canada stood beside the newsprint mill he had planned and dreamed of, the one he and Lord Beaverbrook almost built, then lost in a bitter struggle, and later acquired because he had the patience to wait until the time was right. Fleets of trucks and ships carried Irving products around the Atlantic provinces, up the St. Lawrence River, into Quebec and Ontario, into the United States, across Canada, and around the world. New service stations and convenience stores were sprouting everywhere, foods, fresh and frozen, were finding their way to the supermarket shelves.

And most important of all, his sons had taken over this vast complex just as he had planned it. They were not simply holding the line. They, too, were builders. Grandchildren, too, were part of management, part of the standards that had been set almost a century ago by a man who never once thought that he might be wrong. He would heal a broken-down pulp mill and make it successful by the sheer strength of his will. He would build and rebuild and then build it over again. And when engineers or architects or scientists or politicians or bankers told him he was wrong he'd only become more obstinate. He would do this in business time after time until the pattern became policy.

Soon great-grandchildren would be starting as their fathers and grandfathers had started before them — at the bottom, down in the cellar.

Now Kenneth Colin Irving could look back on a life of accomplishment, as on one day, in his eighties, when he agreed to a tour of the city that is the crux and the heart of it all.

He wore a navy-blue tam, a blue raincoat, and a pair of the shoes he had had resoled four times. He was in a chauffeur-driven car made by Ford: he had never forgotten his early association with Ford. He passed a new building, an SMT bus terminal and office building that started out to be four storeys high, ended up at nine, and later was expanded to twelve-and-a-penthouse. "You have to change your plans from time to time, and you can change them more easily when you have no shareholders, no outsiders, to worry about." He passed a city bus on the rounds he fought Fred Manning twelve years to get, a service that never did become a very good investment and that, like virtually all city bus services elsewhere, had now been sold to the community.

Just past the site of his first garage-showroom and his first apartment was captured, in one astonishing glimpse, a measure of what he meant to Saint John: the newspaper building, the broadcasting building, the building housing various other headquarters, the old textile mill, the causeway he built across Courtenay Bay, the land he got for it, the offices of his shipping line, his towing company, his oil terminal, some of his tankers, the shipyard, the land he fought Rothesay Paper to get and their newsprint mill he got in the end, the thin towers of his oil refinery, spewing flame.

It was an area seething with memories for him, of the Americans, Britons, Germans, and Swedes he brought in to run things, of the many, often harsh, struggles with governments and corporations and unions over land and water and taxes and the things he wanted to do, conflicts that transformed this low and often muddy soil from an intermittent battleground into a great industrial complex.

He came to the oil terminal where Irving tankers load. Nearby are the railway tracks where he drove a truck through union pickets in 1948, and he remembered the men who stood with him: "The Cobham boys were worth their weight in gold." He asked for Gordon Ebbett who ran it then, and when, he was told Ebbett had retired at seventy-two, he was surprised.

From a platform he had built you can look down into the shipyard he bought from Charlie Wilson in 1958 for $4.5 million. Now it was the busiest, most modern shipyard in Canada. His interest shifted quickly as he passed an Irving service station. It wasn't good, he said, to have them, like this one, at corners without traffic lights: "There are certain guidelines you learn from experience."

There was a brief tour of the largest oil refinery in Canada. Nearby was the Canaport supertanker terminal that feeds it crude, the first of its kind when it was built in 1970. He came to another corner with another Irving station, this one beside traffic lights, across from the place at Three Mile House where he came out that day long ago to soothe drivers who had found water in their gas. He drove slowly past the site of his Strescon Ltd., wildflowers bright on land he acquired with Canada Veneers: "The boys might cut the bushes." He passed a Speedy Propane outlet, and remembered that he got into selling propane because it was either that or burn what the refinery made. He passed the expanded version of the service station he bought in 1928 from K.B. Reed, whom he first got to run a bus line to Rothesay: "Tom Enright wanted to get rid of it. It was a good gas user. I suppose that's the main reason we bought it." He passed the old red brick building used by Universal Sales, a building that was used for many "activities." He talked of people, of dealing with "a shrewd old gentleman; he'd sit there with his eyes closed and when he opened them it was in wisdom." He recalled, as he passed City Hall, a clerk who amended an agreement for a new Irving building, of the lawyer who advised him that it "made no material change," told of how he "happened to read it over" and cancelled out because it was no longer a good deal. "It's very easy," he said, "to have a champagne appetite on a beer pocketbook."

He stopped at Ocean Steel, across from his big Thorne's Hardware building, to ask for Hans Klohn. Klohn was out: "Please tell him I called." He came to the pulp mill and wanted to see the sign that told how much it was producing: 826 tons yesterday. He nodded in satisfaction. He remembered when he bought the mill and the struggle to hold production at 80 tons a day. In 1990 it would turn out 300,000 tons of air-dry kraft pulp.

Now, however, as the Reversing Falls churned below, he brooded about the river, the loss of his log drives and, with them, tens of thousands of logs from Maine: "Good logs. The best." Lost because the Mactaquac dam provided no passage. The memory of Mactaquac had not left him. There was a touch of bitterness in his voice.

Ducks flew in formation over the waters, but he saw the falls, the dam that might have been built above them to expand the harbour on which he might have built more industries if he'd won his fight for the Chignecto Canal. He went to South Bay, past Irving Equipment and all the machinery, past Joe's Machine Shop, and came to ground where, he said, "We built the best sawmill in New Brunswick. The machinery was just broken in when Mactaquac ended it. . . . I knew every spike in the place."

Now he was on a rocky bluff overlooking the pulp mill, the logs being shepherded by a small boat into its maw. His wife and the chauffeur stopped to pick blueberries on land he owned. He recalled the time two prominent Maritime businessmen wanted him to go into a partnership with them, and he didn't, and he recalled Lord Thomson, whom he liked and admired, who wanted to buy his Saint John papers, who invited him to go with him into Britain's North Sea oil venture, which he didn't do and said he didn't regret: "You can't regret things."

He clambered over high rocks for a better view of the mill, talked of the time it had non-Irving managers who "couldn't run it worth a darn," and he put in others with practical ideas. Talked of the man in charge of maintenance when he took it over: "He could keep it going with haywire and a wrench. A good fellow. A born mechanic."

At lunchtime he sat in a restaurant and answered questions. What had the tour meant to him? Was he proud of all he'd done? "I wouldn't say proud," he said, fiddling with a napkin, "but at least we stirred things up. There is nothing remarkable about it. Plenty of people could have done it." Was he the last of a breed, in that what he'd done could no longer be done by any individual? "I think," he said, "there are as many opportunities now. Maybe more." Had he ever thought of what might have happened if he'd settled elsewhere? Someone once suggested that if he'd gone to New York he'd own half the state: "If I'd gone away, I wouldn't be near the woodlands I like so much."

He talked quietly, diffidently; throughout the morning not one hint of a boast had come from him. Much of what he said was not about his achievements but about the things that died or didn't come to be. Staggering though those achievements were, his dreams outvaulted them, and were in him still: "You never know about things until the last bugle blows." Yet, for this man who didn't like to be told what to do, age had finally become his master, and he found it a cross to bear. "If," he said wistfully, "Aimé Gaudreau and Frank Lang and I were thirty-five we'd have something going."

It was perhaps his most profound statement of the day. The spark was still there, the will, and the desire. The flame still burned.

a

On another day, in the apartment atop the new Irving office building in Saint John, he mentioned he was staying there as a guest, and not as a residence in Canada. It is something he did from time to time when the thought occurred to him. His heart was in New Brunswick, but his residence was in Bermuda. It was a moment tinged with sadness but it passed quickly.

He picked through old books and papers on a coffee table, pulled out his gunnery report from the Royal Flying Corps, written almost seventy years earlier. His mark? Excellent. He smiled and talked about those days, about England, and his first hair-raising flight with his cousin Leigh Stevenson.

Ever courteous, he insisted on helping his visitor with his coat when it was time to leave. Then he walked the visitor to the stairway.

At that time, before the addition of extra floors, the elevator came only to the eighth floor. When he was eighty-two and the building was under construction, he once climbed eight flights of stairs to see what was going on. Chastised by son Arthur, he bade him hold his tongue: "The last time I was up here I climbed up the ladders." Now, the apartment was on the ninth. In deference to his age, his sons put in a chair elevator from the eighth to the ninth floor. It was for his personal use. They didn't want him walking up that flight of stairs.

He looked at the chair elevator, and in a way he was embarrassed. "The boys did this," he said with a touch of defiance, and also of pride. He didn't want to admit he needed the chair, and often he ignored it, but he was pleased that they cared.

He was almost eighty-seven. He looked at the chair and the strap he was supposed to buckle up. He shook his head, his expression containing both resentment and resignation. He couldn't turn back the clock and he knew it.

"It's terrible to get old," he said, then quickly added, "but it sure beats the alternative." As the two men stood laughing at the top of the stairway, K.C. Irving said it again: "Yes, it sure beats the alternative."

૨&

Another day. Two years on. He was approaching eighty-nine and becoming frail, but only when compared to the K.C. Irving of earlier years. His eyes were alert, his grip firm, his questions penetrating.

What did his visitor think of Free Trade? The new premier? Was the new premier going to be able to do a better job for New Brunswick? Yes, the frigate program at the shipyard was wonderful, providing hundreds, thousands of jobs. Too many people had been out of work for too long. That was bad. It was bad for the economy but worse for those who were out of work. "It breaks their spirit and they lose the incentive to work. They lose the work habit."

He walked across the living room to move a small electric heater from the window sill. "I put that up there just to get it out of the way," he said. He placed it on the floor. He didn't want his visitor to think he needed a heater. It was just something in the apartment. Maybe he used it to keep his legs warm. Maybe not. It was the sort of thing that embarrassed him, as old age embarrassed him. It was like living in a foreign country where he had to learn a new language and new rules.

His youngest son, Jack, dropped in to see him and when he was about to leave he said: "I've got to go now. . . . I've got some things to do." It was the way he'd been himself. There had always been things to do, problems to solve, things to build, decisions to be made. "Yes," he said to his son. "Yes, you've got things to do, I know. . . ."

But the Old Man also had things to do. He hadn't slowed down completely. Earlier in the week he'd been to Bouctouche, to

Kent County, to see some old friends. There weren't many left, not many of the oldtimers. Still, he liked to go back to Bouctouche whenever he could, to walk once more the streets of his boyhood, to go to the modern Irving convenience store and to remember the original store, where as a young man he had bought those neckties of many colours, where he had built his first service station, where he had made his first big potato deal. He liked to look over the harbour and remember the boat he had launched . . . and maybe he thought of the young boy who was fast with his fists, not because he was tough or mean, but because that's what boys did in those days.

But now it was Christmas Eve, 1987, and already it had been a busy day. He had gone to the sandwiches and cakes reception at the J.D. Irving office in the new building on Union Street and he'd stayed so long that he was late for a similar party at the Irving Oil offices in the old Golden Ball building nearby.

Now he would have his own lunch — cream of mushroom soup, unsalted crackers. No butter. And then apple pie and ice cream. Finally tea, weak, with milk. Would he like more tea?

"Yes, why, yes, thank you . . . but no more milk. . . . I have some milk in the cup," he said to his wife in a soft voice. It was more an observation than a complaint. Then as the cup was returned to him, he added: "The tea's weak. I saw that when you poured it."

"Yes, well, that won't keep you awake," he was told. "Well, that's all right." He wasn't complaining. He was learning the new rules, the rules of the old. No salted crackers. No butter on the table and now weak tea. It was all right. He could play by the rules if he had to, but he didn't want anyone to think he didn't know when he was being given weak tea with too much milk.

&

"Do you have your longjohns on?"

"What?"

"Do you have your longjohns on?" Jim Irving asked his brother Jack.

"Sure. What do you think? Do you?"

The oldest of the three brothers pulled up a pantleg and displayed a length of winter underwear above his socks. Jack opened his shirt to reveal he was wearing a sweater underneath it in addition to his longjohns.

They had spent the day with a reporter from *Maclean's* magazine who was trying to do what reporters had been trying to do for half a century or more: to get to the core of the so-called Irving Empire.

At first they had said no to his request for an interview. It was the normal answer. They were not interested. They didn't have the time. But he was determined. He kept calling — one brother after another. He wanted to get their side of the story. He wanted to be fair. Finally, he broke through. They agreed to see him.

They took him on a tour of some of the companies — the shipyard, the oil refinery, the pulp and paper mills. They took him on board one of their ocean-going tankers and had lunch with him. They took him to the Irving Tank Farm overlooking the harbour and the bay and the Irving Deepwater Terminal — and, to get the proper view, Arthur insisted they climb a ladder to the top of one of the tanks.

It was January. The temperature was –19, and the winds were high and bitterly cold. "I don't think he enjoyed that part of it," said Jack as Arthur entered the office and joined his brothers around a conference table. "Have you got your longjohns on?" asked Jack.

Arthur looked perplexed. "No, why?" Arthur answered, at the same time throwing up his right leg and revealing an expanse of bare leg above his sock. "What's all this about longjohns?"

Jim and Jack slapped the table and laughed. "You must have frozen out there today," said Jim.

"Are you wearing longjohns?" Arthur asked.

"Sure," said Jim, "you don't think we're crazy enough to go out in that weather in summer clothes, do you?"

"Why didn't you tell me?"

"Why didn't you ask?" said Jack.

It was a meeting of three of the most powerful men in Canada, and it sounded more like a group of teenagers sitting around in a school locker-room after some sporting event. The brothers Irving were relaxed, verbally horsing around at the end of another long day.

A day with a reporter was an unusual experience for the brothers, but this writer had pestered them until they finally agreed. His name was John DeMont. He was from Halifax, a fellow Maritimer. He was bright, articulate, congenial. He'd made a good impression.

But still, something bothered them. He hadn't asked many questions. He wrote very little down, used no tape recorder. He was a good conversationalist but he didn't seem to be after a lot of information. This led them to the uneasy conclusion that the story was already written and that he was looking only for an angle, perhaps for one or two facts to support some preconceived position. Was it to be another journalistic hit job? Had they been suckered? They didn't think so, or they didn't want to. He seemed straightforward enough, a decent young man. But why hadn't he asked more questions. Why didn't he write things down?

"He kept coming back to that article in *Forbes*," said Jim.

Arthur: "Well, that's just a lot of crap and we told him so."

In 1988 a story in *Forbes* magazine had identified K.C. Irving as one of the richest men in the world. It said he was worth $8 billion, and that placed him in third position behind Japan's Yoshiaki Tsutsumi, $18.9 billion, and Taikichiro Mori, $18 billion.

This, the brothers thought, had become an obsession with DeMont. He'd tried to get confirmation from the three of them both together and individually. They said they didn't know, and they didn't, but this hadn't satisfied him. It did strengthen their suspicion that the story was already written, much of it from old clippings and probably much from unfriendly sources. Now, was he just looking for confirmation or denial of the $8-billion figure to give it some freshness?

They were going to see DeMont the next day and they wished he'd get off that subject of the richest men in the world. They found it embarrassing. They didn't flaunt or hoard their money. They poured it back into their businesses. They expanded. They bought new businesses, they modernized — and they resented it when articles speculated on the worth of the so-called Irving Empire.

"It's a lot of hogwash," said Jim, "and it isn't true."

"Well," said Arthur, "just tell him that. It isn't true. It's a lot of crap. That's it. Chapter closed."

Jack replied: "Yes . . . but then he'll want to know what is true? Is it more or less?"

Finally, Jim: "We don't know and we don't care, and we don't spend any time worrying about it. We've got enough to do just running our businesses. Right?"

Arthur: "Right." Jack: "Right."

And then, an afterthought from Arthur: "And if *we* don't know — and we don't — no one else does either. So let them speculate all they want to." The three brothers looked over the conference table at one another, paused and then nodded. The meeting was over.

Now they were relaxed again. Then Jack said: "We should have had Dad give them his answer." They broke into laughter as they remembered how their father had handled the same question when he was being honoured by the Rotary Club in his boyhood home of Bouctouche the previous summer. Asked by a reporter if the *Forbes* figure was correct, Kenneth Colin Irving, then eighty-nine, had replied by asking: "What figure?" When told the magazine had said he was worth $8 billion, he smiled an inscrutable smile and remarked: "Is that all?"

Then he walked away.

❧

When he was within five months of his ninetieth birthday his interest in seeing wheels turn was as strong as ever.

With Jim he was making an unannounced night visit to Rothesay Paper, their long-sought Saint John newsprint mill, soon to be renamed Irving Paper Limited. Together, they walked through the plant as newsprint was churned out in a never-ending production cycle. At the end of a long walk they entered a small office where Jim often stopped for a few minutes on his regular visits. It was hot in the mill, cooler in the shed-like cubicle. It was a place where someone kept a small container of eyeglass cleaner and, as was his habit, Jim polished his glasses with a couple of sheets of toilet paper, kept there for that purpose. Then he asked if his father would like his glasses cleaned.

"Why, yes, that would be fine," said K.C. Irving. He handed his glasses to his son who squirted them and then pulled on the roll of toilet tissue and unwound, with a flourish, about ten or twelve sheets.

"Jimmy, Jimmy, what are you doing?" his father asked, with more than a touch of alarm in his voice.

"I'm going to clean your glasses," his oldest son answered.

"Well, you're being a bit extravagant aren't you?" asked the patriarch of the Irving family, looking in disapproval at the long ribbon of tissue.

Jim Irving, sixty years of age, quietly rewound the paper and tore off two sheets. He shined his father's glasses, returned them, and they left the mill.

Later, he told of the incident with pride in his father's sharpness. "He was as fast as a whip when he saw how much paper I was going to waste. No," said Jim Irving, approvingly, in answer to a question that hadn't been asked, "he isn't going to change. Not now. Not ever."

&

At ninety-one, he knew that his heart was not as strong as it once had been. He knew he should be taking it easy. What he didn't know was how to do it. How to slow down. His pace worried his family but there was little they could do about it, so on a day in late 1990 it came as no great surprise when he was taken exhausted to hospital in Saint John, and later to the Lahey Clinic in Boston.

There he remained for six weeks in seclusion, confined to intensive care while his heart was monitored, while the media tried daily and persistently to learn something about his condition. The family was noncommittal, the hospital professionally vague in response to reporters' questions. The sons flew back and forth between Boston and Saint John, tight-lipped and worried. Then, in his office in Saint John, Arthur received a telephone call.

"Is that you, Art?"

"Yes, Dad."

"Art, I'm in hospital and I want to get out."

"Are you feeling better, Dad?"

"Yes, and I want out of here."

"Well, Dad . . ."

"Today, Art. Get me out of this place."

Within an hour a plane was on its way to Boston. Kenneth Colin Irving checked out of the hospital, flew to Bermuda and slept that night in his own bed. His body had grown old, but nothing had weakened his will.

ىه

Twelve years had slipped away since that memorable night in Toronto when Irving was given national recognition and acclaim during his induction into the Canadian Business Hall of Fame. It was a night to remember — and, since he was in his eighty-first year, there were those who thought it might be his final, public tribute.

But now, on November 20, 1991, Irving was fêted once again — for his lifetime contribution to the economic development of Atlantic Canada — this time by an audience of business and political leaders. They turned out at the Saint John Trade and Convention Centre hoping to see and pay tribute to this legendary figure. As he neared his ninety-third birthday, he was to receive the Distinguished Service Award of the Atlantic Canada Plus Association, an organization dedicated to the cause of economic prosperity for Atlantic Canada.

For days there had been speculation as to whether he would be there. He no longer enjoyed robust health. Many did not expect him to show, yet there was a sense of disappointment when he didn't. But as the evening unfolded disappointment was replaced by enthusiasm, excitement, and finally an almost euphoric feeling of goodwill and appreciation.

The crowd of more than 500 came from all corners of the four provinces. Tributes poured forth from federal and provincial politicians, from Derek Burney, Canada's ambassador to the United States who, as a boy growing up in Northern Ontario, knew that the New Brunswicker had a reputation "as being as tough as they come." What Canada needed was "more people like Irving."

The mayor, the irrepressible Elsie Wayne, serving her ninth record-breaking year as the city's chief magistrate and soon to be elected for another three-year term, praised the Irvings for the businesses and employment they created. An unabashed and unapologetic ham, she couldn't resist telling the audience about Arthur Irving's beautiful legs. How did she know? It didn't have anything to do with this night or the tribute to K.C. Irving, but the mayor told the story anyway. It happened one night in a Bangor hotel where she and her husband were staying on a return trip to Saint John. The fire alarm went off in the middle of the night and her husband shouted: "Get your slacks on, Elsie, we're getting out of here."

They had rushed to the lobby and the first person they met was Arthur Irving, who also had wasted no time in responding to the fire alarm. The mayor said she couldn't help admiring his plaid shirt. It was a beautiful shirt, she claimed, but that wasn't all that caught her eye, because Arthur hadn't taken the time to put on his pants. "So I can tell you that he has beautiful legs," she exclaimed to a delighted audience.

Dorothy Sutherland, an Atlantic Canada Plus director from Halifax, was lavish in her praise of the industrialist as she read the official citation. She said Irving would be remembered as one of the great architects and builders of industry in Atlantic Canada. Atlantic Canada Plus founder Harvey Webber, from Sydney, N.S., recalled that when he had first sought support for his idea of a more aggressive and more co-operative role for Atlantic business-es, he had called on Art and Jack Irving. They told him he was on the right track and wrote him a substantial cheque. That was it. Atlantic Canada Plus was a fact of life.

Now, with the formalities just about over, it was time for Arthur Irving to speak. Himself a recent heart surgery patient, he bounded up from the audience to accept the trophy that honoured his father. For a moment it appeared that he was about to give a formal, thank-you-on-behalf-of-Dad response. But almost imme-diately his thoughts, his feelings for his father came bubbling forth. It was the no-notes, no-preparation, strictly off-the-cuff speech of his life. It was also typical Arthur Irving: fractured delivery, banking, turning, shifting gears in mid-sentence, and all the time driving his points home with his own, personal staccato delivery with one thought pounding its way forward, pushing others aside, and then veering off in a new direction.

What was it like to work with K.C. Irving, to be a son of K.C. Irving? It was, said Arthur, like being in the stands of a great sporting event. There was excitement every day. Every day there was something new. His father was a fighter, a competitor, a winner.

"Every day was a new game. The score was three to two. We were two and the other guy was three. We had about 10 seconds to play — and we had to win. He got a big charge out of being successful."

And, yes, K.C. Irving was tough. It was a tough world "and he was as tough as they come. I would put him up against any businessman in the world." But there was another side to K.C. Irving. He was a man of his word. He would make huge deals on a handshake. His word was his bond.

He was a man who could be humble. In the home he was always polite. He never used bad language. He appreciated the efforts of loyal employees. If the senior Irving had been present, he would have said that anything that had been achieved could not have been done without "all the good and faithful employees" in the Irving organization. He was not present, said Arthur, because he had had a "bad spell" and had just been released after spending two weeks in hospital. But he had talked to his father by phone just before dinner and his father had told him three times to "make sure you thank everyone."

It had been an unusual speech, a shifting and darting talk in which a son had given the audience a fleeting glimpse of a remarkable man, but more importantly it was a penetrating, even naked view of the warmth, affection, and love of the Irving sons for their father. And then, just as it seemed that everything had been said, there was one final point and it was made in a moving and touching way: "He's been a great father," Arthur said. "A great friend."

CHAPTER THIRTY-EIGHT

✦

The Shoeshine Boy

"I should have shined my shoes this morning."
– 93-YEAR-OLD K.C. IRVING REPROACHING HIMSELF FOR SHOES
THAT DID NOT SPARKLE THE WAY A SALESMAN'S
SHOES SHOULD.

BERMUDA. A WARM DAY IN APRIL 1992. THE TEMPERATURE is in the seventies. It had rained earlier but now the sun is shining and the yachts of the wealthy bob in a gentle breeze in Hamilton Harbor. It is a restful scene far removed from the driving, hardball world where the Old Man spent so much of his life.

K.C. Irving sits on the patio of his home high on a hill in this quiet place that dates back to another time, another era, another way of life. He is impeccably turned out, grey flannels, a blue blazer with his First World War Royal Flying Corps crest, a sweater under his jacket and a neatly knotted tie at the neck of his white business shirt. He wears the dark blue beret that has become his trademark in recent years.

He takes in everything with eyes that are still inquisitive. His gnarled hands, close to the texture and colour of sun-baked leather, suck in the warm rays of the afternoon sun. He is a warrior from another time and finally his wars are behind him. In Bermuda he rode a bicycle into his nineties, but now that is behind him, too. He has been told and has accepted that this is no time for a spill and broken bones. But being grounded is not something that makes him happy. He does not give in easily to change. He does not bow readily to age.

He has invited his visitor to stay for dinner and now he is restless, fidgety. He glances at his watch and wonders if his guest will check on how long it will be until dinner is ready — "but tell them not to hurry." He has not changed. Kenneth Colin Irving remains a curious combination of impatience and courtly consideration. The old saying "Hurry up and take your time" comes to mind. Dinner will be ready in half an hour.

There is time for a walk and the two men stroll at a leisurely pace along the paved driveway. It is slow going at first but then the Old Man picks up the pace, the strides are longer, faster. At ninety-three, K.C. Irving still has difficulty slowing down, even when it is a simple turn around the grounds of his Bermuda home.

"You don't use a cane," he observes, acknowledging in his own way that he himself has a cane, another concession to age.

"No," he is told, "no, I don't use a cane . . . not yet."

"Well, I noticed that and I just thought I'd ask. How old are you?"

The visitor admits to sixty-nine years.

"Oh, well," the older man smiles, "you're just a boy . . . just a boy."

They both laugh.

Now, at the end of the driveway, they pause and sit on a bench, partly to rest and partly to enjoy the warmth of the afternoon sun.

"Are you comfortable?" the older man asks. He is the host. It is his home, his grounds. He is, as always, thoughtful, courteous. He wants to be sure his visitor is warm. "There's a bit of a breeze, you know." He is assured that the breeze is no problem. His visitor is enjoying the break from colder weather in Canada. "Well, that's all right, then. I just thought the breeze might be too cold for you."

Later, back on the patio, they sit again and the Old Man leafs through a photo album, seeking out pictures of his friend Leigh Stevenson. They appear together in several snapshots taken at reunions of old flyers — daring young men who flew those flimsy planes in the First World War. In some of the snapshots he and Stevenson are shown together, friends to the end, both in blue jackets, berets, and grey flannels. They are old, very old, but there is something jaunty and carefree about the way they pose at the Canadian War Museum with the famous Sopwith Camel, that ancient relic of several wars ago, the plane they flew in England when Stevenson was in his early twenties, Irving still in his teens.

He remembers it was in 1918 that he went overseas. "I just missed the fighting."

Missed the fighting. The visitor smiles at the paradox of that comment from a man who spent an entire life in turmoil. But the visitor keeps his thoughts to himself. He says nothing. For the older man it is a moment of memories, a time of quiet nostalgia.

Now the warrior of so many battles sets down the photo album and looks out over the grandeur of Bermuda, at the rolling hills, the white and pink homes of this tranquil island that has been his home for many years. His home. It is in truth his place of residence, never the home of his heart. That forever will be New Brunswick.

After a moment his gaze leaves the beauty that surrounds him and he glances at his shoes. They are sturdy, black oxfords, but on this occasion they are not sparkling the way a salesman's shoes should, not the way K.C. Irving's shoes shone when he went to see bankers and politicians and business associates, not the way they would have glistened in that time so long ago when, at twenty-one, he went to every dance he and Leigh Stevenson could find in Kent County, the year he danced himself "right down to skin and bones" before the summer was over. His shoes, on this day, have probably picked up a few particles of dust in his walk along the driveway.

K.C. Irving shakes his head in self-reproach. "I should have shined my shoes this morning," he remarks.

And then it is time for dinner.

Epilogue

THE THREE BROTHERS STAND NEAR THE FOOT OF THE
casket, greeting mourners, chatting with friends. As an old
associate of their father's approaches, Arthur steps forward
to give him a smiling, gracious welcome. The man had known
Arthur's father for, what, thirty or forty years? Yes, closer to forty.
A long time. The man had not seen K.C. in recent months and as
he draws close to the casket to pay his respects he finds it a troubling, emotional experience. The once-robust frame of the man who
dominated more than half a century of industrial development in
New Brunswick seems small, too frail in death. Eyeglasses are
perched on his aquiline nose and the visitor wonders if it was
unanimous or perhaps a two-to-one vote that put them there.
Then he remembers there would have been four votes: K.C.'s wife
Winnifred, Jim, Arthur, Jack. No vote would have been necessary
for what next catches his eye. K.C. is wearing his favourite blue
blazer, that proud uniform of old age, with its First World War
Royal Flying Corps crest. Appropriate, the man thinks. The Old
Warrior is going to his grave with at least a vestige of a fighter's
regalia. Soon he will join his first wife Harriet in Christ Church

K.C.

Presbyterian Cemetery in Warwick, Bermuda. It is a moment of sadness, a realization that this giant of New Brunswick's twentieth century is gone. Arthur breaks the silence: "He looks good, doesn't he?" The man chokes up and can't speak. The brothers back off, leave him for a moment to compose himself. The man's reaction is a scene that is repeated over and over. The city mourns. The province mourns. In his memorial service, Rev. Philip Lee will say: "All New Brunswick weeps today." It is true. A sense of sadness and loss has gripped the province.

❧

K.C. had come from Bermuda to spend the Christmas season with family, back to the home of his heart, to the penthouse on top of the new Irving Building in the centre of Saint John. The address was 300 Union Street, the very site where he had established his first Ford dealership sixty-seven years earlier.

Now a freeman of the city that had seemed so cold and forbidding those many years ago, he was exactly where he wanted to be, in a place of memories and vast accomplishments. In the days ahead he would visit with his sons and their families, see grandchildren and great-grandchildren. He was ninety-three and there was growing concern about his health, about a weakening heart. The sons visited him regularly and he was accompanied everywhere by his wife. The Irving company doctor kept an anxious eye on his activities.

Irving businesses were as he would want them to be, under the absolute control of his sons and their children. That control met his own personal definition of what majority ownership should be: 100 per cent. Partners of convenience and necessity in the oil refinery, the oil company, the pulp and paper mills had been bought out and were gone. Everything was in order. His work was done.

It was here, then, in Saint John, where so much of it had started, that it came to an end. Death occurred early Sunday morning, December 13, 1992, three months short of his 94th birthday. On Monday morning the *Telegraph-Journal*, that newspaper he believed had given him more than his share of black ink so the editors could "keep their skirts clean," used eight pages of words and pictures to trace his life from a lively, rambunctious boyhood to international success, power, and recognition. Editorially, it came to this conclusion: "His good works will live long after him. They will benefit countless thousands of New Brunswickers who will have access to better lives because of the doors he opened and the opportunities he created — because of the dreams and enterprise of one man. There are those, presumably, who will say he did only what someone else would have done if he had not been here. They are wrong. He was mortal but he was also special. Different. Unique. One of a kind. K.C. Irving, dead at 93. He was a builder."

Public and private tributes would support that view. Many had a common thread: It was the end of an era and Irving's accomplishments were monumental. Liberal leader Jean Chrétien attended the funeral, as did New Brunswick premier Frank McKenna and members of his cabinet. Prime Minister Mulroney, busy in Ottawa honouring Toronto's World Series Champion Blue Jays, issued a public tribute and called members of the family to express his regrets. Messages of sympathy poured in, from people of power, little people, employees, and strangers.

Harrison McCain, head of New Brunswick's internationally renowned food processing company, recalled his early training with the Irvings in the 1950s and the influence Irving had had on his life and the lives of others. To the pleasure of the family, he remembered a man few people knew, a relaxed, fun-loving Irving. "He was good fun to be with, a great storyteller — with plenty of stories to tell." R. Whidden Ganong, the 86-year-old patriarch of the New Brunswick candy-making family, had known Irving since the 1920s, when they had business operations on opposite sides of a street in Saint John. He recalled asking Irving for advice occasionally and remembered one of Irving's rules of business: "Always be honest in what you do." It was, said Ganong, good advice.

Among those at the memorial service from Irving's hometown of Bouctouche was Jean-Paul Robichaud. He had worked for the Irvings for twenty years and remembered K.C. with fondness and awe. The previous summer he had been asked to trim the trees in front of Irving's house in Bouctouche so that K.C. could sit in the window and watch the activity at a nearby Irving service station. "He was 93 and he wanted to see how many cars were going in to buy gas!"

Old adversaries were among those who commended Irving's lifetime of accomplishments. Retired Senator Charles McElman, one of the most persistent critics of Irving's media ownership in the 1960s and '70s, had used bitter words about that ownership, but never about Irving himself. His assessment now of Irving's achievements was unequivocal: "Of all the contacts I've had over the years in public affairs and otherwise, nationally and internationally, he is the one person I've known whom I would say was possessed of absolute genius, in business and finance. He made money work for him, he didn't work for money. That resounded to the benefit of New Brunswick." McElman made other points that could have been taken directly from the Irving bible on business: All benefits were poured back into New Brunswick, and he believed that if the head office were in New Brunswick, decisions would be made in New Brunswick and profits retained there as well.

Senator Louis Robichaud, the former New Brunswick premier who had had a falling out with Irving in the 1960s, said he still admired the man. "I have admired K.C. Irving ever since I was a kid growing up in Kent County, and that admiration has never ceased in my life. We had our ups and downs, but I never lost my admiration for his courage and determination." But Robichaud also acknowledged that their personal rift had never been healed. Of their differences, he said, Irving "had a memory like an elephant."

Longtime New Brunswick politician Gerry Merrithew, then Federal Minister of Veterans' Affairs and previously Minister of Forestry, had special praise for Irving's reforestation program. He also recalled that the Saint John newsprint mill "was going nowhere when the Irvings took it over in 1982" and "the shipyard was a collapsing company" when it was acquired. "The Irvings never took a cent out of it. They poured it back in to make it one of the most modern shipyards in the world."

A more personal anecdote came from Fredericton Member of Parliament Bud Bird. Once, as a young man living in Saint John, he had become stuck in a snowbank. A stranger stopped, took him to a nearby Irving service station and told the attendant to give him good service and help him out of the jam he was in. It was only after the man left that the service station worker told him his Good Samaritan was K.C. Irving.

Then there was the message penned by Eddie Sheehan, that tough-minded straight-talking engineer from Boston who had lived through classic confrontations with Irving during construction projects at the Irving Pulp and Paper mill in Saint John. Seventy-nine, long retired and living in Plymouth, Massachusetts, he sent this note to the sons: "Your Dad went through life providing richly for others, leaving footprints that will be indelible forever."

❧

The Reverend Philip Lee was one of those with a special Irving story and he told it during the memorial service. It involved plans for Harriet Irving's funeral at which an overflow crowd was anticipated: "Mr. Irving and, I believe, all three sons, were busy arranging things downstairs in our hall. He wanted tables set up and flowers arranged so that the people down there would not feel left out of the worship service. Mr. Irving was close to eighty at the time and I was a much younger man. I started to move one of our folding tables when he said, 'Reverend Lee, don't move that table. My sons and I are used to this kind of work.' Now, maybe he didn't trust a preacher with that kind of work, but whatever his motive — his courtesy and modesty left me speechless."

That sermon, paradoxically, was preached in the Presbyterian Church of St. John and St. Stephen, the church whose construction Irving had so staunchly and stubbornly opposed in the 1960s. The property was too cramped, he maintained. The church itself was too small and there was no parking space. It was, he insisted, a terrible location for the church — so bad a choice that he would not give a cent to the building fund. Instead, as a face-saving measure for himself and probably more particularly for his church-going wife, he paid the minister's salary for several years.

Now, at his own funeral, overflow crowds watched the service on closed circuit television in the church basement and on giant screens set up in a nearby school auditorium and gymnasium. They arrived by limousine, taxis, public transportation and on foot, after a worried police chief had made a city-wide appeal through the media: "Leave your cars at home," he pleaded. "There is no parking at the church."

Kenneth Colin Irving, that remarkable huckleberry from Bouctouche, New Brunswick — stubborn, obstinate, and so often right — had made his point. This time, virtually from the grave.

Index

393